Teaching with
The Norton Anthology of
American Literature
SIXTH EDITION
A Guide for Instructors

Teaching with
The Norton Anthology of
American Literature

SIXTH EDITION

A Guide for Instructors

Bruce Michelson
UNIVERSITY OF ILLINOIS AT URBANA-CHAMPAIGN

Marjorie Pryse
STATE UNIVERSITY OF NEW YORK, ALBANY

W. W. NORTON & COMPANY
New York • London

The text of this book is composed in Fairfield Medium
with the display set in Bernhard Modern.

Cover art (front): Interior view of the Capitol Dome in Washington D.C.
Photo: Richard T. Nowitz/Corbis. *Cover art (back)*: Joseph Stella, *Coney Island*
(detail), 1917–1918. Oil on canvas. The Metropolitan Museum of Art, New York.
Photo: Geoffrey Clements/Corbis.

ISBN 0-393-97795-1

W. W. Norton & Company, Inc. 500 Fifth Avenue, New York, NY 10110
www.wwnorton.com

W. W. Norton & Company Ltd., Castle House,
75/86 Wells Street, London W1T 3QT

Contents

Acknowledgments

This instructor's guide is a constant process, evolving from conversations, suggestions, and a great deal of direct observation. In the following pages, many fine teachers have made their mark, by talking and writing to us and letting us see what they do as they refresh the literature and culture of North America for new generations of students. *Teaching with the Norton Anthology of American Literature* owes all of these hard-working imaginative people a great debt of thanks. We hope that you will continue to share with us, and with one another, to keep our literary histories relevant and alive.

Instruction is always empowered by memory—of great moments in the classroom, when our own teachers and friends opened vast possibilities to us, and convinced us that this profession is supremely worthwhile. We remember Roy Barker, Frank Hodgins, and Carol Kyle—teachers.

CHAPTER 1

Getting Started

The Norton Anthology of American Literature (NAAL) has been used with great success in many different instructional and cultural situations, and the new edition responds to requests and suggestions that have come in from a broad array of experienced teachers. *NAAL* is a big, versatile, rich, thoughtful collection—a resource and touchstone in countless history, American studies, and cultural studies courses as well as in college and high school English classrooms. Priding themselves on their independence and sensitivity to changing cultural contexts and student interests, teachers of American literature and culture often develop their own strategies and styles in moving through this trove of material. In this *Guide for Instructors*, several kinds of courses are suggested and developed, but there are many resources here that can be selected, mixed, or adapted in countless other ways.

When we engage a swath of literary history, or open questions about ideas and crises in American cultural life, finding our own way as instructors and students is part of the pleasure. Even when uncertainty reigns, about describing *America* or *history* or *culture* or deciding which writers to spotlight, some intentions seem to remain steady in the classroom. One of these is a hope that our students will achieve informed, open-minded responses to authors we encounter together and to larger questions that take shape in an extended experience with American literature.

- What relationship should we achieve with texts that are proposed as part of a cultural inheritance?

- What blend of credence and robust skepticism should figure in our own "literacy," especially in an age of hypermedia and other sensory engagements?
- What can imaginative works offer, in terms of lasting value, in an age of quantum newness and change, when even the latest computer on which you write is likely to be a relic in a matter of months?

As teachers, we probably want our students to appreciate a variety of literary styles and to speculate intelligently on relationships among these styles and the historical situations in which these works took shape. We probably want our students to think effectively about thematic and stylistic connections *among* texts. We want our students to encounter the lucidity and emotional power that are possible in American literary utterance. Perhaps we also want them to recognize an element of the irrational, or even a touch of complacency, or intellectual or moral blind spots that can also turn up in these works. No matter what conception of the American past may evolve in the give and take of a good class, intellectual independence is something that most of us hope to "teach"—lucid, patient affirmation of the self against or within the pressures of culture, including perhaps the culture of the classroom—and delight in the potentialities of the printed word.

The Instructor's Guide to *The Norton Anthology of American Literature,* Sixth Edition, is therefore intended to help with the following challenges:

- Deciding what your course is going to be about, and recognizing implications of that decision
- Choosing and presenting texts consistent with those intentions
- Sustaining provocative, informed discussions about those texts
- Choosing appropriate subjects for papers, essay examinations, and independent work

Planning a Course: Preliminary Considerations

Individual personalities and enthusiasms have much to do with success in teaching writers and themes. So do time constraints. Since survey courses in American literature have been around for about a hundred years, some wisdom does circulate about how *not* to plan a survey tour, if you want students to stay with you and with this material for fifteen weeks or longer.

It can be tempting to think of an American literature survey as a kind of flu shot against barbarism. Wouldn't it be nice if we could perfect a one-time downloading of names, dates, and "-isms" so that students wouldn't lack such reference points when they take more specialized courses or go into the world and never look at "Am Lit" again? Such an education would be inert, however, if it conveyed no sense of the vigor with which some of these texts have been debated and set apart as special. Inciting curiosity about this material seems essential to achieving staying power in a student's mind.

Though students may come without inborn or conditioned zest for reading Paine's "The Crisis" or Bryant's "To a Waterfowl," they can and do wonder why readers at other times have found these works compelling. Without presenting such texts as obsolete, we can open them as old sources of a kind of intensity and speculate on the transience or permanence of that spirit or cultural frame of mind.

A survey course can offer *reasons,* even if they are only speculative, for why such literary works have remained stubbornly with us or have been recovered for close, compassionate reading now.

Amid controversies that have also been around for a long time, courses can nonetheless go forward without addressing the question of what *literature,* or in this case *American literature,* is or has come to mean. Perhaps to avoid pedagogical chaos and outbreaks of back-row nihilism, or perhaps out of weariness, some instructors seem to affirm, or concede, that *literature* is whatever is included in literary anthologies, or shelved under appropriate headings in the bookstore. One of our colleagues recently referred to this teaching strategy as "tying a knot in the end of the rope, and just hanging on."

But uncertainty can be an advantage too, if we want students to engage directly with the open question of who and what we are. Because your students may want to discuss such issues, you may find it provident to reopen them frequently during the term. *Why* are we reading this material? Why might a young nation or culture yearn for a list of classics? What are the values by which some literary books are valorized and some are not? In constructions and reconstructions of our literary heritage, there are odd-looking choices to account for—especially, perhaps, in regard to texts that date from before the Civil War. Between the Revolution and "The Great Revolution in Publishing," which began in the 1840s—high-speed steam-powered presses, cheap paper, telegraphs and railroads, easy long-distance shipping, and better copyright laws—the new American books published in any given year could all fit comfortably on a single library table. If you wrote a good play or readable poems in those early years, and subsidized the printing (as most early American authors had to), the competition for publicity was not keen compared to now. Are these old works privileged merely because they are scarce? Some of our canonical texts were indeed huge best-sellers like Stowe's *Uncle Tom's Cabin;* but anemic print runs were common for new books by Emerson and Child and Cooper before 1845, and William Cullen Bryant's most famous collection of verse sold fewer than three hundred copies in its first two years in the shops. And what about Bradford's *Of Plymouth Plantation* and Edward Taylor's *Poems,* neither of which were published until centuries after these writers were gone?

To sum up: whatever else we might be doing, we are not teaching the Top Hits of the last few centuries. So as teachers we face an important problem: how some of these recovered texts, which did not shake the world on their first appearance, can be, or can become, important now.

Although our students may not seem to us especially well read or culturally literate, they can be quick to perceive differences between exploring a body of literature and pressing it into other service. If one objective of a college literature course is to help students improve as makers of distinctions and askers of questions, our students still need help achieving those skills that have been taught for generations in good humanities courses but that are rarely expressed in the catalogs. Such objectives include

- Acuity and sensitivity in the art of reading
- Practice in the arts of adult-level writing and conversation
- A heightened sense of what comes after what, and possibly *because* of what, in the onward flow or tumult of cultural history

Teaching the survey as a large lecture or in small sections, instructors often report that they change strategy, and fundamental assumptions, every time they do the course. And experienced instructors have often winced, in retrospect, over things they may have said from the podium, Great Profundities that turned out to be ludicrous. In reviewing your own assumptions as you begin planning your course, you might want to spend a few minutes thinking over the following questions, because they can underlie decisions (conscious or otherwise) that shape a syllabus and class presentations:

• *Should this course center on answers or on questions?* We often tell students that a course can help them *begin* thinking about a complex and evolving arrangement of cultural experiences and that if their thinking continues (as it should) long beyond the end of the course, they should experience at some point the pleasure of some or all of what gets said in this classroom.

• *In a personal or a guided quest for cultural literacy, do some perceptions naturally and helpfully come before others?* Everyday and professional realities, realities that students must be ready to face, seem to require a measure of familiarity with "major" and "canonical" authors. Familiarity doesn't have to signify reverence; literate, passionate antipathy can sometimes work just as well to bring a student into independent, intense relationships with a challenging author, text, or literary period. As Richard Wilbur remarked, "All revolutions in art are palace revolutions," performed by brilliant people who understand what they are rising up against. To dismiss the canonical and the major author idea out of hand may be to deny students their chance to join that conversation.

• *Has the question of an American cultural identity, discoverable in our literary heritage, been settled or laid aside?* If each generation of readers redefines the literary heritage and infuses it with its own values and imagination, then a survey course can be designed to open this issue and keep it alive, rather than close it down.

• *Can the survey course itself be interesting as cultural practice?* There are more than three thousand four-year colleges in the United States, about two thousand community colleges, and even more public and private high schools. Most of the collegiate campuses have at least one or two historical courses in American literature; and many of these classes are very large. It is a reasonable bet, therefore, that when you and your students open *NAAL* to discuss Bradstreet or Douglass or Wharton, legions of other students and their instructors at that moment are doing pretty much the same thing. In itself, the survey course is a standard American cultural practice—possibly a rite of passage. It is not just an inquiry into cultural history but an actual part of its making, its transformation, and its continuance. When you comment about this to students early in the term, you can provoke interesting responses and a heightened attention to what you are doing together.

The Small Class: Special Considerations

If you review student questionnaires about humanities courses, you may see correlation between how much high-quality discussion students experienced in a given class and how much they valued it and feel they learned from it. Your students may want to talk about a lot of things, including the course itself, as well as specific authors and readings. If you're doing a literary history and you want to take advantage of this willingness to participate, then you will have balances to work out—between getting historical facts sufficiently into mind and helping your group speculate, rearrange, play, and achieve some kind of direct and durable connection with the assigned material. Tromping through an anthology chronologically may seem unimaginative, but the process can work well if you and your students pull back once in a while and open some freewheeling dialogue about where you are. What kinds of questions and uncertainties are they facing just now, about specific literary and cultural moments or the value of the tour?

Though a reading list and a discussion sequence probably have to be established right away, certain decisions about strategy might wait until, say, the second week of the term, when you have a better sense of the energy and tone of your class. You might ascertain if there are pockets of special interest in the room: enthusiasms for particular writers, periods, or issues. You could get a sense of this by handing out index cards on the second day (or whenever enrollment has stabilized), and asking students to write something about other English courses that they have taken, the best college course they have had so far (or high school class, if they are college freshmen), their plans or options for a major, and some strong personal interest or achievement that they feel comfortable mentioning, academic or otherwise. With a smaller class, you can pick up cues from their answers and develop a sense of who in your group might be attracted to a particular writer, cultural predicament, or large-scale issue.

If you do see a pattern of such interests, you might think about asking each student to be a resource person on a particular subject (or writer or literary era), or on a recurring and evolving question, or on some topic parallel to literary concerns (architecture, race relations, the status of women, religious minorities, book publishing and technical innovations). Students need room to choose, so you might want to hand out a list of available subjects, with one or two standard resources listed for them to consult for a few hours sometime in the opening weeks of the term. Students may not be ready or willing to chime in with deep-background information every time a question comes up; but if you and they feel comfortable with their offering insights once in a while, then you can hope for these benefits: more voices participating in class discussion, better opportunity for some students to connect to the class, better preliminary thinking by students, and more enthusiasm in regard to the design and writing of major papers.

If a plan like this seems incompatible with your students or your own design for this small class, then you might want to try other options that can work well with groups of under thirty people.

Teaching the Art of the Good Question

Some students may tell you (in an office visit or, alas, when the course is over) that they don't talk in class because they "don't have anything say." Some students are just naturally quiet, of course; and their silence doesn't signify boredom, hostility, stupidity, or lack of preparation. One common problem, however, that can injure their efforts and morale and your ability to keep the class moving is their belief that "anything to say" means pronouncements and grandiose summaries rather than measured, provocative questions about the material or ways of reading it. Students are sometimes driven into unhappy silence by previous courses, where a human jukebox of semiuseless observations has convinced them that class participation amounts to a game of Having the Last Word. If you can convince students that one or two well-aimed questions per week can be wonderful contributions to a class, valued not only by the instructor but by peers who were hoping that *somebody* would ask that, then you will be doing them a service. The craft of conversation is important to survival in adult professional life, and if some of your students can grow comfortable with the notion that in many situations asking is wiser and more humane than telling, that benefit may stay with them long after their textbooks have fallen apart or been sold back to the bookstore.

A Course as a Process of Discovery

There may be correspondence between the size of a given section and the percentage of students who feel puzzled by any variance from a march through time. But with a smaller group, some of the nonlinear arrangements, outlined elsewhere in this guide, become easier as options.

Even with larger groups, instructors can successfully open a course with some "big" work: major in terms of its sales, its mass-cultural impact, its staying power in the academic mind, and its durable appeal to a larger public. The *NAAL* excerpts from *Uncle Tom's Cabin* can be a good choice, if you want to open questions that subsequent readings could help answer. Where do the moral values that inform this book come from, and how could this novel find such a huge receptive audience? If a creed or a body of religious thought lies at its heart, shaping not only the personages in the story but the narrative itself, what roots do these qualities have in the American literary experience? What are the sources of the novel's ideas of goodness, of evil, of salvation and damnation, of the well-lived life and the subtle ways in which well-intentioned people fall into terrible error? What kind of cultural landscape makes it possible for a novel, a tale about people who in a strict sense never existed and events that never took place, to figure centrally in an immense political and moral upheaval? In other words, you could work backward from a book of this magnitude, laying groundwork for a reconsideration of Calvinism, the Enlightenment, Romanticism, Transcendentalism, and the evolving idea of the writer, the imaginative text, and the individual self-not as closed historical issues but as perceptions, crises, and questions that carry forward and shake the foundations of the country.

Adventures of Huckleberry Finn, which is included as a complete work in *NAAL,* could also work well, considering that this novel's status, as a required text in many high school and college curricula, is still being hotly debated. How did this meandering tale of a river trip, a novel attacked as immoral at the end of the nineteenth century, achieve such high placement in official and popular lists of the "best" American novels? If the remarkable staying power of this mass-market adventure story suggests something about American culture (as it really is, or was, or as we want to imagine it is or was), then what are those qualities that it suggests, and where else in our literature might we see them in evidence?

The Lecture Course: Special Considerations

In undergraduate sections ranging from a dozen students up to hundreds, American literature survey courses seem to flourish. With high-tech support in our lecture halls, and because many of us have lectured often enough to have memorized our orations, we can move around a big room, ask questions, work for actual discussion, apply active-learning strategies, and make the gathering feel smaller and more human in scale than it really is. Technology and cautious theatrics: these things can help—up to a point. But a lecture is still a lecture, and when you try to lead a group through many authors and complex issues in American cultural history, there are times when you may have to explain at length, and students may have to listen, if the alternative is TV talk-show exchanges of enthusiastic ignorance.

In a smaller class, discussion can be freewheeling at times without creating anxiety among your students. In the large lecture, however, the interesting sidelight, the digression, or the periodic discussion that intrigues some students can lose others, and cause them to fear that you're rambling or that all of what's being said must be reverently remembered. To try to allay such worries, you might consider producing "lecture summaries" and making them available on-line and at a local copy shop. These summaries should not be transcripts of the lectures, and you would have to make clear that they are not a substitute for coming to class and taking notes. Rather, such summaries can provide core considerations, major dates, names, events, and key questions, so that students can actually think with you when an interesting question is posed, rather than sweat to catch up with whatever was being declaimed just before. Such lecture summaries can be drawn out of your own presentations, and the copy shops will be eager to accommodate you and your students—provided copyright laws are respected.

Using the Web Site to Accompany *The Norton Anthology of American Literature*

Designed as a springboard to help students extend their exploration of American literature and develop subjects for writing and research, this free Web site offers additional pedagogical materials and connections to authoritative resources on the Web. Included on the site are quick-reference timelines, historical-literary outlines, maps, self-grading quizzes, and searchable "exploration" sections that provide generative questions and projects that help students draw connections, close-read texts, and link texts to contexts for 120 of the anthology's authors. In addition, nearly every author in the anthology appears with a brief biography and annotated links to other Web sites. These materials can be used in countless ways. An instructor can assign explorations as writing assignments; students can use the entire site as a sort of "electronic workbook" and as a venture into current literary criticism on specific authors and problems.

CHAPTER 2

Planning the Historical Survey Course

NAAL is organized chronologically by authors' birth dates. Although as teachers we often construct required reading lists that loosely follow such an order, chronology in and of itself doesn't provide historical perspective. Historical approaches to teaching American literature can empower students to ask questions about writers' lives; about ethnic, literary, geographical, and political environments within which they wrote; and about beliefs that influenced the readers they were trying to engage.

In teaching a historical survey, we can see ideas unfold and become powerful in our literary culture. From the selections written before the Civil War you can choose works related to specific historical events; these events can inform the presentation of readings and give students a good basis for exploring questions in class or developing writing topics. Such an approach encourages students to situate literary works in the context of American history courses they may have taken. After the Civil War, as American literature develops such an expanded variety of voices, themes, and degrees of connection to actual events, you can emphasize that diversity while teaching the individuality of writers and a rich array of aesthetic movements.

As you plan, you may need to guess how much you are going to be teaching *literary* history and how much you'll need to teach history of a more basic sort. Contrary to horror stories about how little American college students know of the major events in the development of Western civilization, you may find that most of your students actually do have, or can quickly acquire, passable familiarity with

Puritanism, the Enlightenment, Romanticism, and Transcendentalism, although they may have more stubborn problems with murkier formulations such as Realism, Naturalism, Aestheticism, and Literary Modernism. They probably know, or can reaquire, the dates of the American Revolution and the Civil War; and they likely know about the settling of New England and the Spanish Southwest, about the Industrial Revolution, westward expansion, slavery, and the displacement and decimation of native peoples. What they may lack, and what historical surveys can begin to give them, is voices relating and responding to these cultural moments.

Such an approach, however, does not have to be a tour through antique "-isms." The period introductions in *NAAL* do a fine job of describing historical and cultural landscapes through which a literary history survey course must move; and your own presentations can, therefore, avoid the numbing assumption that the only way to read each writer is as a mouthpiece for some supposedly dominant idea system or list of aesthetic stipulations. The poorer essays that you will read this year and the most inert answers on midterm tests and final examinations may reflect this unhappy misapprehension: if you describe to us the *zeitgeist* (in twenty-five words) we can apply it, forcibly if necessary, to every writer whose career happens to fall within the defined dates of a literary "period."

For such reasons, it seems important to present literary history as lively interaction between prevailing values (or moral conflicts) of a given time, and individual minds and talents, with emphasis on *distinctions* among those minds, and differences in how they each engage with a historical predicament. It's hard to imagine that any student or teacher really wants to read Bradstreet as an undifferentiated voice of New England Puritanism rather than as a many-sided sensibility responding to that culture and creed. If the idea is only to find Romanticism or abolitionist ideology in Stowe, rather than see Stowe as an individualized writer working *amid* a landscape of Romanticism and moral crisis, then there would really be no need to read Stowe after hearing a general description of American Romantic thought or a summary of mid-nineteenth-century politics and race relations. In fact there would be little need to read anything other than the author headnotes.

To teach the historical survey now is to take on a compound responsibility: to offer students background and context, and to investigate authors as remarkable individuals within it. If we can accomplish something like this, we stand a chance of avoiding hypocrisies that students intuitively recognize and resent: the implicit notion that everyone (except, of course, an elite contemporary "us") has been a hopeless mental prisoner of easily summarizable value systems, and that what we do in reading back through American historical periods is hear that system reverberate in the words of any and every given writer. You won't lose conscientious students if you can engage, at least now and then, with paradox instead and with contradictions that we seem to assume are essential to selfhood and modern literary identity. If we begin planning a historical survey course from the idea that the American self is and has been commonly defined in terms of internal conflicts, ambivalence, and some sort of dialogue between reason and received ideas on the one hand and emotions and irrational urgencies on the other, then we can bring some of these texts to life as literature and discover in them lasting relevance and appeal. One key objective, then, can be to look for a humanizing, unhomogenized mix of motives, aspirations, and values.

If you have been teaching for a while, you know that many of your students haven't accepted the possibility that modern identity involves a measure of turmoil. Such students could be both comforted and inspired by a recognition that even in eras that seem overwhelmed by dogmas and idea systems (e.g., Puritanism, Transcendentalism, literary Naturalism), something in the self may stand apart; and that a text offering access to that unreconciled presence within is a text worth remembering.

Accordingly, as you move from one literary era to the next and offer your own review of how historical and cultural situations have evolved around individual writers, you might want to talk about particular situations in regard to the act of writing itself and about what, at those times, it meant to read something. For instance: in talking about the religious and political tumult of seventeenth-century Europe and conditions that propelled thousands of English Puritans to try to establish a theocratic colony in the New England wilderness, you can lose students in a footrace through historical events that do not successfully open up the texts of that period, however huge those events might seem. American students in this sometimes-overwhelming "information age" can gain imaginative entry into the seventeenth century if attention is paid to the printing and literacy revolutions that made the Reformation possible. For the first time in history, those revolutions allowed direct engagement of the ordinary citizen with the sacred text; consequently, new theologies developed and spread, including theologies that placed immense importance on that encounter between mind and text and on the urgencies of reading *right*. In other words, the northeast coast of the United States was being settled at a time when, as never before, the printed word and its interpretation energized not only personal and community life but also the private encounter with belief and Divine Will.

Similarly, a discussion of the literary scene of mid-nineteenth-century America benefits from attention to the technology and business of book publishing in those years: the sudden move to mass production and cheap, easy shipment deep into the American heartland, thanks to the rotary press, the reliable sheet feeder, and the web of railroads. Quite quickly, authorship in America offered an unprecedented chance for high profit, large-scale cultural impact, and real celebrity, not just in the United States but also elsewhere in the English-speaking world. A look at literary Modernism and Postmodernism will seem more plausible to students if it takes notice of situations in which they themselves are reading: with the college and university as major presences in the establishment of literary value and taste and with film and television having a very great impact on what gets written, published, and noticed by the larger culture.

As suggested earlier, the historical survey course is also a good place for spending some time talking about what literary history *has been* in the last century and in the thousands of survey classes taught on our campuses up to this moment. Reviewing this development need not mean condescending to it or congratulating ourselves for achieving some eleventh-hour wisdom that generations of benighted students and instructors had never glimpsed before. If the historical roots of the survey lie in an early-twentieth-century wish to acculturate an increasingly diverse population and stave off chaos by requiring a kind of collective homage to a sequence of supposedly heroic (and mostly white male) American authors, then at the millennium's end, one valid subject for us to discuss is the survey itself, and the cultural work that it can do, and the right of students to participate in reviewing and defining that mission. This need not be a posture: you may find that your students take the course much more seriously if they understand themselves to part of a collective process, rather than audience for an overperformed ritual.

The suggested readings listed here promote the presentation of important historical situations, of the rise and transformation of literary eras and values, of the complex engagement between individual talents and their immediate contexts, and of a literary legacy. The teaching notes for individual authors included in this guide are intended to help address these questions.

Suggested Readings

Volume A: Literature to 1700

NATIVE AMERICAN LITERATURE

The Iroquois Creation Story
Pima Stories of the Beginning of the World
Native American Trickster Tales

LITERATURE OF COLONIAL EXPANSION

Columbus: "Letter to Luis de Santangel"; "Letter to Ferdinand and Isabella"
Harriot: *A Brief and True Report of the New Found Land of Virginia*
Smith: *The General History of Virginia*

LITERATURE OF WITNESS AND ENCOUNTER

Casas: *The Very Brief Relation of the Devastation of the Indies*
Díaz del Castillo: *The True History of the Conquest of New Spain*
Cabeza de Vaca: *The Relation*
de la Vega: *The Florida of the Inca*
Champlain: *The Voyages*

NEW ENGLAND PURITAN WRITERS

Bradford: *Of Plymouth Plantation* ["The Mayflower Compact"]
Winthrop: "A Model of Christian Charity"
Bradstreet: "The Prologue"; "A Dialogue between Old England and New"; "Contemplations"; "The Flesh and the Spirit"; "The Author to Her Book"; "Here Follows Some Verses upon the Burning of Our House"; "As Weary Pilgrim"
Wigglesworth: *The Day of Doom*
Rowlandson: *A Narrative of the Captivity and Restoration*
E. Taylor: "Psalm Two"; *Preparatory Meditations* (including "Prologue"); "The Preface"; "The Joy of Church Fellowship Rightly Attended"; "Upon Wedlock, and Death of Children"; "Huswifery"; "A Fig for Thee, Oh! Death"
Sewall: *The Diary*

BEYOND PURITANISM AND THE BAY COLONY

T. Morton: *The New English Canaan*
Steendam: poems
Van der Donck: *A Description of New Netherland*
Pastorius: *Positive Information from America*

THE NEW ENGLAND PURITAN VISION: CRISIS, REVIVAL, METAMORPHOSIS

Mather: *The Wonders of the Invisible World;* "Galeacius Secundus: The Life of William Bradford"; "Nehemias Americanus: The Life of John Winthrop"; *Pillars of Salt*
Sewall: "The Selling of Joseph"

NATIVE PEOPLES AND THE NEW ARRIVALS

Bradford: *Of Plymouth Plantation*
R. Williams: *A Key into the Language of America*
Rowlandson: *A Narrative of the Captivity and Restoration*

WOMEN IN THE NEW WORLD

Bradstreet: poems
Rowlandson: *A Narrative of the Captivity and Restoration*
Mather: "The Trial of Martha Carrier"

Volume A: American Literature 1700–1820

PURITANISM IN THE EIGHTEENTH CENTURY

Knight: *The Private Journal of a Journey from Boston to New York*
Byrd: *Secret Diary; History of the Dividing Line*
Edwards: *Personal Narrative;* "A Divine and Supernatural Light"; "Letter to Rev. Dr. Benjamin Colman"; "Sinners in the Hands of an Angry God"

FEDERALISM, DEISM, AND THE ENLIGHTENMENT SPIRIT

Franklin: "The Way to Wealth"; "Information to Those Who Would Remove to America"; "Remarks Concerning the Savages of North America"; *The Autobiography*
J. Adams and A. Adams: letters
Paine: *Common Sense;* "The Crisis, No. 1"; *The Age of Reason*
Jefferson: The Declaration of Independence; *Notes on the State of Virginia*
Freneau: "On the Emigration to America and Peopling the Western Country"; "The Wild Honey Suckle"; "The Indian Burying Ground"; "On the Religion of Nature"
Tyler: *The Contrast*

SLAVERY, IDENTITY, AND PERSONAL ETHICS

Byrd: *The Secret Diary*
Woolman: *The Journal*
Moses Bon Sàam: "The Speech"
Crèvecoeur: "Letter IX"
Jefferson: The Declaration of Independence
Equiano: *The Interesting Narrative*
Freneau: "To Sir Toby"
Wheatley: "On Being Brought from Africa to America"; "To the University of
    Cambridge, in New England"; "Thoughts on the Works of Providence"; "To
    S. M., a Young African Painter, on Seeing His Works"; letters
S. Morton: "The African Chief"
Hammon: *Narrative*

NATIVE AMERICANS AND THE WHITE IMAGINATION

Franklin: "Remarks Concerning the Savages of North America"
Occom: *A Short Narrative of My Life*
Freneau: "The Indian Burying Ground"

COLONIAL AMERICAN WOMEN AND THE PREVAILING ETHOS

Knight: *The Private Journal of a Journey from Boston to New York*
Byrd: *The Secret Diary*
Edwards: "[Sarah Pierrepont]"
J. Adams and A. Adams: letters
Murray: "On the Equality of the Sexes"
S. Morton: poems

IMAGINING WOMEN IN THE NEW REPUBLIC

Rowson: *Charlotte*
Brown: *Wieland* (Chapter IX)

Volume B: American Literature 1820–1865

THE NEW AMERICAN-NESS OF AMERICAN LITERATURE

Irving: "Rip Van Winkle"; "The Legend of Sleepy Hollow"
Sedgwick: "Cacoethes Scribendi"; "A Reminiscence of Federalism"
Bryant: "Thanatopsis"; "To a Waterfowl"; "The Prairies"
Emerson: "The American Scholar"; "The Divinity School Address"; "Self-
    Reliance"; "The Poet"; "Experience"
Hawthorne: "Young Goodman Brown"; "The May-Pole of Merry Mount"; "The
    Minister's Black Veil"; *The Scarlet Letter*
Longfellow: "A Psalm of Life"; "Excelsior"; "The Jewish Cemetery at Newport";
    "My Lost Youth"

Poe: "The Raven"; "Annabel Lee"; "Ligeia"; "The Fall of the House of Usher";
   "The Philosophy of Composition"
Melville: "Hawthorne and His Mosses"; *Moby-Dick;* "Bartleby, the Scrivener";
   Billy Budd, Sailor

AMERICAN TRANSCENDENTALISM

Emerson: *Nature*
Fuller: "The Great Lawsuit"
Thoreau: *Walden*
Alcott: "Transcendental Wild Oats"

NARRATIVES OF WESTWARD EXPANSION

Cooper: *The Pioneers*
The Cherokee Memorials
Kirkland: *A New Home*
Clappe: "The Shirley Letters"
B. Taylor: *Eldorado*

LITERATURE OF A HOUSE DIVIDED

Emerson: "Last of the Anti-Slavery Lectures"
Lincoln: "A House Divided"; Gettysburg Address; Second Inaugural Address
Stowe: *Uncle Tom's Cabin*
Thoreau: "Resistance to Civil Government"; "Slavery in Massachusetts"
Douglass: *Narrative of the Life*
Whitman: *Drum-Taps* poems
Melville: "The Paradise of Bachelors and The Tartarus of Maids"; *Battle-Pieces*
Dickinson: 49; 185; 199; 241; 258; 303; 305; 348; 435; 441; 510; 536; 547;
   709; 732; 754; 824; 1099; 1129; 1138; 1545 (poems about being alienated)

PUBLIC VALUES AND DEMOCRATIC PROSPECTS

Lincoln: Second Inaugural Address
Douglass: "The Meaning of July Fourth for the Negro"
Whitman: "Preface to *Leaves of Grass*"; *Leaves of Grass* ["Song of Myself"]; "Let-
   ter to Ralph Waldo Emerson"; "From Pent-up Aching Rivers"; "Facing West
   from California's Shores"; "Scented Herbage of My Breast"; "Crossing Brook-
   lyn Ferry"; "Out of the Cradle Endlessly Rocking"; "As I Ebb'd with the
   Ocean of Life"; "When Lilacs Last in the Dooryard Bloom'd"
Dickinson: 67; 214; 249; 280; 303; 315; 328; 341; 448; 465; 501; 505; 528;
   632; 712; 822; 1540; 1593; 1651; 1732 (poems about struggle, triumph, and
   vision)
Davis: *Life in the Iron-Mills*
Lazarus: poems

Volume C: American Literature 1865–1914

REGIONALISM AND LOCAL-COLOR WRITING

Harte: "The Outcasts of Poker Flat"
Harris: "The Wonderful Tar-Baby Story"; "Mr. Rabbit Grossly Deceives Mr. Fox"
Jewett: "A White Heron"; "The Foreigner"
Freeman: "A New England Nun"; "The Revolt of 'Mother' "
Chesnutt: "The Goophered Grapevine"; "The Wife of His Youth"
Garland: "Under the Lion's Paw"
Zitkala Ša: "Impressions of an Indian Childhood"; "The School Days of an Indian
    Girl"; "An Indian Teacher among Indians"

AMERICAN LITERARY REALISM

Twain: *Adventures of Huckleberry Finn*; "Fenimore Cooper's Literary Offenses"
Woolson: "Miss Grief"
Bierce: "Occurrence at Owl Creek Bridge"
James: "Daisy Miller"; "The Real Thing"; "The Beast in the Jungle"; "The Art of
    Fiction"; "The Jolly Corner"
Wharton: "Souls Belated"
Cahan: "A Sweatshop Romance"
Sui Sin Far: "Mrs. Spring Fragrance"

NARRATIVES OF MINORITY STRUGGLE AND RESISTANCE

Cochise
Charlot
Washington: *Up from Slavery*
Du Bois: *The Souls of Black Folk*
Chesnutt: "The Wife of His Youth"
Eastman: *From the Deep Woods to Civilization*
Native American Chants and Songs
Wovoka, "The Messiah Letter"
Zitkala Ša: "Impressions of an Indian Girlhood"

LITERARY NATURALISM

Chopin: *The Awakening*; "At the 'Cadian Ball"; "The Storm"
Freeman: "A New England Nun"; "The Revolt of 'Mother' "
Gilman: "The Yellow Wall-paper"
Du Bois: *The Souls of Black Folk*
S. Crane: "The Open Boat"; "The Bride Comes to Yellow Sky"; "The Blue Hotel";
    "An Episode of War"
Dreiser: "Old Rogaum and His Theresa"
London: "The Law of Life"; "To Build a Fire"
H. Adams: *The Education of Henry Adams*

Volume D: American Literature between the Wars, 1914–1945

LITERARY NATURALISM IN AMERICAN VERSE

Masters: poems

Robinson: "The House on the Hill"; "Richard Cory"; "Miniver Cheevy"; "Mr. Flood's Party"

Sandburg: poems

MODERNIST THEMES

A. Lowell: poems

Stein: *The Making of Americans*

Frost: "Mending Wall"; "The Death of the Hired Man"; "After Apple-Picking"; "An Old Man's Winter Night"; "The Oven Bird"; "Birches"; " 'Out, Out-' "; "Nothing Gold Can Stay"; "Stopping by Woods on a Snowy Evening"; "Two Tramps in Mud Time"; "Desert Places"; "Design"; "Neither out far nor in Deep"; "The Gift Outright"; "Directive"; "The Figure a Poem Makes"

Anderson: *Winesburg, Ohio*

Stevens: "The Snow Man"; "A High-Toned Old Christian Woman"; "The Emperor of Ice-Cream"; "Disillusionment of Ten O'Clock"; "Sunday Morning"; "Anecdote of the Jar"; "Thirteen Ways of Looking at a Blackbird"; "The Idea of Order at Key West"; "Of Modern Poetry"

Yezierska: "The Lost 'Beautifulness' "

Williams: "Portrait of a Lady"; "The Widow's Lament in Springtime"; "Spring and All"; "To Elsie"; "The Red Wheelbarrow"; "The Dead Baby"; "The Wind Increases"; "Death"; "This Is Just to Say"; "A Sort of a Song"; "The Dance"; "Lear"; "Landscape with the Fall of Icarus"

Jeffers: "Shine, Perishing Republic"; "Hurt Hawks"; "November Surf"; "Carmel Point"

Eliot: "The Love Song of J. Alfred Prufrock"; "Tradition and the Individual Talent"; *The Waste Land*; "The Hollow Men"

O'Neill: *Long Day's Journey into Night*

McKay: poems

Porter: "Flowering Judas"; *Pale Horse, Pale Rider*

Cummings: "Buffalo Bill's"; "the Cambridge ladies who live in furnished souls"; "Poem,or Beauty Hurts Mr. Vinal"; " 'next to of course god america i"; "i sing of Olaf glad and big"; "anyone lived in a pretty how town"; "pity this busy monster,manunkind"

Toomer: *Cane*

Fitzgerald: "Winter Dreams"; "Babylon Revisited"

Faulkner: *As I Lay Dying*

Hemingway: "The Snows of Kilimanjaro"

Hughes: "The Negro Speaks of Rivers"; "Mother to Son"

FORMAL AND TECHNICAL EXPERIMENTATION

Pound: "A Pact"; "In a Station of the Metro"; "Villanelle: The Psychological Hour"; *The Cantos*

H. D.: "Oread"; "Leda"; "At Baia"; "Fragment 113"; "Helen"; "The Walls Do Not
   Fall"
Moore: "Poetry"; "To a Snail"; "Bird-Witted"; "The Mind Is an Enchanting Thing"
Eliot: "Burnt Norton"
Dos Passos: "The Big Money"
Bogan: poems
Faulkner: *As I Lay Dying*
H. Crane: "Chaplinesque"; "At Melville's Tomb"; *The Bridge*

SOCIAL AND POLITICAL WRITING

Yezierska: "The Lost 'Beautifulness' "
Glaspell: *Trifles*
Larsen: *Quicksand*
Hurston: "The Eatonville Anthology"; "How It Feels to Be Colored Me"
Parker: "General Review of the Sex Situation"
Taggard: "Everyday Alchemy"; "With Child"; "A Middle-aged, Middle-class Woman
   at Midnight"; "At Last the Women Are Moving"; "Mill Town"
S. Brown: poems
Hughes: "I, Too"; "Refugee in America"; "Madam and Her Madam"; "Madam's
   Calling Cards"; "Silhouette"; "Visitors to the Black Belt"; "Democracy"
Steinbeck: *The Grapes of Wrath*
Rukeyser: poems

THE NEW NEGRO MOVEMENT

McKay: poems
Larsen: *Quicksand*
Hurston: "The Gilded Six Bits"
Toomer: poems
S. Brown: poems
Hughes: poems
Cullen: poems
R. Wright: "The Man Who Was Almost a Man"

WOMEN WRITERS, MINORITY WRITERS, AND
THE AMERICAN REALIST LEGACY

Cather: "The Sculptor's Funeral"
Porter: *Pale Horse, Pale Rider*
Bulosan: "Be American"; "Homecoming"
McNickle: "Hard Riding"

Volume E: American Literature since 1945

Rather than apply historical labels to contemporary writers, you might choose a
few who suggest the various gatherings and traditions representative of later-twen-
tieth-century literature.

POSTWAR AFRICAN AMERICAN WRITERS

Ellison: *Invisible Man*; "Cadillac Flambé"
Baldwin: "Going to Meet the Man"
Marshall: "Reena"
Morrison: "Recitatif"
Baraka: *Dutchman*
Reed: *The Last Days of Louisiana Red*; "The Neo Hoo Doo Manifesto"
Bambara: "Medley"
Walker: "Everyday Use"
Parks: *The America Play*

SOUTHERN WRITERS

Welty: "Petrified Man"
Ransom: poems
Wolfe, "The Lost Boy"
T. Williams: *A Streetcar Named Desire*
O'Connor: "The Life You Save May Be Your Own"; "Good Country People"
Walker: "Everyday Use"

AMERICAN JEWISH WRITERS

Malamud: "The Magic Barrel"
Bellow: "Looking for Mr. Green"
Paley: "A Conversation with My Father"
Ginsberg: *Howl*
Levine: poems
Rich: poems
Roth: "Defender of the Faith"

POSTWAR AMERICAN DRAMA

T. Williams: *A Streetcar Named Desire*
Miller: *Death of a Salesman*
Baraka: *Dutchman*
Mamet: *Glengarry Glen Ross*
Parks: *The America Play*

WRITERS OF THE POSTWAR EAST COAST

Cheever: "The Swimmer"
Updike: "Separating"
Beattie: "Weekend"

NARRATIVE EXPERIMENTATION

Le Guin: "Schrödinger's Cat"
Barthleme: "The Balloon"
Pynchon: "Entropy"

Carver: "Cathedral"
Powers: *Galatea 2.2*

POSTWAR NATIVE AMERICAN WRITERS

Momaday: *The Way to Rainy Mountain*
Vizenor: "Almost Browne"
Silko: "Lullaby"
Erdrich: "Fleur"

LATINO AND LATINA WRITERS

Ríos: poems
Cervantes: poems
Anzaldúa: "Towards a New Consciousness"
Anaya: "The Christmas Play"
Ortiz Cofer: "The Witch's Husband"

GROUPING INDIVIDUAL POETS

From the contemporary poets included in *NAAL*, here are a few who demonstrate a variety of themes, techniques, and traditions.

Penn Warren
Roethke
Bishop
Berryman
R. Lowell
Wilbur
Brooks
J. Wright
Simic
Rich
Plath
Graham
Collins

EXPLORING INDIVIDUAL AND "SIGNATURE" POEMS

Roethke: "My Papa's Waltz"
Bishop: "In the Waiting Room"; "The Moose"; "One Art"
Hayden: "Middle Passage"
Jarrell: "The Death of the Ball Turret Gunner"; "Well Water"
Berryman: *Dream Songs* (especially 1, 14, 40)
Merrill: "Lost in Translation"; "Family Week at Oracle Ranch"
R. Lowell: "Memories of West Street and Lepke"; "Skunk Hour"; "For the Union Dead"
Brooks: "kitchenette building"; "the mother"; "a song in the front yard"
Wilbur: "Love Calls Us to the Things of This World"; "The Mind-Reader"
Ginsberg: *Howl*

J. Wright: "Autumn Begins in Martins Ferry, Ohio"; "A Blessing"
Sexton: "Sylvia's Death"
Snyder: "Riprap"; "Straight-Creek—Great Burn"
Rich: "A Valediction Forbidding Mourning"; "Diving into the Wreck"
Plath: "Lady Lazarus"; "Daddy"
Lorde: "The Woman Thing"; "Black Mother Woman"
Pinsky: "The Figured Wheel"; "The Want Bone"
Baraka: "An Agony. As Now."
Dove: *Thomas and Beulah*

POETS EXPLORING THE DIVERSITY OF CONTEMPORARY AMERICAN LIFE

Hayden
Brooks
Levertov
Merrill
Ortiz
Ginsberg
Rich
Lorde
Harjo
Baraka
Harper
Dove
Ríos
Cervantes
Song
Lee

CHAPTER 3

A Course in Traditions, Minority Voices, and Literary Diversity

The literature of the United States encompasses many ways of imagining experience. As the latest edition of *NAAL* once again makes clear, our literary diversity is a treasure, and as an instructor you may decide that it warrants more attention and development in your course than chronological surveys usually allow. The Sixth Edition features an especially fine representation of eighteenth- and nineteenth-century American women writers, Latina and Latino writers, Asian American writers, Native American voices and authors, and recent texts from other North American minority communities. *NAAL* can also help students explore populist and vernacular voices that both express and transcend gender and ethnicity. These voices contribute to a literary chronicle of working-class experience in the United States.

It is no secret, however, that as a community of teachers, we are in the midst of important conversations about identity politics and its relationship to literary study and that there are competing perspectives about where, in a course about traditions and diversity, the emphasis should fall: on the text, on the historical moment, on long-term or timeless political and moral concerns. No instructor's guide can presume to solve such riddles. For thinking about them on your own, we can offer only this proposition: if we want our students to remain engaged with literary texts, then those texts do have to be opened as something more than repositories of themes. In other words, the advice in this chapter is organized around the assumption that a key purpose of a course in literary traditions and literary diversity is to explore the text, rather than situate it—to help students talk about voice, style, poetics, rhetorical strategy, and understand how community affiliation, minority status, or other pressures on a given artist affect the choice and ordering of words on the page. The range of voices in NAAL do much more than allow mapping out of an array of divergent political and moral positions. They enrich, complicate, and expand our collective power to imagine and to tell.

Strong central questions for a course in traditions and diversity, therefore, can be questions about poetics:

- How might differences in gender, in ethnicity, in social power, and in historical circumstances affect literary imagination and style?
- Where and how do we see minority or marginalized voices challenging or complicating the prevailing aesthetic values of their own time and the literary legacy they inherit?
- In terms of style, structure, and imaginative possibilities, how do these works extend or resist the idea of an American literary tradition?

Questions like these can help tie a course together, but there are hard choices to make: if you decide to structure your course as an exploration of literary diversity, and of contrasting or competing poetics, you will need to decide on a limited array of communities and traditions to emphasize and to select authors who represent them well. Necessitated by the time constraints of the academic year, those choices can be painful; but if you can describe that selection process at appropriate moments in your class discussions and presentations, your students will understand why you have made certain choices, and how as readers they themselves can explore further on their own.

A Course or Unit about Gender and American Poetics

One enduringly relevant "traditions" exploration is the evolution of gender-related discourses in American poetry and prose: there are two strong traditions here, sometimes at odds, sometimes complementary, and students are often delighted to explore them together. There are moments in our literary history when male-promulgated assumptions about negotiating experience and creating literary art are challenged openly by women writers or are subverted with wit or are repudiated with a bold move in new aesthetic and epistemological directions. In American letters, these revolutionary women continue to have enormous impact on the way we think and write. In a long story running from Winthrop through Emerson and Whitman and on into twentieth-century male poets, fiction writers, and literary critics, there is an emergent masculinist poetics that favors thematic and moral finality, a dominion over worldly experience not unlike what Emerson valorized in "The Poet"—the author as bard, as namer, as prophet. And beginning as early as Bradstreet and continuing through Fuller, Dickinson, Hurston, Welty, Bishop, Rich, Parks, and many others, there is an alternative tradition, a tradition that emphasizes an "us" rather than Edward Taylor's and Emerson's masculinist "I." This feminist tradition values intense yet open-ended engagement with experience rather than final or reductive moralizing. This American feminist poetics accepts and celebrates collectivity, indeterminacy, living without "knowing," a tomorrow replete with more possibilities, rather than confined with yesterday's answers.

Some core questions for a course in gender and American poetics:

- What do various canonical American male writers assume to be the intention of imaginative literature? Where are those assumptions made clear?
- Compared to the values implicit in Bradford, Winthrop, and Mather, how is Bradstreet a radical writer? How do nineteenth-century American women poets continue her quest?
- Consider the way that Romantic and Transcendentalist American male poets end their poems. Why is there such emphasis on a firm philosophical or spiritual conclusion? How do women writers of the same period respond to that expectation?
- In the twentieth century, where do we see authors of either gender learning from the American feminist poetics that Bradstreet, Fuller, and Dickinson pioneered? Where do we see women writers affirming and resisting values that trace back to Emerson?

A Course or Unit about American Minority Voices

From *NAAL*'s substantial collection of minority authors and voices, it is not difficult to assemble a syllabus representing African American, Native American, Jewish American, and Latina and Latino communities. Again, the challenge is to organize such a course around compelling questions, questions that your students will find intellectually and culturally interesting. Good students will enjoy complication; they will value paradoxes and special predicaments that allow writers to emerge as individuals as well as constituents of a tradition. Here are some large-scale questions that can provide continuity as well as complexity in an encounter with literature by American minorities:

- When minority writers work within or against a dominant literary culture, how does a minority "literary tradition" take shape? Does it begin in a large-scale cultural movement? Can traditions arise, over time, from the creativity of isolated artists?
- What connections do we see between such literary traditions and popular culture or folk practices?
- How do American minority writers convey in their texts an understanding that they are participating in a tradition, or resisting one?
- How is a concept of minority literary traditions useful to us in writing about or discussing American literature?
- What dialogue do these minority writers maintain, willingly or otherwise, with the dominant culture or the literary mainstream of their own time?

Throughout most of the history of the United States, the printing presses, the bookshops, the literary reviews and journals were predominantly controlled and operated by people who were white and male; the potential audience, with the education and affluence to be readers, was also mostly white; and from the middle of the seventeenth century, the language of North American literary discourse was overwhelmingly English. What are the challenges here for minority American writers who seek access to such an audience and market, and what accommodations, in any given historical moment, might have to be made?

A Course about Marginality and Inclusion

For intellectually adventurous students, you can construct an exciting course that finds additional dimensions in concepts like *marginality, minority,* and *diversity.* Some of your students may come to your class already be puzzled as to whether there can be an "American literature" at all, as opposed to a Babel of competing values and voices, a chaos forced into shape and continuity by scholars and teachers. That question is difficult and serious—and in discussing it with your class or organizing a syllabus to investigate it, you might want to develop the possibility that in America, *everyone* can feel like an outsider, and that many American writers, regardless of ethnicity or gender, have struggled with marginalization, alienation, or exclusion. Paradoxically, this powerful feeling of being outside seems to unite many authors into a large-scale community. Does a collective sense of exclusion provide a tradition that includes us all?

Therefore, you could develop a unit or a course that compares traditions and discourses of marginality—in other words, a marginalized status as a conscious artistic decision or as a lasting or inescapable predicament. In such a unit, you could explore differences between, for example, Thoreau's deliberate choice to write from the physical and social isolation of Walden Pond, to dramatize himself as an eccentric, and the kind of crisis that his contemporary Frederick Douglass faced throughout his life. As a black slave at birth, and subsequently as a fugitive, and later as an African American author in the company of white abolitionists, with a measure of acceptance in white literary culture, Douglass had none of the freedom that Emerson or Thoreau enjoyed to take up or put aside a constructed public identity. For educated white American men in New England, marginality was an artistic option, a way of achieving an individual voice. However, they could make that decision with confidence in their own literary authority and social position, a confidence that nineteenth-century women writers, and writers from ethnic and racial minorities, could not share.

This contrast continues throughout the nineteenth and twentieth centuries, between artists who adopt or affect a marginalized status, writers who seem to feel deeply and inescapably alienated from every community, and writers who, regardless of what they do or say, are categorized by others as belonging to a specific minority. Bellow, Baldwin, Ellison, Ginsberg, Rich, Momaday, and many other modern writers, over the course of their careers, dissented from constituencies within a minority to which they supposedly belonged, and paid a price for doing so. In a nation and a culture that place such value on individuality, how is isolation or marginalization to be avoided by a writer with an independent mind?

Some core questions for a course or unit on marginality and inclusion:

- For specific writers and historical periods before Romanticism, what were the consequences of writing from a minority or marginalized condition? How do those conditions compare with the predicaments of marginalized American authors after 1850?
- When nineteenth-century popular and official culture begin to celebrate rugged individualism and independence, how do these values empower marginalized artists or complicate their situation?
- Since the 1970s, much has been said about "radical chic" in American popular culture—an affectation of marginalized or outlaw status for the purpose of achieving celebrity and profit. Your students will think of many examples. If this is indeed a presence in our culture, where are its historical roots, and what might the consequences be in a quest for cultural diversity and inclusion?

A Unit on American Persuasion and Polemic

Another way to organize a syllabus is to group writers who share a particular rhetorical or political style or intention. The tradition of the jeremiad and the polemic go back to the Bay Colony, and in the nineteenth century a passionate didacticism becomes a powerful presence in American poetry and fiction. Winthrop, Edwards, Paine, Rowson, and Jefferson; Emerson (including the March 7, 1854, antislavery speech), Stowe, Fuller, Whitman, Douglass, Du Bois, Ellison—in following this tradition, students can explore varieties of rhetoric intended to change minds quickly and utterly, and the interactions between the freewheeling individual imagination and moral imperative.

Some core questions for a unit on American persuasion and polemic:

- In the opening century of European settlement, the dominant published literary form was the sermon. As New England opens to the Enlightenment, the Federal period, and American Romanticism, where does the sermon tradition show itself in imaginative literature?
- From Rowson's *Charlotte* onward through Whitman's *Leaves of Grass,* flagrantly didactic passages turn up in the midst of novels, poems, and plays. How are these didactic passages integrated into secular imaginative works, and with what degree of success?
- When American minority and women authors moralize on the printed page, what rhetorical strategies do they employ?
- In modern American literature, have imagination and polemic parted company? If so, why? If not, can you give examples of poems, fiction, or plays that are didactic as well as imaginative?

Suggested Readings

Alternative Voices and American Literary Diversity

Volume A: Literature to 1700

EUROPEAN MALE LITERARY PRACTICES AND POETICS

Bradford: *Of Plymouth Plantation*
T. Morton: *The New English Canaan*
Winthrop: *A Model of Christian Charity*
Cabeza de Vaca: *The Relation*
Steendam: "The Praise of New Netherland"
E. Taylor: "Psalm Two"; "Prologue"; "Meditations" (8, 16, 38, 42); "The Preface"; "Upon Wedlock, and Death of Children"; "Huswifery"; "A Fig for Thee, Oh! Death"
Mather: *The Wonders of the Invisible World*

ALTERNATIVE WAYS OF TELLING: NATIVE AMERICAN TRADITIONS

Stories of the Beginning of the World
Native American Trickster Tales

ORIGINS OF AN AMERICAN POETICS BY WOMEN

Bradstreet: "The Author to Her Book," "Contemplations," "The Flesh and the Spirit," "Here Follows Some Verses upon the Burning of Our House," "To My Dear Children," and the elegies for her grandchildren

Volume A: American Literature 1700–1820

POLITICS AND WHITE AMERICAN MALE VOICES

Edwards: *Personal Narrative;* ["Sarah Pierrepont"]; "A Divine and Supernatural Light"; "Letter to Rev. Dr. Benjamin Colman"; "Sinners in the Hands of an Angry God"
Franklin: "The Way to Wealth"; "Information to Those Who Would Remove to America"; "Remarks Concerning the Savages of North America"; *The Autobiography*
Jefferson: The Declaration of Independence; *Notes on the State of Virginia* ("Query XVII")
Paine: "The Crisis"
Crèvecoeur: *Letters from an American Farmer*
J. Adams: letters to A. Adams

AMERICAN MEN CREATING WOMEN'S VOICES

Tyler: *The Contrast*
C. Brown: *Wieland*

RESPONSES AND RESISTANCE BY WOMEN; MINORITY PERSPECTIVES

Knight: *Private Journal*
Stockton: poems
Wheatley: poems
S. Morton: poems
Hammon: *Narrative*
Equiano: *The Interesting Narrative of the Life*
Rowson: *Charlotte*
A. Adams: letters to J. Adams
Occom: *A Short Narrative of My Life*
Murray: "On the Equality of the Sexes"

Volume B: American Literature 1820–1865

GENDER, ROMANTICISM, AND AMERICAN POETICS

Poetry

New England "Men of Letters"
Bryant: "Thanatopsis"; "To a Waterfowl"; "The Prairies"
Emerson: "The Poet;" "Experience"
Whittier: *Snow-Bound*
Poe: poems; tales; "The Poetic Principle"
Longfellow: poems
American Gay and Women Poets
Dickinson: poems, esp. 199, 249, 303, 341, 435, 441, 449, 465, 650, 712, 1138, 1473, 1601, 1732
Whitman: "Preface to *Leaves of Grass*"; *Leaves of Grass* ["Song of Myself"]; "Out of the Cradle Endlessly Rocking"

Fiction

"Men of Letters"
Irving: "The Legend of Sleepy Hollow"
Poe: "Ligeia;" "The Fall of the House of Usher"; "The Cask of Amontillado"
Hawthorne: "The Minister's Black Veil"; "Young Goodman Brown"; "Rappaccini's Daughter"
Melville: "Bartleby, the Scrivener"; "Benito Cereno"; "The Paradise of Bachelors and the Tartarus of Maids"
American Women Writers
Stowe: *Uncle Tom's Cabin*
Davis: *Life in the Iron Mills*
Alcott: "Transcendental Wild Oats"
Spofford: "Circumstance"

AMERICAN PERSUASION AND POLEMIC

"Men of Letters"
Emerson: "Nature"; "Fate"; "Last of the Anti-Slavery Lectures"

Thoreau: *Resistance to Civil Government*; *Walden*; "Slavery in Massachusetts";
  "Walking"
Poe: "The Philosophy of Composition"
Lincoln: "A House Divided"; Gettysburg Address; Second Inaugural Address
Women Writers
Sedgwick: "A Reminiscence of Federalism"
Child: "Mrs. Child's Reply"
Fuller: "The Great Lawsuit"
Fern: "Male Criticism on Ladies' Books"
Minority Voices
Apess: "An Indian's Looking-Glass for the White Man"
Jacobs: *Incidents in the Life of a Slave Girl*
Douglass: *Narrative*; "The Meaning of the Fourth of July for the Negro"

MEN, WOMEN, AND TRAVEL

Kirkland: *A New Home*
Clappe: "The Shirley Letters"
B. Taylor: *Eldorado*

Volumes C and D: American Literature 1865–1914 and 1914–1945

MINORITY VOICES IN AMERICAN FICTION

Chesnutt: "The Goophered Grapevine"; "The Wife of His Youth"
Yezierska: "The Lost 'Beautifulness' "
Cahan: "A Sweatshop Romance"
Larsen: *Quicksand*

WOMEN WRITING MODERN AMERICAN FICTION

Woolson: "Miss Grief"
Jewett: "A White Heron"; "The Foreigner"
Chopin: "At the 'Cadian Ball"; *The Awakening*
Freeman: "A New England Nun"; "The Revolt of 'Mother' "
Gilman: "The Yellow Wall-paper"
Wharton: "Souls Belated"
Porter: *Pale Horse, Pale Rider*
Cather: "The Sculptor's Funeral"; "Neighbour Rosicky"

LITERATURE ON THE THEME OF MARGINALITY AND INCLUSION

Charlot: "[He has filled graves with our bones]"
Eastman: *From the Deep Woods to Civilization*
Washington: *Up from Slavery*
Du Bois: *The Souls of Black Folk*
Sui Sin Far: "Mrs. Spring Fragrance"
Oskison: "The Problem of Old Harjo"

Zitkala Ša: "Impressions of an Indian Girlhood"; "School Days of an Indian Girl"; "An Indian Teacher among Indians"
Bulosan: "Be American"; "Homecoming"

AMERICAN WOMEN POETS, 1914–1945

A. Lowell
Moore
H. D.
Millay
Taggard
Stein

AFRICAN AMERICAN POETS AND PROSE WRITERS, 1914–1945

McKay
Toomer
S. Brown
Hughes
Cullen
R. Wright
Hurston

THE NATIVE AMERICAN EXPERIENCE

Black Elk: *Black Elk Speaks*
McNickle: "Hard Riding"

Volume E: American Literature since 1945

VOICES OF DIVERSITY AND INCLUSION, 1945 TO THE PRESENT

Fiction by Women

Welty: "Petrified Man"
Paley: "A Conversation with My Father"
O'Connor: "The Life You Save May Be Your Own"; "Good Country People"
Beattie: "Weekend"

Fiction by African Americans

Ellison: "Cadillac Flambé"
Baldwin: "Going to Meet the Man"
Baraka: *Dutchman*
Reed: *The Last Days of Louisiana Red*; "The Neo Hoo Doo Manifesto"
Marshall: "Reena"
Morrison: "Recitatif"
Bambara: "Medley"
Walker: "Everyday Use"

Fiction by Native Americans

Momaday: *The Way to Rainy Mountain*
Silko: "Lullaby"
Erdrich: "Fleur"

FICTION BY LATINA AND LATINO AMERICANS

Cisneros: selections from *Woman Hollering Creek*

POETRY BY WOMEN

Bishop: "The Fish"; "The Bight"; "At the Fishhouses"; "Questions of Travel";
"The Armadillo"; "In the Waiting Room"; "One Art"
Levertov: "To the Snake"; "In Mind"
Sexton: "The Truth the Dead Know"; "Sylvia's Death"; *The Death of Fathers*
Rich: "Snapshots of a Daughter-in-Law"; " 'I Am in Danger—Sir—' "; "A Vale-
diction Forbidding Mourning"; "Diving into the Wreck"
Plath: "Morning Song"; "Lady Lazarus"; "Daddy"
Oliver: "Poppies"; "Hummingbird Pauses at the Trumpet Vine"
Glück: "The Drowned Children"; "Illuminations"; "Appearances"; "Vespers"

POETRY BY AFRICAN AMERICANS

Hayden: "Middle Passage"; "Homage to the Empress of the Blues"
Harper: "American History"; "Martin's Blues"
Brooks: "kitchenette building"; "a song in the front yard"
Lorde: "Coal;" "The Woman Thing"; "Black Mother Woman"
Dove: *Thomas and Beulah*

POETRY BY NATIVE AMERICANS AND BY LATINA AND LATINO AMERICANS

Ortiz
Harjo
Ríos
Cervantes

CONTEMPORARY LITERATURE BY ASIAN AMERICANS

Lee: "The Gift"; "Persimmons"; "Eating Alone"; "Eating Together"
Song: "Beauty and Sadness"; "Lost Sister"; "Chinatown"; "Heaven"

The Southern Tradition

The southern tradition is represented in *NAAL* by the following authors.

Literature to 1700

Smith

American Literature 1700–1820

Byrd
Jefferson

American Literature 1820–1865

Thorpe
Douglass

American Literature 1865–1914

Twain
Harris
Chopin
Washington

American Literature between the Wars, 1914–1945

Porter
Hurston
Faulkner
Wolfe

American Literature since 1945

Penn Warren
Welty
T. Williams
Dickey
O'Connor
Walker
C. Wright

American Literature and Representations of Gender

If you are interested in examining representations of lesbian and gay experience, you will need to make this category more visible for students. The following list includes writers believed to be lesbian or gay, writers whose work raises questions concerning what Adrienne Rich has called "compulsory heterosexuality," and writers who have produced works of interest in the study of cultural representations of lesbian and gay experience.

Volume A: Literature to 1700 and American Literature 1700–1820

Representations of Pocahontas in Smith suggest that colonization follows the paradigm of heterosexual conquest.

Bradford: *Of Plymouth Plantation* (Book II, Chapter XXXII) establishes Bradford's concept of sexual deviance.

Sewall: *The Diary* offers a sometimes comic portrait of a thoughtful man trying to reconcile firm Calvinist beliefs, an elderly man's romantic inclinations (toward Mrs. Winthrop), and a wish for worldly comfort and prosperity.

Byrd: *The Secret Diary* represents marriage as an economic pact, a source of power and convenience for men, and a source of (to Byrd) amusing rivalry and domestic skirmish, in which African Americans are the pawns and casualties.

Bradstreet (poems) and **J. Adams and A. Adams** (letters): These writings celebrate loving heterosexual relationships as the paradigm for the republic.

Rowson: *Charlotte* provides stern lessons about the dangers of sexuality and passion, mixed with celebrations of prudent middle-class love and marriage and of obedience to family elders.

Volume B: American Literature 1820–1865

Irving: "The Legend of Sleepy Hollow" pits the "masculine," ignorant Brom Bones versus an "effeminate" or asexual and scholastic Ichabod Crane; the real relationship in the story may not be Ichabod's heterosexual interest in Katrina Van Tassel but rather the rivalry between the men, ending in a caricature of erotic conquest.

Emerson: "The Poet," which helped shape American aesthetics for generations, codifies a poetics of dominion over experience, of an agonistic relationship between the male "bard" and a vast and essentially female natural order.

Hawthorne: *The Scarlet Letter* contrasts the erotic and even sadomasochistic relationship between Dimmesdale and Chillingworth with the very different sort of passion between Dimmesdale and Hester Prynne.

Poe: "The Sleeper," "The Raven," "Annabel Lee," and other elegiac poems seem to celebrate dead women as the ideal subject for the poet and the ideal consorts for the truly sensitive male lover; "Ligeia" seems to construct heterosexuality as a form of death.

Fuller: "The Great Lawsuit" critiques the reality of modern American bourgeois marriage.

Thoreau: How much does misogyny or unconventional sexuality figure into *Walden*, which, according to its opening chapter, offers essentially economic advice to "poor students" and supposedly genderless counsel on how to live "deliberately"?

Whitman: The *Calamus* poems contrast powerfully with the *Children of Adam* poems.

Melville: "Hawthorne and His Mosses" depicts the pervasive single-sex world of Melville's fiction. The *Moby-Dick* selections foster discussion of power structures and love relationships among this company of men, thousands of miles from women and standard family life.

Dickinson: 249, 520, and others suggest both homoerotic and heteroerotic themes. Her poems, which avoid a discourse of domination in regard to worldly experience, make up an eloquent rebellion against Emersonian poetics.

Volume C: American Literature 1865–1914

Twain: Like the relationship between Dimmesdale and Chillingworth in Hawthorne's *The Scarlet Letter*, the relationships between Huck and Tom and Huck and Jim in *Adventures of Huckleberry Finn*, as Leslie Fielder observed many years ago, may exemplify a homoerotic bond that turns up frequently in American narratives by male writers: Hawkeye and Chingachgook, Ishmael and Queequeg, Jay Gatsby and Nick Carraway, Chief Bromden and Randall McMurphy.

James: *Daisy Miller* and *The Beast in the Jungle*, along with other narratives, raise questions about male narcissism, the social and sexual predicament of upper-class, late-century women, and the fate of heterosexual and homosexual eroticism in the Gilded Age.

Jewett: Rejecting the requirement of "compulsory heterosexuality," Sylvy, in "A White Heron," refuses to tell the heron's secret to the attractive male hunter.

Chopin: The enduring feminist novel *The Awakening* can be read as a critique not merely of an exhausted bourgeois existence but of all conventional descriptions and confinements of sexuality.

Freeman: In "A New England Nun," Louisa Ellis rejects overwhelming social and economic pressures to marry.

Volume D: American Literature between the Wars, 1914–1945

A. Lowell, Stein, H. D., and H. Crane: All offer poems with homoerotic themes and radical critiques of conventional (post-Emersonian) ways of seeing and dominating experience.

Parker: The poems and prose piece "The Waltz" offer razor-edged satire of twentieth-century bourgeois constructions of love and marriage.

Volume E: American Prose since 1945

T. Williams: *A Streetcar Named Desire* explores various forms of modern sexuality, socially sanctioned and otherwise.

Baldwin: "Going to Meet the Man" is a narrative of a white racist, his memory of a lynching, and a forbidden sexuality entwined with both the bigotry and the crime.

Volume E: American Poetry since 1945

Duncan, Merrill, Ginsberg, Rich, and **Lorde:** All bring gay perspectives to poems about contemporary life.

CHAPTER 4

A Course in
Major American Authors

To thoughtful teachers in any season, *major authors* rarely signifies an immutable array of Greats. In regard to American literature, our academic, commercial, and public conversations about ephemeral fads and lasting quality date only from the end of the nineteenth century. A browse through old American literature collections and college reading lists will provide plenty of evidence that each generation challenges and changes the Parnassus, lifting up new writers and nudging others down the slope. When Stowe died in 1896, *Uncle Tom's Cabin* was commonly regarded as America's *Les Misérables*; only thirty years later, high-profile professors were condescending to it as misshapen, sentimentalist, and hopelessly mass-market. Two generations further on, Stowe's best-seller was back on the lists of national classics, and available in half a dozen scholarly editions. Toward the end of his career, the discriminating Henry James declared that the best novelist then writing in the English language was Hugh Walpole—an author whose works didn't break into anyone's retrospective "top hundred" for the twentieth century. And Twain enthusiasts have seen the reputation of some of his works whipsaw up and down like stocks on an over-the-counter exchange. Other examples of shifting valuations will occur to you—and the lesson that they teach is clear.

Such realities, however, need not be grounds for debunking any selection of great American texts; and a "major authors tour," mixed with a little healthy and playful skepticism, can be stronger and more pleasurable for good students than either a solemn presentation of the timelessly sublime or a protracted exercise in iconoclasm. If we are having luck in fostering honest conversation in the classroom, then these worries over majorness and greatness may take care of themselves. For our own good as teachers, and for the continued worth of the discussions we encourage about American cultural history, we need vigorous participation from our students-and a survey course runs no great risk of collapse if it welcomes that participation at the outset, and sustains it throughout the term.

If that intention makes sense, you might consider opening your course with a discussion of how literary worth is determined and how modern Western culture has deliberated issues like the ones above. Who makes those choices? Why should they have an impact? What cultural forces and aesthetic values might be in play, and how much should they matter? What about mass appeal, as measured by sales in a given year or over several decades? What about popularity of another sort— among professors in literature departments and regular mention in august histories of American letters? What is the effect of big-budget Hollywood screen versions, with high-profile stars? Students will have impressions to share—and if in sharing them and in noting the strengths and limitations of these modes of selections, they see the whole process as a complex and open-ended one, then so much the better.

In a major authors survey, as in a more general historical tour, we can present some of these canonical writers as figures who *have been* regarded as important— by other well known writers who came after and either adapted from them or quarreled with them; or by influential critics and historians; or by a large and steady reading public, as was true for Longfellow and remains true for Melville, Twain, Douglass, Cather, Ellison, and many others. In a semester-long course, you might open with some authors who have been recently added to the lists of the Famous and talk about *why* they might have been rediscovered. You may also want to add writers whose place on the major authors lists is still controversial. Again, the inclusion of a few such writers encourages students to think not just about literary meaning but also about the open-endedness of creating and re-creating an American canon and about the ways in which we use such texts to conduct a dialogue with ourselves about ourselves.

Presenting a course as a study of major authors makes it possible to read and discuss more of each writer's work. This approach does not have to eliminate the historical context or the literary history within which any given writer wrote, although such a course usually emphasizes the development of each writer's career, rather than broad historical and cultural contexts. If you require students to read the excellent *NAAL* period introductions, you can allocate class time to intensive discussion of writers and individual works.

The major authors model works well in a multicourse curriculum in which first-year students take an introduction to literature course and upper-division students study literary periods in detail. The major authors course can be an intensive reacquaintance with writers that students have read before, either in high school or elsewhere on your campus, and an incentive to read other writers who were contemporaries of these major figures or who owe them a literary debt.

As a start, you might find it useful to review your own ideas or intuitions about majorness. Some of the words we might casually resort to, in explaining choices of certain writers over others—*great, universal, enduring,* and *major* itself—can be cloudy, evasive. Your students are sure to have questions of their own: How does this particular author become major? Is his or her greatness open to debate? Is there a "dictionary" somewhere that establishes criteria for inclusion or does inclusion of any particular author reflect the opinions of many readers over a long stretch of time? Why do there appear to be so many major American authors in one brief period (e.g., 1820–65), and so few in other eras (e.g., 1620–1820)? If the theaters were open and thriving in America during the Gilded Age, why don't anthologies include those plays?

One way to open up questions about literary reputation is to allow students to choose a favorite author who is not on the syllabus and ask them to write about this author's literary value. Asking questions like these can help keep the conversation refreshingly open-ended and encourage students to consider that this whole issue of majorness and greatness is one in which they can participate as informed and thoughtful adults. At one of the opening sessions, you might want to see if your class can evolve its own tentative criteria. If you help them keep track by writing their suggestions on the board, you may end up with a list like the following, regarding authors we could call major:

- They still appeal to a variety of readers, and serve as points of reference in conversations about cultural history.
- They wrote works that influenced more than one other major author.
- They contributed at least one acknowledged "masterpiece" to American literature.
- They sustained a literary career beyond a single *tour de force*.
- They were pioneers or innovators in subject matter, literary tradition, technique, or genre.
- They have also been recognized as influential literary critics or historians.

Phrases like *major authors* and one of its classroom variants, *major-minor authors*, can add to students' confusion. We might need to distinguish between *major* meaning "significant" in some way and *major* as "mainstream." One of the larger challenges in teaching the major authors course is helping some students reconsider assumptions that *major* always equals "Euro-American" or "male" and that women, Native American, African American, and other minority writers— because they take up fewer pages in *NAAL* and most other comprehensive anthologies—are certified "minor" writers.

Suggested Readings

Volume A: Literature to 1700

There are several authors here whose voices have echoed strongly in recent reconstructions of cultural history.
Columbus
Díaz del Castillo
Cabeza de Vaca
Smith

Winthrop: "A Model of Christian Charity"
Bradstreet
E. Taylor

Volume A: American Literature 1700–1820

Most of these writers have been touchstones in American literary history courses and comprehensive anthologies since the beginning of the twentieth century.

Edwards
Franklin: including *The Autobiography*
Jefferson: including *Notes on the State of Virginia* and The Declaration of Inde-
    pendence
Tyler: *The Contrast*

Volume B: American Literature 1820–1865

These are some of the seminal figures and perennial favorites in descriptions of
the American Renaissance.

Emerson: including *Nature*
Hawthorne: including *The Scarlet Letter*
Poe
Stowe
Thoreau: *Walden*
Douglass: *Narrative of the Life*
Whitman
Melville: including *Billy Budd, Sailor*
Dickinson

Volume C: American Literature 1865–1914

Since this was a period remembered better for narrative and nonfiction prose
than for poetry and drama, the usual choices are influential novelists of the Realist tradition and essayists on social moral questions. Since the republic's awareness
of its own diversity was increasing in these years, however, it makes sense to
include voices from communities recently recognized by centers of literary power
and production.

Twain: including *Adventures of Huckleberry Finn*
James
Chopin
Wharton
Du Bois
Washington
Native American Chants and Songs

Volume D: American Literature between the Wars, 1914–1945

Again, an accumulation of older anthologies and cultural histories provides good evidence of who can be, or was, regarded as major in the age of American High Modernism.

Cather
Frost
Stevens
O'Neill
Eliot
Fitzgerald
Hemingway
Steinbeck
W. C. Williams
Hurston
Faulkner
Hughes

Volume E: Prose since 1945

The closer we come to the present, the greater the controversy. We have celebrities here, and prize winners, and classroom favorites, and figures who command vigorous attention in American high schools as well as scholarly journals and conferences.

T. Williams
Malamud
Ellison
Bellow
Miller
O'Connor
Momaday
Walker
Beattie

Volume E: Poetry since 1945

Roethke
Bishop
R. Lowell
Brooks
Wilbur
J. Wright
Rich
Dove

A Broader American Canon?

Part of the fun of teaching and reviewing a parade of major writers is encouraging your students to second-guess it. Below are listed some *NAAL* works that can not only lengthen a list of The Greats but also enrich our conception of the culture that these "Great" works are about.

Volume A: Literature to 1700

Stories of the Beginning of the World
Champlain
Native American Trickster Tales
Bradford
T. Morton

Volume A: American Literature 1700–1820

Grainger
Crèvecoeur
Rowson
Stockton
Equiano
S. Morton

Volume B: American Literature 1820–1865

Irving
Fuller
Sedgwick
Fern
Davis
Alcott
Lazarus

Volume C: American Literature 1865–1914

Jewett
Freeman
Chesnutt
Eastman
S. Crane
Cahan
Dreiser
Native American Chants and Songs

Volume D: American Literature between the Wars, 1914–1945

Stein
Anderson
Pound

H. D.
Moore
Porter
R. Wright

Volume E: Prose since 1945

Welty: "Petrified Man"
Malamud: "The Magic Barrel"
Le Guin: "Schrödinger's Cat"
Anaya: "The Christmas Play"
Kingston: *Tripmaster Monkey*
Silko: "Lullaby"
Powers: *Galatea 2.2*

Volume E: Poetry since 1945

Kunitz
Olson
Hayden
Berryman
Levertov
Ammons
Merrill
Ashbery
Sexton
Plath
Merwin
Creeley
Simic
Pinsky
Lorde
Song
Lee

Works by Noncanonical Writers Especially Suited for a Major Authors Course

Volume A: Literature to 1700

We can look for works that focus on exploration and discovery in other locales than the New England coast or what became the Spanish colonies in North America.

Wigglesworth: *The Day of Doom*

Volume A: American Literature 1700–1820

For this period, one of the best-sellers of the age (Paine) might be played off against compelling works from the margins.

Occom: *A Short Narrative of My Life*
Paine: *Common Sense;* "The Crisis, No. 1"
Wheatley: poems

Volume B: American Literature 1820–1865

As Emerson and others around Concord take up the public project of imagining and defining an American public and an array of national values, what traditions and social realities are they including, and what are they leaving out?

Bryant: poems, especially "The Prairies"
Apess: "An Indian's Looking-Glass for the White Man"
Jacobs: *Incidents in the Life of a Slave Girl*
Davis: *Life in the Iron-Mills*

Volume C: American Literature 1865–1914

Here we can revisit writers who were eased out of the limelight after their careers ended or who were regarded as "regional" in ways that kept them on the margins.

Harte: "The Outcasts of Poker Flat"
Harris: tales
Garland: "Under the Lion's Paw"
Gilman: "The Yellow Wall-paper"

Volume D: American Literature between the Wars, 1914–1945

In America between the wars, what else was going on besides High Modernism?

Black Elk: *Black Elk Speaks*
Masters: poems
Hurston: "The Eatonville Anthology"; "How It Feels to Be Colored Me"
Parker: essays
Cummings: poems
Toomer: *Cane*
Wolfe: "The Lost Boy"

Volume E: Prose since 1945

As we approach the present, who's major and who's not becomes a very cloudy issue. Here are some strong candidates not listed earlier.
Cheever: "The Swimmer"
Baldwin: "Going to Meet the Man"
Updike: "Separating"
Roth: "Defender of the Faith"
Pynchon: "Entropy"

Powers: *Galatea 2.2*
Erdrich: "Fleur"

Volume E: Poetry since 1945

Oppen
Jarrell
Wilbur
Creeley
Snyder
Harper
Song
Lee

CHAPTER 5

A Course about Genres and American Literary Themes

This chapter offers reading lists for a course emphasizing the development of specific genres of American writing:

The personal and historical account
Forms of poetry
Narrative fiction
The drama

A course of this kind can be organized to open several large-scale questions:

- In a given historical moment, how do favored genres reflect and converse with conventional thought and cultural values?
- How does a specific literary work follow, resist, or reinvent standard forms and rules of the genre?
- In the American traditions, why do certain genres gain dominance, at various times, for the exploration of moral, political, philosophical, or spiritual themes?
- In a literature with a proliferation of genres and a sizable inheritance from European literary traditions, what constitutes originality or creativity?

In discussing literary history, what are the advantages and drawbacks of imagining an evolution of American genres, a process by which new experiments develop from an accumulated legacy? Does an American cult of newness or a succession of cultural innovations in England and western Europe complicate our wish to see each powerful new text as related to whatever came before?

A course that pays special attention to the development of American genres may need to look carefully at the *literary* circumstances of each author—meaning his or her formal or informal cultural experience, the strength (in that historical moment) of indigenous and imported literary models and influences, the availability of other texts, the supporting community and intended audience, the clarity or uncertainty (at that time) of the function and responsibilities of authorship. Luckily, however, we can keep at least two different dialogues going in such a course: an investigation of literary history from this general perspective and a freer and (to some students at least) more pleasurable review of American genres from *our* viewpoint, whereby texts are read as engaged in a dialogue (author-intended or not) with a long sequence of other texts.

Suggested Readings: Genres

Volume A: Literature to 1700

INDIGENOUS NARRATIVES BEFORE THE COMING OF THE EUROPEANS

Stories of the Beginning of the World
Native American Trickster Tales

THE AGE OF DISCOVERY AND COLONIZATION

Columbus
Casas
Díaz del Castillo
Cabeza de Vaca
Harriot
Champlain
Smith
Bradford
T. Morton
R. Williams
Winthrop
Steendam
Van Der Donck
Rowlandson
Mather

POETRY

Bradstreet
Wigglesworth
E. Taylor

Sermons, Philosophical and Theological Inquiry

Winthrop
E. Taylor: "Sermon VI"
Mather

Political Nonfiction Prose

Bradford
R. Williams

Volume A: American Literature 1700–820

Historical Chronicles and Personal Accounts

Knight
Byrd
Edwards: *Personal Narrative*
Franklin
Woolman
Crèvecoeur
Jefferson
Occom
Equiano

Poetry

Freneau
Wheatley
Grainger
S. Morton
Stockton

Sermons, Philosophical and Theological inquiry

Edwards: "Sinners in the Hands of An Angry God"; "A Divine and Supernatural
Light"

Prose Fiction

Rowson
C. Brown

American State Papers and Political Nonfiction Prose

Franklin
Crèvecoeur
Paine
Jefferson
The Federalist
Murray

DRAMA

Tyler

Volume B: American Literature 1820–1865

FICTION

Irving
Cooper
Sedgwick
Hawthorne
Poe
Stowe
Thorpe
Melville
Davis
Alcott
Spofford

JOURNALS AND LETTERS

Child
Whitman
Dickinson

LITERARY ESSAYS

Emerson
Hawthorne
Poe
Whitman
Melville

LYRIC POETRY

Bryant
Longfellow
Whittier
Poe
Whitman
Dickinson

PERSONAL NARRATIVE

Kirkland
Jacobs
Douglass

Philosophical Essays

Emerson
Thoreau

Travel Accounts

Fern
Clappe
B. Taylor

Southwest Humor

Thorpe

Political Nonfiction Prose

The Cherokee Memorials
Apess
Lincoln
Fuller
Fern
Thoreau
Douglass

Volume C: American Literature 1865–914

The Folk Tradition in American Literature

Harris
Chesnutt

Humor

Twain
Harris

Literary Criticism

Twain
James

Local Color

Twain
Harte
Harris
Garland
S. Crane

LYRIC POETRY

Piatt
S. Crane

LITERARY NATURALISM

Bierce
Chopin
Gilman
S. Crane
Dreiser
London

PUBLIC AND POLITICAL WRITING

Native American Oratory
Washington
Du Bois

REALISM

Twain
Woolson
James
Wharton
Cahan
Far

REGIONALISM

Jewett
Chopin
Freeman
Chesnutt
Oskison
Zitkala Ša

NATIVE AMERICAN ORAL LITERATURE

Cochise
Charlot
Navajo Night Chant
Chippewa Songs
Ghost Dance Songs
Wovoka

AUTOBIOGRAPHY AND PERSONAL NARRATIVE

Washington
Eastman

Gilman
Zitkala Ša
H. Adams

Volume D: American Literature between the Wars, 1914–1945

African American Fiction

Larsen
Hurston
Toomer
R. Wright

Drama

Glaspell
O'Neill

Experimental Prose

Stein
Faulkner

Humor

Parker
Welty

African American Lyric Poetry

McKay
S. Brown
Hughes
Cullen

Populist and Folk Lyric Poetry

Masters
Sandburg

Longer Poems

W. C. Williams
Pound
H. D.
Eliot
H. Crane

MODERNIST LYRIC POETRY

Robinson
Frost
Stevens
W. C. Williams
A. Lowell
Pound
H. D.
Jeffers
Moore
Eliot
Ransom
Millay
Cummings
Bogan
H. Crane

POLITICAL/FEMINIST LYRIC POETRY

Taggard
Rukeyser

REALIST FICTION

Cather
Anderson
Yezierska
Porter
Steinbeck
Hurston
Fitzgerald
Bulosan
McNickle
Dos Passos
Faulkner
Hemingway
Steinbeck

SOUTHERN FICTION

Porter
Faulkner
Wolfe
Welty

NATIVE AMERICAN AUTOBIOGRAPHY

Black Elk

Volume E: Prose Since 1945

DRAMA

T. Williams
Miller
Mamet
Parks

AMERICAN JEWISH FICTION

Malamud
Bellow
Roth

FICTION FROM AND ABOUT NEW YORK CITY

Cheever
Malamud
Ellison
Bellow
Updike
Beattie

SOUTHERN FICTION

Welty
O'Connor
Walker

AFRICAN AMERICAN FICTION

Ellison
Baldwin
Marshall
Baraka
Morrison
Dixon
Bambara
Walker
Reed

NATIVE AMERICAN FICTION

Momaday
Vizenor
Silko
Erdrich

Simic
Levertov
Merrill
Ginsberg
Sexton
Rich
Plath

THE BEATS

Ginsberg
Snyder

AFRICAN AMERICAN POETRY

Hayden
Brooks
Lorde
Harper
Dove

LATINO/LATINA POETRY

Ríos
Cervantes
Ortiz

WOMEN POETS

Rich
Bishop
Plath
Lorde
Harjo
Graham
Dove

SHORT LYRICS

Jarrell
Wilbur
Ammons
Merwin
J. Wright
Pinsky
C. Wright
Simic
Collins
Graham
Glück

LONGER POEMS

Wilbur
Merrill
Ginsberg
Rich
Dove

NATIVE AMERICAN POETRY

Ortiz
Harjo

NATURE AND LANDSCAPE POETRY

Niedecker
Penn Warren
Roethke
Bishop
Wilbur
Ammons
Merrill
J. Wright
Snyder
Oliver

NEW YORK SCHOOL

O'Hara
Ashbery

"PROJECTIVE VERSE"

Olson
Levertov

PROTEST AND POLITICAL POETRY

R. Lowell
Levertov
Ginsberg
Rich

EXPERIMENTAL POETRY

Oppen
Creeley
Duncan

Suggested Readings: Themes

Any catalog of major themes in American literature, and of works in which those themes appear, will necessarily be incomplete and reductive. The following listings refer to certain themes that are characteristic of, though not necessarily exclusive to, the American experience

The Problem of American Identity

This theme so pervades American literature that it might serve as a basis for organizing an entire course, especially for students broadly interested in American history and culture. Following are lists of some of the works in *NAAL* grouped by the issues they raise.

Volume A: Literature to 1700 and American Literature 1700–1820

THE NEW WORLD AND ITS LANDSCAPE

Stories of the Beginning of the World
Casas: "The Coast of Pearls"
Harriot: *A Brief and True Report of the New Found Land of Virginia*
Smith: "A Description of New England"
Bradford: *Of Plymouth Plantation*
R. Williams: *A Key into the Language of America*
Van der Donck: *A Description of New Netherlands*
Rowlandson: *A Narrative of the Captivity and Restoration*
Pastorius: *Positive Information from America*
Crèvecoeur: "Letter X"
Freneau: "On the Emigration to America and Peopling the Western Country";
     "The Indian Burying Ground"; "On Mr. Paine's Rights of Man"
Wheatley: "On Being Brought from Africa to America"

ACHIEVING A PERSONAL VOICE IN THE BAY COLONY

Bradstreet: poems
E. Taylor: poems
Sewall: *The Diary*

PRIVATE PAPERS AS A WAY OF KNOWING

Díaz del Castillo: *The True History of the Conquest of New Spain*
Sewall: *The Diary*
Knight: *The Private Journal*
Byrd: *The Secret Diary*
Woolman: *The Journal*
J. Adams and A. Adams: letters

THE SELF AND DIVINE REVELATION

Bradstreet: "Contemplations"; "To My Dear Children"
Wigglesworth: *The Day of Doom*

E. Taylor: poems
Mather: *The Wonders of the Invisible World*
Edwards: *Personal Narrative;* "A Divine and Supernatural Light"; *Images or Shadows of Divine Things*
Woolman: *The Journal*
Wheatley: "Thoughts on the Works of Providence"

INVENTING THE SELF IN THE EIGHTEENTH CENTURY

Franklin: "The Way to Wealth"; *The Autobiography*
Occom: *A Short Narrative of My Life*
Equiano: *The Interesting Narrative of the Life*
Tyler: *The Contrast*

PUBLIC DISCOURSE AND THE FORMATION OF A NATIONAL CHARACTER

Crèvecoeur: *Letters from an American Farmer*
Stockton: poems
Paine: *Common Sense;* "The Crisis, No. 1"; *The Age of Reason*
Jefferson: The Declaration of Independence; *Notes on the State of Virginia; The Federalist Papers*
Murray: *"On the Equality of the Sexes"*
Rowson: *Charlotte*

Volume B: *American Literature 1820–1865*

FICTION, POETRY, AND THE QUESTION OF AMERICAN IDENTITY

Irving: "Rip Van Winkle"; "The Legend of Sleepy Hollow"
Cooper: *The Pioneers*
Bryant: "The Prairies"
Sedgwick: "Cacoethes Scribendi"; "A Reminiscence of Federalism"

DEFINING THE AMERICAN INTELLECT

Emerson: "The American Scholar"; "The Divinity School Address"; "Self-Reliance"; "The Poet"; "Fate"
Fuller: "The Great Lawsuit"

PROBLEMS OF SELF-KNOWLEDGE

Hawthorne: "Young Goodman Brown"; "The Minister's Black Veil"; *The Scarlet Letter*
Stowe: *Uncle Tom's Cabin* (especially Chapters III, IX, XX)

FANTASY, DREAMS, AND THE PRIVATE SELF

Poe: poems; "Ligeia"

SLAVERY AND THE ACHIEVEMENT OF SELFHOOD

Jacobs: *Incidents in the Life of a Slave Girl*
Douglass: *Narrative of the Life; My Bondage and My Freedom*

THE SELF TRIUMPHANT

Emerson: "Self-Reliance"
Longfellow: "A Psalm of Life"; "Excelsior"
Thoreau: *Walden* (especially "Economy," "Where I Lived," "Spring," "Conclusion")
Whitman: *Leaves of Grass* (esp. "Song of Myself"; "Live Oak, with Moss")
Melville: "Benito Cereno"
Dickinson: 214, 249, 303, 324, 435, 441, 632, 1072, 1125

THE SELF AS CONTINGENT, OR IMPERILED

Whitman: "Facing West from California's Shores"; "When Lilacs Last in the Dooryard Bloom'd"
Melville: *Moby-Dick* (Chapter I); "Bartleby, the Scrivener"; *Billy Budd, Sailor*
Dickinson: 185, 241, 258, 280, 305, 341, 348, 435, 448, 465, 505, 510, 520, 547, 664, 754, 822, 986, 1099, 1129, 1581, 1651, 1732
Davis: *Life in the Iron-Mills*
Spofford: "Circumstance"

Volume C: American Literature 1865–1914

In works after the Civil War, the question of American identity joins with other compelling issues, and nearly every writer engages with it somehow. Here are some works useful for addressing issues of personal identity in the modern era.

Twain: *Adventures of Huckleberry Finn*
James: *Daisy Miller;* "The Beast in the Jungle"; "The Jolly Corner"
Chopin: *The Awakening*
Gilman: "The Yellow Wall-paper"
Freeman: "A New England Nun"
Washington: *Up from Slavery*
Chesnutt: "The Wife of His Youth"
Eastman: *From the Deep Woods to Civilization*
Du Bois: *The Souls of Black Folk*
Oskison: "The Problem of Old Harjo"
Chippewa Songs
Zitkala Ša: "Impressions of an Indian Childhood;" "The School Days of an Indian Girl"; "An Indian Teacher among Indians"
H. Adams: *The Education of Henry Adams*

Volume D: American Literature between the Wars, 1914–1945

Black Elk: *Black Elk Speaks*
Masters: poems

Robinson: poems
Frost: poems (esp. "Once by the Pacific"; "The Gift Outright"; "Directive")
Sandburg: "Chicago"
Larsen: *Quicksand*
Yezierska: "The Lost 'Beautifulness' "
Jeffers: "Shine, Perishing Republic"
McKay: poems
Cather: "The Sculptor's Funeral"
Hurston: "How It Feels to Be Colored Me"
Taggard: "Mill Town"
Cummings: "Buffalo Bill' s"; "Poem,or Beauty Hurts Mr. Vinal"; " 'next to of course god america i"; "i sing of Olaf glad and big"
Toomer: *Cane*
Fitzgerald: "Babylon Revisited"
Dos Passos: *U.S.A.*
H. Crane: *The Bridge*
Hemingway: "The Snows of Kilimanjaro"
S. Brown: "Mister Samuel and Sam"; "Master and Man"
Hughes: "Refugee in America"; "Madam and Her Madam"; "Madam's Calling Cards"; "Visitors to the Black Belt"; "Democracy"
Steinbeck: *The Grapes of Wrath*

Volume E: Prose Since 1945

Ellison: "Cadillac Flambé"
Bellow: "Looking for Mr. Green"
Miller: *Death of a Salesman*
Paley: "A Conversation with My Father"
Baldwin: "Going to Meet the Man"
Marshall: "Reena"
Momaday: *The Way to Rainy Mountain*
Reed: *The Last Days of Louisiana Red*
Kingston: *Tripmaster Monkey*

Volume E: Poetry since 1945

Penn Warren: "American Portrait: Old Style"
Bishop: "The Armadillo"
R. Lowell: "For the Union Dead"; "Skunk Hour"
Wilbur: "Love Calls Us to the Things of This World"
Ginsberg: *Howl*; "A Supermarket in California"; "Sunflower Sutra"
Rich: "Diving into the Wreck"

The Individual and the Community

Bradford: *Of Plymouth Plantation*
Mather: *The Wonders of the Invisible World*
Jefferson: The Declaration of Independence

Hawthorne: "Young Goodman Brown"; "The May-Pole of Merry Mount"; "The Minister's Black Veil"; *The Scarlet Letter*
Thoreau: "Resistance to Civil Government"; *Walden*
Douglass: *Narrative of the Life*
Whitman: *Leaves of Grass* ["Song of Myself"]
Melville: *Moby-Dick*; "Bartleby, the Scrivener"; *Billy Budd, Sailor*
Twain: *Adventures of Huckleberry Finn*
James: *Daisy Miller*; "The Beast in the Jungle"
Jewett: "A White Heron"; "The Foreigner"
Chopin: *The Awakening*
Freeman: "A New England Nun"; "The Revolt of 'Mother' "
S. Crane: "The Bride Comes to Yellow Sky"; "The Blue Hotel"
Oskison: "The Problem of Old Harjo"
Zitkala Ša: "Impressions of an Indian Childhood"; "The School Days of an Indian Girl"; "An Indian Teacher among Indians"
H. Adams: *The Education* (Editor's Preface, Chapters I, XIX)
Cahan: "A Sweatshop Romance"
Masters: poems
Robinson: poems
Frost: "The Tuft of Flowers"; "Mending Wall"; "The Death of the Hired Man"; "Departmental"; "Neither Out Far Nor in Deep"
Anderson: *Winesburg, Ohio*
Eliot: "The Love Song of J. Alfred Prufrock"; "Tradition and the Individual Talent"
Cummings: "the Cambridge ladies who live in furnished souls"; "anyone lived in a pretty how town"; "pity this busy monster,manunkind"
Ellison: *Invisible Man*
Morrison: "Recitatif"

The Problem of Literary Authority

Bradstreet: "The Prologue"; "The Author to Her Book"
E. Taylor: "Prologue"; "Meditation 22"; "Upon a Wasp Chilled with Cold"; "Huswifery"
Edwards: *Personal Narrative*; "Sinners in the Hands of an Angry God"
Franklin: "The Way to Wealth"
Wheatley: "To Maecenas"; "To the University of Cambridge, in New England"; "To S. M., a Young African Painter, on Seeing His Works"
Rowson: *Charlotte*
Irving: "The Legend of Sleepy Hollow"
Emerson: "The American Scholar"; "The Divinity School Address"; "Self-Reliance"; "The Poet"
Hawthorne: *The Scarlet Letter* ("The Custom-House")
Poe: "The Philosophy of Composition"
Fuller: "The Great Lawsuit"
Thoreau: *Walden*
Douglass: *Narrative of the Life*

Whitman: "Preface to *Leaves of Grass*"; *Leaves of Grass* ["Song of Myself"]; "Letter to Ralph Waldo Emerson"; "Trickle Drops"; "Here the Frailest Leaves of Me"; "As I Ebb'd with the Ocean of Life"

Melville: "Hawthorne and His Mosses"; *Moby-Dick*

Dickinson: 185, 441, 448, 505, 528, 754, 1129, 1545, 1651, "Letters to Thomas Wentworth Higginson"

Alcott: "Transcendental Wild Oats"

Twain: *Adventures of Huckleberry Finn* (Chapter 1); "Fenimore Cooper's Literary Offenses"

Washington: *Up from Slavery*

Chesnutt: "The Goophered Grapevine"

Gilman: "The Yellow Wall-paper"

Du Bois: *The Souls of Black Folk*

H. Adams: *The Education* (Editor's Preface, Chapter I)

Black Elk: *Black Elk Speaks*

Stein: *The Making of Americans*

Frost: "Directive"; "The Figure a Poem Makes"

Stevens: "A High-Toned Old Christian Woman"; "Thirteen Ways of Looking at a Blackbird"; "Of Modern Poetry"

W. C. Williams: "Portrait of a Lady"; "The Red Wheelbarrow"; "A Sort of a Song"; "The Dance ('In Brueghel's great picture, The Kermess')"

Moore: "Poetry"; "The Mind Is an Enchanting Thing"

Eliot: "The Love Song of J. Alfred Prufrock"; "Tradition and the Individual Talent"

McKay: "Outcast"; "If We Must Die"; "O Word I Love to Sing"

Ellison: *Invisible Man* (Prologue)

Paley: "A Conversation with My Father"

Pynchon: "Entropy"

Bambara: "Medley"

Hannah: "Midnight and I'm Not Famous Yet"

The American Dream

Columbus: letters

Smith: *A Description of New England; New England's Trials*

Native American Trickster Tales

T. Morton: *The New English Canaan*

Winthrop: "A Model of Christian Charity"

Franklin: "The Way to Wealth"

Equiano: *The Interesting Narrative of the Life*

Irving: "Rip Van Winkle"

Emerson: *Nature*

Hawthorne: "Young Goodman Brown"

Fuller: "The Great Lawsuit"

Thoreau: *Walden* (Chapters 1, 2)

Douglass: *Narrative of the Life*

Whitman: *Leaves of Grass* ["Song of Myself"]

Davis: *Life in the Iron-Mills*

Twain: *Adventures of Huckleberry Finn*
James: "The Jolly Corner"
Jewett: "A White Heron"
Chopin: *The Awakening*
Garland: "Under the Lion's Paw"
Masters: poems
Cather: "Neighbour Rosicky"
Anderson: *Winesburg, Ohio*
Fitzgerald: "Babylon Revisited"
Dos Passos: *U.S.A.*
H. Crane: *The Bridge*
Steinbeck: *The Grapes of Wrath*
Ellison: *Invisible Man* (Chapter I); "Cadillac Flambé"
Miller: *Death of a Salesman*
Updike: "Separating"
Mamet: *Glengarry Glen Ross*

The American Landscape

Bradford: *Of Plymouth Plantation* (Book I, Chapters IX, X)
T. Morton: *New English Canaan* (Chapter I)
Knight: *The Private Journal of a Journey from Boston to New York*
Byrd: *History of the Dividing Line*
Crèvecoeur: *Letters from an American Farmer*
Jefferson: *Notes on the State of Virginia*
Freneau: "On the Emigration to America and Peopling the Western Country"
Irving: "The Legend of Sleepy Hollow"
Cooper: *The Pioneers*
Bryant: "Thanatopsis"; "The Prairies"
Thoreau: *Walden*
Whitman: *Leaves of Grass* ["Song of Myself"] (section 33); "Crossing Brooklyn
    Ferry"
Twain: *Adventures of Huckleberry Finn*
Jewett: "A White Heron"
Garland: "Under the Lion's Paw"
London: "To Build a Fire"
Cather: "Neighbour Rosicky"
Frost: "The Wood-Pile"; "Birches"; " 'Out, Out-' "; "Design"; "Directive"
Sandburg: "Chicago"; "Prairie Waters by Night"; "Grass"
Jeffers: "November Surf"; "Carmel Point"
Momaday: *The Way to Rainy Mountain*
R. Lowell: "The Quaker Graveyard in Nantucket"; "Skunk Hour"
Penn Warren: "Bearded Oaks"
Brooks: *A Street in Bronzeville*
Ginsberg: "Sunflower Sutra"
J. Wright: "A Blessing"
Snyder: "Milton by Firelight"; "August on Sourdough, A Visit from Dick Brewer";
    "The Blue Sky"

Immigration and Wandering

Bradford: *Of Plymouth Plantation*
Franklin: "Information to Those Who Would Remove to America"
Crèvecoeur: *Letters from an American Farmer* (Letter III)
Equiano: The *Interesting Narrative of the Life*
Freneau: "On the Emigration to America and Peopling the Western Country"
Wheatley: "On Being Brought from Africa to America"
The Cherokee Memorials
Bryant: "The Prairies"
Thoreau: "Walking"
Whitman: *Leaves of Grass* ["Song of Myself"]; "Crossing Brooklyn Ferry"
Davis: *Life in the Iron-Mills*
Lazarus: "In the Jewish Cemetery at Newport"; "1492"; "The New Colossus"
Twain: *Adventures of Huckleberry Finn*
Native American Oratory (esp. Cochise)
Jewett: "The Foreigner"
Eastman: *From the Deep Woods to Civilization*
Garland: "Under the Lion's Paw"
Dreiser: "Old Rogaum and His Theresa"
Oskison: "The Problem of Old Harjo"
Cather: "The Sculptor's Funeral"
Yezierska: "The Lost 'Beautifulness'"
Hughes: "Vagabonds"; "Refugee in America"
Malamud: "The Magic Barrel"
Marshall: "Reena"
Roth: "Defender of the Faith"
Kingston: *Tripmaster Monkey*
Ginsberg: *Howl*; "A Supermarket in California"

Family Relationships

Cabeza de Vaca: *The Relation* (esp. ["The Malhado Way of Life"], ["Our Life
    among the Avavares and Arbadaos"], ["Customs of That Region"])
Bradstreet: "To the Memory of My Dear and Ever Honored Father Thomas Dudley
    Esq."; "To Her Father with Some Verses"; "Before the Birth of One of Her Chil-
    dren"; "To My Dear and Loving Husband"; "A Letter to Her Husband, Absent
    upon Public Employment"; "Another [Letter to Her Husband, Absent upon Pub-
    lic Employment]"; "In Reference to Her Children"; "In Memory of My Dear
    Grandchild Elizabeth Bradstreet"; "In Memory of My Dear Grandchild Anne
    Bradstreet"; "On My Dear Grandchild Simon Bradstreet"; "To My Dear Children"
Wigglesworth: *The Day of Doom*
Rowlandson: *Narrative of the Captivity and Restoration*
E. Taylor: "Upon Wedlock, and Death of Children"
Sewall: *The Diary*
Byrd: *The Secret Diary*
J. Adams and A. Adams: letters
Irving: "Rip Van Winkle"

Hawthorne: "Young Goodman Brown"; "Rappaccini's Daughter"; *The Scarlet Letter*
Fuller: "The Great Lawsuit"
Stowe: *Uncle Tom's Cabin*
Jacobs: *Incidents in the Life of a Slave Girl*
Douglass: *Narrative of the Life*
Twain: *Adventures of Huckleberry Finn*
James: *Daisy Miller*
Jewett: "A White Heron"; "The Foreigner"
Chopin: *The Awakening*
Freeman: "The Revolt of 'Mother'"
Gilman: "The Yellow Wall-paper"
Wharton: "Souls Belated"
Du Bois: *The Souls of Black Folk*
Dreiser: "Old Rogaum and His Theresa"
Zitkala Ša: "Impressions of an Indian Childhood"; "The School Days of an Indian Girl"
H. Adams: *The Education* (Chapter I)
Cahan: "A Sweatshop Romance"
Masters: poems
Yezierska: "The Lost 'Beautifulness'"
Cather: "The Sculptor's Funeral"; "Neighbour Rosicky"
Frost: "The Death of the Hired Man"; "Home Burial"; "Birches; "'Out, Out-'"
Anderson: *Winesburg, Ohio* (esp. "Mother")
O'Neill: *Long Day's Journey into Night*
Taggard: "With Child"; "At Last the Women Are Moving"
Cummings: "if there are any heavens my mother will (all by herself) have"; "my father moved through dooms of love"
Faulkner: *As I Lay Dying*
Wolfe: "The Lost Boy"
Hughes: "Mother to Son"
Steinbeck: *The Grapes of Wrath*
Welty: "Petrified Man"
Cheever: "The Swimmer"
O'Connor: "The Life You Save May Be Your Own"; "Good Country People"
Barthelme: "The Balloon"
Updike: "Separating"
Walker: "Everyday Use"
Beattie: "Weekend"
Silko: "Lullaby"
Roethke: "My Papa's Waltz"
R. Lowell: "My Last Afternoon with Uncle Devereux Winslow"
Brooks: "a song in the front yard"
Ginsberg: "To Aunt Rose"
Sexton: "Little Girl"; "The Death of the Fathers"
Rich: "Snapshots of a Daughter-in-Law"
Plath: "Daddy"
Ríos: "Madre Sofía"
Cervantes: "Uncle's First Rabbit"
Song: "Lost Sister"

Race, Segregation, and Slavery

Casas: *The Very Brief Relation*
Cabeza de Vaca: *The Relation*
Smith: *The General History of Virginia*
Bradford: *Of Plymouth Plantation* (Book I, Chapters IX, X; Book II, Chapter XIX)
R. Williams: *A Key into the Language of America*
Rowlandson: *A Narrative of the Captivity and Restoration*
Byrd: *The Secret Diary*
Franklin: "Remarks Concerning the Savages of North America"
Woolman: *The Journal*
Occom: *A Short Narrative of My Life*
Crèvecoeur: *Letters from an American Farmer* (Letter IX)
Jefferson: The Declaration of Independence
Equiano: *The Interesting Narrative of the Life*
Freneau: "The Indian Burying Ground"; "To Sir Toby"
Wheatley: "On Being Brought from Africa to America"; "To S. M., a Young
    African Painter, on Seeing His Works"; letters
The Cherokee Memorials
Apess: "An Indian's Looking-Glass for the White Man"
Emerson: "Last of the Anti-Slavery Lectures"
Longfellow: "The Slave's Dream"
Lincoln: "A House Divided"; Second Inaugural Address
Stowe: *Uncle Tom's Cabin*
Jacobs: *Incidents in the Life of a Slave Girl*
Thoreau: "Resistance to Civil Government"; "Slavery in Massachusetts"
Douglass: *Narrative of the Life*; "The Meaning of July Fourth for the Negro"
Whitman: *Leaves of Grass* ["Song of Myself"]
Melville: "Benito Cereno"
Twain: *Adventures of Huckleberry Finn*
Native American Oratory
Harris: "The Wonderful Tar-Baby Story"; "Mr. Rabbit Grossly Deceives Mr. Fox"
Jewett: "The Foreigner"
Chopin: *The Awakening*
Washington: *Up from Slavery*
Chesnutt: "The Goophered Grapevine"
Eastman: *From the Deep Woods to Civilization*
Du Bois: *The Souls of Black Folk*
Oskison: "The Problem of Old Harjo"
Native American Chants and Songs
Zitkala Ša: "Impressions of an Indian Childhood"; "The School Days of an Indi-
    an Girl"; "An Indian Teacher among Indians"
Black Elk: *Black Elk Speaks*
Hurston: "The Eatonville Anthology"; "How It Feels to Be Colored Me"
Toomer: *Cane*
S. Brown: poems
Hughes: poems
Cullen: poems

R. Wright: "The Man Who Was Almost a Man"
Ellison: *Invisible Man*
Baldwin: "Going to Meet the Man"
Walker: "Everyday Use"
Hayden: poems
R. Lowell: "For the Union Dead"
Brooks: poems
Lorde: poems
Harper: poems
Dove: *Thomas and Beulah*

Gender Issues: Women's Lives, Work, and Vision

Winthrop: *The Journal*
Bradstreet: "The Prologue"; "The Flesh and the Spirit"; "The Author to Her Book"; "Before the Birth of One of Her Children"; "To My Dear and Loving Husband"; "A Letter to Her Husband, Absent upon Public Employment"; "Here Follows Some Verses upon the Burning of Our House"
Rowlandson: *A Narrative of the Captivity and Restoration*
Sewall: *The Diary*
Mather: "The Trial of Martha Carrier"
Knight: *The Private Journal of a Journey from Boston to New York*
Byrd: *The Secret Diary*
J. Adams and A. Adams: letters
Jefferson: The Declaration of Independence
Irving: "Rip Van Winkle"
Hawthorne: "Rappaccini's Daughter"; *The Scarlet Letter*
Poe: "The Sleeper"; "The Raven"; "To ———. Ulalume: A Ballad"; "Annabel Lee"; "Ligeia"; "The Fall of the House of Usher"; "The Philosophy of Composition"
Fuller: "The Great Lawsuit"
Stowe: *Uncle Tom's Cabin*
Jacobs: *Incidents in the Life of a Slave Girl*
Whitman: "Preface to *Leaves of Grass*"; *Leaves of Grass* ["Song of Myself"]; "Letter to Ralph Waldo Emerson"
Melville: "The Paradise of Bachelors and The Tartarus of Maids"
Dickinson: 67, 214, 249, 303, 312, 348, 435, 441, 505, 510, 520, 528, 732, 754, 952, 1099, 1129, 1545
Davis: *Life in the Iron-Mills*
Twain: *Adventures of Huckleberry Finn*
Harte: "The Outcasts of Poker Flat"
James: *Daisy Miller;* "The Real Thing"; "The Beast in the Jungle"
Jewett: "A White Heron"; "The Foreigner"
Chopin: "At the 'Cadian Ball"; "The Storm"; *The Awakening*
Freeman: "A New England Nun"; "The Revolt of 'Mother' "
Gilman: "The Yellow Wall-paper"; "Why I Wrote *The Yellow Wall-paper?*"
S. Crane: "The Bride Comes to Yellow Sky"
Dreiser: "Old Rogaum and His Theresa"

Oskison: "The Problem of Old Harjo"

Chippewa Songs

Zitkala Ša: "Impressions of an Indian Childhood"; "The School Days of an Indian Girl"; "An Indian Teacher among Indians"

H. Adams: *The Education* (Chapter XXV)

Masters: "Serepta Mason"; "Margaret Fuller Slack"; "Lucinda Matlock"

A. Lowell: "The Captured Goddess"; "Venus Transiens"; "Madonna of the Evening Flowers"

Frost: "The Death of the Hired Man"; "Home Burial"

Anderson: *Winesburg, Ohio*

Yezierska: "The Lost 'Beautifulness' "

W. C. Williams: "The Young Housewife"; "The Widow's Lament in Springtime"; "To Elsie"; "The Dead Baby"

Pound: "The River-Merchant's Wife: A Letter"

H. D.: "Leda"; "At Baia"; "Helen"; "The Walls Do Not Fall"

O'Neill: *Long Day's Journey into Night*

Millay: poems

Parker: "De Profundis"; "Résumé"; "General Review of the Sex Situation"; "The Waltz"

Taggard: "With Child"; "A Middle-aged, Middle-class Woman at Midnight"; "At Last the Women Are Moving"

Cummings: "the Cambridge ladies who live in furnished souls"

Toomer: *Cane* ("Fern")

Dos Passos: *U.S.A.* ("Mary French")

Faulkner: *As I Lay Dying*

Bogan: "Women"; "Cassandra"

Hughes: "Mother to Son"; "Song for a Dark Girl"; "Madam and Her Madam"; "Madam's Calling Cards"

Rukeyser: "Effort at Speech Between Two People"

Welty: "Petrified Man"

T. Williams: *A Streetcar Named Desire*

Malamud: "The Magic Barrel"

Ellison: *Invisible Man* (Chapter I)

O'Connor: "The Life You Save May Be Your Own"; "Good Country People"

Updike: "Separating"

Walker: "Everyday Use"

Beattie: "Weekend"

Silko: "Lullaby"

Erdrich: "Fleur"

Niedecker: poems

Roethke: "Frau Bauman, Frau Schmidt, and Frau Schwartze"

Bishop: "In the Waiting Room"; "The Moose"; "One Art"

Hayden: "Homage to the Empress of the Blues"

Brooks: poems

Levertov: poems

Ginsberg: "To Aunt Rose"

Sexton: poems

Rich: poems
Plath: poems
Lorde: poems
Dove: *Thomas and Beulah*
Ríos: "Madre Sofía"
Cervantes: poems
Song: poems

Politics and War

Columbus: letters
Casas: *The Very Brief Relation*
Díaz del Castillo: *The True History of the Conquest of New Spain*
Cabeza de Vaca: *The Relation*
Stories of the Beginning of the World: "The Story of the Flood"
Bradford: *Of Plymouth Plantation*
Rowlandson: *A Narrative of the Captivity and Restoration*
Franklin: *The Autobiography* (esp. [Part Three])
J. Adams and A. Adams: letters
Paine: *Common Sense*; "The Crisis, No. 1"; *The Age of Reason*
Jefferson: The Declaration of Independence
The Federalist Papers
Freneau: "On Mr. Paine's Rights of Man"
Wheatley: "To the Right Honorable William, Earl of Dartmouth"; "To His Excellency General Washington"
Irving: "Rip Van Winkle"
The Cherokee Memorials
Hawthorne: "My Kinsman, Major Molineux"
Lincoln: "A House Divided"; Gettysburg Address; Second Inaugural Address
Thoreau: "Resistance to Civil Government"
Douglass: "The Meaning of July Fourth for the Negro"
Whitman: *Drum-Taps*; "When Lilacs Last in the Dooryard Bloom'd"
Melville: *Battle-Pieces*; *Billy Budd, Sailor*
Bierce: "Occurrence at Owl Creek Bridge"
Native American Oratory
Eastman: *From the Deep Woods to Civilization*
S. Crane: "An Episode of War"
Native American Chants and Songs
Black Elk: *Black Elk Speaks*
Taggard: "Mill Town"
Roth: "Defender of the Faith"
Jarrell: "The Death of the Ball Turret Gunner"; "Second Air Force"
R. Lowell: "For the Union Dead"
Brooks: "The White Troops Had Their Orders But the Negroes Looked Like Men"; "The Blackstone Rangers"

CHAPTER 6

Teaching Notes for Authors and Works: Volume A, Literature to 1700

Because *NAAL* contains excellent period introductions, author headnotes, and bibliographies at the end of each volume, these teaching notes emphasize the following:

- Comparisons among individual authors
- Ways of relating literary works to large-scale questions that may work for you as central issues in your course

The main purpose here is to suggest ways to *introduce* material to intelligent, reasonably mature readers who may not initially feel any bond with it or see an access into it. These notes, which are arranged chronologically following the *NAAL* tables of contents, also suggest ways of encouraging students to think across periods and genres and to sense the development of literary traditions at given historical moments.

Since the mid-1980s, scholars have grown accustomed to talking about "the literature of the Discovery" as a literature about cultural conflict. In bringing together these works from the century or so before the English colonies really began to take root, we have found a compelling drama in the opening encounters between a European and a Native American ethos and about the effect that each wider culture had on the other. Nonetheless, some of your students, who probably know little of that academic dialogue, will have questions like the following in mind:

- How is this material American literature or even a significant precursor of American literature? Much of it was written by Europeans who never thought of themselves as belonging to any place other than their homeland; much of the rest wasn't really "written" in the strict sense at all, but spoken by members of cultures without written language—and in contexts that no commentary can make fully accessible to most of us. And all of this indigenous material was set down—or overheard, translated, and transcribed by outsiders—a long time ago.

• If many of these works were never even published (in the modern sense) until recently and were not written for publication, then what sort of "reading" are we engaged in here? Are we reading as a literary public? As antiquarians? As intruders?

• Since much of this material was not originally written in English and had no direct impact on later writers who used English—and since this is (in all likelihood) an "English" or "American Studies" class, labeled as such in the catalog, why are we bothering with it? Are we paying politically expedient homage before getting on with the real course?

Actually, bewilderment of this kind can be a resource. It can help open up not just honest access to material from early historical periods, but also core issues related to the creation, teaching, and learning of literary history.

This section can also help students reconsider the idea that the most interesting early writings from North America, writings in which the continent and its indigenous people had an impact on the consciousness of the European visitor, were all products of the English explorations and migrations. A drama begins here: a hubbub of voices in different languages, from different places, the verbal record of what Franklin later described as a "great mixing of peoples from the whole Atlantic basin" and as "a many-sided process of influence and exchange that ultimately produced the hybrid cultural universe of the Atlantic world." Indeed, as the Native American creation narratives indicate, the continent was already "peopled" when the Europeans arrived, and the languages of the native inhabitants of the Americas would also contribute to this hybrid cultural universe. One good effect of including this section in your syllabus is that students can glimpse American experience as multicultural from the beginning, with an array of European peoples encountering a variety of nations already here.

To give students a sense that this many-voiced beginning of American literature is not a dead-end historical moment, you might briefly jump ahead to Cervantes's poem "Visions of Mexico While at a Writing Symposium in Port Townsend, Washington," from Volume E. Here is a living Latina American writer writing in English as the dominant language of the United States, yet reopening for herself the colonial experience and speculating on its connections to her own, and our own, identity. The "Literature to 1700" collection invites students to encounter the possibility that American literature is more fluid than these boundaries; it invites students to cross them.

Literature before 1620

Stories of the Beginning of the World

As Arnold Krupat writes in his introductory notes to these creation stories, both the Iroquois and the Pima narratives included here are in a Western chronological sense misplaced, since these versions date from the nineteenth and early twentieth centuries. However, including creation stories in the "Literature to 1700" period of *NAAL* is pedagogically appropriate. First, these written narratives are transcriptions or translations of oral stories whose origins long precede such transcription. Second, the Iroquois and Pima narratives present a worldview that contrasts markedly with the worldview the colonizers brought with them. Although these mythological narratives do not address the relatively more recent historical period of contact with the European invaders, they serve as representations of early Native American culture. Teaching them side by side with European narratives of invasion and colonization allows students to view their own reading as encounters of cultures as well as of historical persons.

Instructors who assign these materials in an American literature course will probably be coming to them from Western cultural perspectives—on mythological or cosmological origins and on narrative forms and elements. And students will probably be in the same situation. Is there a way for most of us to teach Native American materials in the American literature classroom without expertise in these cultures?

The answer has a great deal to do with what we, as teachers, assume that a survey course is about, on the most basic level. A survey, or an introduction, can mean a paying of perfunctory attention or it can mean the opening of a longer acquaintance, deepening and broadening over the years, with many different texts that now belong, or that *might* belong, in a diverse culture's conversation with itself about its own nature. If you have the latter intention in mind, then two mistakes to avoid in regard to these early Native American materials are probably obvious: (1) a cursory glance that conveys, implicitly or otherwise, the sense that these texts are somehow beside the point; and (2) a presumptuous "analysis" or dramatized empathy, either of which can work the same kind of harm.

We are still rethinking, as a culture, nearly everything having to do with our relationship to these recovered materials: how to read them, in what sort of context, and why. The best strategy, therefore, may be to keep such questions open with your class, assuring students that such issues are not to be dismissed quickly or lightly and that their participation is needed to help move our collective thinking forward. Good strategies for reading these Native American materials, in the very Euro-American context of a modern college or high school classroom, will take shape if literary culture and history can be presented as something changeful, alive, and available to all who read patiently and in good faith.

One influential essay on teaching Native American texts is Barre Toelken and Tacheeni Scott's "Poetic Retranslation and the 'Pretty Languages of Yellowman,' " in Toelken, ed., *Traditional Literatures of the American Indian: Texts and Interpretations* (1981), a volume with many strong suggestions and perspectives. Without discouraging readings by cultural outsiders, Toelken draws our attention to complications of approaching Native American texts, across barriers of translation and dislocation. His encouragement to us, to try to proceed in spite of these obstacles and in full cognizance of them, is worth bearing in mind:

> I have encouraged—even forced—my students in recent years to go beyond mere reading of native literature and into the troublesome, frustrating, and often impossible task of recovering something of the original. "But what if we can't

speak Tsimshian?" they ask: "How are we to presume we can reconstitute the original presentation properly?" My response is to suggest that—using the materials at hand—we can at least come *closer* to real presentation than is now provided for us in the awkwardly serviceable and often primitive—sounding prose translations of linguists who were not anyhow as involved in the study of live literature as in the recovery of almost moribund languages (p. 69).

Another good essay about the complications of reading these texts in English translations, and in the context of the American college campus, is Paula Gunn Allen's "Kochinnenako in Academe," in Robyn Warhol and Diane Price Herndl, eds., *Feminisms* (1991). Allen proposes a "feminist-tribal" approach to Native American narrative, allowing readers to understand the kinds of agency that Native American narratives give women. For Allen, these stories can be read as about balance rather than conflict, about agency rather than heroism, and about background rather than a possibly overvalued foreground. The art she speaks of, running counter to Western expectations, is about a "living web of definition and depth" with an "importance of balance among all elements." As Allen describes it, "tribal art functions something like a forest in which all elements coexist, where each is integral to the being of the others." See also Allen's *The Sacred Hoop: Recovering the Feminine in American Indian Traditions* (1986).

Obviously there are limits to how much contextualizing material can be included in anthologies covering four hundred years and many North American voices. Nonetheless, the help in this quide, along with the headnotes and other Native American materials in *NAAL* can take us fairly far—at the very least into a recognition that other cultures were present, active, and imaginatively engaged at the time of European settlement. Students should understand that the American experience was being looked at passionately, and from many perspectives, as European and native cultures encountered one another.

The Iroquois Creation Story

Because of the shifts in context and expectations required to engage with these works, it is important to devote some class time to close reading of these stories. But close reading, the way one closely reads Bradstreet or Eliot, will not take students where they want (or expect) to go—that is, to a full understanding of the human sensibility in these texts. That may have to wait, and you may need to reassure your students that patience and comfort with uncertainty are required of all mature readers who seek to move across time, landscape, and large cultural barriers. As you assign other Native American texts, these will create an intertextuality, and instructors will receive much help from the headnotes and introductory materials in *NAAL* in providing the historical and oral/literary contexts for Native American stories and storytellers.

For this first experience with Native American mythology, you might encourage your students to read comparatively, bearing in mind the creation stories that most of them already know and scrutinizing the differences between these Native American creation myths and accounts from other cultures. Two interesting differences to note right away: first, these Native American stories do not enforce a distinction that most students are used to—a distinction between the Creator and world created—and second, these stories do not talk about a world somewhere else—an Eden, a Mount Ararat, or some other landscape far away from the experience of the listener or reader. The world spoken of is a world that is right here, to be gazed on and known firsthand as the tale is told again and again.

These differences matter because, for most of your students, reading these stories will require a recognition of certain habits of mind, habits of imagining and telling, that are culturally contingent and yet rarely recognized by us as paradigms, as ways of organizing not just experience, but also our narratives about experience.

As an exercise to stimulate discussion and an awareness of such differences, construct with students a visual "map" or interpretive sketch of the events of the Iroquois Creation Story. You will probably develop a diagram with a vertical axis: the woman who conceived (note Krupat's reference to one version in which she conceives parthenogenetically) begins in the "upper world" but falls to the "dark world," where "monsters" collect enough earth to make a seat for her, on which she gives birth to the twins, the good mind and the bad mind. In *Native American Literature* (1985), Andrew Wiget provides a useful diagram that suggests connections between specific events in origin stories and genres of Native American oral narrative. The twins transform the earthen seat, the Great Island that the monsters have created for the woman who fell, into a world that begins to resemble a world of humans rather than of mythical people; indeed, the story ends with the twins retiring from the earth, as the creation has been accomplished. Wiget's diagram maps three "generations" of beings: the original parent (the woman who fell from the sky), the twins (one of whom, the good mind, creates the earth and, through deceiving the bad mind, sets in motion the "nature of the system" we know as the world), and the first people with souls (who come to inhabit the universe).

Within these three levels, numerous narratives are possible; the Iroquois Creation Story that students have before them is only one variant of a story whose main elements may be relatively fixed but that relies on communal and participatory retelling. Communal participation results from viewing creation as a process of descent rather than as a one-time construction in a single god's image.

Students may also read the creation account in the Book of Genesis and compare elements: descent in the Iroquois story suggests a *process* of creation rather than the completed act of a single creator; the woman who fell from the sky may have become parthenogenetically pregnant, thereby linking the origins of the world to women (or to an asexual being capable of parthenogenesis) rather than to a patriarchal god (note that the Iroquois were matrilineal); and the monsters in the "dark world" are benign compared with the devils that inhabit Western conceptions of hell, and these monsters actually help the falling woman give birth. The good twin creates "two images of the dust of the ground in his own likeness," unlike the single male image the Western God creates in Genesis, where the female image is later created from a rib of the male.

Another exercise that helps open up the Iroquois Creation Story for Western-oriented students involves making a list of the characters in the myth and trying to determine each one's particular contribution, without which the creation would not be complete. While a Western narrative might suggest that the woman who fell from the sky and the good twin are "central" characters, the Iroquois story highlights the importance of the other characters and the interdependence of all. The turtle, for example, who offers to endure the falling woman's weight and who enlarges to become an island of earth is essential to the origin of the world, as are the contrivances of the bad twin, without whom we would not have mountains, waterfalls, reptiles, and the idea that even the good twin's powers are limited (as are those of humans). This suggests that there is no human agency without help from a variety of participants and that all creative powers must know their limits. If possible, read Wiget's beautiful interpretation of the story of the woman who fell. He says, in part,

> The Earth-Diver is the story of the Fortunate Fall played out against a landscape more vast than Eden and yet on a personal scale equally as intimate. It is a story of losses, the loss of celestial status, the loss of life in the depths of the sea. But it is also the story of gifts, especially the gift of power over life, the gift of agriculture to sustain life, and the gift of the vision to understand man's place as somewhere between the abyss and the stars.

PIMA STORIES OF THE BEGINNING OF THE WORLD

As Wiget's diagram of Native American oral narrative genres makes clear, there are two main story lines within various Native American creation myths: the stories that center around the "woman who fell from the sky," and those that depict the "emergence" of the world. The Pima Story of the Creation provides students with an example of the second kind, although students who wish to explore very different conceptions of emergence myths may want to read, or read about, Navajo or Pueblo myths. One of the images that distinguishes the emergence narrative, and here gives the Pima myth some elements of that genre, is the ability of Juhwertamahkai to poke a hole in the sky with his staff and to "emerge" through this hole into another dimension, where he begins his act of world creation anew. Some scholars have associated the emergence of a people through a hole in the ground or sky with the numerous migrations of Native American peoples. These myths may implicitly record those migrations.

In discussing this story, students can compare and contrast within Native American traditions—locating similarities and differences between Iroquois and Pima myths—as well as among other Native American and Western versions of "genesis." The point to make here is that even though some of the Native American creation stories follow two main story lines, the very concept of creation, or origins, itself seems to have inspired the creation of many variations on creation itself. Unlike the Judeo-Christian story told in Genesis, which favors one story of origin, Native American traditions offer many different creation stories, as if the fecundity of the creation process presupposed multiplicity rather than monotheism or the construction of a single dominant *mythos*. And this particular Pima story does not include many elements of other emergence narratives.

At first glance, the Pima Story of the Creation resembles the narratives of Genesis more closely than the Iroquois story. In the Pima, as in Genesis, the world begins "in the beginning" with a person who floated in the darkness; in Genesis, the spirit of God hovers over the darkness. Understanding the perils of the transcription of Native American legends is crucial to "reading" the opening of this story, because the language of the transcription itself echoes the language of Genesis. This leads to the question of whether this language truly characterizes the original Pima oral narrative or if it represents that oral story as viewed through the eyes of a translator who, despite his intentions to transcribe the stories of Thin Leather, still views creation through the lens of the Western Bible.

As the story progresses, it ceases to resemble Genesis. Indeed, Juhwertamahkai makes several mistakes in the process of creating the world. Unlike the Western god, whose destruction of the world by flood is blamed on human behavior, Juhwertamahkai takes a trial-and-error approach to creation, starting over or letting the sky fall each time the creative act sets in motion a process that will not sustain life. As the headnote points out, he makes the world four times before he is satisfied with his creation, establishing the number four (corresponding to north, south, east, and west) as significant in Native American cosmology.

The Pima Story of the Creation includes the birth of Coyote, the trickster of many Native American legends, and the arrival of Seeurhuh, or the elder, who in this story seems to move the creation into a world of negotiation between powerful personages who "claimed to have been here first," perhaps suggesting the process of relating stories about the organization of the social world into native cultures.

In the narrative that follows, the Pima Story of the Flood, Seeurhuh, or Ee-ee-toy, and Juhwertamahkai seem to engage in a struggle to determine, as the headnote points out, not creation but re-creation, "the reestablishment or rebirth of the divine, natural, and social orders." Ask students in reading Story of the Flood to note images or details that indicate imbalance in this social order. For example, even though Juhwertamahkai has already created people, Ee-ee-toy makes a man of his own, arming him with bow and arrow. Then, when this man marries, word of him strikes fear in the marriageable daughter of the South Doctor (presumably a "doctor of the earth" or shaman with powers that resemble those of Juhwertamahkai and Ee-ee-toy). The arrival of the flood itself is an image of turmoil, as is the array of plans the doctors and other persons/animals make for escaping the flood. As the story unfolds, the arrival of the flood is linked to the birth of a child from the young man who turns into a pregnant woman; the birth produces springs that "would gush forth from under every tree and on every mountain."

The struggle between Ee-ee-toy and Juhwertamahkai may also be an attempt to achieve balance. One way of showing this is to ask students to trace and try to account for Juhwertamahkai's behavior during and after the flood. The two doctors, Juhwertamahkai and Ee-ee-toy, and the person/animal Toehahvs (Coyote) face directions that may imply territories or tribal lands, and they make new dolls, or persons, to replace those who have drowned. Juhwertamahkai deliberately makes dolls that will not survive, "because he remembered some of his people had escaped the flood thru a hole in the earth, and he intended to visit them and he did not want to make anything better than they were to take the place of them." But the defective dolls break to pieces; Juhwertamahkai turns into waste and excretion, and the original creator of the world in the Pima Story of the Creation brings sickness and death into that world. While The Story of the Flood may help listeners to understand death, and especially war, it may also associate such things with the work of the spirits; Juhwertamahkai's creation ultimately includes both birth and death, and this establishes order in the world.

CHRISTOPHER COLUMBUS

Using Columbus to get the course started and open questions about the "literary" status of personal accounts and letters written centuries ago in languages other than English, and in immensely different cultural situations, can be ideal, because Columbus became a huge figure in the mythology of the Americas. You could loosen the class up with a quick review of old and newer artifacts of that legend: the cities, rivers, and countries named after him, the countless statues in public parks and squares, the two handsome tombs (he is buried in grand style in Havana and also in Seville, and there is still no settlement to the dispute over which church has the real remains!), and the two big-budget films released in 1992 to mark the five hundredth anniversary of the San Salvador landing. The literary impact of Columbus shows up in the hagiographic biography by Washington Irving; the once-popular epic poem by Joel Barlow; and even the jokes in Twain's *Innocents Abroad,* in which European guides expect American tourists to be floored by the sight of any object related to the Great Discoverer. All this can raise student interest in trying to hear the actual voice (more or less) of the actual human being who started the whole drama of European conquest and settlement.

To find an element of psychological familiarity in Columbus, these letters can be read as showing us a figure of deep and unresolved conflict. There is piety here, and covetousness, and self-righteousness, and pride, and political servility and manipulation; and these mingled inclinations and drives, even when seen through the thick distorting glass of so much intervening time, can make him seem eminently real. If one of your course objectives is to make these readings memorable and accessible, then attention to these very familiar contradictions can take the discussion in good directions.

What happens if you read Columbus's 1493 letter with his 1503, in which he complains bitterly of his own abandonment and betrayal and reveals his disillusionment with the experience of colonization? What do these letters suggest about the relative value of kings and great cities, the power of Spanish explorers, and the relative "importance" of the "people without number" who already inhabit the islands?

BARTOLOMÉ DE LAS CASAS

The selection from Casas's *Very Brief Relation* will open up interesting questions about assumptions held by Spanish explorers in their treatment of the Native Americans and challenge the notion that all these explorers were blind to the human worth of the people they encountered or mindless apologists for colonialism. Ask students to speculate on Casas's motives as a writer. Casas witnesses horrors in the Spanish treatment of native peoples, and the moral outrage expressed by this rough-and-tumble soldier-adventurer is based in Judeo-Christian teachings and ethics. This is the opening of a long and very important dialogue, as writers on the American continent try to reconcile political and social practice with religious values and to close the rift between professed creeds and actual practice. Equiano, Douglass, and Stowe are just three of the upcoming writers who will base their interventions on similar principles. A bit of foreshadowing can be effective here, in regard to the ways in which America will quarrel with itself.

Bernal Díaz del Castillo

Like Casas, Díaz del Castillo writes a narrative of witness. Ask students to explore the differences between the imagined audiences for these narratives and those by Columbus, who was writing official missives to the Spanish Crown. Does the difference in the implied reader make for differences in the kinds of observations Casas and Díaz del Castillo make and the images they choose? Does literature result in part from the choice to write for almost anyone other than the king and queen?

Díaz del Castillo's narrative "[Gifts Presented to Cortés]" provides good social context. Students can find evidence in this brief narrative that the meeting between Spaniards and Aztecs served as an encounter on both sides. The description of the physical resemblance between "our Cortés" and "the other Cortés," the Aztec chief Quintalbor, provides an emblem of the facing off between invaders and indigenous people. The first battle between Cortés and Montezuma is presented as a rhetorical one: whose insistence will allow the speaker to make the next move—Montezuma's that Cortés not try to travel to the Aztec capital to meet him or Cortés's that he must account to his own king and, therefore, must see Montezuma in person?

An instructor's role in this text, as in the following segment, "[The Approach to Tenochtitlán]," might be to help students locate moments of tension between Cortés and his forces and Montezuma and the Aztecs. Otherwise, the descriptions of violence and the quick shifts from apparent negotiations to killing and conquest, from gift giving to conflict, seem inexplicable. On Montezuma's side, Díaz del Castillo reports, the Aztecs call the Spaniards *teules*, or "gods," and this may explain why Montezuma does not simply crush Cortés, even though his own gods and priests (*papas*) urge him to do so. Yet such quick shifts perhaps convey the astonishment of Díaz del Castillo himself that such a marvelous place as Tenochtitlán should have been destroyed so quickly.

Another moment that also conveys both the tensions between Cortés and Montezuma and the volatility of their encounters occurs near the beginning of the "[Cortés in Difficulties]" segment. Díaz del Castillo writes, "On hearing Cortés say that he would have to come with us and visit the Emperor, Montezuma was even sadder than before." This "excited conversation" leads the soldiers to wonder "when the fighting would begin," but the shift from apparent diplomacy to anxiety continues to signal the understated conflict of the encounter between Cortés and Montezuma. The fact that Montezuma delays any attack and instead resorts to persuasion, expressing his annoyance that Cortés does not tell him about the arrival of Narvaez's ships and claiming to be "delighted" that "now you can all return to Spain without more discussion," suggests that Montezuma is simply not confident of victory over Cortés and Cortés's god.

Implicit in *The True History of the Conquest of New Spain* is the myth that has been perpetuated in Mexican history and culture that it was a native woman, Doña Marina—often called "La Malinche" to refer to the fact that she is believed to have been Cortés's mistress (Cortés in this text is referred to as Malinche)—who betrayed the Aztec Empire. She is visible in this text at the moment when Cortés first meets Montezuma, and she serves as his translator ("Cortés, speaking through Doña Marina, answered him"). Later, she seems to be in Cortés's power or employ and continues to serve as a translator. Discuss with students the effect of introducing a woman as the cultural translator. In attempting to translate, or to mediate, between two such oppositional interests as those of Cortés and Montezuma, Doña Marina is said to have betrayed her country. By implication, without her treachery, the Aztec Empire might not have fallen. Ask students to consider this rationally by focusing on the behavior of the Spaniards in this and in other narratives and to speculate on the reasons for the survival of the myth of La Malinche.

The narrator of *The True History of the Conquest* writes as if he experienced the effects of colonial conquest in his own body. Ask students to locate the passages where this becomes clear and to speculate on his responses. Help students see connections between the narrator's role in the Conquest of Mexico and his inability to sleep "even when I go to the villages of my *encomienda*."

ÁLVAR NÚÑEZ CABEZA DE VACA AND GARCILASO DE LA VEGA

By considering these two writers as a pair, students might achieve a breakthrough in their thinking about these narratives as *literary* texts—that is, as texts that are strongly informed by imaginative and literary traditions as well as by independent minds operating with intensity, and in some measure against the expectations of their respective audiences. Amid this broad array of exploration histories and reports, Cabeza de Vaca, even in translation, achieves a voice that actually sounds unique and human, and students may respond strongly to the sense that finally, among all of these accounts, a distinct personality is in evidence. His interest in detail is different: he writes of customs and people with respect and genuine curiosity. His *Relation* attempts to present the native peoples' way of life as much as possible from the inside. Ask students to look for moments in which Cabeza de Vaca's observations and opinions suggest unorthodox thinking for his time and culture, an imaginative wanderer.

Students might examine his attention to women's lives in particular. Cabeza de Vaca's interest in and concern for women (he writes in "[The Long Swing-Around]" that "among this people, women are better treated than in any part of the Indies we had come through") help compensate for the lack of attention most other narrators of texts in the "Literature to 1700" period give to women except as myths—such as the myth of Doña Marina in Díaz del Castillo's narrative or, later, the myth of Pocahontas in the writings of John Smith.

Cabeza de Vaca comes closer than any writer yet encountered to understanding and communicating with various American Indian groups. Locate with students those moments in his narrative when he seems to come closest to communicating—one rich episode is his description of "[Our Life among the Avavares and Arbadaos]," in which he describes dressing, eating, and dwelling in the way of his hosts.

At times, Cabeza de Vaca sounds like a missionary or an anthropologist in his approach to the native peoples he encountered: "They are a substantial people with a capacity for unlimited development." Perhaps the most significant test of how the Native Americans themselves received Cabeza de Vaca's respect and understanding for their way of life emerges in "[The Falling-Out with Our Countrymen]", when the American Indians refuse to believe that Cabeza de Vaca and his group were from the same race as the "Christian slavers." The passage near the end of the excerpt that begins "Conferring among themselves, they replied that the

Christians lied" conveys the Indians' view of Cabeza de Vaca in imagery that comes close to giving them voice in this narrative.

In this beautiful work, students can deepen their understanding of "encounter" narratives. Cabeza de Vaca makes ample room in his work for readers to see the native people's view of their encounter with him as well as his encounter with them. In a further complication of the term, the *Relation* shows Europeans encountering their own internal contradictions. If resistance to the brutal practices of conquest and colonization was itself capable of transforming one group of Spaniards (Cabeza de Vaca and his group) into men the American Indians no longer recognized as "Christian slavers," then who are the true Europeans? Was it conquest and colonization that turned civilized men into monsters (so that Cabeza de Vaca may be viewed as someone who resists that transformation), or was it encounters with the native peoples themselves that turned Spaniards into potentially civilized men? In any event, the *Relation* offers an encounter between the elements of internal contradiction within European conquest itself.

When read in conjunction with Cabeza de Vaca, Garcilaso de la Vega's account of the torments and miraculous survival of young Juan Ortiz may suggest a voice much more imbued with narrative conventions and archetypes. These "histories" can be vexing to read, because we can sense that some of the account is fact, while some of it is enhanced or made up to resonate with those conventions—and that we can never can be sure where the truth leaves off and imaginative license begins. To begin with, you might ask students what this account reminds them of, what stories seem to echo here. Some of them may think of Old Testament narratives of long stoic suffering ultimately rewarded, of mercy coming from unexpected directions (Good Samaritans), or of accounts of the lives and martyrdom of Medieval Christian saints. All of these traditions may resonate in the story of Juan Ortiz.

But archetypal or not, how does this narrative present Native Americans and the encounter with Europeans? We have a story of sadism—monstrous yet not unbelievable, as there are eerie similarities here between Juan Ortiz's torments and the horrific tortures and executions that European Roman Catholic and Protestant groups were inflicting on one another and hapless minorities at home, as this text took shape. The tale of the noble and merciful Mucoco, and the contrast with the vicious Hirrihigua keeps us in familiar imaginative territory—heroes and villains in an exotic new land—but is the presentation of Mucoco important for other reasons? How often before this narrative have European writers countenanced the possibility of inherent goodness or universal humanity, unconnected to a specific religious education?

THOMAS HARRIOT

As noted in the comments on Cabeza de Vaca and Garcilaso de la Vega, encounters between the Spanish explorers and the American Indians reveal contradictions within the Conquest, perceptions, motivations, and imaginative habits that cause moral and imaginative crisis for some of these writers. This internal contradiction may seem more muted to students in early English narratives, but there are enough similarities between Spanish and English encounters to suggest patterns.

After reading Cabeza de Vaca and Garcilaso de la Vega, students may find Harriot much less perceptive or curious about the native peoples he encounters. You might ask students to look for signs in Harriot's text of seeing the world from fresh perspectives: early in his *Brief and True Report,* he writes, "In respect of us, they are a poor people, and for want of skill and judgment in the knowledge and use of our things, do esteem our trifles before things of greater value." In his view, Native American mythology demonstrates the ignorance of these peoples, and there is little sign that Harriot has any curiosity about understanding the world in fresh ways. When Harriot dismisses as absurd the Native American belief that "a woman was made first, who by the working of one of the gods, conceived and brought forth children," what values and unquestioned assumptions are implicit in his judgment?

SAMUEL DE CHAMPLAIN

Champlain's narratives suggest a different relationship with native peoples than some of the earlier Spanish and English explorers. His *Voyages* conveys a keener awareness of how to negotiate with people in an established, indigenous, and powerful culture. The story that Champlain tells recognizes the agency of the native peoples he meets, takes them seriously, and acknowledges the limitations of his own expedition and European power.

Suddenly, in these narratives of encounter, exploration, and conquest, we find ourselves in a world of negotiations, celebrations, pacts, maneuvers, and political deliberations. Students might find all this a blur and worry that they might be quizzed on who's allied with whom and what Champlain's objective is at each stage in this meandering business. It might be well to suggest that they consider the whole fabric, the strong implication that in Champlain's New France, power is achieve through shrewdness and talk, choosing the right friends, playing "our savages" against "their savages," and recognizing and respecting where authority resides—until the colonizers grow strong enough to overwhelm it.

As a narrative, the material from "The Voyage of 1618" takes an odd turn, which students might want to discuss. Until Etienne Brule is suddenly attacked by the people of an outlying native village (ignoring the will of their chief), Brule is presented as an entirely secular man, an opportunist who pleases himself and is a bit slack in following orders. In the midst of the attack, however, the story takes on the trappings of a hagiography: a Christian symbol around Brule's neck momentarily checks the heathen; and when they continue the mayhem, thunder and lightning miraculously intercede. Students will wonder about this turn of events— whether to believe it, and whether it fits the fabric of this narrative. In this account, what is the Divine? A source of inspiration and values? A weapon deployed suddenly or luckily to turn the tide of a conflict? The Europeans are moving into this vast territory for reasons as ostensibly religious as mercantile. Champlain's narrative allows us to speculate on the relative importance of each motive to this leader.

JOHN SMITH

Smith is an imaginative writer, a dramatist and self-dramatist as well as a chronicler and advocate for European settlement. With Smith, many students may find themselves in comfortable territory—not just because Smith, an Englishman, has become part of the American mythology but also because his narrative is different, and more familiar in shape and pace, than the others encountered thus far. Students may want to look at *The General History of Virginia* as an American adventure story and observe ways in which it configures actual events and experiences to appeal to a London audience. The moment of encounter has passed, for Smith, and the shift to settlement and exploitation has begun. Indeed, Smith's job was to make the Americas safe for colonial growth; and as his *General History* demonstrates, when "trade and courtesy" failed, he resorted to force.

Smith's account of Pocahontas may be highly fictionalized; and students may want to take note of another instance of this archetypal story of a young woman who crosses cultural boundaries and changes the world. If students want to talk about the Disney restyling of this story or other ways in which it has been reworked to reflect values of other times in our cultural history, why not encourage them? What we have here, after all, is a supremely literary moment—a moment that not only unfolds by the rules of old tales of love and adventure but also inspires a long succession of other American imaginative texts.

Pocahontas does not survive as a cultural myth in the United States in the way La Malinche does in Mexico. Ask students to speculate on why this is the case. In Mexico, the myth of a treacherous Doña Marina represents the betrayal of one culture to another, in a nation where native peoples and Europeans have commingled and where native strains remain strong but culturally subordinate. In the myth of La Malinche, she betrays Mexico itself.

NATIVE AMERICAN TRICKSTER TALES

The headnotes to this section will be invaluable for your students to read carefully, not just for their cautions and its suggestions about historical context but also as a basis for considering whether "literature" can have any stable description across times and cultures, and whether transformations worked by the passage of time and change of context and language are invariably a loss, harm, or gain.

One cautious generalization that we can begin with is that these stories are about change, about shape-shifting: change in physical form; change in relationships among natural and supernatural creatures (including human beings); changes of mind and intention. Furthermore, from a European perspective these narratives seem to shape-shift in terms of mood and mode: farce gets mixed up with the sacred; bawdiness and scatological humor break out in places where a listener from outside these cultures might least expect them. There are elements in these stories that can make them seem like caricatures of a creation story; there are also tales here that seem didactic or etiological—lessons in how to be careful and how the natural world came to be as it is.

How can we account for this? If you live in a subsistence culture in the midst of a vast natural landscape and, therefore, see indications, every day, that creation is an ongoing process, rather than something that happened far away and long ago, what might be the effects on the way that stories are told? In other words, if you perceive the events and consequences of one of these trickster tales as timeless or as a process that not only continues but involves the participation of the teller and listener as the *story* happens as a literary and cultural event, how might those very different assumptions affect the shaping of a narrative?

Students could have much to say, therefore, about the way that the world is categorized and stabilized by certain basic structures in narratives constructed in the European tradition and the way that emotional and psychological experiences are blended in some of these Native American texts. Even so, to go from that generalization, or from any other, into conventional close reading or a hunt for parallels or universal themes and motives is to run into troubles that the headnotes caution us against. No amount of academic guidance, in the context of a broader and ongoing survey, can prepare us to read and understand a Chinook tale from a Chinook perspective, a Navajo tale from a Navajo point of view, and so on, because the very ideas of telling, of listening, of fiction, of truth, and of belief can vary so much among Native American cultures.

So what else can we talk about of relevance to these tales and the anthology and survey course in which they are located? We can take guidance from that recurring emphasis on change, on shape-shifting, and talk about the shape-shifting of literary texts—Native American or otherwise—from the oral to the written, from one culture to another, from the popular world to the solemnity and supposed high seriousness of academe, from the notepad or the popular edition to the footnoted portable Hall of Fame that an anthology can signify to so many students who, with no small measure of anxiety, crack it open for the first time and expect to find greatness, profundity, and permanence everywhere. These Native American storytellers and listeners seem to participate in the making of the world by the very act of saying, by repeating reverently and irreverently, and adapting boldly; by conserving lore and visions, dreams and wisdom; and by giving them new shapes for new cultural situations.

When students eventually consider contemporary Native American writers like Leslie Marmon Silko and Louise Erdrich, they will see writers in a quest to accomplish something akin to what their ancestors did: to keep old tales alive by reconfirming their relevance and making them new. A discussion that entertains such problems can broaden into important considerations for your students as they negotiate these texts and wonder about the process and ritual of the survey course and what they themselves are being asked to do, and are doing on their own, as they infuse these deeply foreign, deeply American texts with their own imagination. That process is going on in everything they read; and if on that level they understand a commonality between this one reading experience and others, they will have a surer and more plausible basis to maintain interest in native American literary culture and to achieve some measure of passionate engagement with the whole course.

Literature between 1620 and 1700

To open this period, you could ask students first to imagine the passage from seventeenth-century England to the New World: the violence and disruptions of the old country and the unknown terrors of the new one; the loss of home, of kinship, of worldly possessions (these ships were very small), of so much that matters to one's personal and cultural identity. It's also a good idea to spend some time on the sheer physical risk of this kind of dislocation. The Roanoke Colony had been wiped out without a trace; a year after the landing at Plymouth Rock, half of the *Mayflower* Pilgrims were dead. Religious warfare raged in Europe; civil war would soon break out in the English homeland, and a succession of religious upheavals and political changes over the previous half century had claimed tens of thousands of lives.

If you're hoping that your students will find ways to empathize with the New England Puritan mind and not regard the whole group as grumpy, hopelessly repressed, inhuman zealots, then it may be a good idea to establish what mortality meant to these people, how very close at hand it was, and how it could affect all phases of life—not just belief but ideas of family, of career, of the worth of any human action or enterprise.

The Massachusetts Bay Colonists were primarily, though not exclusively, Puritan in ideology, which meant that most believed in the literal authority of the Bible. They saw the Bible as a topological model for their own lives (Puritan writers use biblical metaphors to explain the Puritan condition; they often refer to themselves, for example, as Israelites, and the New World becomes Canaan). You will probably need to outline several basic tenets of Puritan thought: original depravity (we are born sinners), limited atonement (no worldly ritual or prayer will ensure salvation; no human action or gesture of faith obliges the Almighty to respond), and predestination (God has chosen his elect before we were born).

For the sake of keeping this a *literature* course and avoiding disappearance into theological arguments that very few of us are competent to handle properly, you might want to approach predestination (if you approach it at all) as an example of the rigorous logic that flourished in Reformation theology, partly as a result of the unprecedented empowerment of the reader and the exhilaration and terror of trying to discern Divine Will on our own. From the perspective of ordinary life and the writing of imaginative literature, predestination is almost a moot point, and students who go round and round with the matter run the risk of doing so at the expense of attention to the texts you are reading together.

Here a few key matters:

• Puritans viewed the Bible as God's covenant with them; they saw themselves as a Chosen People and identified strongly with the tribes of Israel in the Book of Exodus. In reading both Testaments, they concluded that God, though sometimes arbitrary in His power, is neither malicious nor capricious.

• Doers of evil suffer and are destroyed; true believers and doers of good may suffer as well, as worldly misfortune is both a test of faith and a signifier of God's will.

In sum, covenant theology taught that although no human being can ever know for certain whether or not he or she is among the saved, the only hope lay in rigorous study of Scripture; relentless moral self-examination; and active, wholehearted membership in these congregations.

Again, if we are looking for lasting cultural effects, ways in which this theological system, and the consciousness it shaped, continue down through many generations and cultural moments, then it's worth backing away at the end of your summary to ask students to speculate on what those effects might be. The list you come up with might run something like this:

• With no central religious authority, and an expectation that each member of the community should encounter Scripture and theological prose firsthand, New

England Puritanism would be strongly influenced by a drive toward solidarity and consensus and by a championing of individual thought. These conflicting values would become clear in the collision between the Colony's elders and Anne Hutchinson, less than ten years after the founding of Boston.

• An emphasis on individual responsibility, on a direct and personal relationship with God, and on the acquisition of knowledge in anticipation (or hope) of the coming of Divine Grace could be a powerful force for the education of women, and eventually for their political and social equality.

• A belief that salvation required, and would be signified by, achievement of absolute integrity among faith, worldly conduct, private life, and the spoken and written word would eventually figure centrally in the rise of abolitionist sentiment: race slavery becomes not an economic expediency or a social problem to be overlooked and eventually remedied but a mortal sin, threatening the moral condition of the society and every individual within it. The long-term effects of this kind of thinking are enormous. Nearly two centuries later, *Uncle Tom's Cabin* was constructed around a similar proposition.

• A belief in a special destiny and a conviction that what was unfolding in New England was the last and best hope of the Christian world. Cataclysmic changes in London in the middle of the seventeenth century and the erosion of solidarity in the colony after the Restoration and with the passage of years would bring those convictions into crisis at century's end.

• A special emphasis on reading correctly—not only holy texts but commentaries and the events of ordinary life. The New England Puritans were an intellectual people who believed firmly in portents, symbols, and the significance of all that happened in private and public life.

WILLIAM BRADFORD

Of Plymouth Plantation is an excellent foundation for the study of colonial American literature, as it offers a thorough portrait of hopes and expectations central to the New England Puritan mind, and it shows us how an idea of destiny, and an expectation that all worldly experience is meaningful and must be "read," organizes Bradford's account of the colony's first years. Everything seems to matter: prosperity, misfortune, natural events, even outbreaks of indecency, which modern readers (including your students) will probably find hilarious. If you are hoping to demonstrate key qualities of the seventeenth-century Puritan consciousness, assumptions and beliefs that echo down through New England literature for hundreds of years, those qualities are strongly evident in Bradford.

The earlier selections from *Of Plymouth Plantation* help students visualize the practical and spiritual concerns of the earliest colonials. In trying to find a harbor (Book I, Chapter X), the "lusty seaman" on board the shallop reminds the pilot to row, "or else they were all cast away." Bradford's account reveals the necessity for self-reliance among the first Puritan settlers; only after they reach "the lee of a small island" can they afford to give thanks to God "for His mercies in their manifold deliverances." Students are surprised to discover how secular and pragmatic the Puritans had to be in the process of creating their spiritual New World. In Book I, Chapter IV, Bradford cites physical hardships, premature aging, lack of control over their children, and only last (if not least) their hope of "propagating and advancing the gospel of the kingdom of Christ" as the Puritans' reasons for "removing" to the "vast and unpeopled countries of America." How does Bradford's text challenge undergraduate students' preconceptions of the Puritans and their literature?

Among the selections from *Of Plymouth Plantation,* "[The Mayflower Compact]" deserves special attention in class discussion. Bradford writes that the document was "occasioned partly by the discontented and mutinous speeches that some of the strangers [non-Puritans aboard the *Mayflower*] amongst them had let fall from them in the ship." How does what Bradford calls "the first foundation of their government in this place" establish a Puritan community from the beginning as one that excludes "strangers"? What evidence is in the compact that even before landing the Puritans defined themselves as an elect group? And what implicit effect does writing and signing the Mayflower Compact have? Putting their first agreement into written form was an act of major significance for the Puritans, who believed in the Bible's literal truth and authority. Written words, from the beginning of American culture, carry the associative power of God's word.

What does the writing of the Mayflower Compact indicate about the Puritans' need for divine authority? From the point of landing in the New World, the Puritans were already setting in motion the necessity of inventing for themselves solutions to material concerns that the Bible does not address. In "[The Mayflower Compact]" we see them trying to create other documents that would, like the Bible of their covenant theology, possess the power to compel respect and obedience.

Students can read later segments as if Bradford's own text were a prefiguring: in what ways do the excerpts from *Of Plymouth Plantation* recall for students later moments or patterns of thought in American history, even in our own time? Compare Book I, Chapter IV with Book II, Chapter XXXII: both demonstrate early attempts to rationalize colonial life, but in the latter, Bradford's own logic breaks down. In his "endeavour to give some answer hereunto," he ends by raising an unanswerable and prophetic question: "And thus, by one means or other, in 20 years' time it is a question whether the greater part be not grown the worser?" As Bradford records successive years in his history, he continues to convey a pattern of rise and fall, of end prefigured in the beginning. In "[Proposal to Remove to Nauset]," he describes the split in the church that resulted from the removal to Nauset and characterizes the "poor church" as "an ancient mother grown old and forsaken of her children." Do the selections from Book II in particular suggest a less-than-optimistic view of our colonial origins? Social problems existed from the beginning: corruption, dissent, falling away from the "ancient mother," abandonment, lack of fidelity.

THOMAS MORTON

Morton makes a wonderful pairing with Bradford, especially if you want to focus on relationships between cultural values and literary style. Morton, as the headnote tells you, was anything but a Puritan, and his intentions in settling at Merrymount were worldly pleasure and profit, not the fulfillment of grand destinies or the founding of the New Jerusalem. We know little about his life, but his prose speaks volumes.

Ask a student to read aloud a few opening lines from the Morton selection, and when the student gets lost in the forest of show-off prose and esoteric allusions, offer some reassurances: this kind of writing is *not* meant to communicate clearly but to strike a posture and convey a certain kind of social position and comradeship. Morton seems to know what he is doing, and he is sending his London audience a message that unlike these dour and austere colonists, he is "one of us," an urbane Englishman who loves a good time, fancy dress, courtly manners, and florid writing styles. If your students are coming to you with some experience of Renaissance English literature, urge them to stop worrying about the allusions that break out everywhere in Morton and ask them what this prose *sounds* like. Somebody will say Shakespeare, which is a good connection to build on; you're closer to the mark if they say Sir Toby Belch or Falstaff, affable rascals who escape blame and accusations not by denying the charges against them, but by being charming and by creating farce as an act of self-defense. Morton knows what he is doing: in retelling the taking of his settlement by Standish and the other Puritans, he makes the event a slapstick encounter between good-natured revelers and a sneaking band of Malvolios, who threaten to close down all good times in the New World.

As you move in a bit closer, observe that Morton's allusions and metaphors come from a different storehouse than do Bradford's or Winthrop's. The earlier Puritan writers (with the exception of Bradstreet, whose refreshing independence and range we shall look at it in a moment) have turned away from the classical (favored by Shakespeare, Donne, Jonson, and most of the best writers of the English High Renaissance) and draw their metaphors from Scripture. Compared to Morton's, their prose is as plain and clear as the dress they favored—and a stop with *The New English Cannan* will bring home the fact that the difference between the Puritan sensibility and that of the non-Puritan English middle class affected the choice of words and the workings of the imagination.

JOHN WINTHROP

"A Model of Christian Charity" gives students the earliest example of a Puritan sermon delivered in the New World (or en route to the New World, because Winthrop delivered it on board the *Arbella*). Students can comment on the image patterns by which Winthrop characterizes the community he envisions, and they can discuss the discursive form of this sermon as an example of the key literary genre of seventeenth-century Puritan culture. If students in a historical survey course are beginning to wonder whether these early writings have any resonance in our own time or show us any literary motifs or imaginative habits that continue to this day, then it's worth spending some time with the City on a Hill metaphor, unpacking its meaning, looking for its analogues in Judeo-Christian history and noticing where similar core beliefs—that Boston or Chicago or the whole United States is a beacon for humanity and the destiny of the world—continue to show up in our own culture and public discourse.

The Journal offers examples of typology and evidence of the principle of exclusion by which the Puritans founded their New World government. Ask students to assess Winthrop's comments on Roger Williams (possibly asking them to read the selections from Williams) and Anne Hutchinson. How can we account for the fervor of Winthrop's reaction against Hutchinson and her doctrine of personal conscience, which would seem, from some perspectives, quite in keeping with the general religious tenets of the colony? Why does Winthrop go to such lengths to seek evidence that Hutchinson is dangerously wrong and has lost favor with God? What are the implications and possible dangers that can arise from that kind of close reading of worldly experience?

ANNE BRADSTREET

Bradstreet can be a breakthrought moment in a historical survey or major authors course; after a sequence of historical accounts that may be interesting chiefly as artifacts rather than as living and compelling literature, we suddenly come upon creative genius, a writer whose verse still seems limpid, courageous, and profound and who would command substantial space in any good anthology of Anglo-American verse. As one delighted student recently described the discovery of Bradstreet: "Finally, I can hear one of these writers breathing!"

Bradstreet's poetry may "breathe" because it presents a conflict, a conflict that may have been inherent in living a secular and a spiritual life in a Puritan colony. In the small city of Boston (never more than a few thousand people in her lifetime), she was a public figure, a leader in her congregation, and eventually the wife of the governor. She was also a mother and a grandmother, and as such she had to reconcile Holy Writ with human love, and human fear, for her immediate and extended family. And in Bradstreet's verse we can hear as well the voice of a woman pleased by the richness of non-Puritan English literature, by the sometimes outlandish art of Renaissance verse, and by the whole alluring, and dangerous heritage of the Western imagination.

To begin discussion of Bradstreet, you might suggest that there are two voices operating here, sometimes in harmony, sometimes in conflict. You might call them "Mistress Bradstreet" and "Anne." Mistress Bradstreet is the poet-voice who speaks as she ought, in full accord with religious doctrine, public duty, and conventional belief; "Anne" is the woman who loves, grieves, fears, feels pride, and experiences the full range of emotions and curiosities that the teachings of her faith were supposed to put to rest. In the drama of her poems, sometimes one side of her seems to win out and sometimes the other; sometimes a reassuring harmony is reached, and sometimes not.

Poems that students respond to in line-by-line analysis include "The Author to Her Book," which has a dangerous metaphor embedded in it; students will want to comment on that. The darkening mood of the three elegies for her grandchildren, a sequence in which the doctrinal consolations seem to console less and less, will also catch the attention of your class and increase receptiveness to the great poems of family love and domestic life: "To My Dear and Loving Husband," "Here Follows Some Verses upon the Burning of Our House," and "Before the Birth of One of Her Children." Pause over this last one and offer some word about the risk of bearing a child in the seventeenth century, the frequency with which young women died of "childbed fever," and the situation of orphans in a near-subsistence culture with no social services. Students need to know that Bradstreet was looking at very real possibilities.

Students respond to the personal voice and the element of self-disclosure in Bradstreet that make for moving lyrics and can lead into a discussion of the constraints on individual expression in Puritan society. Some additional questions: What does "The Prologue" reveal about Bradstreet's struggle to locate literary authority within herself? Is she really as self-deprecating as a quick first reading of the poem might suggest? How does she assert her own achievement despite the poem's apparent apologetic tone? What are the several meanings of the line "It is but vain unjustly to wage war" in the context of Bradstreet's self-assertion?

Other selections in *NAAL* underscore Bradstreet's self-disclosure and search for personal voice in her work. The contrast between form and feeling in "Another [Letter to Her Husband Absent upon Public Employment]" emphasizes the radical nature of Bradstreet's writing. Although she builds her verse on a series of closely connected conceits and the conventional forms of iambic pentameter and end rhymes, she writes a deeply personal, rather than conventional, love poem. And in "To My Dear Children," she further explores her own doubts and perplexities "that I have not found that constant joy in my pilgrimage . . . which I supposed most of the servants of God have."

Even more striking and apparent in "In Reference to Her Children, 23 June, 1659" and in "To My Dear Children," Bradstreet conveys her sense of God as a mother. She writes in "To My Dear Children" that when she has been troubled "concerning the verity of the Scriptures," she has found comfort in the order of things, "the daily providing for this great household upon the earth, the preserving and directing of all to its proper end." How does the language of "providing" help her view herself in God's image? She, too, has preserved and directed a household and speaks a language of provisions. Here, too, Bradstreet's vision expresses a departure from conventional Puritan thinking. In Puritan typology, it was the father, not the mother, who figured divine authority and power; and the literature of the colonial period noticeably omits references to mothers. In "In Reference to Her Children," she writes lovingly of her children and gives central importance, at the end of the poem, to the relationship between mother and children: "You had a dam that loved you well, That did what could be done for young." What students may initially pass over as commonplace in this imagery (as a result of the nine-teenth- and twentieth-century institutionalization of motherhood) in effect was Bradstreet's address to the invisibility of mothers in Puritan society and Puritan theology.

JACOB STEENDAM, ADRIAEN VAN DER DONCK, FRANCIS DANIEL PASTORIUS

If you are teaching an English course, a sudden move to any or all of these three writers from the Middle Colonies can be a jolt. Why are we reading texts written in Dutch and German? Before going here, some preliminaries are obviously in order. One of the popular themes for a course in literary and cultural history is ways of seeing the New World, the impact that this vast and unexpected landscape could have on European sensibilities and literary modes. These three authors can be read and discussed to accomplish more than a simple recognition that others besides English speakers were feeling the challenge of writing about North America.

Because again we are reading imaginative literature through a scrim of transla-tion, a conversation about Steendam will likely be more plausible if it stays with large-scale themes and strategies in his verse. If you're situating Steendam amid the New England Puritan writers who were his contemporaries, you might have a livelier dialogue than if he is read along side John Smith or other English explorers a generation or more before him. Like Bradstreet, Wigglesworth, and Rowlandson, Steendam writes from a Puritan tradition—but both Amsterdam and New Amsterdam, as port cities founded by pragmatic believers, were places where worldly wealth and delights seemed to hold more favor in the imagination than up the coast in the vicinity of Boston. The Almighty is present in "The Praise of New Netherland" but He comes at the very end of a poem that reads at times like a tour of an opulent Dutch *Markt* or haven of fishmongers.

Divine benevolence is invoked at the opening of "Spurring-Verses"—but once again, the bulk of the poem is a celebration of nature's abundance, a wilderness that feeds and comforts the Europeans who come there seeking those worldly values. How does this perspective compare to Bradford's? To Bradstreet's? Where in Steendam's verse do you see the merchant and the pious Christian operating in harmony? Where do you sense conflict? How does the flood of details in "Praise of New Netherland" (fish, otters, raccoons, elk, even eels, dried manure, and fetid gas!) bolster his credibility as an observer, and as a devotee of this new world?

Adriaen Van der Donck and Francis Daniel Pastorius, both describers of Colonial North America, come to us as isolated figures—a German writer and a Dutch writer amid a verbal sea of English sensibilities, traditions, and discourse. Also, we read them through translation and intervening time. Since students therefore face a measure of frustration in talking about or situating these excerpts as literary texts, it's a good idea to consider them together, as evidence of the range of imagination that the North American wilderness provoked in European newcomers. What are the differences in their ways of seeing? Which of these authors shows a special relish for raw wilderness and natural beauty? Is one of these landscapes, as surveyed and written about, more empty and unpopulated than the other? Does one writer seem to have a more utilitarian temperament than the other? What moments in each excerpt lead you to contrast the writers in this way? Do both of them seem different somehow, from John Smith or Champlain or other explorers in regard to the art of seeing? When Native Americans are observed in this natural setting, what are the explicit and implicit judgments about them?

MICHAEL WIGGLESWORTH

The Day of Doom may presents difficulties for students unless you suggest what to look for as they read. This was the first New England best-seller, a fact that will astound some members of your class. Ask them to speculate why it lasted so long and did so well. What does it tell us about what New England Puritans thought a poem was *for*? Ask them to find specific evidence of the tenets of Puritan theology, to characterize the contrast between Wigglesworth's sheep and goats, to summarize the portrait of hell in the poem, and to locate passages that suggest the nature of family relationships in Puritan society. And to reveal an important and durable premise in Puritan doctrine, ask students to discuss the poem's refusal to soften at any point, to imagine any last-minute mercy for the hosts of well-intentioned "good" people caught suddenly by death and Judgment, people who simply had not had time (or so they thought) to make ready. No quarter is given—off to hell they go, suddenly and irretrievably.

In some ways this is a tale of terror, making use of some of the same horrifying surprises and rhythms that propel our endlessly popular Gothic fiction. The moment makes a reappearance in works centuries after, like *Uncle Tom's Cabin*, in which St. Clair, as a decent and supposedly Christian and humane sort of slave-holder, is almost ready to free his slaves when without any warning he is stabbed and killed, bringing doom not only to himself, but to his entire household.

In discussion, ask students to contrast Wigglesworth's descriptions of place (heaven and hell) with Bradford's in *Of Plymouth Plantation* and to reread Bradstreet's "Here Follows Some Verses upon the Burning of Our House" in light of Wigglesworth's 1662 poem.

MARY ROWLANDSON

A Narrative of the Captivity and Restoration will fascinate students and help them make thematic connections between several Puritan writers. Ask students to speculate on Rowlandson's purpose in writing this narrative: is it a personal account, or didactic, or some mingling of both intentions? Rowlandson's story will come alive for your class, not merely because it includes mayhem and heartbreaking suffering but also because Rowlandson shows us a more conflicted sensibility than does Bradstreet. Her conflict grows straight out of two Puritan premises: first, that the Indians are agents of Satan, emblems of the Philistines, and the unforgivable enemies of her own Bay Colony group; and second, that as a Puritan she is obligated to look steadily and carefully at worldly experience, and understand fully what it signifies. Therein lies the conflict: though she suffers terribly among her captors and sees much to confirm her impression of some of them as creatures from hell, she encounters others who *do not* seem so, who indeed seem capable of humanity and even of charity.

How does the narrative compare with other Puritan works that show triumph or redemption after suffering? What do the poems of Bradstreet and the *Narrative* of Rowlandson together reveal about the fears, anxieties, and accommodations that shadowed ordinary life for women in Puritan society?

EDWARD TAYLOR

The success by which Taylor works through his extended metaphors to imagery of salvation demonstrates the energy that must have been required for the Puritan to engage in spiritual introspection. Help students focus their attention on Taylor's use of poetic form. Ask them to describe the stanzaic pattern of any of the *Preparatory Meditations,* to locate and examine his use of the extended metaphor and to discuss the imagery of the poem. "Prologue" works well for line-by-line analysis, especially by way of contrast with Bradstreet's poem of the same title, to show Taylor's awareness that his spiritual salvation and his poetic imagination depend on each other. Taylor's problem as a Puritan is to demonstrate to himself over and over again that he is one of the elect, and he does this by using the metaphysical conceit as a focus for literal and poetic meditation. If he can turn the mark or spot—the poem's central metaphor—into an image of salvation, then he will have proven his election both spiritually and aesthetically. How does Taylor resolve the problem of literary authority? Does he have difficulty seeing himself as God's pen? What does his struggle for poetic inspiration suggest about those who wrote poetry in Puritan society? Examine "The Preface" from *God's Determinations* to elicit Taylor's Puritan vision. What is the relationship between "nothing man" and "Might Almighty"? Ask students to trace the formal as well as thematic cohesion Taylor achieves through repetition of "nothing" and "might," "all might," and "almighty" throughout the poem. Trace Taylor's references to children in some of his poems; analyze his use of erotic and scatological imagery or trace the triumph over death in "A Fig for Thee, Oh! Death," possibly asking students to compare the poem with John Donne's "Death Be Not Proud."

Discussing Bradstreet's "To My Dear and Loving Husband" side by side with Taylor's "Huswifery" can demonstrate the contrast between the two poets. Bradstreet is interested in physical life, is aware of love as a physical tie, views heaven as a consequence of human faithfulness, and chooses imagery from daily life and classical mythology; Taylor depicts spiritual rebirth, his dependence on God and love as a spiritual tie and depends on the poetic conceit and biblical imagery to carry the power of his poems. Bradstreet gives us the sense of the individual; Taylor's poetry stifles or subordinates the individual to the spiritual type. Bradstreet's poetry allows her to express her doubts; Taylor tries to contain his within the tight form of the extended metaphor.

SAMUEL SEWALL

Of the judges who presided at the Salem witch trials, Sewall is remembered as the most intellectually rigorous, and courageous. We have a sampling here of his private thoughts and some of his more stunning public utterances. Sewall seems a slow, thorough thinker, willing to acknowledge error in his own life and his community, and to accept consequences. If students are surprised by the moral conclusions of "The Selling of Joseph," published at a time when Boston economic and religious life were largely oblivious to race slavery, they can be encouraged to think about how Sewall arrives at this controversial affirmation: through exegesis, the same kind of rigorous reading and interpretion of Scripture that had propelled the Puritan quest and community through much of the seventeenth century. Students can contrast the form and style of the diary with Taylor's poetic forms in *Preparatory Meditations* and consider the relationship between Sewall's commitment to "great exercise of mind," "Spiritual Estate," and his interest in ordinary daily life. We have indications here of a Puritan temperament and intellect both on duty and off, and struggling for a reconciliation among the various sides of the self. These excerpts can open a lively discussion about personal life, public responsibilities, spiritual obligations, and human relationships in Puritan society more than sixty years after the Colony's founding.

COTTON MATHER

The headnote to Mather points out that the *Magnalia Christi Americana* "remains Mather's most impressive work" for its portraits of Bradford and Winthrop. Students find more interest in the excerpts from *The Wonders of the Invisible World,* Mather's history of the Salem witch trials, though they may be angry with him for his militant fundamentalist enthusiasm for these inquests, trials, and executions. As the best-remembered justifier of this persecution, he is often presented as an hysterical last gasp of Puritan fervor before the Enlightenment washed up on New England shores. The extract from *Pillars of Salt* can help us balance that view of Mather. If students read the excerpts from the *Magnalia*, you might begin with a discussion of Mather's concept of greatness and its deep connection with *good*ness.

Compare these biographical writings to contemporary biography: in a supposedly true representation of a personality and a life, what do we look for now, compared to what Mather was seeking as he reviewed the lives of the Colony's founders? *Pillars of Salt* supplies an important complement to both the *Magnalia* and *Wonders*, because it demonstrates an interest in the sinner as well as in the saint—it puzzles over the mind and soul that commit great crimes and seeks a root cause of that depravity. Why does he attribute such eloquence to these men and women as they head for the gallows? If the dialogue is not "realistic," does it have some other intention? If this dialogue represents the first stirrings of drama as a New England genre, what qualities in these human beings seem to matter the most?

CHAPTER 7

Teaching Notes for Authors and Works: Volume A, American Literature 1700–1820

The previous chapter opens with a summary of basic tenets and lasting intellectual and imaginative effects of New England Puritanism. As you move forward from the turn of the eighteenth century, you might need to emphasize to your students that Puritanism did not evaporate, as a powerful religious, moral, and literary presence, right after the Salem witch trials; or with the end of the Great Awakening; or with the unpacking, on American shores, of a few popular texts from the English and continental Enlightenment. The eighteenth century and the first years of the nineteenth can be effectively presented as an ongoing interaction between an Age of Reason and an Age of Faith, a time when new ideas and older ones commingled in sharp minds and strong American literary texts. We begin to shift attention southward, toward colonies where other values were growing and local culture was taking different directions. The colonists visit each other, compare, and experiment with the pluralism and empiricism that played a major role in the thinking of the Revolutionary period, and the intellectual and imaginative courage that supported a new literature for a new republic.

SARAH KEMBLE KNIGHT

Knight writes as one of our first homegrown tourists, visiting down the East Coast with a keen eye and a playful curiosity. Students may enjoy the secular truculence of her voice and want to compare it to Rowlandson's, perhaps speculating on what may be happening to the status and voice of colonial women. Students might be puzzled by the apparent strangeness of New York to Knight's Boston sensibility, especially now, when the territory between Beacon Street and Manhattan can seem like one amalgamated supercity.

Ask students what insights Knight affords about the different European-based cultures that were flourishing in what we now regard as close proximity, and the challenge of forging one nation out of these differences and the attendant mutual suspicions. Also, we can look at Knight as a moment in the evolution of a feminist voice on this continent: what are the implications of seeing independently, of establishing a distance between the self and the visited world, of reporting one's judgments crisply in words, even if only in a "private" journal? A larger and more ungainly question might be posed now and revisited later: in constructing a history of American feminist discourse, do we transform Knight somehow when we encompass her journal, bring it into the light, and situate it with works which were written more forthrightly for public response?

WILLIAM BYRD

Students need continual reminding that by no means all who settled the New World were Puritans and that we emphasize them as founders by choice, not historical necessity. Ask them to compare Sewall's *The Diary* with Byrd's *The Secret Diary*. How does the Virginian Byrd's view of life differ from that of his New England Puritan counterpart? In form and apparent intention, Byrd's regular writing in his "secret diary" resembles the Puritan practice of introspection and meditation. But students will find it a refreshing contrast. Is Byrd's repetition of his prayers for "good health, good thoughts, and good humor" a cynical response to religion or an expression of well-being that we should take at face value? And what *does* he mean by doing his "dance"?

JONATHAN EDWARDS

The Edwards selections can be introduced as visits to the highest, fullest achievement in New England Puritan prose but also as the epitome of the male Puritan mind: in New England literature before 1750, only Bradstreet ranks with him in creating, on the printed page, a passionate, intellectual, complex, yet integrated sensibility.

Students should understand that so long after his death, Edwards still ranks as a major American philosopher and theologian—a rigorous, systematic thinker. His brimstone sermons are more widely read by modern undergraduates than are his careful readings of scripture and the natural world, and his gentle personal narratives. This contrast in his tone can cause problems: conditioned by contemporary pop culture, some students may assume that any preacher with a fiery delivery is a hypocrite. It may be important, therefore, to make clear from the start that Edwards lived what he believed, and that the blameless life (which has withstood generations of skeptical review), the rhetoric, the devotion to family, and the relentless scholarship and theological inquiry coalesce into an integrated self, and into the first great intellect to emerge in Puritan New England.

A reading of *Personal Narrative* allows us to contrast the Puritan Edwards to the Quaker John Woolman; it also shows us Edwards responding to the richness and theological challenge of Enlightenment thinking. Edwards took on the challenge of organizing and strengthening Calvinist theology to meet eighteenth-century scrutiny, a scrutiny based in logic, in science, and in a belief that the individual mind, propelled along by healthy skepticism and common sense, could find its way to truth. The contrast between Edwards and Franklin, therefore, and the response of Edwards *to* the likes of Franklin, offer a dramatic opposition, and a way to move from the New England Puritans to the secular world of the Federalists.

If you decide not to have students read all of the Edwards selections, you can make headway reading "Sinners in the Hands of an Angry God," not as a work of antisecular fanaticism but as relentless logic and powerful belief. The earlier sermon "A Divine and Supernatural Light" helps provide a context, a demonstration that those same commingled intentions—to read Scripture accurately, to follow logic wherever it might take you, and to believe wholeheartedly—could guide a Puritan consciousness to a vision of grace and peace, and to a vision of damnation.

In analyzing "Sinners" in the classroom, consider tracing the evolution of semantic meaning in the sermon. Edwards takes a verse from Deuteronomy as his text: "Their foot shall slide in due time." Applying exegetical attention to the verse, he achieves this interpretation: "There is nothing that keeps wicked men at any one moment out of hell, but the mere pleasure of God." Hereafter, the logic moves relentlessly, and the passion of the sermon rises with it. Even in the "Application," where attention turns from the "they" of the Old Testament to the "you" of the congregation before him, the relentless, Scripture-founded inquiry never subsides or disappears, and the tone of "Sinners" remains one of enlightened compassion, not condescension or wild accusation. This is a way of describing the intellectual genius of the sermon, its rhetorical power, and its commonality with the many far gentler discourses for which Edwards is also remembered.

If you turn to the excerpts from *Images or Shadows of Divine Things*, there are opportunities here to explore Edwards's epistemological thought—in other words, the way that Edwards "reads" the natural world and similarities to the way he reads Scripture. These short paragraphs that draw analogies between landscapes, rivers, trees, and the Divine Will have a striking gentleness of tone and suggest a love of the details of worldly experience. If you are covering a long stretch of literary history in your course, it would be a good idea to keep these passages in mind when you come to Dickinson: in regard to ways of seeing and drawing conclusions about this world as an emanation of the supernal, there are many striking parallels between "Images" and Dickinson's verse about the landscape around Amherst. If you are looking to complicate your thinking about Edwards as a poetic sensibility and a theologian, you might pause over the long "[Rivers]" passage, which follows a "graceful analogy" to the point where one belief seems to come under challenge—the belief in a personal salvation. If there is great peace in the recognition of all rivers flowing into the sea, and in the aura of union and final return that it conveys, what about the implicit loss of individual identity? Does the passage seem especially Puritan in its thinking? Or incipiently Transcendental?

In "A Divine and Supernatural Light" and the short sketch "[Sarah Pierrepont]" (the woman who became his wife), Edwards tries to define religious conversion and describe its outward signs and inner life; "Sinners in the Hands of an Angry God" terrifies the unconverted—and like Huck Finn, students may feel that hell has more interesting literary possibilities. But we can emphasize the challenge of writing about the supremely beautiful: in "A Divine and Supernatural Light," and in "[Sarah Pierrepont]," Edwards tried to find words for the infusion of the Holy Spirit; "Sinners" creates an experience for its listeners, as if Edwards believed that sinners wouldn't have the equivalent sense of being damned that the elect have of being filled with grace.

BENJAMIN FRANKLIN

For your students, the transition to Franklin is easy, because they have known Franklin since the second grade as a benign and grandfatherly American icon and because (for the first time since Morton!) they are now in the company of someone with a modern-style sense of humor. Overall, Franklin is going to seem (in contrast to the Puritans) refreshingly modern; and a good way to begin engaging with him is to ask *why* he strikes us that way.

What would be shocking about Franklin, from the point of view of a Jonathan Edwards or any fervent New England Puritan, is his breezy acceptance of unreconciled conflicts and discontinuities in his own system of values. The Puritan quest for complete integrity among all of one's words, public actions, private life, and cherished principles is replaced by a quest for maximum worldly *effectiveness* and exemplary *citizenship*—and the condition of the soul seems to have little to do with his plan.

One can begin with a look at the famous rules that he lays out for himself in *The Autobiography* as a method for achieving a kind of perfection. With delight, students will notice the hedge about "venery"—to be used "rarely" for purposes other than "health or procreation," meaning that it's okay to go on a tear once in a while, provided you do it discreetly and don't disturb others. And they may jump at the world of paradoxes inherent in trying to "imitate" both "Jesus and Socrates," as if there were no fundamental differences between these moral models and as if such "imitation" weren't in itself a problem for someone trying to achieve "humility." When Franklin encounters such dilemmas (as he does here), he escapes with a joke; and students will have much to say about that as an intellectual and moral strategy and about whether or not a Puritan thinker would ever allow himself or herself an evasion of that kind.

Ask students how Franklin's "Project of arriving at moral Perfection" is similar in form to Puritan introspection and meditation. (He writes that "daily Examination would be necessary," and he uses a "little Book" duly lined, "on which Line and in its proper Column I might mark by a little black Spot every Fault I found upon Examination to have been committed respecting that Virtue upon that Day.") Franklin's life and his "instruction" through his *Autobiography* transform daily routine into something resembling a religious practice. Practical life itself seems to become his secular or deistic "religion," governed by more precepts, self-discipline, and a consistent desire for worldly self-improvement, so that Franklin's work both derives from Puritan religious method and is a reaction against it. You might need to make clear that materialism and greed evidently aren't the motives that propel Franklin but an assumption that civic, intellectual, scientific, and charitable *action* constitute the only self worth caring about and the only self that the Almighty (who Franklin imagines as somebody much like himself—busy, intellectual, reasonable, benign, undogmatic, and forgiving) cares about either. Students will have fun considering the implications of Franklin's use of *erratum,* in describing moral failings and his refusal to use the word *sin.*

The discussion of Franklin may include the following questions: How does *The Autobiography* reveal Franklin as an eighteenth-century man? In what ways does he adapt what he calls the "Age of Experiments" to political and personal life? What does Franklin's plan for the "union of all the colonies" have in common with his thinking about other matters? Discussion of *The Autobiography* can prepare the way for The Declaration of Independence, for which Franklin offered some revisions and influenced Jefferson's conceptual thinking. Franklin is motivated by the advice he receives to "invite all wise men to become like yourself," and students can get a clear picture of Franklin as both a self-made man and a "self-invented" one. Franklin offers his life as a blueprint, a repeatable experiment, evidence that an American can resolve the confusion involved in being a colonial by inventing himself or herself as a new kind of person.

Franklin's other prose both confirms and enlarges on his self-portrait as a rational man. Discuss Franklin's use of satire, especially in "Rules by Which a Great Empire May Be Reduced to a Small One," as an eighteenth-century rhetorical device. Compare the form of "Rules" with the numbered, discursive, rational forms that William Bradford attempts (see *Of Plymouth Plantation,* Book I, Chapter IV) and Jonathan Edwards perfects (see especially "Sinners in the Hands of an Angry God") and evaluate the power of Franklin's work. Recast each satirical point into a direct statement, and examine the quality of Franklin's logic.

JOHN WOOLMAN

Read in conjunction with the Jonathan Edwards materials, Woolman's *Journal* extracts can help students see that many core values of Puritanism endured throughout New England as deism gained favor, and flourished in the thinking of writers who belonged to very different congregations. In reading Woolman's *Journal,* students may wonder what was so alien about the Quakers that the Puritans felt a need to persecute them. This curiosity may lead into a good discussion of similarities and differences between Woolman's beliefs and those of major writers of the Bay Colony. What does Woolman mean when he writes that "true religion consisted in an inward life?"—and how is this different from the theology of Edwards?

Woolman's emphasis on the inward life or "inner light" of the Quakers may recall the development of individual voice in the poetry of Anne Bradstreet, rather than the didactic poetry of Taylor or Wigglesworth. Woolman's *Journal* suggests a yearning for faith connected more to feeling than to the kind of "delight" that Edwards celebrates, a delight connected to rigorous reasoning and close reading of Scripture. Are there other ways in which the *Journal* illustrates a split within colonial religious and philosophical thought, and a different orientation toward worldly experience? Ask students to think about connections between expressions of self-reliance as early as Bradford's *Of Plymouth Plantation,* Woolman's "inward life," and the assumptions that promoted Franklin's popularity in Quaker Pennsylvania.

In the selection included from *Some Considerations on the Keeping of Negroes,* students can see an example of the application of Quaker values to the problem of race slavery. Even before the American Revolution Woolman reveals the chagrin concerning the "general disadvantage which these poor Africans lie under in an enlightened Christian country." Students can be encouraged to locate fundamental assumptions of Woolman's argument—an argument addressed to empathy and derived from the attempt to "make their case ours." In this Age of Enlightenment, Quakers like Woolman demonstrated that rationality must also involve "life guided by wisdom from above," that both individual and collective decisions must derive from moving beyond self-love to considering what is "truly beneficial to society." Woolman implies that logic without a moral dimension leads to a "darkness in the understanding."

Woolman's position did not prevail, yet the terms of his plea and his awareness of the politics involved in arguing against slavery remain of interest to twentieth-century readers. He portrays a society more interested in gain than in moral action, and he holds that sometimes it becomes necessary to advocate "the cause of some" to promote "the good of all."

JAMES GRAINGER

When students enter literary study through the portals of an anthology or a tour of annotated classics, the impression grows that in centuries when output was relatively sparse compared to now, every poem and poet found an audience, a sprig of laurel, and a place in some literary Parnassus. The exhumation of Grainger's epic, variously engrossing, morally grotesque, sporadically humane, and in its overall fabric bizarre to modern eyes, allows a glimpse into an age when poems were cranked out by people of varying talents on almost every imaginable subject. But this is also a moment when the sensibility and imagination of English-speaking America is extended into the Caribbean, and students may want to talk about that extension as an imaginative leap, or a kind of imperialism. Grainger's voice is distinctive, even beneath the ponderous conventions of eighteenth-century formal and neo-Classical verse. A personality can be imagined here that is neither brilliant nor barbarous; if he is myopic, he is not villainous, as he applies to tropes of genteel poetry to produce effects that are sometimes apt, sometimes ludicrous or catastrophic.

Imbued with the neo-Classicism that influenced English intellectual and cultural life in his time, Grainger gives us a Georgic—in other words, a poem that emulates Virgil in celebrating the details and rhythms of pastoral life. If Georgics are long gone as a popular poetic form, what about the imaginative and moral questions that pertain to Grainger's use of the form?

When an artist adopts a form, and implicitly a long tradition, in engaging with new experience, what are the risks that form and tradition will alter or constrict the "seeing" of that new experience?

Tradition often comes down to us with an aura of gentility, and there is plenty of evidence in Grainger's poem that he intends to sound genteel—that this is meant to be read as the reflections of a cultured and educated gentleman. In his Georgics, Virgil wasn't rough-hewn as he wrote about rustics; Grainger keeps a similar distance. To what extent does this gentility strengthen the poem, and how might it get in the way?

To engage this strange poem, you might delve into specific sections that have caught the eye of students, rather than open with an overview conversation about a poem that some of them might have a hard time seeing as a whole or that might have exasperated them in ways that impeded their reading to the end. If they are too puzzled to fix on any especially interesting or egregious passage, you might suggest moments when the poem reads like a planter's field guide to the diseases of his human livestock, for example, lines 244–305, comparing these to the hymn to commerce that follows (especially lines 322–364). Do these sequences belong in the same poem? Why is this celebration of commerce here at all, and how does it unfold? What standard rhetorical devices (for that time) does Grainger make use of in these passages, and to what effect? What are the implications of putting health advice into a poem? What kind of authority is thus imparted to that advice, or subtracted from it, when it is loaded into sonorous pentameters? If Grainger heaps on the florid language at various moments in the poem, what is he celebrating—and what might he be evading or covering up? Specifically with regard to the "commerce" passage, where does he address the moral dimensions of this worldwide venture? If it reads like an engaging spectacle, a kind of heroic mural fit for the forecourt of an English public building, what are the implications of that kind of praise?

To step back from these perilous moments and consider the poem as a whole: how is Grainger's poem imaginably an American literary document? What insight does it suggest into a moral struggle? What collisions and interactions are interesting here, as a rhetoric borrowed from London and the neo-Classical mode is applied to a firsthand experience of life on plantations in the New World?

SAMSON OCCOM

Occom is a fascinating historical figure, a man who lived in two opposed cultures and became a respected leader in both of them. Though he embraced Christianity at an early age and became an ordained minister and teacher—mastering the theology, the language, and the rhetorical strategies of his chosen faith—he seems to have done all this without losing sight of, or compromising, his identity as a member of the Mohegan people or his understanding that white Christian America would always see him as an Indian.

The writings by Occom that come down to us are sparse: the often republished "Sermon on the Execution of Moses Paul" (an American Indian hanged for murder in New Haven in 1772), a collection of devotional songs and hymns, and *A Short Narrative of My Life* (which appeared in print only twenty years ago). Because students will want to understand the "literary" dimensions of Occom and his unadorned narrative, you may want to begin there, inviting some speculations on how a representative life, in and of itself, can become important to our literary legacy and our ongoing conversation about who and what we are. As questions of plurality, inclusivity, and multicultural identity abound in the contemporary United States, we can look about for historical forebears who faced such difficult questions throughout their lives and who constructed identities and wrote them with measure and dignity.

At the end of the *Narrative*, Occom writes curtly about the injustice in the compensation he received for a career of ministry and teaching, and the pittance he mentions compared with the normal earnings of a white man in similar profes-

sional life is astounding-as is the brevity and the matter-of-factness with which
Occom describes the difference. Students may want to talk about that understatement as a rhetorical strategy: how dignity is maintained, how a life thus narrated
is not reduced to a protracted grievance, and how Occom's firm and abiding profession of Christian values is not compromised or contradicted by his clear sense
of worldly injustice.

Moses Bon Sàam

From early times in the literary history of the Americas, this is a ghostly voice.
Many literary traditions begin that way, with texts that modern readers cannot
ascribe to an historical figure, a single authorial hand, a specific incident in cultural history. It is very difficult, therefore, to open a good discussion of Bon Sàam's
personality or motives, or to discern if his speech is transcribed, filtered, or imagined by others far away. But those problems, when recognized, can allow us to
open larger questions: when we encounter such documents far down in the lower
strata of a literary-archaeological quest, how should we read them at all? This
seems to be a text in which aspirations are blended: the aspirations of African
slaves but also, perhaps, the hopes of white abolitionist thinkers imagining the
consequences of revolt or liberation. In Bon Sàam's speech, students will hear
some familiar Puritan values and habits of mind and rhetoric. Bon Sàam's people
are reenacting events in Scripture, perhaps fulfilling a covenant or playing a part
in some great historical and divine plan, and you could ask about moments where
that kind of thinking comes clear. Bon Sàam describes their situation as not unlike
the Children of Israel or the first generations in the Massachusetts Bay Colony,
keeping to themselves, firm in their cause and self-interest, prepared for sacrifice
and defense.

J. Hector St. John de Crèvecoeur

Letters from an American Farmer meditates on the now-famous question "What
is an American?" If there is a measure of truth in the old adage that one universal
American trait is the constant reopening of this very question, then a very long and
culturally important discussion may begin here, with Crèvecoeur's attempt to make
an answer. Crèvecoeur asserts that in America "the rich and the poor are not so far
removed from each other as they are in Europe" and implies that the United States
is founded as a classless society. Crèvecoeur also notes the near-barbarousness of
some of these pioneers and finds strength and cultural promise in that lack of a
European-style sophistication. Indeed, as his narrative reveals in Letter XII, he
prefers to accommodate to life with the Indians more than with some of the Europeans who have become settlers in the American woods.

A variety of European philosophers and historical crises seem to influence
Crèvecoeur's thinking, and it might be worth asking your students to suggest what
these are. There are moments when he sounds like Hobbes, like Locke, even like
Rousseau—and students may want to discuss this key issue: is this a body of
thought that grows out of American experience or is his thinking, and his hope,
imposed on American experience or adapted to it from some other culture or body
of wisdom? Throughout a discussion of Crèvecoeur, asking students to locate both
his assumptions and his contradictions will help them read his letters within

Crèvecoeur's own historical context and identify their significance for present-day readers.

Letter IX offers an implicit contradiction to Crèvecoeur's affirmation in Letter III that "we know, properly speaking, no strangers," when he describes coming on the caged African who has been left to die. The letter ends with his report that when he asked why the slave had been punished in this manner, "they told me that the laws of self-preservation rendered such executions necessary." Letter X, in which he writes about the mortal conflict between a black snake and a watersnake, seems a rather gloomy parable, and students may want to speculate on its implications. If we read this parable as being about the relationship between power and corruption, then even within the brief period from the composition of Crèvecoeur's earliest letters (about 1769), to the Declaration of Independence and American Revolution (1776), to the composition of his later letters and their publication (1780–82) his altered perception of American life may more accurately reflect the contradictions inherent in the creation of the United States than the utopian vision reflected in Letter III, particularly when Crèvecoeur writes, "we have no princes, for whom we toil, starve, and bleed; we are the most perfect society now existing in the world." In response to Crèvecoeur's question "What is an American?" some students may want to ask, What does he mean by *we*?

JOHN ADAMS AND ABIGAIL ADAMS

In the letters of John and Abigail Adams, students can see the rare intersection of public and personal life in colonial America and evidence of an intimate human relationship between two people. Organize class discussion of the letters by asking students to list the various conflicts that each of these writers reveals in his or her letters: Abigail is concerned with smallpox, a lack of pins, and other domestic troubles; she fears war with England; she's afraid that others might read her letters; and she takes pride in her connection with John's work. John is concerned about keeping his private identity alive, even as he attends to the affairs of the new Continental Congress and labors to ensure the survival of a new country. Both are capable of praising and chiding in the same letter and of complaining about the other's lack of attention or expression of feeling. John's letter of July 20, 1776 (less than three weeks after the signing of The Declaration of Independence), opens, "This has been a dull day to me," because a letter he had expected to receive from Abigail did not arrive.

John and Abigail Adams transcend the formal requirements of eighteenth-century letter writing and allow feeling to interrupt form. Indeed, Abigail statedly prefers those letters in which John transgresses conventional form, writing about one of his letters, in hers of July 21, 1776, that "I think it a choise one in the Litterary Way, . . . yet it Lacked some essential engrediants to make it compleat." She wants from John more personal discourse and more words "respecting yourself, your Health or your present Situation." These letters exist within the dual contexts of personal relationship and political change, and the rapid shifts in the discourse reflect the way attention to audience changes the use of language, even in the late eighteenth century.

Annis Boudinot Stockton

The recovery of Stockton adds refreshment and variety to the eighteenth-century materials in *NAAL*. Stockton is, among other things, a love poet, really the first that students reading chronologically have encountered since Bradstreet. In her lyrics and satires, Stockton works with a vocabulary that explores the power of the vernacular, ordinary words and speechlike cadences that would distinguish the poetry of leaders in the American Renaissance (Emerson, Thoreau, Fuller, Whitman, Dickinson). Students may prefer Stockton's style to Wheatley's, because Wheatley often shows stronger fidelity to the Grand Style, working from limited experience and seeking to prove her prowess as the first African American poet. For that reason, it may be important to ensure that Wheatley's verse retains its importance and value when set against Stockton's, and that students spend some time considering the strengths of ornate expression, as well as plain speech. Stockton's satires seem intended to poke a hole in something, and in her ode to sensibility she seems to be responding against conventional assumptions. What is the mentality that Stockton is working against? Comparing Stockton's and Wheatley's odes to George Washington, what are the key differences—in the characteristics of the "Washington" addressed, and the political and cultural climate from which the poet speaks?

Thomas Paine, Thomas Jefferson, The Federalist, and The Declaration of Independence

Throughout the 1700–1820 period, we have been observing the way in which each shift in thinking retains old forms. The need that the *Mayflower* Puritans felt for a document to clarify and stabilize their shared values is the earliest example of the pattern. In the writings of the Federalist period, the pattern continues. Madison, in *The Federalist* No. 10, argues that one advantage of union is "its tendency to break and control the violence of faction." By 1787, when Madison wrote his paper, his concern that factions be controlled by means of a union laid out in writing suggests his close kinship with Puritan thought in regard to the authority of the written word.

Like Franklin's *Autobiography*, The Declaration of Independence is a blueprint, an experiment that the French would soon emulate, and another important moment in the invention of an American polity and identity. Yet some students may not do more than skim it out of class, because they read it in high school or because they feel that they are somehow "living" it. It has the aura of a sacred text, and you may find it necessary to discuss, for a while, the legitimacy of looking at The Declaration as a literary work, a work with special rhetorical qualities and power, a work that was actually edited by human beings, not dictated from the heavens. Ask your students to consider the way it "invents" history, as Franklin invents his own life in *The Autobiography*. Do they see resemblance, in sheer use of the English language, between The Declaration and the sermon form, especially in "Sinners in the Hands of an Angry God?" Compare the language with Franklin's in "The Way to Wealth." Whatever else you choose to teach from Jefferson and the Federalist era, The Declaration of Independence can be a central work to read closely with students.

THE ISSUE OF SLAVERY

An approach to teaching American literature that neglects the evidence of dissenting voices within the apparent union makes it difficult for the classroom teacher to explain why anything changed—why writers in any historical period began to think differently, and why they experimented with different genres. Given the principle of exclusion that is our heritage from the Puritans (however far back and from whatever origin we are able to trace our personal lineage) and looking ahead to the Civil War of the 1860s, how our founders saw fit to deal with factions, with social difference, and in particular, with the issue of slavery can help us describe the tensions that have always been, and still remain, a part of American life. In the literature of the Federal period, then, in addition to discussing major figures and ideas of the Enlightenment, you can also focus on the ways various writers and works address the issue of slavery.

Long before the early nineteenth century, slavery was a national issue; and in failing to resolve it, Jefferson, Madison, and the Continental Congress helped create another "new world" with its own stresses; students of American literature will welcome a discussion of the relationship between liberty and literary authority. The language of liberty that makes Paine's writing and The Declaration of Independence particularly effective suggests that it is the very articulation of the "United States of America" that makes revolution possible and thereby brings the country into being. The documents of the American Revolution achieve their power much as Bradford does in "[The Mayflower Compact]": they focus the nebulous thinking of a larger group and they offer the familiar form of written covenant. The writers of the Federal period put language in the service of human liberty—for some but not all.

And it seems important to point out to students that the unspoken omissions from the language of "all men are created equal" will require other internal revolutions—for the abolition of slavery and the fight for women's suffrage—before the liberty that makes possible the literary achievements of the 1820–65 period will also support the literary authority of black men, white women, and black women.

Students can find discussions of slavery in several writers whose works may otherwise seem difficult to connect. Woolman, in his *Journal,* records being reluctant to write a bill of sale for a black woman as early as the 1740s, and in *Some Considerations on the Keeping of Negroes* he argues that his listeners must empathize with the plight of the slaves and apply moral reasoning to their "considerations." Byrd of Virginia writes casually of whipping black house servants in his *Secret Diary.* Crèvecoeur, in Letter IX, describes the miserable condition of the slaves in Charles-Town. Jefferson, in *Notes on the State of Virginia,* objects to slavery as much for what it does to the masters as for what it does to the slaves and fears "supernatural interference" and even the "extirpation" of the masters—yet makes no concrete proposal for ending slavery (and he himself owned many slaves). The Declaration of Independence, in its original version (*NAAL* includes the original document Jefferson submitted to the Continental Congress, with the changes as adopted noted in the margins), clearly shows Jefferson's abhorrence of the institution of slavery.

The passage in The Declaration that begins "He has waged cruel war against human nature itself," which was completely excised from the document based on objections from representatives from South Carolina, Georgia, and some northern colonies engaged in the slave trade, helps students understand the inherent contradiction in the document's reference to "all men." The textual revisions show that the Continental Congress addressed the issue of slavery and then decided to eliminate it from consideration in The Declaration. One essay that can be especially useful in preparing to teach The Declaration is Edwin Gittleman's article "Jefferson's 'Slave Narrative': *The Declaration of Independence* as a Literary Text" (*Early American Literature,* 1974).

OLAUDAH EQUIANO

One of the first questions you might raise with students concerns the inclusion of Equiano's *Narrative* in *NAAL*. What makes it interesting as "American" literature? Equiano's *Narrative* gives students a new perspective on life in the American colonies. Although the original version of The Declaration of Independence includes a reference to the slave trade (see the changes Jefferson notes in the text included in his *Autobiography*) and although during the writing of the Constitution the prohibition of the slave trade was discussed, stipulations concerning slavery were omitted from the Constitution, and Congress was formally prohibited from abolishing the slave trade for at least twenty years. Equiano's narrative exists within the context of that history and provides a rare and stirring firsthand account of life in Africa, the internal African slave trade (Equiano's own father owned slaves), and conditions on the slave ships themselves.

The American world that Equiano depicts enshrines the merchant. King, the Philadelphia merchant, eventually keeps his promise and allows Equiano to buy his freedom. Equiano does so by becoming a merchant himself. Cargo thus becomes central to Equiano's freedom; he begins as "live cargo," becomes a trader in various goods, and literally reverses his fortunes. Unlike the authors of later slave narratives, such as Frederick Douglass, Equiano does not achieve freedom by finding his voice. Neither does he feel compelled to keep silent. By including his manumission papers in his *Narrative,* he seems to suggest that, indeed, it is only a reversal of fortune, not his own power, that has produced his freedom, for the "absolute power and domination one man claims over his fellow" that allowed Robert King to emancipate Equiano equally allowed other white men to enslave the freeman Joseph Clipson.

JUDITH SARGENT MURRAY

Murray offers a polemic about gender inequality—but before settling in to discuss the underlying logic of her attack, there are some long-term benefits to spending some time with the *tone* and rhetoric of this essay and its epigraph poem. That tone is subtle and blended, and it may take your class a while to hear some of its components, the playfulness and wit mixed in with the aggression and rage. By this point in the course, students should be developing a sense of how to hear various rhetorical strategies, how to listen to verse like this, for example—rhymed couplets and relatively simple language—as opposed to the declamatory classical style put on by S. Morton. They may also be able to hear the exuberance and the agility in that first, almost endless onrush of a paragraph, that torrent of rhetoric and rhetorical questions with which Murray overwhelms a supposedly male reader. What stereotypes is she playing with here, in the very structure of her prose? When does she good-humoredly seem to give ground, concede small points or cliché characterizations of women to move around or to pass these minor issues to get to major ones? Where does the tone change—and at what points is the reader, put at "his" ease by the easy flow of this mostly genial and civil argument, caught by surprise? These are important matters to dwell on: when we get to a different sort of argument-by-inundation, with Emerson, students can keep in mind, thanks to Murray, that the discourse of human liberty has more than one tradition within it, more than one way of accomplishing its purpose. When Fuller comes up in the sequence of your readings, be sure to stop and do some comparison to Murray and see how the two of them gang up on the likes of Emerson, offering a Fabian, supremely mobile prose strategy in contrast to his more ponderous forward movement. When you come to talk about differences between male poetics and female (or feminist) poetics in the American tradition, a comparison of these rhetorical styles will serve that discussion well.

Philip Freneau

In a provocative mix of voices, Freneau's poetry addresses the social and historical events of his day and attends to both moral issues and small details from nature, in anticipation of the Romantic poems like *The House of Night* and "On Observing a Large Red-streak Apple." "On the Emigration to America and Peopling the Western Country" and "On Mr. Paine's Rights of Man" derive their force from their historical situation. The poems suggest that the American Revolution made the development of American poetry possible; and yet, as Francis Murphy notes in the *NAAL* headnote, Freneau was not "the father of American poetry."

Ask students to think about what limits Freneau. Freneau's brand of eloquence as it survives in his poetry (he also wrote political pamphlets) has not appeared to be as lasting in its significance as our country's founding documents; the political covenant and the autobiography absorb almost all of the literary energy available during the Revolutionary and Federal periods and serve as the major literary genres of the late eighteenth century. Still, Freneau's choice to respond to political and social conditions in "To Sir Toby," written about slavery (although he addresses a sugar planter in Jamaica rather than a southern slaveholder), demonstrates his faith in the power of language used in the service of political and social change. This faith has its roots in the Puritan belief in the literary authority of the Bible, but it also anticipates the First Amendment to the Constitution and the idea that freedom of speech is the most important freedom, because it is speech that leads to freedom itself.

Phillis Wheatley

Wheatley is a fascinating poet, for she reflects Puritan influence, wrote poetry that imitates Alexander Pope, and was the first African American to publish a book. Wheatley writes about liberty as an abstract or spiritual condition, rather than as freedom from slavery. In "On Being Brought from Africa to America," the kind of enslavement she seems most concerned with is that of her former ignorance of

Christianity and redemption. Her letters provide a valuable addition to students' understanding of Wheatley's life, documenting her correspondence with abolitionist groups in England and America and with other Africans in servitude in America. The correspondence continues to suggest that she views spiritual salvation as "the way to true felicity," as she expresses in her letter to Arbour Tanner, but also that she is aware of the needs of both Africans and American Indians. Her letter to Samson Occom comes closest to revealing the development of Wheatley's voice as an advocate for the natural rights of blacks.

Ask students to compare Wheatley with Bradstreet as poets on public subjects. What explains the absence of personal voice in Wheatley? Is her emulation of eighteenth-century British poets a kind of performance or does this poetic style allow her both to achieve and to evade a distinct literary voice? Wheatley does make a connection between achieving exalted language in poetry (or in art, as in "To S. M., a Young African Painter, on Seeing His Works") and rising on "seraphic pinions." Wheatley resembles the earlier colonial writers (such as Wigglesworth and Edward Taylor) for whom personal concerns and personal voice are largely absent, but the powerful images of "rising" and racial uplift will reappear in black prose and poetry from Booker T. Washington to Countee Cullen.

"To the Right Honorable William, Earl of Dartmouth" and "To Maecenas" can be looked at as a good deal more than polished performances in a borrowed genteel mode, an African American woman working in a form perfected by Pope, Cowley, Lee, and a score of other British Augustans. When Wheatley addresses Dartmouth and Mæcenas, she addresses individuals who achieved (as she says of Mæcenas) a "partial grace," who lived lives of talent and achievement but who somehow exist on the periphery, either of history or cultural memory or the mainstream of contemporary action. Terence and Virgil were "happier" in the arts than was Mæcenas; Dartmouth did "once deplore" injustice, but he has taken sides against freedom now, as the revolutionary movement in America rises to what Wheatley portrays as irresistible strength. In each case, as she frames her address, Wheatley reveals something of herself, as if to achieve some commonality with the individual she speaks to. What does she turn to within herself and why?

ROYALL TYLER

At last, a play! Even if you haven't been moving through NAAL chronologically, logging time with explorers and historians and sermonizers and folktales, you may need to pause and engage the class, right away, with the oddities of reading a play, and what kinds of imaginative leaps might be necessary to enjoy it and understand a text that was meant to be acted and heard, and written more than two centuries ago. Because this is a comedy and a satire, a work meant to inundate a happy audience from a proscenium stage, some boundaries and inhibitions might need to be broken when we open it as a text in a classroom, several hundred pages into a daunting anthology.

In class discussion of The Contrast, a point of arrival might be the play's quest to affirm a separate, superior American identity and an ethos of pragmatism and rough-hewn Yankee nobility, while borrowing heavily from the drama traditions of England, the culture from which The Contrast supposedly turns away.

Is Tyler trying to have it both ways? Is it legitimate for him to play by the rules of the cultural tradition that he wants to scorn? The conversation might engage with these paradoxes if it starts from the familiar—what students recognize as archetypes in the opening scenes and the major characters, and the oddities in those archetypes as they are exploited even now. The first American comedy opens with two lively young women and a conversation centered on fashion, "shopping" and "visiting." Exactly how unusual is this? Do Lettia and Charlotte have posterity in the suburban shopping malls now, and on the screens at the movieplexes? The superficiality and materialism of the American young are major clichés in our culture, and in the stories that Hollywood spins of that culture—with this extra spin, that the stories on the screen can influence the values and behavior of the real people in the audience. When students see modern-day analogs for this opening scene, do they also see cues here for how it should be played? If *The Contrast* were being staged for a twenty-first-century audience, what should these young women sound like? How fast should they talk—and how much attention would and should an audience pay to what they say? In other words, if the dialogue of the first scene is bright patter of talk among intimates, what are the conventions of listening to it?

This last question can open up a consideration of the dynamics of stage comedy, and of how *The Contrast,* as a performed work, can strike the ear and the mind. If speed is essential not only for getting through that first scene but for understanding the temperament of the people on the stage, then that speed runs counter to the habits of people in classrooms working their way laboriously through a text, slowing down to decode and evaluate every speech, every joke. If young people in our own moment are expected to speak in codes and patterns that affirm an in-group and a generation, then how well do you suppose Tyler, a man of thirty when he wrote this play, understood the special discourses of young women in *his* time?

The second scene—between Maria and her father, Van Rough—can also be nudged for familiar patterns. The encounter will be familiar to students who have been through some Shakespeare comedies or the Jane Austen novels, which come a bit later than *The Contrast*—a sensitive, courageous young woman sparring with a loving but stodgy and obtuse father about—marriage. This is supremely familiar territory, and the stuff of comedy since the Renaissance, and a dilemma that we still exploit: young love and exuberance defying custom and parental rules. What kind of suspense is established at the end of Act I? There might be at least two varieties: a simple sort, having to do with whether these women will know and get whatever they want—but also a richer sort as well, a suspense about whether this play will at some point become American, affirm a sensibility or offer us heroes and heroines who do not come from the collections that populated standard comedies in England and on the Continent.

Charlotte is the sister of Colonel Manly, a hero of the Revolutionary War, a friend of the great Lafayette, and a prime specimen of the honest and virile new Yankee. You might point out that Manly's name is itself borrowed from the English tradition, that William Wycherley nearly a century before Tyler had established a "Manly" as a brash "Plain Dealer" cutting a swath through London foppery and pretense. Students will see other resemblances: the strong stoic type, unpolished yet keenly intelligent, turns up everywhere in our popular literature as the handsome prince, rescuer of damsels in the distress of impending bad marriage. Manly and Maria have met on their own, without the manipulations of elders of chaperones, and a bit like the young in Crèvecoeur's *Letters from an American Farmer* they love and ultimately marry without regard to background or community approval. Dimple, the insidious fop in pursuit of Maria, is duly driven from the scene: ask students to suggest what progeny Dimple has in novels or films that they have recently seen.

But then a larger question might take shape. Class discussion could now center on the admiration we affirm, or the lip-service we pay, to simple styles and virtues. Here we are, back at the very beginning of American drama and the genre that would eventually give birth to American film and television, and already there is this championing of the simple, good-hearted, untutored, fashionless hero, not "rough" like Van Rough in his insensitivity, but rough in his surfaces, with inherent good nature shining through. But this is a play in a theater, aimed assumedly at people of fashion, and the popular cult of the simple hero is strong in a contemporary America that spends more money on clothes, cosmetics, and status symbols than any other culture on earth. When as a public we watch and value plays of this kind, what are we really doing?

SARAH WENTWORTH MORTON

Morton compares in interesting ways to Wheatley: two American women poets in a complex predicament. They are both writing in a time when the prevailing style of English poetry was very grand; the simplicities of Bradstreet, commonplace language, and metaphor drawn from Scripture and ordinary life have given way to the kind of adornment that Morton had indulged in playfully and that had become fashionable again in London. Classical allusions are back with a vengeance, and Horace, Juvenal, and highly oratorical poets from antiquity are again being celebrated as the highest achievements in formal verse.

The problem for Morton and Wheatley isn't that women can't play the high-style game and match male London court poets metaphor for metaphor; the problem may be instead that even the most accomplished grand-style verse by American women writers could not escape seeming like a performance, like a *tour de force* rather than an expression of any genuine insight or sentiment. Another and more profound problem may transcend even issues of gender and involve instead an incompatibility between this kind of verse and emerging American democratic values. In other words, the high-flown language that was still expected from pre-Romantic poets may have been inherently inappropriate for this new republic, in which much of the power now rested not with hereditary nobles but with scattered yeoman farmers, small-town merchants and tradesmen, and a populace that survived by hard work rather than inheritance or hereditary privilege. America had yet to evolve a poetics that could accommodate the values that were expressed in the The Declaration of Independence and the Constitution.

Still, it makes little sense to present Morton as some kind of victim of her time, a woman poet born too soon. If the best of eighteenth-century English poetry locks itself in chains and still manages to dance somehow, then where are the moments in Morton where she breaks through the high formality that she accepts and achieves lasting rhetorical power—where, in other words, is she convincing as a poet of feeling? When she writes "The African Chief," a poem with much in it of the epic and the heroic elegy, is she convincing? Does she convey empathy for the plight of this nameless African? Or is he only an excuse for a grand-style dream, a co-opted Hector for a pocket-size *Iliad,* safely distanced from our own experience?

Here you can reach for your slides and bring in some heroic-academic paintings from right around this time (earlier work by David, for example, or any large canvas of handsomely realized dying Noble Romans) to suggest how this kind of extravagant imagining *could* be a mannerism. Students may want to fight about this—and the debate may open up important issues having to do with poetics and tastes in the Federal period and in the literary eras soon to come in your course.

BRITON HAMMON

Hammon's brief telegraphic narrative is a recovered document whose significance, for students, is likely to be as a point of comparison. For example, you could contrast the closing of Hammon's account with moments in Wheatley where she offers praise for the faith and the culture she was forced to join. A stronger comparison is with Equiano's personal narrative, which is far more elegant, detailed, and reflective as an account of servitude and liberation, of survival against great odds, of constructing and affirming a personal identity out of that amazing array of experience. Hammon gives us a sequence of terrible ordeals, and a closing paragraph of thanks and benediction. But we have little to work with, in imagining a distinct voice here, an individual. If countless stories of peril and loss and endurance are woven into the American experience, what does it take for some of them to situate themselves in the legacy of this culture? In other words, what qualities in such narratives cause us to pay special attention?

SUSANNA ROWSON

Charlotte: A Tale of Truth still makes a bumptiously good read; and once students get a few pages into it, they are likely to enjoy it. After all, it has seduction, abduction, sex, betrayal, lots of desperation and misery, a grand *tableau* death scene, and ghoulishly fitting retribution for the malefactors—all the elements of the daytime soap operas that some of your students may be scheduling your course around! Students will be glad to discuss the similarities between this first best-seller of the American republic and pop entertainments of the present day: the discussion will get more complex, and more far-reaching, when you ask whether the overtly didactic tone and intentions of *Charlotte* are justifiably there in the novel or read like hypocritical add-ons, dignifying an essentially sensationalistic text? A question like this can lead in many directions. You may open up interpretive problems relating to differences between intention and effect. You may hear objectives to imaginative fiction having any moral design at all, or to reading it for such designs. As one of the very first American novelists, Rowson was engaged not only in helping invent the form but also in inventing an audience and cultural purpose for the form. She draws on many established traditions and sanctioned habits: the Puritan sermon, suspicion of Redcoats and of women with vaguely French connections, a myth of an innocent America vulnerable to seduction and undoing by European-style deceit and sophistication. This is a literary work that expresses fierce suspicions about imaginative literature, a novel that seems very uneasy about novels and the power they can have over guileless readers. The conversation can radiate outward, therefore, to speculations about America's uncomfortable relationship to its own literary practices and legacy and its habit of turning out powerful works that seem to turn against weaknesses and failings in their own form. As you close, you might suggest that the uncertainty will continue down through Thoreau and Stowe and Whitman and James and onward to the debates in today's newspapers about the worth of the literary arts.

CHARLES BROCKDEN BROWN

Students may find this *Wieland* chapter a bit of a wild ride and a puzzling one. We are plunged into the company of characters with strange names and scant introduction; a narrator talks breathlessly of late-night trysts and a tangle of affections. Also there are outbreaks of extravagant self-accusation and many moments when the narrator seems, as she says, to be tormented "by phantoms of my own creation." If students are drawn into sorting all this out and trying to locate a plot in it, disaster is likely. To set up the chapter, you may need to encourage them to read for tone and atmosphere and style, rather than for who's connected to whom and where and what's going to happen next. The chapter can be provocative as a quick trip into the tastes and temperament that made the Gothic work in America, and gave rise to a long stream of popular, overheated emotional narratives of which *Wieland* is one of the first.

To establish a workable approach, ask students to skip through the chapter again, reading those passages that presume to offer truths about the self, the soul, inner experience: "Ideas exist in our minds that can be accounted for by no established laws." "Solitude imposes least restraint upon the fancy. Dark is less fertile of images than the feeble lustre of the moon." "My scruples were preposterous and criminal. They are bred in all hearts, by a perverse and vicious education." As readers, how are we supposed to respond to such pronouncements? As great truths that provide a foundation for a good Gothic sensibility? Do they parody the kind of truth telling that Jane Austen occasionally and playfully includes in her novels? Do they give us some guidance into the character of the narrator? Why does this kind of narrative appeal to readers? Wherein lies the pleasure of losing our way in a text, and not knowing psychologically or in any other sense where we are? If you are moving on to Poe soon after visiting Brown, you might compare the paragraph beginning "Ideas exist in our minds . . ." to one of the longer paragraphs of Poe's "Ligeia" in which, alone and late at night, the narrator slips into a morbid, self-indulgent, and strangely pleasurable reverie.

CHAPTER 8

Teaching Notes
for Authors and Works:
Volume B,
American Literature
1820–1865

One way of creating a context for discussing early-nineteenth-century authors is to analyze closely with students several works related in theme. You might ask students to read "Rip Van Winkle" (see discussion of Rip's dream below) in conjunction with "Young Goodman Brown" (another story that shows the male protagonist waking from a dream), "Bartleby, the Scrivener" (where Bartleby's "dead wall revery" becomes a variation on the dream motif), and Thoreau's "Resistance to Civil Government" (in which he describes his night in jail as "a change [that] had to my eyes come over the scene"). Students have heard the phrase *American Dream* used as a cliché; beginning in the nineteenth century with works in which American dreams actually figure in the plot helps them look for new meanings in the theme. In these four works the dreamers share confusion concerning the nature of reality. Your students should keep in mind the larger historical context— the abolitionist movement; early manifestations of the women's rights struggle in the temperance society; the emerging American economic system; the near extinction of the American Indians in the settled Northeast and Midwest; and the various conflicts with Canada, Britain, and Mexico—as they study a literature that explores the power of the imagination and struggles with or evades the conflicts at the center of early-nineteenth-century American social and political life.

As Hershel Parker notes in the period introduction in *NAAL*, by the 1850s "there was some elusive quality about [the country's] new literature that was *American*." Even though many of our early-nineteenth-century writers may have turned inward—to the world of romance, Gothic fantasy, dreams, idealized portraits of the

West and the American Indians, or to the microcosm of individual perception, or to the single-sex universe of Melville's sea fiction—even the transcendentalist Thoreau, in separating himself from society at Walden Pond, tries to give imagery of the waking literal—and literary—body. Is an American identity the creation of a few early-nineteenth-century dreamers or does it result from rhythms of dreaming and waking, of separation and engagement, of evasion and confrontation?

As the literature of the 1820–65 period shows, writing helps Emerson, Hawthorne, Dickinson, and others discover who they are in what they see and the language they find to express that vision. What we are exploring, in part, as we read American literature is the development of ways of thinking and seeing the world as well as ways of imagining and creating the self. In rejecting the rationality of the Enlightenment, early-nineteenth-century writers were evolving their own vision. Thoreau, in *Walden,* exchanges Enlightenment thinking for mystical enlightenment. Can students see this period's writers' rejection of rationality as part of a pattern in American literary history? The Puritans were typological; the eighteenth-century writers exalted reason and logic, but the early-nineteenth-century writers were analogical in their way of seeing. Perhaps the emergence of an "American" imaginative literature in the early nineteenth century may itself be seen as evidence of evolution in epistemology. Once writers became capable of inventing metaphors for their own imagination or for telling stories about either private or public life, they became equally capable of exploring the meaning of their experience and of defining it as "American."

In one sense, Transcendentalism took the separatism of early-nineteenth-century writers to its limit, yet "Nature" and *Walden* both show us that the transcendentalist theory of language is the basis for another American spiritual movement. In fact, every prior moment of separation in colonial and American literary history may be seen in retrospect as a variation on that pattern. When the Puritan reliance on God's word seems in need of strengthening, Edwards rewrites the Bible; when theology fails to solve material problems, Franklin invents a language with which to address the common people and to create himself as a blueprint; when Britain no longer speaks for the colonists, Jefferson writes a document that enacts the very independence it declares; and in the early nineteenth century, Emerson calls for a literary separation ("We have listened too long to the courtly muses of Europe," from "The American Scholar") and for an American poet capable of finding the language for the "as yet unsung" American experience ("Yet America is a poem in our eyes," from "The Poet"). The evolution from typology to logic to analogy is progressive, even though the early-nineteenth-century writers were the first to see the pattern. The "forms of being" change and the theories of language change, but American writers become increasingly aware of their powers to name themselves and thus to write themselves into being. From Rip Van Winkle's dream to Adrienne Rich's "dream of a common language," the meaning of both American identity and American literary history are intimately tied to the evolution of an American language.

By the end of their study of the first two volumes of *NAAL,* students can see that while American writers may continue after the Civil War to struggle with language and literary forms that will make it possible for them to write an American literature, from the Revolution on they look to themselves for their literary authority and to their own experience for the emotional and aesthetic power of their work.

Despite Stowe's comment about taking dictation from God, American writers after the Federal period no longer have even the illusion, as Edward Taylor had written, "that Thou wilt guide my pen to write aright." Nineteenth-century authors make creative literature out of the economic and spiritual self-reliance of which Franklin and Emerson wrote. Nevertheless, the prohibitions against writing and speaking that American white women and black and Native American men and women suffered throughout the 1620–1865 period in American history would mean that many Americans, then and now, continued to be silenced and that the act of writing for white women and for black writers would reflect acts of heroic rebellion.

WASHINGTON IRVING

"Rip Van Winkle" is a good place to open the 1820–65 period, and we can analyze it closely. If this story is the first "American dream" in American literature, we can talk about the implications of that dream. Students make connections between the confused state of mind the earliest colonists must have experienced and Rip's confusion on "waking" to discover that he is a citizen of a new country, an event that must have seemed to many to have taken place overnight. In one central passage in the story that recurs almost as a template in later American literature, Rip asks, "Does nobody here know Rip Van Winkle?" Irving writes, "The poor fellow was now completely confounded. He doubted his own identity, and whether he was himself or another man. In the midst of his bewilderment, the man in the cocked hat demanded who he was, and what was his name?" Rip's reply echoes with contemporary resonance to undergraduate students: " 'God knows,' exclaimed he, at his wit's end; 'I'm not myself—I'm somebody else—that's me yonder—no—that's somebody else, got into my shoes—I was myself last night, but I fell asleep on the mountain, and they've changed my gun and every thing's changed, and I'm changed, and I can't tell what's my name, or who I am!' " The story suggests that, like Rip, we may be deeply confused and years behind in accepting or understanding our own history and destiny. The new country begins in uncertainty; the new American's sense of identity falters, then gains confidence, much as the tale itself shows Rip, by the end, invested with new authority and self-assurance.

But what is the nature of that authority? For Rip, who becomes "reverenced" as a storyteller, a "chronicle of the old times 'before the war,' " is the same person who, twenty years earlier, owned the "worst conditioned farm in the neighbourhood" and was "ready to attend to any body's business but his own." It is only *after* history catches up with Rip, in a sense, and he manages to wake up after the Revolution that he finds his vocation. Is the story in some sense Irving's meditation on imaginative literature before and after the American Revolution? What happens to Rip's cultural identity that makes it possible for the townspeople to produce their first storyteller? The story seems to document the transition between the moment in which the new country had a potential chronicler (Rip Van Winkle) but no history to the moment just a "dream" later when its new identity gave it both a storyteller and a story to tell. Like the moment of the decline of Puritanism and the emergence of Enlightenment thinking that we see in Franklin's *Autobiography* (where Franklin respects the general form of Puritan introspection but dramatically alters its content), there is a similar moment of transition between prerevolutionary and postrevolutionary thinking for the new American Rip Van Winkle. In changing only the red coat of King George to the blue coat of George Washington on the sign that used to stand over the village inn (and now advertises the Union Hotel), Irving suggests that the "singularly metamorphosed" country may have undergone radical change in some ways, but that in other ways it may have changed very little indeed.

At the end of the story, Irving turns Rip's confusion into a joke at Dame Van Winkle's expense: "But there was one species of despotism under which he had long groaned, and that was—petticoat government." Here Irving establishes a theme that would become characteristic of much nineteenth-century fiction, in which the male character represents simple good nature, artistic sensibility, and free spirit and the female character signifies the forces that inhibit that sensibility. Dame's "curtain lectures" vie only with Puritan sermons in their severity, and it is her "dinning" voice, her tongue that was "incessantly going," that Irving blames for silencing the budding artist in Rip. ("Rip had but one way of replying to all lectures of the kind. . . . He shrugged his shoulders, shook his head, cast up his eyes, but said nothing.") American fiction seems to begin, therefore, in the silencing of Dame Van Winkle—for Rip's real victory is not the one he wins over the British, but the one he wins as a result of Dame's death. One might speculate that for Irving—as for Cooper, Poe, Hawthorne, and Melville—the real American Dream is of a world in which women are either silent, dead, or in some other way excluded from the sphere of action.

If students are interested in reading Irving for allegorical resonance or for the indication (or betrayal) of certain archetypal fears in the emerging American male author, then "The Legend of Sleepy Hollow" can provide them with more possibilities along this line. What if we read the conflict between Ichabod and Brom Bones as suggesting somehow a larger opposition—between Ichabod as the product of a new-style book learning that conceals but does not eliminate foolishness and superstition and Brom Bones, who flat-out refuses intellectuality and intellectual pretensions and who makes his way through the world on personal intuitions and common sense? Ichabod reads and reasons and teaches, but he cannot escape his childish fears; Brom says no! in thunder to Ichabod's kind of thinking—is it significant then that this horseman of his is headless? About two hundred years before Irving wrote this story, Anne Hutchinson was banished from the Bay Colony for trusting her own mind and heart above any printed word or reasoned argument; playfully or otherwise, has her spirit made its return in Irving's story? Does the last line of the story suggest, perhaps, that the story itself celebrates a buoyant distrust of the spoken and printed word? If the students remember Anne Hutchinson, you might ask a question like this: To what extent are latter-day Antinomians and Headless Horsemen heroic figures in American imaginative literature? Such a question is worth keeping in mind as we move forward from Sleepy Hollow.

JAMES FENIMORE COOPER

You have small bits here of a writer known for sprawling works, and some special care may be required so that students read him sympathetically. You might want to open with some notes about Cooper's huge popularity in his own time and after—to the extent that later nineteenth-century writers (like Mark Twain) felt that he was a ponderous Romantic legacy that realism had to push out of the way, just as British realism had to rise up against Sir Walter Scott. Cooper remained a rite of passage for young American boys until the middle of the twentieth century; and his grander yarns, in which Hawkeye (Natty Bumppo, the old hunter in these excerpts) was young and a superhero in buckskins, did much to shape not only the popular conception of the eastern woods in the French and Indian War and the Revolution but also popular ideas of what Indians were like and how to tell the Noble Savages (mostly Delawares and Mohegans in these tales) from the skulking, villainous Hurons.

Back before academics began to fuss about literary modes and schools, Cooper was engaged in doing several kinds of cultural work at once in these novels about Natty and the early days of settlement in the neighborhood of Otsego Lake, Lake George, and Lake Champlain. He was writing an epic, with the classic purposes of Virgil's epic: to lay claim to a heroic heritage, to infuse a landscape with an aura of grandeur and elegy, to inspire his contemporaries with paragons of various virtues. He was also writing romance, in the manner of Scott, who not only had imbued Scotland with magic, legend, and melancholy beauty but also had made a fortune in the process. And Cooper was also a man of political and social causes: environmentalist ethics burst forth at times in these novels, as do moments of prophecy. It's worth telling your students that these floods of pigeons, slaughtered with cannons and so thick that they blot out the sky, are indeed the passenger pigeons that were driven to extinction in the opening decades of this century. As you read more closely, talk at some length about Cooper's slow-developing sentences; his delight in the carefully composed tableau; and the affinity of such a style to the dark, emotion-charged, ceremonial canvases of the Hudson River School of painters, to which Cooper was closely allied.

THE CHEROKEE MEMORIALS

The memorials themselves were written in response to the Indian Removal Act of 1830, which authorized the removal of Indian groups to lands west of the Mississippi. The memorials reveal inconsistencies in the U.S. government's treatment of the Cherokee: on the one hand viewing them as subjects and on the other negotiating with them as independent people of a separate nation. "The answer must be plain—they were not subjects, but a distinct nation." Furthermore, the memorials hold that treaties enacted between the Cherokee and the U.S. government were "always written by the Commissioners, on the part of the United States, for obvious reasons: as the Cherokees were unacquainted with letters." In each of these arguments, students can see evidence of awareness on the part of the Cherokee themselves, and reading the memorials may help them recognize that even at the time of their own removal, the Cherokee were articulate analysts of their own situation and of U.S. policies and accurately predicted the disastrous outcome of the Indian Removal Act. In the document dated November 5, 1829, the authors note that the doctrine will be "fatal in its consequences to us" and urge the House and the Senate to take action so that "our national existence may not be extinguished."

The Cherokee had built roads and houses, become Christianized, published books in an alphabet invented by Sequoyah, and adopted a national constitution.

In light of these efforts, students may see in the hope that "our national existence may not be extinguished" a double meaning: the Cherokee do not wish to lose either their cultural identity or their new attainments as "civilized" or "national" persons. They doubly express their feelings of betrayal, because they are asked not only to leave their ancestral lands but also to understand that their efforts to "improve" their society have not merited what they had expected—"the voice of encouragement by an approving world." In a literature course, it is particularly important to look at the structure and language of these memorials and understand how they work. They are not a mindless copycatting of language in The Declaration of Independence and sections of The Constitution of the United States; they employ those by-now "self-evident" truths and principles, and the language in which they were expressed fifty years earlier, to give special emphasis to the facts that "all men" are not being treated equally by the Washington government, and that those most feared sins of the New England Puritans—hypocrisy and deep inconsistency between principle and action—are overshadowing relations with indigenous American peoples.

CATHERINE MARIA SEDGWICK

Think twice before you pass over Sedgwick. For several reasons, she can be an important inclusion in a historical survey course, especially if you are following the development of an American voice, or voices, and looking for vivid accounts of how large-scale doctrines, creeds, and cultural shifts influenced ordinary life. If you are seeking indications of how we got from the magisterial sound of Irving and the rhetorical stodginess of Cooper to the vital vernaculars of Melville, Twain, and Jewett, then Sedgwick marks an important stage in those developments.

Something is happening to American prose and to American ideas of authorship, and "Cacoethes Scribendi" (take a moment and reassure your class that the story under this pretentious-sounding title is anything but pretentious) is a tale that your students will move through with a speed that may surprise them. It a tale of life and love in a small New England town, and in the context of a survey course it can help shift and extend the view of white American experience. You might select a page or two of Sedgwick and do a quick comparison with Irving in "The Legend of Sleepy Hollow," or Rowson or Cooper, and see if students can hear a difference, hear a prose style that in this case is aptly suited to the context and people that the story is about. This is ordinary America as Sedgwick knew it, and it is also the regular literary scene: the world from which writers and audiences and a literary culture will grow. The story is light hearted; this is no pastoral tragedy or Thomas Gray lament for talent lost under the bushel of rural life. But there are uncertainties here about how people will write, why they will write, and what they will write; and your class can get a good glimpse of the emerging situation of imaginative literature in America, a situation understood firsthand by one of its most successful authors.

"A Reminiscence of Federalism" is perhaps harder to enter into imaginatively. Sedgwick is writing of an era that for herself was long gone, and she is telling a story that is mustier to your students than a tale of small-town love. There is a distinctly eighteenth-century cast to the plot: the early death of a mother and a great deal of anxiety about inheritance, expectations, family name—the stuff of the English gentry as evoked by the likes of Fielding. There is a timeless quality, however, to some of the central subjects of the story: a struggle between political values, a struggle supposedly far away, is having a local effect on the motives of characters in the foreground and on the reasons and rationalizations that they offer (to others and to themselves) for what they do. It's a reasonable hope that some of your students have been wondering about this, about how the big philosophical and political principles encountered so often in a typical survey course sifted down into ordinary thinking and experience. Sedgwick's astute, cool observations of those effects make her work an important moment in the growth of American fiction as social observation and commentary. For those reasons, the Sedgwick materials make an excellent combination with Alcott's "Transcendental Wild Oats."

WILLIAM CULLEN BRYANT

More than Freneau, Bryant exemplifies the new "Americanness" of nineteenth-century literature; yet Bryant will not serve as Emerson's American poet. Ask your students why; and ask them to compare "Thanatopsis" with Freneau's *The House of Night*. Which of Bryant's poems look to eighteenth-century values, both in philosophy and in aesthetics? You can closely analyze "The Prairies" in class, for this poem is the most clearly "American" of the Bryant selections in *NAAL*. Even so, memories of Sarah Morton (if "The African Chief" has been read before Bryant) will cause students to wonder what the core intention is here—a mystical breakthrough into understanding of these bygone Indian nations, these enigmatic mound builders about whom Bryant has no clues but the landscape and its telltale shapes? Or a pretext to write, on a small scale, an American *Aeneid*, and thus claim for ourselves some reassuring romantic ghosts in our wilderness and some oblique claim to an ancient, heroic, and tragic tradition?

What marks the poem as American? You can discuss the way Bryant draws his imagery from the Great Plains, takes as his subject the "dilated sight" of the romantic perceiver, and associates the source of perception with change in the "forms of being." The mixture of styles, philosophies, and attitudes toward poetry that students find in "The Prairies" helps them see that evolution in thinking and writing takes place slowly. Some might argue that the "British" elements in Bryant's poetry contribute greatly to its beauty and power and that the evidence of continued influence is one valid response to the confusion the new Americans must have felt after the Revolution and also serves as a tribute to the enduring cultural and emotional content of the new country's relationship to things British, despite the change in our form of government.

WILLIAM APESS

Both Occom and Apess were Christian preachers, and both worked as missionaries of and reformers to American Indian peoples. Furthermore, in both of the texts in *NAAL*, Occom and Apess are addressing a white audience; Apess, however, is much more direct in criticizing the audience he is addressing.

Ask students to comment on the image of the looking glass. In one sense Apess's essay holds a mirror up to his Euro-American audience, but that mirroring also creates a rhetorical form of encounter, thus linking Apess's text with the "Litera-ture to 1700" period of *NAAL* and hinting at several new ways to interpret this trope in light of the history of native Americans in the nineteenth-century United States.

For the looking glass also shows his audience the reality of the lives of Indians, particularly of women and children in poverty—"Let me for a few moments turn your attention to the reservations in the different states of New England"—thus asking his audience to encounter in a literal sense the lives he describes for them and in a spiritual sense the racism they have condoned and that Apess deems responsible for the material condition of the Indians' lives. The looking glass thus becomes both self-reflexive and reflective of the racialized "others" in American history—a history that for Apess includes the treatment of African Americans as well as American Indians.

In some ways the rhetoric of Apess's text may seem uncomplicated, perhaps part-ly because the arguments he raises to counter racism may be familiar to students in your class. He argues that Euro-Americans use skin color to racialize the dif-ference and hence the inferiority of both Native Americans and African Americans; he reminds his audience that there are by far more skins of color in the world than white skins (he cites the ratio of fifteen to one), he makes his audience aware of the theory that Jesus Christ and the Apostles were themselves persons of color, and he protests the double-standard that has allowed white men to marry Native Amer-ican women but has not allowed Native American men "to choose their partners among the whites if they wish." Many of these and other points of his argument actually seem quite forward looking for 1833, anticipating analyses of racial for-mation in our own time. And Apess cites Scripture to underscore his reasoning.

In another way, his rhetorical strategy is complex and provocative. After all, as a Christian Indian, he is himself the product of a particular aspect of white culture, the aspect he now invokes to affirm his perspective. Thus as he addresses his white audience, he himself becomes a looking glass; in Apess, his Christian audience can see their own creation and their own best selves taken as gospel and then held back up to them. Point out to students that Apess does not base his essay on Scripture and in fact does not even quote from the Bible early in his text. It is only later, when he is looking for support for his own argument, that he quotes. Examine the particular passages he includes; these passages become the ultimate moments of encounter with the self for his Euro-American audience, for they have ostensibly served as models for New England character. When he examines them, he states his purpose, namely "to penetrate more fully into the conduct of those who pro-fess to have pure principles and who tell us to follow Jesus Christ. . . . Let us see if they come anywhere near him and his ancient disciples." The act of examining the principles of Christ—including especially "Thou shalt love thy neighbor as thy-self" and "Let us not love in word but in deed"—becomes the rhetorical act of hold-ing up the looking glass, but in effect, the Indians themselves are what Apess wants his audience to see when they look in a mirror. "Thou shalt love thy neighbor as thy-self" becomes, in Apess's text, "Thou shalt see thy neighbor as—and in—thyself."

Apess's text thus becomes an emblem of American literature viewed as encounter: without the meeting of Native American and Christian cultures in Apess himself, he would not be speaking texts in a language that can be transcribed (but rather, perhaps, be an orator of native myths or songs). What he has to say, as a product of that encounter, is conveyed by the word *looking glass*. Thus the history of relations between Indians and whites explains the emergence of Apess's text: *encounter* serves as a figure for another creation myth, this one for a Native American's creation of American literature and his implied white reader.

CAROLINE STANSBURY KIRKLAND

Kirkland's brief sketches help jar the notion that realist intentions came to America only after the Civil War, but the interest of this material extends further. These are thoughtful observations, and they ask whether high-flown philosophical premises and Romantic perceptions and sentiments have a life in the outback—a life of their own or as transplants from eastern or European intellectual circles. Crèvecoeur is an obvious figure for comparison here: he hardly mentions women in his imaginative and fairly abstract tour of American rural settlements. Kirkland, in contrast, centers on the experience and space of the woman pioneer and builds her larger formulations out of the particulars and domestic details of life on the frontier; in other words, she seems to work from an opposite direction. To what extent does she arrive where Crèvecoeur does, on the subject of freedom and the moral effects of living in the natural world? Where are the important differences?

LYDIA MARIA CHILD

Child was a prolific and adventurous writer; this excerpt is nonfiction prose from fairly late in her career, after the success of *Hobomok* and much of her work in the cause of abolitionism and women's rights. All of her life, Child was a risk taker, out ahead of other reformers and social critics; and students may respond well to a look at the way she frames her defense of John Brown. There is sustained, high-serious intensity here, and Child's argumentative strategy compares in very interesting ways to the tactics that Fuller and Fern adopt for arguing important issues connected to principles of liberty and human worth. The best comparison, however, might be with Thoreau's famous "Plea for Captain John Brown," which could easily be brought in and looked over in class. In defending Brown, each of these writers sees him differently; and those differences open up major comparisons in their temperament, in their social circumstances, and in the motives that shaped their respective careers.

RALPH WALDO EMERSON

If you are focusing on the New Americanness of American literature in the early nineteenth century, one or more of the following essays will help you develop the theme: "The American Scholar," "The Divinity School Address," "Self-Reliance," and "The Poet." If you are interested in discussing Emerson's philosophy and contrasting it with his commentary on social issues of the day, you might want to choose from the list in Chapter 4. Whatever your model of course organization, you can ask students to read all of *Nature,* and then spend several class meetings analyzing it. Understanding Emerson may depend on success with this essay, so detailed suggestions are offered below.

Nature

Emerson can lose students in the opening paragraphs of *Nature,* and it might be useful to read the "Introduction" with them during the class period before you turn them loose on the entire essay. One of his opening premises, "Every man's condition is a solution in hieroglyphic to those inquiries he would put. He acts it as life, before he apprehends it as truth," initially can give students difficulty; but as you talk about it, trying to find something in their own experience that will give them some affinity for what Emerson is saying, they begin to see that for Emerson nature includes our own "condition." He breaks down boundaries between self and body, between our own feeling and the natural world, with the result that he achieves a spiritual vision of unity with nature: "I become a transparent eyeball. I am nothing. I see all. The currents of the Universal Being circulate through me; I am part or particle of God."

Pedagogically, the most important single concept in the essay may be contained in the following sentence: "Each particle is a microcosm, and faithfully renders the likeness of the world." Students can see this visually by turning to an example Emerson uses earlier in the essay, at the beginning of "Language," in which he writes, "Who looks upon a river in a meditative hour, and is not reminded of the flux of all things? Throw a stone into the stream, and the circles that propagate themselves are the beautiful type of all influence." Almost everyone in the class, at some point in childhood, will have done just that; and all will remember the series of concentric circles that radiate out from the point at which the stone enters the water. Ask students to reconstruct what happens as we look farther from that central point; they all remember that the circles grow larger but fainter, and some of them will recall from a high school math or physics class that, theoretically, the circles continue infinitely, even though they might not be visible to the eye.

You can talk about this example as an analogy for Emerson's entire philosophy, for it contains several essential ideas: (1) that our observation of the finite ripples on the water leads us to "see" the ripples that ease out into infinity, (2) that the concentric circles made by the ripples themselves form a series of analogies, and (3) that in the act of throwing one stone we can manage to contact an infinitely enlarging sphere. This discussion helps with the related ideas that "man is an analogist, and studies relations in all objects" and that "the world is emblematic. Parts of speech are metaphors because the whole of nature is a metaphor of the human mind." Each of these points takes time, but the rewards are great. Students begin to see that through analogies we can understand the world and our own relation to it. The chapter "Language" is important to this discussion, because Emerson sees the very process of creating analogies or metaphors as essential to human understanding. Therefore, he can quote Plato—"poetry comes nearer to vital truth than history"—and can state, "Empirical science is apt to cloud the sight . . . a dream may let us deeper into the secret of nature than a hundred concerted experiments." Here you can ask students to compare Emerson with Franklin and Jefferson; Emerson's philosophy is deeply antithetical to the Age of Experiment.

Why do students find *Nature* difficult? Ask them to think about what constitutes the unit of thought for Emerson. Is it the sentence, the paragraph, the section? He uses a linear form, prose, but does not write discursively. Is *analogy* Emerson's basic unit of thought? His ideas seem to move out from an analogical center like the ripples on the pond, even though he is forced to write about them as if he were thinking linearly and logically.

Another concept that students need help with is what Emerson means by *transcendence*. How does an understanding of analogies, or of the microcosm that is nature, help us transcend the limitations of our material existence and our own finite abilities to "see"? Here, understanding Emerson's use of *analogy* as the unit of thought is crucial, for Emerson seems to affirm that if we focus on the analogy and on the single part, we will be able to understand the whole. To this end, he states, "Whilst we behold unveiled the nature of Justice and Truth, we learn the difference between the absolute and the conditional or relative. We apprehend the absolute. As it were, for the first time, *we exist*." If you have any students in your class who have studied transcendental meditation, or any other Eastern meditative technique, you can ask them to talk about how they have understood and experienced the difference between the "absolute" and the "relative." Sometimes these students can explain what it feels like to begin with a mantra in meditation and then "transcend" into an oceanic feeling of oneness with the universe. (This is also an ideal moment to ask students whether they find any lingering Puritanism in Emerson. Are there similarities in form between Emerson's focus on the analogy as the vehicle for transcendence and the Puritan's search for the black mark or spot?)

Ask students to list some American themes that Emerson touches on or invokes in the essay: reliance on the self; the idea that the possibility of redemption lies within the individual; a belief in the perception of the individual and the intimate connection of human beings with nature (if students have studied the British Romantic poets it will help here); the ability, the imperative, of Americans to "build their own world"; and essential to his philosophy, the conflict between empirical knowledge and intuition, between logic and analogy. You can talk about the way that conflict is apparent in students' own lives, even in their own choice of major fields of study at the university: Do they become technologists or humanists? Do they choose applied or theoretical science? Do they elect courses in computer science or poetry? Emerson is certain to challenge their conception of thinking as linear, for he shows that analogy possesses its own logic, and that poetry and imaginative literature can help us live in the world, perhaps better than science and technology—for, if analogy is the means of transcending, then analogy holds ascendancy over logic and helps us reunite body and spirit, thought and feeling. "What we are, that only can we see" brings the essay back to the beginning, to the idea of "solution in hieroglyphic."

The Poet

Emerson's essay "The Poet" makes an argument for the value of poetry and the significance of language that remains compelling in the early twenty-first century. It also reflects a distinctly male sort of poetics that can be contracted to the way in which American women writers from Fuller through Dickinson and onward to Plath and Rich choose to engage with the world.

As the *NAAL* headnote observes, Emerson considered himself a poet, and we can read an Emerson essay as if we were reading the work of a poet; we can respond to individual sentences and to Emerson's specific expression of particular ideas much as if we were trying to close-read a lyric poem. In this essay, we begin with his central idea that all of us "stand in need of expression . . . we study to utter our painful secret. The man is only half himself, the other half is his expression." Asking students to respond to this idea can lead into a discussion of voice, one of their own specific tasks as undergraduates, as well as the ongoing task of American writers throughout our literary history. Emerson suggests that the poet possesses both a complete vision and the tool—language—for expressing what we would all understand if we were just given the analogies for doing so. The poet finds those particular analogies (metaphors, similes, images) that allow us to understand what we might have been just on the verge of seeing but were never able to fully see without the analogies themselves.

Therefore, Emerson writes, "Words are also actions, and actions are a kind of words." Someone who is able to express the inchoate understandings of other human beings allows us to integrate our being and our experience in the world. This idea may generate some controversy for students, unaccustomed to viewing language as action. Ask them to talk about related ideas they find in their reading of the essay, perhaps Emerson's statement that "language is fossil poetry" or that the world is "thus put under the mind for verb and noun." Asking students to explain what it might mean to see the world as "put under the mind for verb and noun" may help them become more conscious about the relationship between words and actions.

Emerson's poet does more than help us create a bridge between what we see and what we can express; the poet also enables us to re-create ourselves. Thus, Emerson writes, "All that we call sacred history attests that the birth of a poet is the principal event in chronology." In direct challenge to particular theologies, Emerson asserts that, as young Americans (whether we interpret him to refer specifically to the young culture of the New Republic, or more loosely to the process of forming American identity in each of us as one of the tasks of undergraduate intellectual development), we look for a poet who will be able to tell us who and what we are. "Poets are thus liberating gods," he writes. "They are free, and they make free," and they keep us from miserably dying "on the brink of the waters of life and truth."

This is a powerful manifesto for poetry in the Transcendental age and after, and Emerson's influence extends down to the present. But ask students to look closely at lines like these: "the man is only half himself, the other half is his expression." "The religions of the world are the ejaculations of a few imaginative men." "Hence the necessity of speech and song; . . . that thought may be ejaculated as Logos, or Word." Here and throughout the essay, Emerson's poetics is aggressively male: all about gaining dominion over experience, playing Adam, naming all things in the natural world, or playing some version of the wild bard that Emerson imagines as powerfully male primordial spirit and force in Anglo-Saxon poetry. It's not just the imagery in the essay that shows this male inflection: it is this assumption that the highest and best engagement with worldly experience is agonistic, a struggle to say the profoundest and most permanent possible thing, and to have the Last Word. What about a poetics based on dialogue with experience, rather than dominion over it? What about a poetics in which each poem is not proffered as the *last* word or the last poem but as momentary perceptions in and of a particular moment? What about a poetics in which a certain mutuality, rather than domination, is the hoped for relationship to the world? Students will want to know what you are suggesting. This is a great time to turn to Dickinson and to read half a dozen poems together, fairly quickly. When students ask whether they "add up" to a consistent theme or aesthetic vision, why not ask where this idea comes from, that all the poems from a complex and changeful sensibility have to add up to some overarching and final profundity? *That* idea comes from Emerson . . . and in Dickinson we see the most brilliant resistance to the idea that Emerson's "Poet" describes *the* Poet, for all times, and for both genders.

Fate

The late essay "Fate" will elicit controversy among your students and give them a glimpse of Emerson responding to the current events and spirit of his own times. Throughout the essay, Emerson variously defines *fate* as the laws of the world, as what limits us, and as unpenetrated causes; he writes that "once we thought, positive power was all. Now, we learn, that negative power, or circumstance, is half. Nature is the tyrannous circumstance." Contrast what he says here about nature with the book *Nature* itself. How do your students respond to Emerson's position that the "fate" of our limitations cannot be transcended, except by accepting it and building "altars" to the "Beautiful Necessity"? Is there no hope for reform in the world if "the riddle of the age has for each a private solution"? Is Emerson asking us to accept what he himself terms the "complicity" of "race living at the expense of race" because "Providence has a wild, rough, incalculable road to its end," and therefore, it is futile to "whitewash its huge mixed instrumentalities"? Is there no hope for environment or the "nurture" side of Emerson's portrait of nature? He writes of the ditch digger that "he has but one future, and that is already predetermined in his lobes, and described in that little fatty face, pig-eye, and squat form. All the privilege and all the legislation of the world cannot meddle or help to make a poet or a prince of him." Is Emerson's own essay itself an example of "organization tyrannizing over character"? If we accept the "Beautiful Necessity" of things, are we enshrining elitism, the New England Brahminism of ideological caste and class? Allowing your students to challenge Emerson is one way of teaching them to take his ideas seriously, to be critical as well as appreciative; it is a way of allowing them to participate in the shaping of ideological debate that characterizes American cultural history.

Last of the Anti-Slavery Lectures

The March 7, 1854, speech is usually overlooked in the Emerson canon, in part because Emerson came to the antislavery movement rather late and because these speeches were not collected and published in book form in his lifetime. From a literary perspective and from the perspective of the American intellectual tradition, this speech can be read as a testing ground, an experiment in which the Emersonian way of thinking, and of organizing perceptions, had to be reconciled with the needs of a New York City auditorium full of sympathetic listeners and an overwhelming moral emergency. There is a struggle under way here, having to do with self-expression and one's own legacy as a great American author and established philosophical leader; and students can be asked to offer their opinions on how that struggle turns out: Emerson loves the vast perspective, the free range through all

Western historical periods, the immense generalization, the durable truth extract-ed from (we are to suppose) a mountain of reading and long rumination. Race slav-ery certainly wasn't something abstract and timeless as a human condition; and obviously the institution was the antithesis of everything Emerson called for, and hoped for, in regard to the possibilities of the free human spirit. How well do these long paragraphs work as a speech on this subject? What turns out to be the sub-ject? Is this a speech designed to be followed logically? Is it meant to be persua-sive? Is it constructed for an audience that needs to be convinced that slavery is a social and moral evil? Or is something else happening here, an effort, perhaps, to connect Emerson the gray eminence with a movement that has a shape, momen-tum, and creed already and to which he can provide only added legitimacy, a bless-ing, and some intellectual grandeur?

NATHANIEL HAWTHORNE

Hawthorne can present a problem for a teacher because students often feel that reading his work is little more than a quest for the "moral" or a game of "find the secret sin." They confuse his use of Puritan subjects and themes with his own val-ues and conclude that Hawthorne is himself a Puritan. They may also need help in understanding the concept of allegory and how it works in Hawthorne and in making distinctions between those stories that seem predominantly or essentially allegories and those in which the allegory is only part of a larger experience or med-itation. "Young Goodman Brown," "The Minister's Black Veil," and "Rappaccini's Daughter" all invite students to find allegorical "equations"; but each of these sto-ries ultimately frustrates the attempt. In each of these stories, see if students can identify the "good" character; in every case, they will eventually come around to qualifying their initial response. If students can grow comfortable with the idea that Hawthorne, as an author and a modern human being, asks complex questions rather than deals in prophecy or reductive moral answers, they will enjoy reading him all the more and see his importance to modern American fiction.

"Rappaccini's Daughter" works particularly well in classroom study of Hawthorne's use of allegory, for students have fun trying to work out the parallels between the Garden of Eden and Rappaccini's garden. The role of the serpent (after the lizard is poisoned by the flower) remains open by the end of the story: who *is* responsible for Beatrice's death? Rappaccini? Baglioni? Giovanni? Hawthorne himself? How does the story, in creating an antigarden, actually affirm the moral universe of the Garden of Eden, despite its attempt to invert those val-ues? Is the story a variation of "Rip Van Winkle," in which Irving triumphs over Dame Van Winkle's power by silencing her at the end?

Asking students to read Melville's "Hawthorne and His Mosses" can lead into a discussion of the "blackness" Melville saw in Hawthorne's fiction. Is that blackness a reference to Hawthorne's moral universe or a reflection of his use of dream imagery (explicitly in "Young Goodman Brown" and implicitly in the atmosphere of his other work)? Suggest to students that the ambivalence they find in Hawthorne actually expresses the mingled self-confrontation and self-evasion that character-ize his protagonists. Rather than try to "solve" the ambiguities one finds in Hawthorne, show students instead that his choice to be ambivalent is deliberate and conscious. You can also talk about the way Young Goodman Brown, Reverend Hooper, Rappaccini, and the speaker in "The Custom-House" (from *The Scarlet Letter*) are all, in part, Hawthorne's self-portraits, or at least portraits of the artist. Unlike Thoreau, who values facing life "deliberately" in *Walden*, Hawthorne goes only so far in trying to see what is there—in his characters and ultimately in himself. Hershel Parker, in the period introduction in *NAAL*, describes the "crucial aesthetic problems" early -nineteenth-century writers faced and suggests that Hawthorne's involved his attempt to "strike a balance between the allegorical and the realistic." What might this mean, if we consider the actual moment of confrontation between the writer and the blank page? "The Custom-House" provides a rich opportunity for students to consider the struggles of the writer and to see that these struggles take place within the depths of the psyche, perhaps at the source of the individual writer's (or the culture's) dream life.

"The Birth-Mark" and "The Celestial Railroad" make a nice pair, especially if students are moving through the anthology chronologically and reading Hawthorne after an experience with Emerson and Transcendentalism. Students will probably have an easier time with "The Birth-Mark," as it seems to play by all the rules and themes that became evident in "Rappaccini's Daughter"—the foolhardiness and depravity of seeking perfection or superhuman power; the fatality of mistaking infatuation and idolatry for love; the reduction, in one's own mind, of other human beings into objects to be manipulated, overhauled, or otherwise controlled. In contrast to this dark fable, "The Celestial Railroad" may strike your class as an outbreak of disorder, a refreshing escape from high formality, provided that students, coming to this story after unpacking and appreciating the high formality of the others, don't frustrate themselves in seeking or enforcing a tidiness and a closure that may simply not be there. It might be well to suggest that Hawthorne writes very much as one of us, a passenger on the train being carried into a future that he, like most of us, only dimly understands, even while he listens to the reassurances of bumptious Emersonian optimists. If this narrative of the modern, post-Emerson situation can be read as open-ended, as an eloquent and sometimes funny expression of worry from a fellow traveler, someone like ourselves, then a tour of Hawthorne can close on a high note and with a stronger sense both of the risks that he takes as a writer of fiction and of the big-scale issues that he enters and necessarily leaves open.

The Scarlet Letter

The Scarlet Letter has been interpreted in many different ways, and most of you have probably written about the book at some point, as students or as critics. It helps to remember what it was like to read the book for the first or second time and to give students a chance to achieve some kind of direct and personal relationship with the text before turning them loose on a writing assignment.

"The Custom-House": As you move into the text, you might want to observe some peculiarities of "The Custom-House," a preface that some students will want to dismiss as a time waster before the real story begins. You might draw attention to the atmosphere of dream or hallucination that accompanies not only Hawthorne's discovery of the letter but also his entire memory of the customhouse itself. Also interesting are (1) the moments in which Hawthorne blames others for his own "torpor" and his consequent difficulty in writing and (2) the image patterns of this opening essay: the meals that he describes, the word portrait of the inspector, and Hawthorne's speculations about reconciling "the Actual and the Imaginary." Consider the statement that Hawthorne makes early: "To this extent and within these limits, an author, methinks, may be autobiographical, without violating either the reader's rights or his own." Is "The Custom-House" a revelation of its author or a veil like the one Reverend Hooper wears?

The novel itself (or the romance—ask students to talk about what they think Hawthorne means by the difference in "Preface to *The House of the Seven Gables*") raises a lot of related questions. Hawthorne bares Hester; does he reveal or conceal Dimmesdale? Examine the imagery of revelation in the book: Hester's first appearance in the prison door; the scarlet letter itself; the scenes on the scaffold; and Chapter XXIII, titled "The Revelation of the Scarlet Letter." Does Hawthorne's symbol, literally fastened to Hester's breast, allow him to bridge "the Actual and the Imaginary"? Compare Hawthorne's use of tangible symbol with Emerson's use of analogies. Is the scarlet letter also a way of seeing and of knowing, for Hawthorne's characters and for himself? What is the relationship between symbol and stigma? And why does Chillingworth, twice in *The Scarlet Letter,* have the privilege of seeing what is on Dimmersdale's breast, while Hawthorne averts his own eyes—and ours? Who are the "good" or "evil" characters in this book?

What limits Hawthorne's sympathy for Chillingworth? What limits his portrait of Hester? In Chapter II he writes, "The women, who were now standing about the prison-door, stood within less than half a century of the period when the man-like Elizabeth had been the not altogether unsuitable representative of the sex." Even so, Hawthorne implies that, by the early nineteenth century, American women have changed. "There was, moreover, a boldness and rotundity of speech among these matrons, as most of them seemed to be, that would startle us at the present day." Is Hester herself a variation on Dame Van Winkle—silenced by her author as much as by her society? And to what extent is *The Scarlet Letter* not "about" Hester Prynne at all? To what extent does she catalyze the "real" drama of the dynamic and developing association between the minister and the physician? And how does Hawthorne use Pearl, particularly at the end of the book, to affirm a certain view of femininity and to reject others? He writes that her tears "were the pledge that she would grow up amid human joy and sorrow, nor for ever do battle with the world, but be a woman in it." Is *The Scarlet Letter* itself an indictment of Hester? And a vindication of Dimmesdale? And how do we interpret the "moral" Hawthorne "presses" on his readers at the end: "Be true! Be true! Be true! Show freely to the world, if not your worst, yet some trait whereby the worst may be inferred!"

EDGAR ALLAN POE

You might find it useful to open with observations about the rediscovery, or reinvention, of Poe: how he faded into obscurity in America for decades after his death; his rediscovery and veneration by Symbolist and Imagist poets in France; his reimportation to America as an imaginative writer of real consequence, rather than as a maestro of Gothic entertainments and a sort of show-off in the tradition of Romantic verse. Did the French get it right? You might also move into speculations on how and why Poe has become so influential in our popular culture, a forebear of mountains of Gothic novels, slash-and-hack films, and gruesome television shows. Poe has changed for us, and he has changed us. The largest and most vexing questions are if, and how, we should take him "seriously" and what our efforts to do so say about our notions of seriousness in imaginative literature.

The dream world characterizes Poe's work, of course; and students may study his dream imagery in the poems "The Sleeper," "Dream-land," and "The Raven." Can we read any of these allegorically, as we might read Hawthorne? Are these poems about the mind? Is there any connection between Poe's dream worlds and those of "Rip Van Winkle" or Hawthorne's fiction? Many writers in American literary history serve as spokespeople for others; does Poe? What effects does his poetry create in the reader and how? His poetry lacks specific references to American places or American life; is it, like Freneau's or Bryant's, derivative of British poetry? If you read "The Philosophy of Composition" and "The Poetic Principle" closely with students, and compare them with "The Custom-House," then how is the act of writing different for Poe and Hawthorne? When Poe asserts that the ultimate subject for a poem is the death of a beautiful woman, is he "serious"? In "The Poetic Principle," when he says that "a poem deserves its title only inasmuch as it excites by elevating the soul," what do you think he means by *soul*? Does he mean something that the New England Puritans would have recognized? When he argues that sheer emotional intensity is the be-all and end-all of a poem, does that fit with the experience of your students? They might cheer for the idea that poems should be brief—but do they agree that emotional excitement is the chief reason for verse? Do they think Poe means what he says—or could this be a posture as much as a work of literary theory? Can you complicate their thinking by turning to "The Imp of the Perverse," and to Poe's famous relish for put-ons and practical jokes? Students have a lot of experience with the way that comedy and horror, deadly seriousness and put-ons, mingle in popular Gothic entertainments, their habit of becoming reflexive and self-satirizing. What about here? Is there an element of the absurd about "The Raven" and is that absurdity possibly intentional?

You can also read "Annabel Lee" in the context of Poe's statement in "The Philosophy of Composition" that beauty moves the soul best when the subject is sad and that, therefore, the death of a beautiful woman becomes the "soul" of poetry. Why does Poe need to kill off Annabel Lee to achieve the male speaker's maturity and poetic inspiration? And if you are willing to let the conversation rove a bit more, you might ask for observations about how Romantic male writers constructed women as subjects in their poetry and fiction.

Among the tales included in *NAAL*, "The Fall of the House of Usher" and "Ligeia" further demonstrate the effects Poe creates at the expense of his female characters. In either case, is the center of interest with the tormented woman or with the psychological torments of the men who bear witness? What happens if we try reading "The Tell-Tale Heart" and "The Masque of the Red Death" this way— as allegories for mental states or emotions? How does Poe's use of doubling in "The Fall of the House of Usher," reinforce the effect of the torture and death of Madeline? Ask students to think about the "organic" relationship between human beings and nature, or the supernatural, in Poe, especially "The Fall of the House of Usher," as another form of doubling. In what other tales does Poe use doubling between characters and events? Does he alter the effects of the dream world by portraying events as nightmares (in "The Tell-Tale Heart," for example)? From the point of view of twentieth-century psychology, do Montresor and Fortunato in "The Cask of Amontillado" represent shadow elements of the same personality?

When students turn to "The Purloined Letter" and enter the familiar territory of the detective story, they might compare this narrative with Poe's tales of the supernatural. What are the different effects he achieves in "The Purloined Letter"? How do Dupin's cleverness and rationality go together with his idea that "the material world abounds with very strict analogies to the immaterial"? Consider the statement in light of Emerson's use of the analogy in *Nature*. Compare Dupin's language with Poe's in "The Philosophy of Composition": is the character a double for his author?

ABRAHAM LINCOLN

You may find that a return to Lincoln's words as significant literature will be a refreshing experience. In American elementary and secondary classes, excerpts from these speeches have echoed so often than students may have tuned them out—and they probably haven't thought about them much as literary documents, crafted for a specific audience and historical moment. The latter two speeches in *NAAL*, the Gettysburg Address and the Second Inaugural Address, are revolutionary moments in discourse of American leaders: plain, brief, taut, and carefully cadenced, they were written to be read as well as heard—and perfect for recitation by others, at a time when declamation was a standard subject in American schools. You might point out that at Gettysburg, the featured speaker on the program was Edward Everett, a Boston Brahmin and famed orator who spoke for more than two hours before Lincoln rose on the platform. Lincoln knew something like that was going to happen: how does his speech respond to that immediate context? Comparing the two Lincoln Civil War speeches to the "House Divided" speech in 1858 can provoke some observations how words can be shaped to be heard, or *overheard*. In "House Divided," what assumptions does Lincoln seem to be making about the thinking and the attention span of his audience, this gathering of weary politicians and reporters at the end of a convention? Have your students ever watched a political convention on the last day? What are the challenges for the person at the rostrum? Why are there so many rhetorical questions here, and none in the two presidential speeches? How has Lincoln grown as a rhetorician and as a leader? In the midst of the Civil War, when newspapers, national weeklies and monthlies, and overloaded telegraph systems are so important to getting the news out and maintaining morale, what kind of speech is going to be more effective—as front page news and an expression of national sentiment?

MARGARET FULLER

The Fuller selections in *NAAL* present a rich experience of Fuller. "The Great Lawsuit," her long essay on the undervaluation of women, ranges widely, through contemporary literature, ancient mythology, philosophy, the arts, history, the realities of public and domestic life; it alludes to Shakespeare, Isabella, George Sand, the U.S. Constitution, Spenser's Britomart, a dreamed-up modern Miranda,

Orpheus and Euridice, Mosaic law, the French Revolution, Isis, Sita, Mary Wollstonecraft, Mesmerism—it seems that nothing is left out. Are these comparisons and allusions random, stream-of-consciousness? In other words, is "The Great Lawsuit" an accretion rather than an organized essay? Or is there a sequence, and a cadence, to the way that these issues and allusions are raised, and to the style that they are raised in?

"The Great Lawsuit" takes a while to warm up, and the opening paragraphs are long and ornate, to the extent that modern students may feel like tuning out before reaching the quick, sharp, imaginary exchanges and short incisive paragraphs that constitute the best-known parts of the essay. Why does Fuller start as she does, with paragraphs like the one that begins "But it is not the purpose now to sing the prophecy of his jubilee"? Compare this paragraph with the short one a few pages later, the paragraph that begins, "Yet, no doubt, a new manifestation is at hand, a new hour in the day of man." Who does this sound like? How is Emerson echoed and invoked in Fuller's essay? Is it pure homage? Does a quarrel open up, at some point, with a failure, among Emersonian Transcendentalists, to extend their gospel of freedom and self-reliance to include women? Does Fuller stay with the Emersonian style, as represented in the paragraph we just looked at? Or does she develop a voice of her own?

"The Great Lawsuit," especially in its lively "Miranda" passages, is an excellent place to open questions regarding the development of a discourse that escapes certain male predispositions, about formal argument and engagement with experience. Fuller shines as a creator of dialogue, and her tighter, more economical paragraphs can make Emerson's symphonic sentences and grand generalizations seem overbearing. To put it another way, Fuller's style, as it gradually comes clear or breaks away from conventionality and formality in "The Great Lawsuit," may represent a very different spirit and style in regard to addressing and persuading others and understanding life: there is a delight in give and take, in open-endedness, rather than in displays of overwhelming rhetorical force and the "settling" of big questions. Fuller calls the essay "The Great Lawsuit"—why? What were lawsuits like in the nineteenth-century Anglo-American legal system? Were clear, quick victories to be expected? Is there anything sardonic or playful about Fuller's title? In comparison to the way Emerson argues or pleads a case, does Fuller's wit weaken hers or get in the way somehow? Does it change, or even satirize, the nature of argument itself, as that ritual has evolved over several centuries, under male governance?

Students may wonder why so much space is given over in Fuller's essay to domestic relations, to husbands and wives, especially considering that Fuller was never married and eventually lived (and died) out beyond the pale, as far as Anglo-American matrimony was concerned. Is this section of the essay a gesture of accommodation? Is it subversive in some way, or Fabian (to borrow an adjective from decades later) in the way that it addresses the American domestic scene?

For several reasons, you may find that your students respond more readily to "Autobiographical Romance" than to "The Great Lawsuit," and not merely because readers tend to like stories more than debate. Fuller's account of her early life resonates wonderfully with several other compelling accounts of growing up and self-creation, the mix of will and hazard that shapes an individual self. Franklin looms here, as both model and adversary, and the relationship that Fuller describes, between her temperament, her intellectual curiosity, and all the received wisdom about the education of (male) children is full of paradox, elements of comedy, and moments of pathos. The opening half of Fuller's account is a comic disaster of good intentions or rather of noble aims dangerously mixed with severity and cold-ness in family life: At a time when women were denied admission to genuine high-er education, Fuller's father sets out to give her a tour of "all he knew," which at least isn't demeaning or diluted down to what an early-nineteenth-century middle-class American male might have believed was a "woman's level." The psychological price is high—in part because of her father's harshness but also because of a larg-er, culture—based assumption that logic and common sense are the virtues to be cultivated above all others. Like John Stuart Mill (who was driven to a nervous breakdown by a similar sort of childhood education), Fuller has to discover, on her own, other ways of thinking and seeing. The arrival of Ellen Kilshaw, the unnamed "English Lady" who comes into Fuller's life in the second half of this account, allows for a handsome portrait of these opposed sensibilities: the logic and "accu-racy and clearness of everything" represented by Fuller's father; the "region of ele-gant culture" represented by Kilshaw, the reassurance that one could "gratify the sense of beauty, not the mere utilities of life."

Nonetheless, there is nothing reductive about Fuller's account of her upbring-ing, and once you establish this opposition between the pragmatic and the aes-thetic (or the Franklinian and the Romantic) in Fuller's upbringing, you might want to complicate the model a bit, by observing what she draws from these opposed ideals regarding education. The stand-off with her father over Shake-speare makes an amusing center for attention: at the age of eight, she affirms her taste for *Romeo and Juliet* over her father's objections, but how has she been pre-pared for that rebellion? Does her playfully recounted taste for things Roman show itself in the way she writes, in the character that she presents on the printed page? You might focus on the paragraph containing the following passage to observe the complex way in which Fuller draws on, modifies, and rebels against the education that her father sought to instill in her: "Thus it was with me,—from no merit of mine, but because I had the good fortune to be free enough to yield to my impres-sions. Common ties had not bound me; there were no traditionary notions in my mind: I believed in nothing merely because others believed in it: I had taken no feelings on trust. Thus my mind was open to their sway." How did Fuller's upbring-ing prepare her to enter the Emersonian circle of thought and to take it farther, in some key directions, than Emerson intended for it to go?

HARRIET BEECHER STOWE

This is a book that was, and is, "big" by any measure. Selling millions of copies in hundreds of editions and having a real effect on American social and moral thought, it's often known to today's students via myth and misconception. Stu-dents can feel some gratification in arriving at a text that, unlike *Moby-Dick* or *The Scarlet Letter*, really shook the world in its own time and achieved vast pop-ular success—but they will want to know what the fuss was about and why the doors of the canon have creaked open lately to admit (after a long lapse) a book that was written for the millions and that plays by so many of the rules of popular fiction.

You might plan to organize class discussion around a few large and important questions:

• Technologically, socially, and aesthetically, how can we account for the huge appeal of this book? As students speculate about this, you may want to bring up the revolution in printing and in transportation that was taking place just before and during the publication of *Uncle Tom's Cabin*. The Hoe Rotary Press had suddenly raised page production from one thousand sheets per hour to about twenty thousand; the web of railroads now allowed publishers to ship large quantities of printed books farther and cheaper than ever before—and suddenly the smash best-seller, selling hundreds of thousands of copies in a few months, was a possibility. But students will want to speculate about the way that the novel works within and against the popular romantic or sentimental narrative, and they can draw on their own experience (with *Charlotte* or popular modern novels that they have read on their own) to look at the way that these representative chapters exploit and resist expectations.

• Where does the moral fire of this novel come from? In other words, *Uncle Tom's Cabin* can be read as a point of arrival in a long American quest to evolve a morality out of the Puritan heritage, the words of the chartering documents of the republic, the ethos of the Enlightenment, the values of Transcendentalism. To put it simply, a suspense had been building: was America going to stand behind what it had been saying about the consequentiality of the individual life, the importance of direct experience and personally acquired wisdom, the equality of all human beings? On what does Stowe's moral fervor seem to be based? In latter-day Calvinism? Concord-style ethics? Franklinian rationalism and self-reliance? Some fusion of all of these sources?

• What is Tom like as a character that he has been variously admired and vilified for his temperament? This can be a complex question: students may have personal and painful experiences with "Uncle Tom" as an epithet, to the extent that they may be surprised and bothered by the way that Stowe lauds him in this novel. Why this kind of character in the foreground, at this particular historical moment?

• If students have heard of Tom before, they may have heard of Simon Legree as the villain of the piece—and if they follow the cue of, say, *The King and I,* they may think of the novel as the agon of the final chapters between the stoic and saintly Tom and the self-hating, Satanic Legree. The other whites in the novel are remembered less well in the popular imagination, but Stowe spends a great deal of time developing them—more, actually, than she spends in developing Tom and his fellow slaves. Why all of this attention to these genteel whites, who carry no whips and do no violence themselves and who have elaborate and sometimes eloquent excuses for their various degrees of noninvolvement in the issue of race slavery? Ask a question like that, and you may reach an area of real importance in Stowe's novel: the book's sustained wrath about the supposedly good men and women who do nothing. Ask how the portraits of these complacent whites might have a special effect in creating the shock and suspense of the novel and in reaching Stowe's overwhelmingly white, middle-class, church-going northern audience where it lives.

FANNY FERN

These brief selections can do more than merely demonstrate, yet again, that women were thoroughly engaged in the battle of words and ideas in the middle of the nineteenth century, including the controversies about various missions of imaginative literature. Fuller and Stowe, however, are hard acts to follow, so you might want to put special emphasis on ways of distinguishing Fern's voice and her strategy as an essayist. Students will notice some similarities, especially to Fuller; and noticing this Fabian, sometimes self-deprecating, highly mobile mode of attack, they may want to think about how this strategy played both with and against conventional male stereotypes of female temperament and intellectual reach. Is this an effective strategy or an accommodation? A discussion of this sort can resonate for a long time and open many perceptions and speculations about how the individual talent interacts with prevailing, and sometimes prejudicial and oppressive, cultural and intellectual habits.

HARRIET JACOBS

The six chapters included here represent a coherent, integrated unit that conveys the power of Jacobs's narrative and shows her raising questions about slavery and particularly the experience of women in slavery. Chapters I and VII focus on family connections. Jacobs contrasts the powerful emotional bonds enslaved families felt for each other and the horrors of a legal system that did not recognize slave marriages or the primary bonds between parents and children. Chapters X and XIV explore what students might term Dr. Flint's sexual harassment of Linda and Jacobs's presentation of Linda's moral right to choose a lover. Throughout Jacobs's description of Linda's relationship with Mr. Sands, she addresses herself to white women readers and is concerned that they will identify with Linda as both a woman and, later, a mother and yet not judge her behavior by their own codes, which prescribed chastity. Jacobs implies that Linda felt she could achieve some measure of protection for children she might have with Sands, and so this proved to be in the short term; later, in part of the text not printed in *NAAL*, Sands marries and, under the guise of taking Linda's daughter Ellen to educate her, turns her into a house servant for his family. Yet she knows that she cannot shelter her child when it is born a girl: "slavery is terrible for men; but it is far more terrible for women." Explore with students differences between Douglass's *Narrative* and Jacobs's *Incidents*. Without *Incidents*, would we know much from Douglass's account concerning the sexual harassment and abuse of enslaved women?

After an abortive attempt to run away, Linda hides in the garret of her grandmother's shed; and Chapter XXI will raise many questions for students. In this chapter Jacob uses the intriguing metaphor *loophole*; what does this mean? The image *loophole* seems accurate to describe the garret in which she hides; she lives in a space that would not be visible to anyone who looked. It is as if she had "escaped" slavery by finding a "loophole" within the institution; has she "all but" escaped Dr. Flint by hiding for seven years in her grandmother's shed? If so, her "freedom" does her little good, and her children might have been better served had she escaped to the North. Why does she stay? She implies that she wants to remain near her children, even though for a long time they do not know she is there; does she remain a mother, except for the "loophole" that her children do not know where she is? She compares herself to Robinson Crusoe; ask students to explore the accuracy of this comparison. Chapter XLI, "Free at Last," serves as an ending for Jacobs's narrative; and as she writes, her story "ends with freedom; not in the usual way, with marriage." Ask students to explore what *freedom* means for Linda and her children. "Free at Last" shows Linda still with no home of her own, and her daughter has not received the education she has wanted for her. The chapter hints at the lingering ravages of slavery and the deficits the newly freed persons experienced by virtue of being propertyless, uneducated, and separated from family members.

HENRY DAVID THOREAU

In Thoreau's "Resistance to Civil Government" and "Slavery in Massachusetts" we see him as the prominent exception among his contemporaries to the pattern of evading confrontation with social and political issues of his day. And *Walden,* despite the premise of separation from society on which it opens, emphasizes the practical aspects of Transcendentalism. Ask students to locate Thoreau in a tradition of American writers from Bradstreet through Franklin who speak in a personal voice and address the common reader. How do the effects Thoreau achieves in "Resistance to Civil Government" or *Walden* differ from those Emerson creates in "Self-Reliance" or "Nature"? Ask students to compare and contrast "Nature" and *Walden* as literary works: how are they conceptually similar but technically different? Many who found it difficult to find logical discourse in "Nature" will perceive a narrative design in *Walden.* How does Thoreau manage a happy balance between logical and analogical thinking?

Walden

You will probably want to spend several class sessions on *Walden.* Here are some questions and issues that can be raised in sequence:

• Focusing on "Economy," ask students to address Thoreau's practical concerns. What, for Thoreau, is wrong with the daily life of his contemporaries? What were his motives for going to Walden? What led him to write the book? How does his version of writing in the first person compare with Hawthorne's in "The Custom-House"? Find evidence that he is making a pun on *I* and *eye;* recall Emerson's "transparent eye-ball" in *Nature.* Are Thoreau's criticisms of his own society applicable to ours? How seriously are we to take his suggestion that students ought, quite literally, to build their own colleges? Compare Thoreau's list of materials for his house at Walden with Franklin's list of virtues in *The Autobiography.* Is there evidence in "Economy" that Thoreau is constructing an analogy, or is he writing a how-to book in the tradition of "The Way to Wealth"?

• In "Where I Lived and What I Lived For," students can consider again the creation of analogies in *Walden,* suggesting here that analogy becomes a method of introspection and religious meditation for Thoreau. Stanley Cavell in *The Senses of "Walden"* suggests that *Walden* is a scripture. You can review ways in which American writers before Thoreau achieved literary authority and what different relationships writers have to scripture, especially the Bible. Does Thoreau achieve literary authority by going back to what he sees as the very source of creation, in nature at Walden? Ask students to comment on the following quotation from Hershel Parker's headnote: "The prose of *Walden,* in short, is designed as a practical course in the liberation of the reader." Thoreau's experience at Walden becomes a record of his way of seeing the world; as it does for Emerson, the process of learning for Thoreau involves making the analogies he discovers as a result of going to the woods. In Thoreau's very ability to create the analogy he has the experience; Transcendentalism can thus be seen as the first American spiritual movement based on a theory of language. That theory is Emerson's as well as Thoreau's, but Thoreau is able to find the analogies he wants in the life he is living on an hourly, daily, and seasonal basis at the pond.

Crucial to considering *Walden* as scripture are the frequent references Thoreau makes to Eastern religious experience. He writes that every morning "I got up early and bathed in the pond; that was a religious exercise, and one of the best things I did." How can bathing in the pond be a religious exercise? (He seems to mean that it is a spiritual experience, not just part of his routine that he follows religiously.) Following his own inclination toward analogy, bathing in the pond metaphorically suggests his daily immersion in the meaning of the experience of the pond. To jump into it suggests, by means of analogy, his daily attempt to understand it. It cleanses, renews, wakes him up—provides a rippling effect by which he can reach Eastern enlightenment, "to reawaken and keep [himself] awake, not by mechanical aids, but by an infinite expectation of the dawn." Bathing in Walden becomes an interim "mechanical aid"; when he becomes able to keep himself awake without the pond, he won't need it anymore.

You can ask students, at this point, how Thoreau's meditation differs from Puritan meditation. Thoreau (like Franklin) is also focusing on a single mark or spot—but instead of looking for his theological or economic salvation, he is attempting to transcend the world of literal limits, what Emerson calls the relative world. Yet there is so much of the literal world in *Walden.* There is a sense in which the very rhythm of working in the physical world, finding an analogy in that work to spiritual life, and feeling—temporarily, at least—at one with the universe become cumulative for Thoreau. The process enables him to make successive leaps between relative and absolute worlds, to transcend the limits of material existence, truly to become eccentric (a word that he cites as particularly important at the end of *Walden*). Walden Pond becomes his eye (see the chapter "The Ponds").

Beginning with "Brute Neighbors," you can trace Thoreau's deep submergence into the character of Walden Pond as nature's "face." Then the last three chapters, "The Pond in Winter," "Spring," and "Conclusion," all build to Thoreau's description of the transcendent moment in which he has the experience of confronting absolute truths. In "The Pond in Winter," Thoreau makes the analogy between sounding the depths of a pond and "sounding" the depths of the human mind, as one might theoretically do by pursuing Eastern meditation techniques. Thoreau has no mantra but his pond; his "depth" of knowledge of the pond prepares him for an even deeper dive into his own imagination, his own consciousness.

"Spring" heralds new life at the pond and new light in the writer. Here he discovers that "the day is an epitome of the year"; the small scale of Walden Pond (and ultimately of *Walden* as book or scripture) is what makes it useful as an analogy. He concludes, at the end of "Spring," that "we need to witness our own limits transgressed, and some life pasturing freely where we never wander." Becoming eccentric, getting outside our own limits, trying to transcend the narrowness of our own experience, can give us the vision of larger life, of some life "pasturing freely where we never wander." The exploration of life by means of analogy possesses a spiritual dimension that logic does not.

But he leaves the pond because he has learned its lessons. When the person becomes enlightened, the vehicle of enlightenment is no longer necessary. The religious technique, or the poetic analogy, is viewed not as an end in itself, but as means to an end. The basic idea in *Walden*, then, is that of self-expression, Thoreau's attempt to find a way to make visible and concrete his sense of who he is. His greatest fear, as he expresses it in "Conclusion," is that his "expression may not be *extra-vagant* enough." It's hard to get students to be extravagant themselves, because it means encouraging them to "wander outside" the limits of everything they have learned as received knowledge, prescribed feelings, and "right" and "wrong" ways to think.

FREDERICK DOUGLASS

NAAL now includes a selection from Douglass's second published autobiography, *My Bondage and My Freedom* (1855), as well as the complete *Narrative*, which was first published in 1845. Therefore, a class interested in Douglass and accounts of American race slavery can look carefully at a retelling, at ways in which the same experience and array of facts can be transformed and restyled, when the intended audience has shifted, along with the author's perspectives on his or her own past.

Since Douglass wrote and spoke publicly with the support and encouragement of New England abolitionists, many of whom were strongly influenced by the values and literature of Transcendentalism, a good start can be made by thinking about the *Narrative* as a complex response to that movement, that way of constructing identity. If students have read a bit of Emerson's and Thoreau's celebrations of the self, as sovereign and safe, somehow, from the brutalities of social life, then the opening of *Narrative* may stun them. *Narrative* opens not with accounts of physical brutality but with slavery's assault on self-knowledge, self-affirmation: the obliteration of basic facts about personal history, facts that Emerson and Thoreau and Fuller could take for granted. When you do not know when you were born or how old you are, or who your father was, what are the psychological effects? What are the complications for achieving the self-knowledge that the Concord writers called for so vigorously? Students may also want to make comparisons with regard to prose, by moving in several directions: from the controlled formal heat of the *Narrative* to the rhetorical capework of Emerson at the start of "Self-Reliance," or the playfulness of self-confident Thoreau, "sure of his dinner" like one of Emerson's imaginary small boys. A comparison of Douglass with Jacobs is more difficult. It is possible that after an encounter with Douglass's composure, *Incidents* will seem overheated. If that is the impression, then attention could be paid to the very different predicaments that Douglass and Jacobs faced, not only in bondage but also in freedom. When Douglass periodically celebrates his hard-won emancipation, is he talking about a condition that could be available to Jacobs or other black women, even when liberated from servitude to white masters? How might gender influence and differentiate the experience of these writers?

When Douglass returns to his personal history in *My Bondage and My Freedom*, he begins the second account with more theatricality. We have more about the harsh landscape and physical privations of slave life on the Eastern Shore, and he moves more quickly into a painful account of life for families—for grandmothers, mothers, and small children. Why are the proportions changed here? Do students sense an alteration in the temperament behind the new account? In compressing some of the experiences of *Narrative* to take up less space in a longer autobiography, what effects have been gained or sacrificed?

WALT WHITMAN

In teaching both Whitman and Dickinson, you can show students how these two poets are pivotal figures, summarizing in their work many of the themes and concerns of earlier writers, yet looking ahead to the twentieth century in their poetic technique and the high level of self-consciousness that each brings to the act of writing. How, in particular, does Whitman express a culmination of American impulses in poetry? Ask students to reread Emerson's "The Poet" and to evaluate Whitman; is Emerson prophesying the kind of poetry Whitman would write, especially in *Leaves of Grass* ["Song of Myself"]? Or are both writers responding to the same cultural need? Ask students to discuss the detailed catalogs of American people, places, and human feelings that Whitman creates in "Song of Myself." How does Whitman's portrait of human life differ from those of earlier writers? You can introduce the concept and complications of realism here, and suggest elements of realism in Whitman's language, looking ahead to the "local color" impulse of some of the post–Civil War writers that students will read in Volume C.

You might consider carefully Whitman's idea of the dream, which illustrates the process by which Whitman works through the "night" of his analogy to "awaken" into a diffused and enlarged sense of self; students can then trace the pattern through "Song of Myself," at the end of which the poet transcends even his physical body, becoming effused flesh that drifts "in lacy jags." How does Whitman's use of analogy compare with Emerson's or Thoreau's? And how does reading Whitman compare with reading earlier writers? What is the conceptual unit of a Whitman poem?—possibly the catalog? What is the effect of the repetitions? What evidence can students find of discursive reasoning in Whitman? Whitman may require a kind of immersion ("religiously," the way Thoreau bathes in the pond). Is *Song of Myself*, like *Walden*, a kind of scripture?

Students understand Whitman better when they locate the same image in several different poems; the imagery shows Whitman's vision of physical life. Harold Aspiz's *Walt Whitman and the Body Beautiful* (1980) is extremely useful reading as you prepare to teach Whitman. Aspiz suggests that "Whitman's physical self is the authentic vital center of *Leaves of Grass*. By idealizing his body, Whitman created a model that his fellow Americans could emulate." Such a reading of the poems makes it possible to suggest pedagogical connections between Whitman and Franklin, for Whitman clearly "invents" himself as the American poet in the same way that Franklin invents himself as the American man. And it may lead students to see that *Leaves of Grass* is as much a poetry of evasion (Aspiz makes the point that for all of Whitman's pretense to health in his poems, from childhood on he had physical problems, was fascinated by physical illness, and spent many years as a sick man) as it is of self-disclosure (as in "I celebrate myself, and sing myself"), in its own way another "Minister's Black Veil."

Ask students to examine "Trickle Drops" and other *Calamus* poems included in *NAAL* for evidence that Whitman's analogue for vision is male sexuality. In "Trickle Drops," they can see most clearly and succinctly the way Whitman views poetry as spermatic fluid; the image is pervasive in his work, including his discussion in "Preface to *Leaves of Grass.*" Male physical health and robustness, in general, becomes a metaphor for vision. Does that make male sexuality, for Whitman, as much a product of the creative imagination as Walden is for Thoreau? Is the version of sexuality Whitman proposes (and suggests, throughout his work, that women share) another variation on the early-nineteenth-century American dream?

The sequence of poems *Live Oak, with Moss* demonstrates more specifically Whitman's interest in male sexuality and in personal as well as public poetry. The headnote and footnote discussions provide the essential literary context for reading the poems in *Live Oak, with Moss* in their own sequence, as they exist in unpublished manuscript, rather than as Whitman collected some of them in his *Calamus* poems. Trace with students the various "narratives" embedded in this poem sequence: (1) a love affair begun, then ended, with the speaker abandoned; (2) the speaker's growing wonder, as in VIII, about whether there are other men like him; and (3) the narrator's emerging awareness of the relationship between poetry and "manly love" and of how this relationship comes to matter more to him (in V) than being the "singer of songs." In a sense, *Live Oak, with Moss* serves as a revision of what Parker calls Whitman's "tributes to the American people" and, as such, invites comparison with Douglass's question "What to the slave is the Fourth of July?" in "The Meaning of July Fourth for the Negro." Consider with students the irony that the "good grey poet" who created himself and has been constructed by critics as our first truly *American* poet should also be our first gay poet struggling for freedom of expression both as a poet and as a lover. In Whitman's time, as in our own, *Live Oak, with Moss* suggests the contradictions between free speech and the expression of sexual orientation; as Whitman writes in XI, "I dare not tell it in words—not even in these songs."

LOUISE AMELIA SMITH CLAPPE
AND BAYARD TAYLOR

A strong-selling adventurer and "fine writer" in the middle of the nineteenth century, Taylor fell into obscurity through most of the twentieth, as his prose style came to seem oratorical and a bit gaseous. "The Shirley Letters," which never enjoyed Taylor's vogue, make a brisk contrast, and together they provide a rich glimpse of California in the tumult of becoming an American place.

If you read these texts together, you have a great opportunity to compare literary styles, ways of seeing, ways of telling—and if you have had a good experience in comparing Emerson and Fuller as stylists, or Bradstreet and Edward Taylor and the early days of an American masculinist and feminist poetics, your class on these

California observations can continue those lines of thinking. Ask your students to run their eyes down the longer paragraphs in Taylor's San Francisco reportage and find moments where he speaks as from a great height, offering a grand overview, foretelling the future, generalizing about culture, real estate, finances, family life, everything. Are there similar moments in Clappe's "Residence in the Mines"? Observe the way that the narration closes in the second paragraph. Is that a gesture that Taylor is capable of? What does that moment do to establish or alter an implicit relationship between writer or text and reader? Which writer do your students find they trust more, and why? "The Shirley Letters" offer us individual people, carefully and closely observed. Is this an effective strategy for conveying something as large as the fabric and character of life among the California pioneers? Can your students find or remember moments in Emerson that sound like Taylor? Moments in Fuller that recall the Shirley letters? With what speculations are they comfortable about some gender-related parting of the ways in the art of seeing and telling?

HERMAN MELVILLE

A few days with Melville can be a high point in a survey course, provided that your students are comfortable about plunging into *NAAL*'s well-chosen selections, especially the chapters from *Moby-Dick*. They may wonder whether these few pieces from such a thick volume can give them a sense of the whole text; and having heard the rumors that this is a Big Hard Great American Novel, they may have their defenses up or come to class expecting that there is some profound overarching theme that pervades every sentence and phrase of every Melville narrative. They *won't* expect wit, humor, changefulness, exuberance, breezy vernacular American English, a host of engaging and brilliantly drawn characters—or any of the other qualities that make Melville delightful to read and not just a collection of cumbersome themes.

One of the virtues of *Moby-Dick* is that it really is about what it is supposed to be about: a voyage on a whaling ship; and you might want to tell your students that what they're *not* reading (the chapters that aren't in the anthology) includes more about the details and bric-a-brac of whaling, sailing, and cetology than most of them would ever want to know. You might start with some facts and speculations about life on one of these whalers—your Greenpeace convictions need not get in the way, as all this happened a long time ago when this dangerous, deadly work was regarded as vital. Take a moment to tell them how small these whaling ships were, how long they went out for, what kinds of crews they picked up (Melville's collection of cannibals, Calvinists, Indians, and seadogs from all over the world is not far from the truth), and what kinds of people would spend a year to three years or more of their lives in such an enterprise? This is life on the edge; and students can sometimes empathize with Ahab's drive to create firm conviction and sublime or monomaniacal purpose amid nothing, if the students understand the work that these characters do and the company that they keep.

When you get around to symbols, you might want to begin with some discussion of what symbols are, not just what they signify about the thing symbolized but about the mind and mood of the individual who creates or gravitates to the symbol. In other words, if symbols can be interesting as provisional *attempts* to penetrate to truth, or express possibly transient perceptions, or seasons of the mind, then the act of reading becomes much less mechanical and deadening than a decoding of the whale or the whalebone leg or any of the gams. These are Ishmael's attempts to make sense of what he sees and what he has been through; and if students can keep that understanding in mind, that these are the creations of an eager human being, trying (perhaps with no permanent success at all) to understand the world and his place in it, then connections can be made on which students will be able to build their own.

"Bartleby," therefore, makes a very nice pairing with the *Moby-Dick* excerpts, both for its apparent oppositeness as a story (a confined, domestic, claustrophobic urban tale) and for its commonalities (its array of characters, its bizarre humor, its intense and possibly unsuccessful struggle to understand life and fellow human beings, its thorough grounding in actual experience). If you began *Moby-Dick* with a conversation about the realities of whaling and then begin "Bartleby" with some talk about mindless, dehumanizing, mind-wrecking work, students will have plenty to tell you. Bartleby is a human photocopying machine, and most students who have worked summer jobs will be quick to tell you that work this grim has *not* gone away with the mechanized office.

In your class you may have erstwhile roofers, corn detasselers, telemarketers, potato fryers, intelligent young people who spent months in front of a computer terminal or on an assembly line to pay for college. Ask them to speculate on what a life of such work would have done to them; also ask if they had the experience in those jobs of working with some other individual whom they could never figure out. It can be very hard, in the long routines of repetitive work, to really know the poet from the fool, the tragic figure from the true machine in human form. If students want to jump to full credence in the narrator's conclusion about Bartleby, that he was a sensitive soul brought to grief by his work in a dead-letter office, see if you can loosen that conclusion without driving them into what they might regard as frustrating ambiguity. Again, if this story is in some ways about the sad, funny quest to understand others and to understand the self (to what extent might this narrator be using Bartleby as an evasion, a way of *not* looking squarely at the emptiness of the narrator's *own* life?), then it is certainly about much and not ambiguous at all about the predicament of the sensitive mind amid the demands of modern life.

Billy Budd, not published until thirty years after Melville's death, is a thrill to read, a posthumous treasure and a supremely crafted tale—so well crafted that students may run the risk of allowing the allegorical rumblings of the tale's first half to determine their reading of the story's ending. Again, you might want to spend some time establishing that Melville had done his homework regarding the predicament of England in the midst of the Napoleonic Wars: most of Europe was in the hands of the enemy, and survival depended on the Royal Navy—and in the navy, conditions were brutal and mutiny was a real possibility. It's important to make that clear, especially if students feel an urge to turn the tale into an allegorical chart and to assign stable values to each character: Billy as Adam or Christ or both; Claggart as Satan or one of his minions; and Vere—what of Vere? If they decide that Vere is Pilate they are no more than half right, which means that they deny themselves much of the modernity and human understanding in the story.

Vere sits in Pilate's seat, to be sure; but he doesn't "wash his hands" of the case. Quite to the contrary, he insists that his drumhead court convene and judge Billy Budd by the strictest and harshest standards, even though a part of Vere (in our judgment the *best* part of Vere) cries out against doing so.

Students will want to know what's going on here. If you want to get into Hobbes and his constructions of both sovereignty and political identity, you can do so here; but if you fear that this will just muddy the issue, you might open the question of how we can willfully and consciously define ourselves—as students; as leaders; as professionals; as clear, firm, limited creatures of one sort or another, acting to the end on contractual and statutory obligations—and *almost* believe that this public or social "us" is the real us. Vere convinced the court: did he convince himself?

EMILY DICKINSON

There is much in the headnote to guide a discussion of Dickinson and her poetry.* *NAAL* includes several of the poems involved in Dickinson's "rebellion against the theology of her town" (for example, 324 and 1068); poems that reflect her deep regard for British writers Elizabeth Barrett Browning (312 and 593), the Brontë sisters (148), and James Thomson (131); and numerous poems that reflect T. W. Higginson's groupings for the first (1890) edition of her work, his response to Mabel Loomis Todd's efforts to secure posthumous publication for Dickinson. Although each individual poem reflects larger formal and thematic interest than its grouping under just one heading indicates, the process of creating the thematic groups (according to the categories Higginson created: life, love, nature, time, and eternity) gives students one way of looking for intertextual connections and, indeed, of beginning to create interpretive patterns within which to analyze and appreciate Dickinson's work. One exercise you might assign students would ask them to group the poems under Higginson's headings, and then, in class, discuss the difficulties involved in doing so.

Here is a thematic arrangement to consider:

Life: 67, 241, 258, 341, 536, 650
Love: 249, 303, 1078
Nature: 130, 285, 314, 328, 520, 978, 986, 1068, 1138, 1397, 1463
Time: 305
Eternity: 214, 216, 280, 287, 315, 324, 449, 465, 501, 510, 528, 547, 664, 712,
   822, 824, 978, 1099, 1125, 1126, 1540

What is interesting about this exercise, rather than how much individual readers agree concerning which poems to include in each group, are their reasons for inclusion and their interpretations of the categories themselves. The categories may express more about the themes and worldview Higginson reflected a century ago than the themes and interests of our own time.

A follow-up exercise would involve asking students to identify the themes by

* The text of Dickinson's poems, in *NAAL* Volume B and Volume C, gives the numbers for both the arrangement of poems by Thomas Johnson (1960) and, to the right, the arrangement of poems by R. W. Franklin (1999).

which they would group Dickinson's poetry, if they were creating their own edition for contemporary readers. As readers still trained to revere modernist and post-modernist aesthetics, some of them may want to include a category that reflects Dickinson's self-consciousness concerning poetic form and practice; the poems they may group together for such a list may include 185, 285, 303, 326, 441, 448, 488, 505, 709, 952, 1129, and 1138. Discussion of this list may also follow from Parker's observation that in a poem like 326, Dickinson reveals her awareness of her own originality, her own "genius."

The exercise also leads into questions of editorial selection. Thomas Johnson's *The Poems of Emily Dickinson* (1955) includes 1,775 poems. *NAAL* includes 81 poems, many of which have frequently been anthologized. One question that emerges from the process of editorial selection concerns the role an editor's interests or tastes play in such a process. Put one of the Johnson editions on reserve and assign individual students clusters of 75 or 100 poems so that all 1,775 are covered. Then ask the students to make a case (either in a class presentation or in a paper) for the inclusion of one or two additional poems. On what grounds would the students argue for inclusion? What different portrait of the poet, or of the body of poetry, would emerge if the poem or poems (and others like them) were included?

Such an approach encourages students to select and evaluate certain poems as representative, in their own view, of Dickinson's temperament and abiding concerns. *NAAL* includes several poems that appear to address women's lives as wives: 199, 732, and 1072. For a different perspective on the life of a wife, students may discover, in one of the Johnson volumes, poems 154 and 219.

If your students are adventurous and willing to rove in a complete edition, you might ask them to look at poems in which fathers—worldly and otherwise—are addressed or considered, and to speculate on the implications. Many scholars prefer to read Dickinson as engaged in resistance against her own father, and credit her with considerable courage in doing so as a daughter and an artist. While many of the poems—indeed the very existence of the poems—provide evidence to support such a reading, students attuned to the way Dickinson tries to "Tell all the Truth but tell it slant—" may find other poems that complicate our thinking about her as rebellious, and her portrait of white middle-class life for nineteenth-century women in New England.

For a more traditional discussion of Dickinson, you might note that many of her poems are transcendental in theme and style, and ask students to select a favorite and discuss affinities with Emerson and Thoreau. But Dickinson is often considered an early modernist, because of the way her poetic technique calls attention to itself and reflects a high level of self-consciousness (see the specific list of anthologized poems discussed above in connection with poetic form and practice). You can begin discussion of Dickinson by asking students to contrast her with Whitman—and not just in the poets' perspectives on same-sex love. Both poets reverse students' expectations concerning traditional poetic form, and comparing and contrasting the ways they do this leads to an extensive discussion of what each poet might have been trying to do in poetry. Sheer size is one of the most striking points of contrast; see poem 185, in which Dickinson writes, " 'Faith' is a fine invention / When Gentlemen can *see* / But *Microscopes* are prudent / In an Emergency." Compared with Whitman's "Walt Whitman, a kosmos" and the "magnifying and applying" of "Song of Myself," Dickinson's small poems seem microscopic. Exploring the freedom with which Whitman creates the vast catalogs in *Song of Myself* and allows himself endless repetition and then contrasting that freedom with Dickinson's 185 or 1099 ("My Cocoon tightens—Colors teaze—") can move the discussion from formal differences to thematic ones, and to the question of literary authority. Where does Whitman find his? How does it appear as an assumption in his poetry, although Dickinson, as in 505, must struggle to achieve it? How does the smallness of her poetry suggest her own assumptions about the nature of literary authority?

Unlike Whitman, Dickinson appears uninterested in the physical body, grounding many poems in a specific image from nature that she then proceeds either to transcend, as in 328 and 348, or to despair in finding her own inability to transcend human limitations and the limits of poetry, as in 465. Like Whitman, Dickinson also writes analogically, following Emerson's technique for transcendental vision. Many poems illustrate her use of analogies to express and contain her vision, particularly the poems that appear to be about death but actually show the poet trying to see beyond the limits of human vision that death, as life's limit, symbolizes for her. 465, 510, and 754 are just three of the many poems that illustrate this pattern; and many others write thematically about the process, as 67 and 528.

Many of the Dickinson poems that initially appear so elusive to students can become deeply revealing of the consciousness of the woman who wrote them—and of the fact that they were written by a woman, as the list above indicates. Poem 1129 also becomes another Dickinson variation on Emerson's use of the poetic analogy to achieve transcendental vision. But her reasons for choosing analogies that move in "slant" fashion rather than in concentric circles (like the ripples that result when Emerson throws a stone) suggest that Dickinson, unlike Whitman, may have seen herself as self-conceived, self-born—not because she has invented a new kind of poetry but because she has dared, as an American woman, to write at all (especially in light of the fact that her models were British women). In inventing herself as woman and poet, how does she differ from other self-inventors: Franklin and Douglass? Does she imagine setting her life up as model for others? And does the biographical fact that she published only seven poems in her lifetime imply self-censorship or feminine reticence? Ask students to reread Bradstreet's "Prologue" and "The Author to Her Book." To what extent does Dickinson's use of smallness in her imagery reflect her sense of inadequacy even as it gives her the analogical vehicle for transcending that sense?

Finally, for some readings of Dickinson that are certain to provoke discussion in the classroom, and that may provide students with some support for their own readings, see, in particular, Mary Loeffelholz's *Dickinson and the Boundaries of Feminist Theory* (1991), William Shurr's *The Marriage of Emily Dickinson* (1983), and essays by Adelaide Morris and Joanne Dobson in *Feminist Critics Read Emily Dickinson* (1983), edited by Suzanne Juhasz.

REBECCA HARDING DAVIS

Davis's story *Life in the Iron-Mills* can allow you to end your course by making thematic connections with earlier writers and introducing your students to an early work of literary realism. Ask students to compare the atmosphere in Davis's mill with Melville's "The Paradise of Bachelors and The Tartarus of Maids" and to compare Davis's nightmarish descriptions with Poe's. Students who have read some Dickens in earlier courses (especially works like *Hard Times, Bleak House,* and *A Tale of Two Cities*) will hear a familiar ring to Davis's grim opening panorama and should join a discussion of how Realist and Romantic motives can intertwine.

They may also want to compare Hugh Wolfe's creation of the korl woman with women characters created by Irving, Poe, and Hawthorne and to think about the korl woman's special hunger in light of Dickinson's own poems about yearning. There are also similarities to note between the bondage of Davis's mill workers and Douglass's portrait of race slavery. Comparing the very last lines of *Walden* ("Only that day dawns to which we are awake. There is more day to dawn. The sun is but a morning star.") to the closing of *Life in the Iron-Mills* ("its groping arm points through the broken cloud to the far East, where, in the flickering, nebulous crimson, God has set the promise of the Dawn") can provoke a far-reaching discussion of hope in nineteenth-century American literature: what that hope consists of and what assumptions it is founded on.

Louisa May Alcott

You might want to teach Alcott out of the Norton chronological sequence and include this selection among your Transcendentalist readings. With a deft blend of satire and affection, Alcott writes of her girlhood here, the years in which her family was most under the influence of the philosophical winds blowing out of the Hedge Club, central Concord, and a certain pond one mile out of town. *Little Women* is one of a handful of nineteenth-century American works that students still read enthusiastically, and in great numbers, without any prodding from academe; and a turn to Alcott, in the midst of Emerson's grand formulations and the cool and crankiness of Thoreau's opening chapters in *Walden,* could provide context and a measure of relief. Alcott's subject is eerily modern: the danger of the totalizing formulation, the great idea or ideal imposed not only on one's own thinking and conduct but also on others.

It's probably good to avoid a too-long immersion in the exact historical sources or analogues for this or that moment or character in the story: if students know a little about Brook Farm, the Fruitlands experiment, Robert Owen and the other Utopians, and Bronson Alcott's other misadventures, they will know the important thing—that this was an era in which some people were actually trying to live Emersonian and Romantic doctrines and that the comedy and near-tragedy in Alcott's story are a sometimes whimsical, sometimes hard-edged commentary on the consequences of "-isms" and the dangers of ideas taken too much to heart.

You might begin with one moment that seems modern to you and work outward from there, speculating about whether this story is relevant only to the Concord neighborhood in the middle of the nineteenth century. You can open the tale by means of the dialogue on shoes and lamps: to avoid any moral complicity with any human activity that this little group finds repugnant—the leather trade and whaling for starters—they decide to go barefoot and lightless until a someday when suitable and morally correct substitutes are contrived. The passage about the evils of cotton and wool works much the same way: it's funny and yet eerily familiar. A good point of arrival, however, might be the specialness of the Alcott voice, the rare mix of exuberance, playfulness, pathos, and moral intensity that keeps her novels fresh and flourishing after all this time.

HARRIET PRESCOTT SPOFFORD

"Circumstance" may seem like an odd selection to conclude Volume B of *NAAL*. The tale is hard to classify, and it certainly doesn't fit neatly into any model of literary development whereby American Romanticism and Transcendentalism give way to Realism and Naturalism. This is in some ways an all-out Gothic, with an aura of symbolic or allegorical intention; and students will probably want to know how to classify it and whether or not pursuing those (possible) symbols is sensible or worthwhile. The story also resonates with that sexuality which got Spofford into trouble as a writer. Oscar Wilde and the English Decadent writers could get away with this—thirty years later—but here again, Spofford seems so far ahead of her time as to be something of a literary orphan or lost soul.

With that in mind, you might want to head off the symbolism anxieties at the start and instead ask students what this story is *like*, what it reminds them of— from their assigned reading and from their experience of American pop culture. For the story does belong to a lively tradition of tales of horror, of women in terrible danger threatened by monsters (human and otherwise), of crises of faith in the wilderness. The trail runs from Rowlandson through "Young Goodman Brown" and *The Scarlet Letter* through *The Turn of the Screw* to Stephen King, the biggest-selling American novelist of the last quarter of the twentieth century. Again, this has to work as a Gothic tale, a tale of terror, before it can work as an allegory; and students have much with which to compare it and on which to evaluate it. Even in the welter of American horror fiction, it has a compelling strangeness; and on that basis you can venture out to speculate (do keep it speculative) on the possible implications of these creatures and events that seem to mean something more.

In other words, "Circumstance" may help open a conversation about how American Gothic fiction connects to symbolism within ourselves, giving form and faces to abstract things that frighten us, whether we read Gothic tales or not: the loss of one's way in life, the sudden irresistible rise of passions and drives from within, the loss of love and family, the loss of whatever faith keeps us going and confers our identity. If students venture out from this tale to test the symbolic reverberations of the latest smash-hit horror novel or popular film, so much the better.

EMMA LAZARUS

Remembered through much of the twentieth century for one poem only, "The New Colossus," Lazarus is recovered here with selections that offer a chance for lively discussion. We can read her as a fervent patriot, an American proud of her Jewish ancestry, and a participant in the construction of a poetics that resisted a masculinist mode promulgated by Emerson in "The Poet" and practiced by many male poets during his lifetime. Consider "In the Jewish Cemetery at Newport" as a friendly quarrel with Longfellow's "The Jewish Cemetery at Newport," a widely circulated elegy in the "Country Churchyard" tradition by the biggest-selling poet of the age. Coming necessarily as an outsider, Longfellow estranges the dead around him, treats them like the remains of a bygone exotic culture. Using the same poetic forms, how does Lazarus visit the synagogue? Over the course of the poem, is there a change in her impression of the place, a closing of the distance between herself and the legacy of the temple? What happens to the word *we* as the stanzas unfold? Does it take on different implications? What about the last line of the poem? Does it try to blend two faiths together? Does Longfellow's poem take such a risk?

Students might also enjoy a comparison between Lazarus's "1492" and Wheatley's "On Being Brought from Africa to America." Both of these poems engage with a paradox, a catastrophe in which each poet finds a measure of good fortune. Compare the personal stake that each poet has in the events she describes. Which poem do you find more convincing as an historical observation? How does the language of each sonnet contribute to or impede the effect?

CHAPTER 9

Teaching Notes for Authors and Works: Volume C, American Literature 1865–1914

Realism and Its Variants: Regionalism, Local Color, and Naturalism

The problems of realism and the genre of narrative fiction dominate the concerns of post–Civil War writers. The meaning of the term *realism* is complicated by the fact that, as the period introduction in *NAAL* suggests, there were "other realists" and there were critical categories that seem somehow both related and different: regionalism, local color writing, and naturalism (which at the turn of the century was often termed "new realism"). Furthermore, this is the period for which we have the richest array of surviving Native American texts; how do these texts intersect with critical categories such as realism or regionalism?

One standard approach to teaching the period is to begin with Twain and James and then touch on those "others." One difficulty with this approach is that American authors (like Davis) began writing in a realistic mode decades before Twain and James published their major works. If we begin teaching the period not with Twain, but with the realistic literary works that were published in the 1860s and 1870s, we can give students a better sense of the evolution of American literary realism, which began as a mode of perception and a way of thinking about American life. It achieved the stature of "theory" only when William Dean Howells (and James) wrote so many editorial columns (and prefaces) in an attempt to define the American "art of fiction."

In American fiction, the realistic mode may have its origins with Stowe and some of her contemporaries, including Davis. Literary historians also see signs of realism in Thorpe. To understand the evolution of American realism, students need to see what happens to these early strains, and what happens is that a group of writers—mostly women—develop the genre of regionalism, represented in *NAAL* by Jewett, Chopin, Freeman, Chesnutt, possibly Oskison, and Zitkala Ša. In conveying features of the earlier literary tradition, you might want to teach Jewett and Chesnutt before Twain, even though all of the particular regionalist texts anthologized in *NAAL* were published after *Adventures of Huckleberry Finn*.

What all of the writers in realistic modes share is a commitment to referential narrative. Despite the evidence of invention, the reader expects to meet characters in the fiction who resemble ordinary people in ordinary circumstances, and who often meet unhappy ends. (The pattern of the unhappy ending is much less prevalent in regionalism, however.) The realists develop these characters by the use of ordinary speech in dialogue, and plot and character development become intertwined. Some writers make use of orthographic changes to convey particular speech rhythms and other elements of dialect peculiar to regional life. They all set their fictions in places that actually exist, or might easily have actual prototypes; and they are interested in recent or contemporary life, not in history or legend. Setting can become conspicuous as an element of theme in local color and regionalist fiction. And the realists rely on a first- or third-person-limited point of view to convey the sensibility of a central character or, in the case of the local color writers, the altered perception of the outside observer as he or she witnesses the scene.

Realism and Native American Literature

The anthologized selections from Native American oratory, songs, legends, fictions, and autobiographical memoirs in one sense belong to a variety of different genres; but they also comment in interesting ways on the intentions and strategies of literary realism.

As the headnotes observe, Native American literature during this period represents an "encounter" between traditional Native American oratory and the new demands of the practices of Euro-American culture, namely the occasions at which Indians used both oratory and writing to try to make beneficial treaties, to achieve their land claims, or to adapt their own practices to meet the demands of the whites. Thus the body of Native American literature represented in this period indeed records an acute consciousness of of white American life and ways of saying. Setting is everything in some of these narratives; land becomes the fundamental source of conflict as well as the source of metaphor, spirituality, and identity for large groups of native peoples. Furthermore, read together and interwoven with Euro-American texts, the Native American materials all imply the existence of and looming threat by an outside observer (sometimes equipped with Hotchkiss guns), who, alas, is also the narrator of a conflicting story of events and the narrator who controls not only the guns but also the language of legal discourse.

Once students explore the suitability of terms like *realism* and *regionalism* for Native American texts, they may find them inappropriate; but the terms may have served the function of pedagogical bridge to an enlarged appreciation for Native

American literature taught, inevitably in a survey course, as part of literature in the United States. To make connections between the anthologized Native American texts and the much more familiar concept of realism—as well as to understand crucial distinctions between the two—encourage students to view realism as a literary effect as much as, if not more than, a genre or a defined body of narrative strategies.

Then even the Ghost Dance narrative—which is told by a variety of narrators in a variety of genres, including Wovoka and his transcribers, Eastman, and tribal songmakers—may be viewed as a collectively told "text" of Native American realism, despite its origins in a vision and its survival in songs and legends. This collectively told narrative also serves as a useful corrective to the theory of realism as articulated by James, which focuses on a single stationary observer and his particular perspective from "the house of fiction" (or what he calls "the posted presence of the watcher, . . . the consciousness of the artist" in his preface to the New York edition of *The Portrait of a Lady*). The collectively told narrative of the Ghost Dance and its aftermath, Wounded Knee, can be viewed from several perspectives at once in Native American literature. The realist observer becomes apparent to the reader, "appears" to the reader (as if reader response to Native American texts involved forming a Wovoka-like vision of his or her own), as a collective, or even "tribal," grouping of observations that confirm each other. These observations share a theme and referentiality (the focus is on the gulch in which the women and children were massacred and buried in snow), emerge from more than one "watcher," are confirmed by more than one pair of eyes, and above all provide a counternarrative to the absence of this story in Euro-American "realism" of the period.

The particular mode of realism that seems to assume the closest kinship to the perspective from which the body of Native American literature is spoken or written is that of regionalism.

While it is certainly true that traditional Native American literature must be viewed as central to itself and not even part of "American literature," American literary history (and canon revision politics) led to the revision of anthologies of "American literature" in the late twentieth century to "include" Native American materials and literary scholarship about these materials. From the perspective of such anthologies (as *NAAL*), both regionalism and Native American literature are noncanonical, marginal representations of American life; both cannot separate setting from the development of character; and both foreground the contrasting perception of persons on the margins of American life in the nineteenth century with those who own the land and the property, who make (and break with impunity) the laws, and who consign certain persons to separate lands, or separate spheres or regions.

WALT WHITMAN AND EMILY DICKINSON

See notes in Chapter 8 (pp. 135–41).

MARK TWAIN

Why read *Huckleberry Finn* again? It's likely that most of your students have read the novel at least once before, in a high school English course, in a history course, or on their own; and if they haven't, they have probably seen some of the many films of the story. However, the chances are good that they haven't considered the novel from the perspectives you are developing in your own course: the evolution of an American vernacular, the imaginative transformation of the North American landscape, the Romantic and Realist traditions, themes of individuality and escape, the sources of wisdom and conscience in this culture, and imaginative fiction's address to race slavery and the predicament of minorities and women. *Huckleberry Finn* can be reread from any or all of these perspectives; but it is probably a good idea to avoid too much zeal in imposing one reading at the expense of all others. The reasons are perhaps obvious; since the early twentieth century, the novel has weathered one systematic interpretation after another: disturbed Freudian dream, New Deal hymn to the Common People, Symbolist poem, formalist masterpiece, radical (or reactionary) political tract . . . the alternatives stack up high, and few of them have had any effect on the popularity and image that this novel enjoys with a worldwide audience. The problem is complicated by the fact that many readers (including perhaps many of your students) feel that this novel is *theirs,* a freewheeling tale told by an ordinary boy, improvising his way through a world presented as it really was—and a story that is, or should be, out beyond the systems and evaluations of modern academe.

If you sense that your class is uneasy about being urged into some overly systematic reading of *Huckleberry Finn,* then it might be a good idea to present the novel, and Twain, as requiring us to do a different kind of close reading than we do on a highly crafted work like *The Scarlet Letter* or a short story by Melville or Poe. "Fenimore Cooper's Literary Offenses" can work well as an hors d'oeuvre before the plunge into *Huckleberry Finn.* Twain's commentary on Cooper and on Romantic fiction is still fresh and funny (especially if your group has experience with Cooper); and this essay is as close as we can come to a forthright statement by Twain about the Realism that he supposedly championed. We can see in this comic piece that Twain's "realism" is reactive, a rejection of the extravagances and illusions of Romantic narrative, and that Twain's mode defines itself by what it isn't at least as much as by what it is. *Huckleberry Finn* can be read many ways, of course; one such way, which follows naturally from a look into "Fenimore Cooper's Literary Offenses," is as a book about the impact of Romantic and sentimental fiction, drama, poetry, and illustration on the Mississippi River world in which Huck and Jim try to survive.

But the first order of business, and perhaps the most important objective in rereading the novel as part of an American literature survey, is to help students find ways to engage with literary works that suggest or demonstrate genius and that may please them deeply but that from some perspectives may be formally flawed. To clear the air, it might be worth drifting through the novel's early chapters to look at the evidence of false starts and abandoned intentions. This book did begin as a potboiler, as *The Adventures of Huckleberry Finn, Tom Sawyer's Comrade,* and it seems also to have begun as a detective story. If we look at the bric-a-brac in the floating house (Chapter IX), which Huck catalogs at such length, and at all the details that are provided in regard to the faking of his own death, we see some of the remains of the plot that Twain eventually abandoned. However, if we ignore those detective-story relics and try to describe the novel's plot as a flight to freedom and as the quest to free Huck's friend Jim, then we have major problems explaining why the two of them continue to flee southward, after missing the confluence with the Ohio River and the route into free territory. And as for formal symmetry and perfection: though you may hesitate to give Ernest Hemingway any last word about American literature, you might toss into the conversation his famous remark that after Chapter XXX—when Jim is trapped at the Phelps farm—the rest of the novel is "cheating." The ending of the book has been debated for fifty years; and students should know that however they feel comfortable reading it (or ignoring it), their views can find validation somewhere in the welter of published criticism.

Another unsettled controversy also requires some attention: the question of how the book is to be read as a commentary on racism and the appropriateness of including in the canon, as required reading on thousands of syllabi, a novel that uses the word *nigger* freely and dozens of times. A strong and time-honored case can be made that *Huck* is very much about racism, about a culture that instills and enforces dehumanization and prejudice, an ideology that can be escaped only for brief interludes when the human social world fades away and something more natural and innocent can flourish. A good case can also be made that if this were the intended theme of the novel, then Twain did not stay with it faithfully: the other Tom and Huck narratives that Twain wrote thereafter fail to show much interest in social justice for African Americans or in Jim as a rounded and interesting character. If students reach an impasse in settling, in some general way, the rightness of listing this novel as an American classic and a must-read for students of all races in all contexts, then see if they want to make distinctions among contexts. When and where would they feel comfortable teaching the novel? To what kind of class? In what sort of historical moment?

As you move into the novel, here are some suggestions for developing a different sort of close reading, a close reading suitable for a work in which high art might be quite different from highly polished formality.

• The opening page can be read carefully, attending to Huck's language and to Twain's strategy in getting the novel going. Huck claims no literary authority; his idea of a story apparently seems to be the simple and unadorned telling of actual events, moving from one incident to the next, without the embellishment of elaborate commentary or even subordinate clauses. Compare the beginning of *Huckleberry Finn* to the opening paragraphs of *The Scarlet Letter*, and students will see why Hemingway felt that the modern novel begins right here. But if the language and the teller have grown simpler in some ways, the narrative, in a broader sense, has grown more complex, more reflexive, more aware of the paradoxes of writing and reading novels. To introduce himself, Huck refers us back to Twain, who "told the truth, mainly" about two boys who do not exist; but then again, "Mark Twain" does not exist either, does he? Is there a playful address to "truth" and to "realism" here, by a writer who is supposed to be a master of the mode? Is realistic fiction a hopeless contradiction in terms? If such questions are asked in an appropriately light hearted way, students may be more willing to enter the novel as, in some senses at least, an epistemological funhouse, a meditation on how illusions and ordinary life get intertwined—in ordinary life as well as in narrative fiction.

• When Tom Sawyer shows up in the novel and Huck acquiesces to being a member of Tom's gang, we see how make-believe, borrowed from Romantic fiction, pervades childhood in this world; soon afterward we will encounter plenty of situations in which adults show themselves susceptible to the same disease. The deeper realism of the novel grows especially clear hereafter, for the nature of the real, of genuine emotion, moral action, and social behavior, all come into vigorous and sustained question. Here and afterward, you can raise questions about Tom's influence on Huck, when Tom is on the scene and when he isn't. Tom, we should remember, is several years younger: do students find Huck's compliance and his occasional admiration, plausible in a fourteen-year-old boy? Does Huck end the novel as morally grown up as we might like him to be?

• As you move past the point in the novel at which Twain put aside the manuscript (Chapter XVI, where the steamboat runs over the raft), it's worth stopping to observe what intentions have been abandoned or outgrown and what has happened not only to the plot but to the characters. Jim, for example, has become much more interesting as a moral presence in the work, Huck's "sound heart" has finally brought him to a full recognition of his friend's humanity and dignity, the Ohio River has been missed somehow, and the novel has cut itself loose from nearly every expectation with which a reader might have begun it. *Huckleberry Finn* is often classified as picaresque, as a way of addressing this escape from conventions and from its own opening; but are we witnessing here not just the liberation of one white boy's mind but also of American narrative fiction? The novel may seem loose, but it should not seem strange: students have read works like *The Catcher in the Rye, One Flew Over the Cuckoo's Nest, Their Eyes Were Watching God,* and *The Bell Jar,* all of which may owe something to the "breakout" of Twain's novel from prevailing habits of literary form. Ask students to talk about what has been gained and lost in this act of escape.

• The Grangerford-Shepherdson feud is based on actual violence that Twain knew about as a young man growing up along the Mississippi. But these chapters about the Grangerford household, their values, pretensions, and impact on their own children, can bring a lot of interesting commentary out of a class, especially now, when the papers are full of senseless mayhem based on family and pseudo-family affiliations and contorted ideas of honor and macho behavior. You can have a good deal of fun with Huck's description of Emmeline's poems and "crayons"—Huck tries comically and poignantly hard to be respectful of her morbid work, but his similes betray his real reactions. It's a bravura piece of narrative description; but beneath the comedy, beneath this struggle between common sense and supposedly genteel aesthetics, there are hints of a tragedy, a young girl destroyed by the sickness of the family values around her and the sickness of the sentimentality being shipped into this home from the "sivilized" world.

• As the duke and the dauphin usurp the raft, some students may wonder if the "cheating" hasn't begun already, in other words, if Twain isn't making Huck and Jim into "extras" in a tale of con artists and fools. It would be worth spending some time, therefore, on the duke-dauphin chapters as a unit in the novel, to observe their overall pattern and the effect on Huck's thinking. The initial scams of the two con men may seem relatively innocuous: if the Pokeville camp meeting is so ignorant and foolish as to believe a wild tale about pirates from the Indian Ocean, perhaps they deserve to be gulled; and the Bricksville we see (the site of the Boggs shooting and the Royal Nonesuch) seems so meanspirited, lazy, and cowardly that we may cheer when the three visitors (for Huck is now an accomplice) fleece them with a bad stage show. But after this, the tone darkens, and Huck's involvement with the duke and the dauphin becomes morally perilous. When and why does he decide to take a stand against them? Does he do it on principle? Is he moved by a pretty face? By his "sound heart?" Or by a touch of that sentimentality or degraded romanticism that have overwhelmed Tom Sawyer and Emmeline Grangerford? You may expect some lively debate over questions of this kind.

  • The Phelps farm chapters, with Jim incarcerated and tormented and Huck and Tom playing children's games with the life and liberty of a grown man, need to be looked at carefully rather than passed over as padding or an awkward coda to a narrative that really came to an end somewhere before this point. Students will want to speculate on Huck's moral situation and psychological development, on the "realism" of his fall back into being Tom's sidekick, on the plausibility of his apparent failure to generalize from the various lessons that Jim and his river adventure have taught him, and on the thematic value of this final sequence. Is the last paragraph of the novel optimistic? Indeterminate? A foretaste of the pessimism that, according to some critics, overtook Twain in the final decades of his career?

SARAH MORGAN BRYAN PIATT

Because Piatt is a recently "recovered" poet who had a mild reputation in her own lifetime and a long period of neglect afterward, situating her work in a specific literary context can help students open a dialogue with it. Piatt was born in the same year as Whitman, and she was only about ten years older than Dickinson. So to make a beginning, we can consider what her voice and intentions share with these two very different contemporaries. In the *NAAL* selections, there are moments that strongly suggest Dickinson (the third stanza, for example, of "The Palace Burner"), and others that seem to echo with Whitman (students can hear the resemblance if they read aloud the first stanza or two of "A Pique at Parting"). Also in the background of Piatt's work are the love poems and sonnets of Elizabeth Barrett Browning—and for good or ill, a long tradition of "graveyard" poetry, elegies of varying quality that were common in the national weeklies and monthlies, sometimes about subjects that the poet had only read about in those same journals. In other words, if Browning, Whitman, and Dickinson were there to be learned from as well as kept at bay, there was also the archetypal Emmeline Grangerford—the manufacturer of "tributes" who gives Huck Finn the shivers. A poet in a graveyard, sighing deep and delivering an elegy—this could be a recipe for disaster.

You might draw the students into an encounter with Piatt by asking them which poems they prefer, and why. There is a good chance that "The Palace Burner" could be controversial, in great part because of the poet's predicament. Piatt is safe at home in the United States, writing about a bloodbath in Paris after the Franco-Prussian war, a street battle that killed more than twenty thousand civilians in a week. How does Piatt address her own situation in the poem? How does she gain credibility with us, although like ourselves she witnesses all this third-hand from afar? Do your students like this poem better than "Army of Occupation," which is about the Union dead at the new Arlington Cemetery on the old Custis estate that belonged to Confederate General Robert E. Lee? If your students have read Whitman's *Drum-Taps* poems, ask them to consider which voice they find more compelling.

Bret Harte

In "The Outcasts of Poker Flat," Harte creates central characters who become the object of perception by someone outside the setting or region. Oakhurst is the outsider; and the reader's views of Madam Shipton, Piney Woods, and the others are all filtered through Oakhurst. When Oakhurst kills himself at the end of the story, Harte presents this scene also as a tableau for other outsiders—his readers— to see. Ask students to consider the humor of the story: does Harte achieve it at the expense of any particular characters more than others? Had he tried to depict the experience of western life from Mother Shipton's point of view, would "Outcasts" have been a different story? How much does Harte assume that his readers will find women, in general, and western prostitutes, in particular, laughable? Is he laughing at or with his characters?

Constance Fenimore Woolson

Woolson's "Miss Grief" is as self-conscious as any short story by Henry James, as aware of the perils of sophistication and literary fashion. The story is energized by its uneasiness about stories as ornaments, and about the slim chance that "power" and raw honesty in the art of telling can weather an age of arty-ness pretending to be an age of realism and truth. Students may want to make connections to other narrators whose voices seem to echo with this one, and other situations in which someone caught in webs of decorum looks with a measure of longing at a tragic figure on the outside. What is the appeal of that kind of story, retold so often in various ways (James's "The Jolly Corner" and *The Aspern Papers*, Fitzgerald's "Winter Dreams" and *The Great Gatsby*, stories they may have read by Hawthorne and Wharton and Conrad and Salinger and Baldwin, especially "Sonny's Blues")? Is the successful writer always in some ways caught or inhibited like the narrator of "Miss Grief?" Look at the way that dialogue flows in this story—how quick it is at the outset, and how rarely anyone, even Miss Moncrief, speaks her heart at length. How does this quick conversing play off against the long paragraphs in which Woolson's narrator, in a manner reminiscent of James and Wharton, pauses to analyze his literary opposite, and analyze himself in the process? How well does he know either person—Miss Moncrief or himself? How honest is this narrator with us, or with himself, in the last paragraph? Do we believe his Jamesian reasons for not publishing "Armor" or sharing it with others? As the story closes, what has been left unsaid?

Ambrose Bierce

"Occurrence at Owl Creek Bridge" is going to be a familiar story to many of your students, as it appears commonly in anthologies and collections for middle and high school use. Students will remember the ironies in the surprise ending; and perhaps with a little encouragement, they will remember other surprising and ironic configurations in other stories from this period by Bierce and his contemporaries: H. Crane, James, O. Henry, Wilde, Wharton, Stevenson. If this was the hey-day of Realism and Naturalism, it was also a golden age of the supremely crafted tale; and if conversation about Bierce flags a bit, because the story is an old-home-week return for too many of your students, then you could have an engaging and far-reaching conversation about irony itself: why it came into such vogue around this time; whether it suggests some belief in large forces governing human experi-ence; whether it is a *substitute* for belief, an orderly, and even tidy, suggestion of an inherent disorder or malice controlling the human situation. You might bring in a few excerpts from Bierce's *The Devil's Dictionary,* which will amuse your stu-dents: the epigram and the adage were also in vogue, and Bierce was a leading practitioner. A few of his more startling one-liners can provide fuel for a conversa-tion about how he saw the world.

NATIVE AMERICAN ORATORY

In his discussion of Native American oratory, Andrew Wiget (*Native American Literature,* 1985) observes that "from the first centuries of white settlement in America, the oratorical ability of Native Americans, their artful talent for persua-sion, was noted by Europeans," and he cites Jefferson's *Notes on the State of Vir-ginia* as offering the "moment of highest praise."

Cochise

Cochise's speech makes a plea for the Apaches, although much reduced in num-ber by the wars with the Euro-Americans, to retain "a part of my own country, where I and my little band can live." As the headnote observes, this is an example of oratory addressed to white listeners, and its theme is land. You can make the speech live for readers in a couple of ways.

First, ask students to recall (and reread) the Pima Stories of the Beginning of the World, for the opening sentence of Cochise's speech makes an indirect refer-ence to the emergence myth of creation of some Southwest Indians, a myth in which humans crawl out from a hole in the ground: "This for a very long time has been the home of my people; they came from the darkness, few in numbers and feeble." It's important that students catch this reference, what Euro-Americans would call a literary allusion, but what for Cochise links the spiritual origins of his people with their present predicament (and the occasion for his oratory). It also provides evidence for the headnote's observation that for Native Americans there were no fixed distinctions between the spiritual and the secular.

In light of Cochise's allusion to the emergence myth of the Pimas and the Apaches (locate for students the reference at the end of the Pima "Story of the Flood" to the origins of the Apaches as "the first ones that talked"), you might want to note that Native American literature itself "emerges" with such power during the years 1830–90, when the Indians themselves were losing their battles with the whites. And yet the emergence myth implies the cyclical destruction and reemer-gence of native peoples as well as their migrations. Perhaps the new "emergence" of Native American literature into the larger canon of American literature through the contest for space or literary "territory" in anthologies represents the triumph, or at least the persistence, of Native American cultures, despite several acts of destruction by the world maker.

Second, trace with students the numerous and pervasive references to land in the speech and all of the different ways in which Cochise configures the meaning of land to his people. Variously, land becomes imaged as "these mountains about us," "home," and "our country," and the Apaches are portrayed as integral to that landscape, as, early in the speech, Cochise compares the way his people "covered the whole country" to the way "clouds cover the mountains." The rhetorical occasion for the speech, namely to arrive at a treaty that would yield "a part of my own country," establishes its form, in the sense that Cochise defines himself and his people as quite "part" of the country. In formal terms, the speech becomes synecdoche: he speaks for all, and the terms in which he speaks establish an identity between people and their land. To take away the land kills the people who are "part" of that land; if the people have been reduced in numbers, then they can survive on "part" of that land, but they must be on that land. Like the deer that flee the hunter in a later image from the speech, the Apaches exist only on the land that has been their home.

Charlot

This speech addressed to Charlot's fellow Flathead Indians lives up to its description in the headnote as "a powerful critique of the white people's ways." Contrast with students the tone and language of Charlot's speech with Cochise's; focus on the evocation of shame in the speech and discuss the way racism attempts to obliterate emotions of shame; compare this with Apess's "An Indian's Looking-Glass for the White Man," another indictment of white treatment of native peoples. Ask students if the rhetorical stance of the speaker reminds them of any historical works in Euro-American literature: for instance, Paine's "Thoughts on the Present State of American Affairs" from *Common Sense,* or especially Jefferson's Declaration of Independence. Students might compare the rhetorical construction of King George III in Jefferson's Declaration with Charlot's rhetorical construction of "the white man" in the Centennial Year of the United States. What are the advantages of using "he," suggesting an individual rather than a government or a general population, throughout the speech? Charlot's speech conveys an expectation of being overheard. Students can consider and compare closely the rhetorical strategy of these documents. How does Charlot center and portray the predicament? A cause has to be made clear: a source of oppression has to be identified, coalesced. How does Charlot accomplish that task? Constructing the Other in each of these political statements designed simultaneously to arouse enmity against "King George," "the white man," and "man" and support for the cause of the oppressed also increases students' perspective on the use of rhetorical devices as part of the process by which writing becomes a form of political action that Native American speakers, perhaps because of their tradition of oral practice and the extent of their own grievances, were quite skillful in employing.

Henry James

"The Art of Fiction" shows that James shares William Dean Howells's theory of fiction, in part. He writes, "The only reason for the existence of a novel is that it does attempt to represent life." However, what James means by *life* and what Howells means by it are two different things. Unlike Howells, who asserts a reality that is referential and shared, James suggests that creation resides in the author's perception. Without the perceiving eye there is no art. James implicitly links realism with point of view and with the "quality of the mind of the producer." He writes, "A novel is in its broadest definition a personal, a direct impression of life: that, to begin with, constitutes its value, which is greater or less according to the intensity of the impression." Thus reality is subjective for James; and he suggests that, far from being referential, Realism reveals aspects of life that cannot be seen. He insists on "the power to guess the unseen from the seen, to trace the implication of things, to judge the whole piece by the pattern"; and he writes, "Experience is never limited, and it is never complete; it is an immense sensibility, a kind of huge spiderweb of the finest silken threads suspended in the chamber of consciousness, and catching every airborne particle in its tissue."

If, as Howells writes, the reader is the arbiter of a fiction's realism and if "the only test of a novel's truth is his own knowledge of life," then many of our students will have difficulty seeing realism in James. The challenge in teaching James is to try to get students to follow the psychological complexity of the relationships James creates—between Daisy and Winterbourne in *Daisy Miller,* and between John Marcher and May Bartram in "The Beast in the Jungle"—and to see his interest in relationships per se as an aspect of realism that makes James stand out among many of his contemporaries. Compare James's analysis of the complexity of emotional and psychological development with Twain's in *Adventures of Huckleberry Finn.* The regionalists link emotional development to the development of community—here portrayed by Mrs. Todd's empathy with the French woman in Jewett's "The Foreigner." And Freeman and Chopin show that the individual develops emotionally within the context of human relationships, but their focus remains the quality and development of individual or shared vision. Only James among his contemporaries focuses on human relationships themselves as the source of experience. The single context within the meaning of human experience may be explored. In the shorter works anthologized here, we see relationships that are primarily dyadic. In the novels, James interweaves pairs of intense personal relationships with each other to form the "huge spiderweb" of his psychological fiction.

The Beast in the Jungle

In this story, James fully develops his theory of the novel as "a personal, direct impression of life," for it is actually such an "impression" that Marcher expects to have and by which he figures his "beast." James's use of third-person-limited point of view to define the unfolding of Marcher's perception serves as a laboratory of the use of technique. Marcher's point of view gives the reader a sense of reality as being bounded by the limits of perception and consciousness; yet James so skillfully creates May Bartram that, without ever entering her consciousness, we know what she is thinking and feeling—even more than John Marcher, despite the fact that he sees and hears everything the reader does.

Ask your students "what happens" in this story. The wide range of responses creates a spectrum of the kinds of experience that constitute "reality" for James. Some will reply that nothing happens—which, in a sense, is true enough. Others will wonder whether Marcher dies at the end of the story—a valid speculation. Some will reply that he discovers he has been in love with May Bartram all along—an assertion that seems both true and false in light of the story. A few will focus on the developing portrayal of character as "what happens" for James. You can help them see what interests James in the relationship between his two characters by asking them which character they, as readers, most resemble. They will certainly align themselves with May, for, in a sense, Marcher and May are acting out the ideal relationship between author and reader. He is his own author, like many American male protagonists before him; she is his ideal reader—she grants him his *donnée*—as, James states in "The Art of Fiction," the reader must do for the novelist. So that when the two meet again after ten years' time and May Bartram remembers Marcher's old impression, he asks, " 'You mean you feel how my obsession—poor old thing!—may correspond to some possible reality?' " "Corresponding to some possible reality" is the precise problem of the story, of James's other work, and of Realism itself. If reality is only "possible" and if two different characters within the same story, in which nothing else happens but their relationship, have such different perceptions of what is real, then what happens to realism itself?

James's interest in convention and social forms in *Daisy Miller* is apparent in "The Beast in the Jungle" as well. Marcher's very "unsettled" feeling about the nature of reality makes it difficult for him to go along with social forms. And so he lives with his "figure" of the beast as the hypothesis by which he understands his life. When the beast springs, in a sense, he will be able to live; until then he can't consider marriage. The beast becomes his disfiguring quality—he calls it "a hump on one's back"—and it is necessary for May to "dispose the concealing veil in the right folds." James, here, continues Hawthorne's fascination with the contradictions between apparent self-confrontation (Marcher tries to think of himself as courageous) and actual self-evasion (even when the beast finally springs, he turns "instinctively . . . to avoid it" as he flings himself, face down, on May Bartram's tomb).

Ironically, his relationship with May contributes to that process of self-evasion. For she helps him "to pass for a man like another"; with her, Marcher appears to be conventional and to be living an ordinary life. He says to her: "What saves us, you know, is that we answer so completely to so usual an appearance: that of the man and woman whose friendship has become such a daily habit—or almost—as to be at last indispensable." Although they aren't married, Marcher believes that he has the "appearance" of it. He uses May to "cover" his apparent deficiencies. But certain kinds of experience and certain kinds of psychological development cannot be acquired by what "passes for" living, and neither can they be taught; they must be lived. Therefore, although the reader perceives that May Bartram understands much more of Marcher than he does of himself, she restrains herself, as James restrains himself, from telling him what it all means. He has to figure it out for himself—or not know it at all.

The story ends "happily" in a sense, because, although Marcher discovers the limitations of his fate, James manages to achieve his own goal—namely, that of portraying a character having a "personal, direct impression"—a literal *impress* of "letters of quick flame." The question becomes, How does Marcher finally achieve that impression? What is responsible, what is the catalyzing moment? Students will remember the scene in the cemetery, when Marcher sees the ravaged mourner, who is apparently a widower and whose manifestation of grief makes Marcher ask, "What had the man *had,* to make him by the loss of it so bleed and yet live?" The apparent answer, and perhaps the only "right" answer, is that the other man has been touched by passion, has loved, whereas Marcher "had seen *outside* of his life, not learned it within." And he concludes, "The escape would have been to love her; then, *then* he would have lived."

But it seems curious that the other man at the cemetery seems—possibly, to Marcher—aware of an "overt discord" between his feelings and Marcher's. The significant thing, to Marcher, is that the other man showed his feelings, "*showed* them—that was the point." And he is aware of his own presence as "something that profaned the air." Perhaps James is more interested in Marcher's inability to find the appropriate *form* for his feeling than in his inability to feel at all. He describes Marcher at May's funeral as being "treated as scarce more nearly concerned with it than if there had been a thousand others." As the author of his own fate, Marcher has failed in its execution. He has failed to find any manifest form for his own "personal, direct impression" that would have allowed him to "learn from within." And James links that failure with Marcher's refusal to make "real" what is only "appearance"—his "daily habit" of relationship with May Bartram. For James, consciousness requires a social context. Therefore, "it was as if in the view of society he had not *been* markedly bereaved, as if there still failed some sign or proof of it." James's characters may defy convention, as Daisy Miller does, but they don't escape having to confront it. The intrusion of convention in James's fiction establishes its social realism, the limitations within which his characters may establish themselves as conscious.

The Jolly Corner

If the students have been reading the James materials chronologically, then some questions may have been forming in your class regarding all these situations in which protagonists and raptly attentive narrators find themselves terribly and sometimes fatally deceived: they have looked at the truth, and for the truth, and they have failed to see it. Somebody may have made the observation in your group that the higher forms of Realism, as practiced by people like James, Wharton, and Twain, often deeply question the nature of the real. If that hasn't come up as a speculation, then you might open it as you move into both of these stories, in which even one's own identity becomes suspect.

It is also an old adage—about sheer storytelling, not specifically about Realism—that to tell a good horror story an author has to find something that scares himself or herself. If that is true, then the ghost story dimensions of these two tales can lead into a very fruitful discussion of what it is that would scare the daylights out of a confirmed realist, an artist who gives his life and his career over to "seeing"—to a belief in a stable self; a coalesced and perhaps transcendent consciousness; and the validity of any quest to understand who we are, where we are, and what we are. A conversation like this can expand outward beyond all of these tales, so that students will be better prepared to read the longer James works and to understand what urgencies, compulsions, and fears underlie all the social maneuverings on the surface of those great texts.

JOEL CHANDLER HARRIS

The Uncle Remus tales depend for their narrative success on the contrast between black storyteller and white audience. Harris includes in his work "instructions" to his readers, writes for a white audience, and yet manages to avoid caricaturing his black characters or turning them into mere entertainment. In his extensive use of southern black dialect and African American folktales as the source of his subject matter, Harris might easily have been perceived in his time, and in ours, as a local-color writer. With your class, you might speculate about the usefulness of distinctions between "regionalism" and "local color." One difference might be that the regionalist narrator looks *with* the regional protagonist, whereas the local-color writer looks *at* regional experience; ask students to consider the location of Harris's own perspective on his characters.

SARAH ORNE JEWETT

In the traditional presentation of late-nineteenth-century American fiction, Jewett and Freeman are often grouped with the local-color writers, and *regionalism* becomes a descriptive term for the entire group. A closer look at American literary history reveals that regionalism and local-color writing developed as distinct but parallel genres and that if we look at chronology, regionalism was the first of the late-nineteenth-century fictional genres to emerge. Stowe published "The Pearl of Orr's Island," the work that influenced Jewett's own development, five years before Twain's "The Notorious Jumping Frog of Calaveras County"; and during the same decade that Hawthorne and Melville were publishing their most significant work (the 1850s), Alice Cary, Rose Terry Cooke (not anthologized here), and Stowe herself were establishing regionalism as a genre. By the time Jewett published "Deephaven" (1877), she already had a regionalist tradition to write within; and although by the chronology of birth order she and her work appear to follow Twain and James, the publication of "Deephaven" precedes that of *Adventures of Huckleberry Finn*, *The Rise of Silas Lapham*, and *The Portrait of a Lady*.

A White Heron

In this story, Jewett chooses as her center of perception a character who lives within the region she is writing about. In "A White Heron," Sylvy (whose name means "woods") is indigenous to the setting (even though she has moved there from the city), because she speaks the language of nature; it is the ornithologist who is the outsider, implicitly resembling the local-color writer in his quest to come into the rural scene, shoot and stuff a bird, and bring it back for urban people to see. In refusing to reveal the secrets of the white heron's nest, Sylvy protects the regional perception from exploitation. The contrast between Sylvy's desire to allow the bird its freedom and the ornithologist's desire to kill and stuff the bird provides a focal point for a discussion of the contrasts among regionalism, Realism, and local-color writing. Consider B. Harte's story "The Outcasts of Poker Flat" and James's "The Beast in the Jungle" in conjunction with "A White Heron," and ask students to describe differences in point of view, the extent to which the story includes the perspective of other characters, and the text's depiction of female characters. Ask them to imagine that "The Outcasts of Poker Flat" included the perspective of the duchess, Mother Shipton, or Piney Woods, instead of turning them into caricatures, or to imagine that "The Beast in the Jungle" included May Bartram's perspective and gave her a voice, and you will begin to convey some of the particular features of regionalism as a genre. In "A White Heron," Jewett shifts the center of perception not only to a poor, rural female character but also to a nine-year-old child and makes it possible for her reader to understand the disenfranchised perspective.

The Foreigner

"The Foreigner" depicts the relationship between the female narrator of *The Country of the Pointed Firs* and her guide in that novel, Mrs. Todd; but Jewett wrote "The Foreigner" after publishing the novel and the story stands alone. In this text, students can experience the power of the earlier, longer work. Like Twain and James, Jewett as regionalist also experimented with storytelling, but "The Foreigner" adds empathy to the requirements of relationship between storyteller and reader/listener/audience. In characterizing the tale Mrs. Todd relates in "The Foreigner" as a "ghost story," Jewett's narrator invites us to contrast her approach with James's narrators in *The Turn of the Screw*. For James, the "impression" the teller makes on the listener becomes the standard of the tale's success. For Jewett, the tale becomes a medium for relationship between teller and listener; and although the narrator of "The Foreigner" says very little while Mrs. Todd tells her story, her choice to remain silent at crucial points in the narrative establishes her as a partner in the telling. The listener/reader has a role to play in Jewett that goes beyond the reader response James's narrator tries to teach in *The Turn of the Screw*. Without relationship between teller and listener, there is no text. The power of Jewett's narrator is that she does not attempt to "read" the meaning of Mrs. Todd's narrative but allows the other woman to tell the story as its meaning deepens and dawns on her. The appearance of the "ghost" at the end is not Mrs. Todd's attempt to frighten her listener or to create a narrative effect but to move beyond her storm fear for her aged mother, who, with Mrs. Todd's brother William, lives on one of the "outlying islands."

The story begins with Mrs. Todd separated from her mother by the raging gale and dramatizes her use of storytelling to ease her anxiety and to regain inner peace. By the end of "The Foreigner," Jewett has taught her readers how to feel a different kind of suspense than they might have expected in a ghost story. The story's climax occurs not with the appearance of the ghost but with Mrs. Todd's recognition that Mrs. Tolland has been reunited with her mother. In the larger story, the narrator also feels the strengthening of her ties to Mrs. Todd; and fiction, for the regionalist Jewett, becomes reparative and inclusive. Neither Mrs. Tolland nor Mrs. Todd is a caricature set up for readers to laugh at; the comedy of "The Foreigner" makes possible the continued "harmony of fellowship" that eases separation anxiety and social isolation.

KATE CHOPIN

At the 'Cadian Ball

This story was Chopin's first significant regional publication, and it establishes an interest in hierarchies of southern society according to categories of race, class, and gender that would characterize much of her regionalist fiction. In the southern Louisiana locale of her work, her characters establish superiority for the Creoles, descendants of the original French settlers of Louisiana, and lower-class status for the Cajuns, descendants of the French Acadians exiled by the British from Nova Scotia in the late eighteenth century. Black characters occupy the lowest social position in this society; and within the rank of Cajuns ('Cadians), status is granted according to racial characteristics that are viewed as European rather than African. Helping students sort out the social codes among the characters will help them understand the way class power and sexual desire are constructed and become interconnected. For example, Calixta, a Cajun woman with a Spanish Cuban mother, has more "status" than other women because she has blue eyes and flaxen hair, even though it "kinked worse than a mulatto's"; but she has no power at all against Clarisse, the upper-class Creole woman, "dainty as a lily." The racial codes in this society are complex. Bruce, the black servant, does not go to the 'Cadian ball, but the 'Cadians are not apparently considered white; for Chopin writes, when Alcee Laballiere arrives, that "anyone who is white may go to a 'Cadian ball, but he must pay for his lemonade. . . . And he must behave himself like a 'Cadian." Once students sort out the intricacies of power and hierarchy in this story, it becomes easier for them to understand Calixta's attraction for Laballiere and yet her decision to marry the "brown" Bobinot. The story leads to a more general discussion concerning the way racial and class status construct sexual desire and even sexual attractiveness in American society.

The Awakening

In seeing Edna Pontellier as yet another American on a quest to become self-reliant and to establish her identity within a hostile society, students might consider whether The Awakening could be titled "Adventures of Edna Pontellier." This can lead into a brief discussion of Huck Finn, and students can see essential differences in design between the two novels. Briefly, Edna Pontellier is not a "picaro," and Chopin does not present her awakening as a linear series of adventures but rather as an interwoven account of the relationships Edna has with other characters and the way in which her awakening becomes her own "education." Conversely, you may ask students whether Twain might have subtitled his book "The Awakening of Huckleberry Finn," and the incongruity of the two portraits of nineteenth-century life becomes even clearer. If you have taught earlier material to these students, you can also make connections between Chopin's novel and earlier American dream fictions, especially "Rip Van Winkle," "Young Goodman Brown," Thoreau's "Resistance to Civil Government," and certainly to Jim's dream in Chapter XV of Huckleberry Finn. In Chopin's successful attempt to present Edna's life from her own point of view—so that students can see that even physical sex is not an end in itself for Edna but rather only one aspect of her artistic and spiritual awakening and her struggle to achieve autonomy—she uses the technique of shifting the center, which characterizes the best of regionalist writing. One essay that will help students place Edna's attempts to reach toward limits that seem radical for women in her time is Elizabeth Cady Stanton's 1896 "The Solitude of Self," which is brief enough to circulate as background reading.

But Edna's attempt to achieve her own limits is thwarted—by her husband; by the attitudes of men, like Robert, whom she respects; and by the society in which she lives. In describing the limitations Edna constantly comes up against, Chopin writes literary Realism, because in *The Awakening*, Edna's identity is finally so contingent on her social context that it becomes impossible for her to reconcile her sense of her own individual identity with society's expectations. But does she commit suicide? Some students may want to argue that her death is not actually suicide, but rather the consequences of Edna's choice to immerse herself quite literally in a context (the sea) that is the only place she can transcend her own limits (with connections here to Thoreau's "immersion" in Walden Pond). To put it another way, if Edna's death is suicide, then Huck Finn's choice to evade the conflicts of civilization is suicide by other means.

You might want to read closely one scene in the novel (the closing scene of Chapter XXIII, in which Edna and Leonce have dinner with Edna's father and Dr. Mandelet) as a way of demonstrating Edna's inability to transform the world she lives in into one that will seem real to her. In this scene, each of the four characters tells a story that reveals a great deal about the teller's character. Leonce tells an antebellum tale of "some amusing plantation experiences" and casts himself as a paternalistic Huck Finn, Edna's father depicts himself as a "central figure" in the Civil War, Dr. Mandelet tells a tale of a woman who moves away from her husband but whose love returns "to its legitimate source," and Edna tells a romantic story of two lovers who paddle away one night and never come back. What is interesting about the scene is that only Edna's story engages the imaginations of her audience. Despite its romanticism, the story possesses some compelling truth. Ironically, the anecdotes the other three relate are equally romantic projections of themselves or, in the doctor's case, of his ability to "cure" Edna; but in each case, the society has provided mirrors that appear to confirm the self-portraits. Leonce can depict himself as Huck Finn without seeming ridiculous, the colonel can aspire to having a war hero's reputation without attracting scorn, and the doctor can presume to understand the nature of women without losing patients. But Edna cannot find in her culture—except in the invention of her own imagination—any ratification of her self-concept.

Edna's confusion can be viewed as a variation on Du Boisean "double consciousness," for throughout the book she constantly lives in a state of tension between her emerging sense of self and the limitations her society imposes on her. You might ask your students if Chopin is portraying Edna as the victim of social forces over which she has no control and if the novel can, therefore, be viewed as naturalistic. To call sexism a social force, in the same way that Darwinism might be seen as a social force at that time, obscures the fact that theories of separate spheres were viewed as the underpinnings of American culture, rather than as new "discoveries." The force over which Edna has no control leads her to look for some other form within which to manifest her double consciousness. In the "real" world of Edna's family and society, the only person capable of understanding her death on its own terms might be Mlle. Reisz, another woman who has engaged in a similar struggle and taken the life of the artist as her own form within which to express the tensions of the solitude (also the title of the piece of music she plays) of self. From a realist's view, Edna's last act appears to be meaningless suicide. From a regionalist's view, however, it becomes the only form of expression available to her.

Yet, perhaps the novel's limitations partly reside in Chopin's limited vision of what an American woman might achieve. Edna isn't strong enough or talented enough to live like Mlle. Reisz, and Chopin doesn't even present this as a serious possibility for her. Neither does she perceive the possibility of extending her own desire for awakening to the countless, and generally nameless, women of color in the novel. Neither Edna nor Chopin herself seems to perceive Edna's concerns as applicable to women of color or different social class. Perhaps Edna's limitations are Chopin's own: for Chopin, implicitly viewing sexism with the naturalist's eye, cannot achieve the full shift of the center of perception that would be necessary to produce works of regionalism in the nineteenth century or modernism in the twentieth, a shift that in Chopin would have to focus on Edna's perception as normal and the perceptions of other characters as skewed. The only nineteenth-century work by a woman writer that really accomplishes this is Jewett's 1896 *The Country of the Pointed Firs* (not anthologized in *NAAL* but available in paperback in a Norton edition).

Mary E. Wilkins Freeman

Like Jewett, Freeman wrote in the genre of regionalism, and also like Jewett, Freeman places women's lives and regional vision at the center of her stories. Freeman's "A New England Nun" makes a useful companion story to Jewett's "A White Heron." Ask your students to evaluate the motivations and final choices of Louisa Ellis and Jewett's Sylvy. Compare and contrast "A New England Nun" with Harte's "The Outcasts of Poker Flat." Although Freeman focuses on Louisa Ellis's experience, she portrays her male character, Joe Dagget, more sympathetically than Harte or Garland do their female characters. "A New England Nun" presents Louisa Ellis's vision and decision not to marry as valid and normal; but Freeman doesn't earn the reader's sympathy for her female character at Joe Dagget's expense. She portrays Joe as well meaning and honorable, if typical of his time and place (many young men left New England to make their fortunes elsewhere in the years following the Civil War). Some critics have called Louisa sexually repressed. A lively discussion will follow if you ask your students whether they agree.

"The Revolt of 'Mother' " earns Freeman a place in the humorist tradition, with a difference. Once again, she includes "Father's" perspective in her story of "Mother's" revolt, and suggests "Father's" ability to enlarge his own capacity for empathy. Unlike writers of the Southwest humorist school, for whom local color implied acceptance of off-color jokes about women, Freeman does not elevate Sarah Penn by caricaturing Adoniram and making him the object of ridicule. Like Jewett's "A White Heron," "The Revolt of 'Mother' " may be read as Freeman's response to local-color writing. From the opening line of the story, what Sarah Penn seems to want most of all is to engage her husband as her audience and to find acceptance for her own voice. *Revolt* may be too strong a word to describe Sarah Penn's attempt to make herself heard; she remains within the family structure, even if she has managed to redefine its terms; Nanny's impending marriage, not Sarah's own frustration, moves her to act.

Freeman contributes to the development of regionalism by collapsing narrator and female protagonist. Ask students to consider the absence of narrators in Freeman's stories and to contrast this with the reliance on narrators by her contemporaries, most notably Jewett and James. Where Jewett makes it possible for a reader to empathize with a regional character and to imagine that character speaking in his or her own voice, Freeman actually stands back from her own regional canvas, allowing her characters' voices, not a narrator's perspective, to create their own stories. Unlike Jewett, Freeman does not dramatize a shift in the center of perception, from, say, the ornithologist of "A White Heron" to the nine-year-old rural child; instead, Freeman writes from a position where such a shift has already occurred. She frames her stories carefully—Louisa Ellis's window and the Penns' barn door carefully limit the world she depicts—but within that frame, she creates a fictional territory in which characters can articulate the perspective of marginal women as central. The tight form of her fiction both fences out and fences in; she writes as if regionalism both opened up and protected that small space within which late-nineteenth-century women were free to express their vision.

BOOKER T. WASHINGTON

The Washington materials give us a real opportunity to talk about the construction of an American identity, of an autobiography, and of a text that converses with other important documents in our cultural history. Writing at the very end of the nineteenth century, Washington was deeply aware of the historical and literary moment in which he was working: Franklin, Jacobs, Douglass, Whitman, Ulysses S. Grant, and many other autobiographers had already done much to establish the pace, subject matter, and general configurations of an American life set down on paper. Your students have probably engaged with some of these forebears (or competitors) in the craft and art of American-style autobiography; where do they see suggestions that Washington is echoing or resisting moments or assumptions that we associate with these other writers?

You might focus on the opening pages of *Up from Slavery* and the way it continues and departs from traditions developed by Douglass; you might spend some time with much-later passages in Washington's book that describe the mature leader's daily schedules, work routines, and conceptions of success, recreation, and personal contentment and compare these to procedures and values laid out by Franklin or Thoreau. Does Washington conceive of his audience as similar, somehow, to Franklin's? Do themes or tones emerge here, in *Up from Slavery,* that might account for the way that Washington's book, which was hailed as a classic for decades, fell into eclipse in more recent years? In what spirit does he distinguish his own upbringing from middle-class conceptions of childhood? When he talks about his strategies as a public speaker, what assumptions might be indicated about complexities of maintaining personal integrity and Emersonian-style honesty, while also striving (as Washington affirms that he does) to please an audience so thoroughly that not one listener would ever leave the hall?

CHARLES W. CHESNUTT

It would be a mistake to present Chesnutt as just another local colorist, an African American working faithfully in the mode and fashion pioneered and dominated by white authors. His situation is in some ways much more complex, and his handling of it is worth our attention—not as a way of excusing him somehow but as a way of recognizing the breadth and depth of what he achieves. In several ways, Chesnutt's situation was supremely paradoxical: he was a black writer narrating black experience into a context already well supplied with narratives of black experience, written by white people. Moreover, the situation of African Americans in the United States had obviously changed immensely in a thirty-year period, to the extent that the perceptions, personal histories, and identities of this minority had never been more scattered and diverse. Chesnutt was a realist by conviction—in which direction did "the real" lie: back in the rural South and the plantation life or as far from it as one could flee? There were also profound ironies having to do with his situation as an artist, working in a mode in which the flashy counterfeit could often strike a reading audience as more "true" than the true article.

Chesnutt, therefore, speaks in a chorus of voices, and he violates expectations, not just in terms of plotting but in terms of the realist mode itself. The motive may be to return his readers to a condition of wonder, of the rapt attention that can come with seeing things freshly or for the first time. Like Twain, like James, like Wharton, Chesnutt will throw plausibility out the window at times, in pursuit of a more important or larger sort of "realism." His frame-tale narrators (as in "The Goophered Grapevine") don't serve merely to give Chesnutt himself some safe distance, or social removal, from the story he tells; the strategy allows us to approach, in stages, something unfamiliar, where (as your students might say) all bets are off—an American reality where the conventional, white, turn-of-the-century audience would find very little that was familiar to it and where, in a sense, anything could happen.

"The Wife of His Youth" is a story with a twist, somewhat like an O. Henry tale; but the twist has the resonance that a plot twist might have in a Hawthorne romance. An old woman wanders by chance into the life of a man who believes, to his core, that he has left his old life and his old self behind and has achieved full amalgamation into sophisticated urban life, or at least into this new African American gentility, where Tennyson's poems have replaced the spirituals that Du Bois lauds in *The Souls of Black Folk*. Is Liza's return, then, the return of Ryder's soul? Is the transformation that simple? What will happen next, after the last page of this narrative? Does Chesnutt offer some forecast here about the future of his people? Or does he puzzle over that future, as Hawthorne does when he engages with present-day New England?

CHARLES ALEXANDER EASTMAN (OHIYESA)

In light of the headnote's assessment of Eastman's assimilationist tendencies, read the chapters from *From the Deep Woods to Civilization* with particular awareness of Eastman's references to whites; to other Sioux, such as Blue Horse, who claim to be "friends" with white men; and to Sioux who are intolerant of relationships with whites. Then recall Charlot's speech, in which "the white man" is portrayed as a monolithic villain. Does Eastman's narrative confirm or refute Charlot's speech? To what extent would students argue that Eastman's assimilationist perspective is the product of his white education in the Indian boarding schools of the period? Is it possible for Eastman to be both an assimilationist and a spokesman for Native Americans? He summarizes the ambivalence of his position at one point

early in the excerpt when he writes about the difficulty parents had separating
from their children who were attending government boarding schools and about
how they would ask him to write letters excusing their children on account of illness: "I was of course wholly in sympathy with the policy of education for the Indian children, yet by no means hardened to the exhibition of natural feeling." Yet
later (in Chapter VII) he seems to give meaning to the phrase he is called, "the
Indian white doctor," when he writes, "I scarcely knew at the time, but gradually
learned afterward, that the Sioux had many grievances and causes for profound
discontent, which lay back of and were more or less closely related to the Ghost
Dance craze and the prevailing restlessness and excitement." Eastman speaks the
Sioux language, has power vested in him by the U.S. government, and yet does not
completely understand the Sioux point of view.

Eastman's powerful narrative conveys details about the day-to-day workings of
the Pine Ridge Agency. Explicate with students the apparent role of the agency in
the lives of Native Americans and the power the agency could exercise; explore the
significance of such "games" as the buffalo hunt on "issue day"; consider the role
of the Indian police force at Pine Ridge Agency. Consider as well the meaning of
the placement of the doctor's offices: "the assembly room of the Indian police,
used also as a council room, opened out of my dispensary."

For the larger narrative of the story of the Ghost Dance religion and the Wounded Knee massacre, Eastman's narrative offers a powerful eyewitness account of
impending conflict and of the aftermath and consequences of the massacre. Trace
references to the "new religion" that has been proclaimed at about the same time
as Eastman's arrival at Pine Ridge. Read the anthologized versions of Wovoka's
Messiah Letters and compare them with Eastman's careful paraphrase of Wovoka's
teachings in Chapter VI (Captain Sword's account of the Ghost Dance religion).
Examine Eastman's narrative for evidence that might explain the resistance of
white settlers to the Ghost Dance religion.

Then examine carefully Eastman's account of the Ghost Dance war itself,
including the U.S. government's use of black soldiers against the Sioux. While not
an eyewitness, Eastman is an "ear-witness," for he hears the sound of the
Hotchkiss guns. Yet what he sees of the wounded and dead when he visits the bat-
tlefield, although it tests his assimilationism, does not ultimately change his course
of action: "All this was a severe ordeal for one who had so lately put all his faith in
the Christian love and lofty ideals of the white man," he writes—and sets his day
of marriage to a white woman for the following June. Recall here, once again, the
words of Apess's "An Indian's Looking-Glass"; in Eastman, we see at least one
Sioux who manages to avail himself of the possibilities of cross-racial marriage.
The times—and the terms of the discourse—are different for Eastman than they
were for Apess sixty years earlier.

HAMLIN GARLAND

Garland's "Under the Lion's Paw" usefully contrasts with both Jewett's "The Foreigner" and Freeman's "The Revolt of 'Mother.'" Although Stephen Council initially helps Haskins get a good start, Garland focuses on the futility of Haskins's
labor; and the concluding scene creates a tableau similar in effect to the end of
"The Outcasts of Poker Flat." Haskins is "under the lion's paw," and Butler (and

Garland) leave him "seated dumbly on the sunny pile of sheaves, his head sunk into his hands." The reader views Haskins—like Mother Shipton, Piney Woods, and ultimately Oakhurst as well—from the outside. Contrast this with the perspective Jewett offers in "The Foreigner," in which she depicts the growth of sympathy between characters and in which Mrs. Todd explores and tries to repair the social exclusion of Mrs. Tolland; Haskins ends as an object of exclusion, viewed from outside the story, whereas Jewett's characters expand their circle of community. Or contrast the poverty of the homeless characters in "Under the Lion's Paw with the inadequately housed Sarah and Nanny Penn in Freeman's "The Revolt of 'Mother.'" Garland bases the power of his story on its portrait of the bleakness of poverty; Freeman bases hers on her protagonists' awareness of their own strengths.

ABRAHAM CAHAN

In the context of the other short stories that cluster in the "American Literature, 1865–1914" volume of NAAL, "A Sweatshop Romance" might seem mild and comparatively unassuming, a bit like a network situation comedy. The interpersonal chemistry and the conflict in Leizer's shop could fill half an hour of air time with mild laughter. We have bashful lovers, overbearing parents, and social hierarchies disrupted by the move from the Old World to the New. Beile loves Heyman; David yearns for Beile; Heyman is too shy to express himself on matters of the heart. When the low-paid lovers-to-be stand up to an arrogant boss and lose their jobs, they find new ones together, and the ending is quick and happy. Students are not likely to find much that's unique in the plot or character list of "A Sweatshop Romance"—but they may be intrigued by peculiarities in the way the tale is told: the tone and position of the narrator, the stylization of the dialogue. Cahan obviously knows these people and this economic and social predicament firsthand, but how would we describe his voice, his implicit relationship to the characters in this story? How is his voice differentiated from the voices of his characters? Does he sound like a dweller in this neighborhood? A knowledgeable visitor from somewhere else? These characters, recent immigrants most of them, might be expected to speak in heavily accented English, or in Yiddish or Russian or some mix of these and other languages. But in Cahan's tale they speak without accents, without a salting of non-English words and expressions—in other words, without any of the dialect that turns up in stories from this period by Harris, Hart Crane, and Chesnutt. If we listen closely however, we can hear a syntactic twist here and there, the reversals and up-and-down swings that *suggest* speech in this ethnic community. Why might Cahan handle the speech of his characters in this way? Whom is he writing to, and for, and with what intention? Is his presentation of life on the Lower East Side charged with the same intentions as Chesnutt's "The Wife of His Youth" or Garland's "Under the Lion's Paw?" What is gained and what is sacrificed with such stylization? What is gained and risked by telling a story of love, reticence, and misunderstanding—in other words, one of the oldest stories in the world?

CHARLOTTE PERKINS GILMAN

Like *The Awakening*, "The Yellow Wall-paper" shows a woman trying to find some alternative context for self-expression. The speaker in the story looks in vain for any referential reflector of her own reality, until she is incarcerated by her husband in a room with yellow wallpaper and, over the course of the story, comes to identify with or project herself onto the figure of a woman who stoops down and creeps about behind the pattern on the wallpaper. Gilman presents her narrator's "double consciousness" as the tension the woman artist must live with in a context that refuses (with absolute denial of her husband) to mirror her self-concept. Like Edna's suicide at the end of *The Awakening*, Gilman's narrator's madness becomes understandable as her only means of self-expression. Ask students to contrast the story with Poe's "The Fall of the House of Usher" and James's "The Beast in the Jungle." Consider the narrator as a type of the artist and apply to her Howells's dictum that the imagination "can work only with the stuff of experience." Does the narrator "compose" elements from real life; and if so, are both her madness and her work of art—the story itself—realistic? What happens to a writer when she wants to write referentially about experience that the world refuses to recognize? What does the story tell us about the prevailing medical attitudes toward women in the late nineteenth century? Reading "Why I Wrote *The Yellow Wall-paper*?" in conjunction with the story makes it clear to students that Gilman was self-conscious about the possibilities for fiction to intervene in the medical treatment of women as well as in women's understanding of the relationship between their own madness and their lack of social autonomy and intellectual choice.

EDITH WHARTON

"Souls Belated" is in some ways a period piece, a story about the institution of marriage and the relatively recent innovation of divorce, as these were construed by members of the Anglo-American upper classes, including people who thought of themselves as independent minded and thoroughly self-aware. But if students can find their way past the historical surfaces of the story, they can follow Wharton into an absorbing contemplation of what *love* means and how our inmost feelings and aspirations can be inextricably tangled up with cultural and social influences. Veteran Wharton readers in the group (students who have already encountered *Ethan Frome, The Age of Innocence,* or *The House of Mirth*) will recognize patterns here: the woman in a socially constructed predicament; the leading man thoughtful, sensitive, self-scrutinizing, but given to destructive and self-destructive irresolution. But within this general pattern, "Souls Belated" can stand out.

You might open by asking a broad question about the tone of the story and about how, finally, we read it: as a tale of star-crossed lovers, a bourgeois tragedy? Is there humor here or an element of bemused detachment in the way Lydia and Gannett are presented? Why open the story with that odd vignette of the nameless "courtly person who ate garlic out of a carpet-bag"? Amid the condescension in that brief description, is there any element of yearning for a life constructed in some other way—other than the genteel and frustrating civilities that keep Lydia and Gannett in their predicament?

If you sense that students are having some trouble believing in these two people as *people*—that is, as individuals with plausible motives and inhibitions—it might be well to center on one of those cadenza passages in which these lovers try to articulate their values and fears. The paragraphs after the surprising line, " 'But I

don't *want* to marry you!' she cried," will offer plenty to talk about—eloquent explanations (chiefly by Lydia) of the way that love and marriage are understood in their
world, and the resistance and accommodation that each of them is forced into to
be together. The conversation may veer outward into a contemplation of Realism
as a mode: the supposed implausibility of this pair of lovers in our own time may
be a function of their perfect plausibility in theirs. And what of these stifling pro-
prieties? Are they unmitigatedly awful, in Wharton's portrayal of them? Or do they
offer identity as well and the matter of life—without which there would be the
"nothing left to talk about" that Lydia dreads in the opening of the story?

SUI SIN FAR

With two names and two identities, Sui Sin Far wrote fiction that also negotiat-
ed several different worlds. She wrote of social and domestic life in West Coast
Chinese American families, which—like East European Jewish families in Cahan's
New York—were in a turmoil of reinvention, reconciling the traditional with the
new, and conditions of alienation with deep drives to belong. A parallel drama may
be under way in regard to narrative fiction itself: Sui Sin Far is appearing in media
dominated by followers of Howells, James, Wharton, Chopin, and others who
established a style and an array of expectations with regard to the Realist short
story. Can we examine the style and structure of "Mrs. Spring Fragrance" as a mingling of acceptance and resistance? If students glance quickly over these pages in
NAAL, what patterns do they see—how long, for example, is a typical descriptive
paragraph here, compared to a paragraph in "Souls Belated" or "The Beast in the
Jungle" or *The Awakening*? If these people, these domestic spaces, might be
expected to seem strange to a typical (white) reader, what might be the reasons for
not meticulously presenting the details and differences? In these encounters
among family members, how are people portrayed as speaking, and what are the
risks of transcribing Cantonese speech in this way? The story ends with Mr. Spring
Fragrance exclaiming about the "detestable" quality of American poetry. Why does
he say that? What might such "poetry" represent as a challenge not only to his aesthetics but to his family values?

W. E. B. DU BOIS

The moral and political problems, and the problems of personal and cultural
identity, raised so eloquently by Du Bois in these selections, can fuel plenty of discussion—about race, politics, and painful continuing differences between professed national values and actual social practice. You may not, however, have to
make an either—or decision as you plan your classes in regard to teaching this
from aesthetic or political perspectives. Du Bois was an uncommonly skillful
writer, and a fully respectful reading of *The Souls of Black Folk* should take note
of his sense of pace; his analogies and extended metaphors; and his expert understanding of when to make use of the rhetoric of the pulpit and when not to, when
to reach into the cultural experience of an educated audience and when to turn to
the details of ordinary life as experienced by African Americans after the Civil War.

You might select an especially strong passage—strong not just in the complexity
of its content but also in the energy of its prose—and work backward, toward the

beginning of the chapter, to observe how Du Bois prepares the way for a rhetorical adventure of this sort. The two paragraphs beginning with "The history of the American Negro is the history of this strife—this longing to obtain self-conscious manhood, to merge his double self into a better and truer self" can provide such a starting point. What are the connections—both logical and intuitive—between these paragraphs and the song selection that opens the chapter and the personal memories that come soon after it? If the long conceit about the "mountain path to Canaan" returns the reader to the familiar imaginative territory of the Calvinist and Evangelical traditions, how has Du Bois prepared us to accept this old (and perhaps time-worn) analogy as something relevant and fresh? How would students describe an overall strategy of *The Souls of Black Folk,* the discernment, in the lines of supposedly simple African American spirituals, of complex ideas of self-hood and self-fulfillment? Is this a writerly *tour de force,* a display of wit, mental agility, and (perhaps) late-Victorian sentimentality by one author working in a mainstream tradition? Or does Du Bois make this venture into cultural anthropology ring true and convince us of the deep wisdom within the ordinary and the plain?

The necessary two-ness of Washington and the "double consciousness" that Du Bois expresses allow students to see the emergence of real stress points in the concept of a referential, universal, or reliable reality. While it would not be accurate to say that the double consciousness of American blacks and of American women, beginning with Stanton's address to the Seneca Falls Woman's Rights Convention and the "Declaration of Sentiments" in 1848 (reprinted as an appendix in this guide), led to ways of thinking that would produce modernism, it was one aspect of the social environment that made and continues to make central concepts of modernism seem relevant to American experience. While neither a naturalist nor a modernist, Du Bois can be interpreted as a transition thinker-someone who observed the social forces at work in his own moment, who wrote to move common people, and who located his vision within the increasing sense that reality and identity might not be inherited or myterious but rather, like myth, invented.

STEPHEN CRANE

For Crane, even our most intimate self-concepts are contingent on our social context and on the forces of natural environment. The selections in NAAL allow students to see the variety of forces against which the protagonist in the Crane universe must fight. "The Open Boat" presents the forces of nature as the elements against which the characters are pitted, and "The Blue Hotel" reveals the rage and ultimate lack of control that govern human behavior. "The Bride Comes to Yellow Sky" is anomalous in the collection. Where does the story get its humor? What are the local-color elements in the story? Crane suggests that marriage itself is a force; how does the story suggest that each character is controlled by that force?

THEODORE DREISER

Dreiser's fiction conveys his sense of forces ranged against the individual; and in most of his work, these forces act directly. In "Old Rogaum and His Theresa," students see a more subtle text, for the forces Theresa and her father must battle are revealed to them indirectly. Unlike other women in Dreiser's fiction, such as Carrie Meeber of *Sister Carrie,* Theresa is not "ruined" during her night out but is given a glimpse of how she might be. And Old Rogaum does not lose "his Theresa," but the blond girl who shows up groaning on his doorstep gives him a glimpse of how the night might have turned out. Dreiser reveals the forces within the family as well. Old Rogaum himself is both a force for his daughter and is taken over by forces of rage and powerlessness beyond his control. His wife is no force at all; compare her with the bride in Crane's "The Bride Comes to Yellow Sky."

JOHN M. OSKISON

"The Problem of Old Harjo" may be discussed both as a Native American text and as regionalist fiction, and the two readings complement each other. In the context of other Native American works anthologized in the 1865–1914 period of *NAAL,* begin by comparing Miss Evans with Charles Eastman's wife-to-be, Elaine Goodale; for Miss Evans is the prototype of the young, white, well-meaning, and often-female Christian missionary to the Indians. Unlike the more experienced and less idealistic Mrs. Rowell, who expresses racism in her attitude toward "the old and bigamous" among the Creek Indian population (stating that "the country guarantees [Harjo's] idle existence" even though the truth is that he is materially solvent on his farm), Miss Evans is capable of seeing Harjo's situation as he sees it himself and withholds moral judgment. Harjo mutely questions her; she questions Mrs. Rowell, then her old pastor in New York, even implicitly church doctrine when she is tempted to say to him, " 'Stop worrying about your soul; you'll get to Heaven as surely as any of us.' " Yet the "problem of old Harjo" becomes Miss Evans's problem; and although the story seems unresolved at the end, since the problem remains insoluble, her "solution" (if not "solvent") is to recognize that circumstances have somehow tied her to this particular mission station, to this particular "impossible convert." Tied to Harjo "until death came to one of them," does Miss Evans become in effect yet another "wife" to the bigamist? Even if not, Oskison is nevertheless suggesting that the real agenda of the Christian missionaries is to suppress Creek culture in the young until the old men die off. What is this agenda but a continuation of the Ghost Dance War in another form?

Readers familiar with Native American literature may recognize Harjo as a figuration of the trickster archetype, which they may have encountered in the Native American Trickster Tales in *NAAL*: a transformative character who represents the dilemmas of change—change for the old Creek but also change necessarily in the Christians, if anyone is to achieve genuine salvation. The story's apparent lack of resolution—"And meanwhile, what?"—conveys the disruptive effect of the trickster figure but also the process of highlighting trouble in the prevailing moral order. Old Harjo brings into relief the basic contradiction inherent in the encounter between the Christian missionaries and some Native Americans, which perhaps might be summed up in Mrs. Rowell's (long) wait for the "old bigamists" to die out. Yet as the story's ending attests, Harjo's powers include tenacity; and he engages Miss Evans in a temporal "problem" for which the only solution would be genuine change in the moral order of things. She becomes his "wife" to the extent that the trickster figure who appears in some Native American legends may represent sexuality and desire; and her wish to assure him of salvation is humorous within a Native American tradition, for the trickster (as students may recall from the Pima "Story of Creation") is already Coyote, the divinely powerful child born when the moon became a mother. So Coyote is another version of the Messiah of the Ghost Dance religion in the sense that, in a "trickster" mode, Coyote—or here, Harjo—becomes incarnate to point up moral failings in the creation.

Read from the perspective of regionalism, the story's portrait of the relationship between Harjo and Miss Evans becomes an exercise in empathic exchange. Miss Evans is capable of moving into Harjo's moral and affectional universe because she is able to look with, not at, the "problem" Harjo presents. At the same time, her sympathy for him works implicitly to challenge the moral, political, and religious control Mrs. Rowell represents. Although Oskison's story may not on initial reading appear to be as sophisticated as Chesnutt's "The Goophered Grapevine," both involve powerless and disenfranchised persons (old Harjo and Uncle Julius) creating a situation that will force whites to reveal their own moral limitations. In both stories, it is the cunning of the powerless that sets up the "looking glass" to white society; in posing his "problem" week after week in the church, Harjo is indeed expressing his cunning, for has Miss Evans converted him or has he converted her?

As a fictional representation of Apess's critique, "The Problem of Old Harjo" has much in common with the work of Chesnutt and other nineteenth-century regionalists. Or, to put it another way, regionalist writers invented the white characters (like Miss Evans) capable of responding to figures like Harjo, whether we view him as a Native American trickster or as a "realistic" problem occasioned by the encounter of cultures, in this story represented by the conflict between the Christian missionary and the "old and bigamous" Creek.

JACK LONDON

London's "To Build a Fire" is a standard in English courses as early as the eighth grade, and some of your students will probably have keen memories of its graphic description of the stages of freezing to death in the Yukon wilderness. If you are approaching the story in the context of literary naturalism, however, you will have new things to talk about: for example, the subtlety or self-evidence of the themes in the tale and the open question of whether the story is inherently a fable advancing the loosely Darwinist doctrines that gave literary naturalism its force around the turn of the twentieth century. Why do works by London and S. Crane make use, so often, of protagonists with limited imagination and intellect? Are they, therefore, representative of the typical human being or of the human condition in general? Or would an extra measure of self-awareness and intelligence spoil the drama somehow by affording the protagonist the power to escape from the vast, indifferent, yet hostile context that provides the world of this tale, Crane's "The Blue Hotel" and "The Open Boat," and London's *The Call of the Wild*? If you feel that the habits and limitations of naturalism might wear thin as a subject, you could escape the "-isms," at least for a while, and speculate on why this kind of narrative, compelling and memorable and powerful as it is, has become the stuff of popular fiction, while supposedly serious fiction has turned in other directions? If James, as a consummate realist, held that literature should be (in his words) "a celebration of life," then what of "To Build a Fire"?

NATIVE AMERICAN CHANTS AND SONGS

Although teaching the chants and songs may not take the central position in your presentation of Native American literature, they are significant because they give the instructor a way to illustrate the truth that there was an American literature on this continent before there was English here. With this brief set of examples of chants and songs, students can learn that there was also literary form on the North American continent before there was formal literature, indeed, that there was drama, in the ceremonial performance of the nine-day Navajo Night Chant; there was dance as a form of language, as the Comanche and Sioux drawings of the Ghost Dance recall; and there was music, particularly represented by drumbeats and tonalities. Chants and songs gave poetry breath, considered by some Native American groups to link human life with the hole from which the earliest people emerged (as in the Pima Stories of the Beginning of the World).

Teaching the Native American chants and songs invites some transformation from the linear to some other mode—whether it be spatial (asking a group of students to enact at least part of the staging directions for the Navajo Night Chant, perhaps without sand!) or aural (asking others to prepare one or two of the songs for presentation). If you have a student talented enough (or courageous enough) on the recorder or flute, you might ask him or her to perform a few such songs in class. These songs must be heard to be appreciated for the way they alternate time signatures. In the Ghost Dance songs of the Arapaho in particular, there seems to be some correlation between elongated time signatures and the address to the gods. In "[Father, have pity on me]," the singer takes longer measures to address the "Father," and the singer does the same thing in "[When I met him approaching]" when re-creating the moment of trance vision. According to Andrew Wiget (*Native American Literature*, 1985), the songs or prayers in ritual Native American poetry seek "to re-create a state rather than an event" and achieve "substantiality and duration in time and space by repeating many different short songs in sequence." Perhaps the alternation of time signatures or rhythmic meters within these short songs also contributes to achieving this "substantiality and duration in time and space."

Students may feel on most familiar ground in reading the English translations themselves, and certainly the Ghost Dance songs will be evocative if you have discussed the Ghost Dance religion and the Wounded Knee massacre previously. These songs convey the losses of the native peoples and their hopes for revelation and salvation. The two excerpts from the Navajo Night Chant may produce the most extensive formal analysis of the (translated) language of the chants and songs.

The Navajo Night Chant

The headnote points out that the chant is a healing ceremony, focused on an individual rather than society as a whole—but clearly understood to be inclusive and relevant to the audience—participants. The patient of the first chant comes onto the "trail of song"; prays to ("walks with") the gods; and follows the rainbow (their promise of salvation, associated with rain) progressively to, then into, then within the "fore part of my house with the dawn," where he meets the gods that symbolize generative and regenerative powers. Upon sitting with these gods, the patient experiences restoration of his own powers ("Beautifully my fire to me is restored") and walks a new trail at the end of the prayer, one marked by the pollen, grasshoppers, and dew that represent generativity (and the dawn).

The second chant, according to the notes, represents the prayer for salvation as the prayer for rain. The progression in this chant moves from the repetitions of invocations to the "male divinity" to bring the rain, to the chanter's association of rain with individual healing, to a joyful acknowledgment that healing has taken place ("Happily for me *the spell* is taken off. / Happily may I walk"), and to a section of the chant leading up to the benediction and conclusion of the ceremony that widens the circle to include others ("Happily may fair white corn, to the ends of the earth, come with you") and ends with the patient's inhalation of "the breath of dawn," signifying the patient's emergence into health. This chant focuses both on an individual's healing and on transforming the social order. The patient's healing symbolizes the well-being of all those who live the Navajo "way" or walk with their gods.

Wovoka

For Wovoka's vision, offered here in two versions as The Messiah Letters, the headnote is as important as the text to the classroom reception of the entire range of Ghost Dance/Wounded Knee narratives included in *NAAL*. Spend time going over the details of the Ghost Dance religion and the subsequent massacre at Wounded Knee. Explore with students the statement from the period introduction that "armed action against the settlers and U.S. troops had failed. Many American Indians turned to spiritual action as a means of bringing about desired ends. From this impulse arose what has been called the Ghost Dance religion." The implication here is that some northern Plains Indians knew that they could no longer defend themselves in battle and, therefore, turned to spirituality to save themselves and give themselves hope. Read the two Messiah Letters carefully with students and identify specific aspects of the letters that link them with Native American traditions and with Christianity. Ask students why Euro-Americans seem to have had such difficulty imagining the concept of religious freedom for Indians. Recall Apess's "An Indian's Looking-Glass for the White Man," and apply his strategy of eliciting shame in his white Christian readers to the white settlers' resistance to the practice of a Christian-inspired religion by a few defeated bands of Indians.

Zitkala Ša

Zitkala Ša's three autobiographical essays invite comparison with other autobiographies by women writers. Students may find it interesting to read Rowlandson's *Narrative* in which the author describes her capture by the Wampanoag Indians against Zitkala Ša's narrative of "capture" by the "palefaces." Suggest that Zitkala Ša's account of her removal from the reservation and attempted assimilation into white culture provides a twist on the Indian captivity narrative of the colonial period. It's also interesting to think about Zitkala Ša as a Native American Daisy Miller.

Although Zitkala Ša's work does not, strictly speaking, belong to the genre of regionalism—it is autobiography, not fiction—nevertheless, there are elements of fictional form, especially in "Impressions of an Indian Childhood." She uses images—learning the "art of beadwork" or the cropped and "shingled hair"—that characterize both her own life and the larger plight of other Native Americans. "Impressions of an Indian Childhood" also possesses an aesthetic distance that students might associate with fiction. At the end of the third selection, "An Indian Teacher among Indians," Zitkala Ša herself acknowledges that "as I look back upon the recent past, I see it from a distance, as a whole." Perhaps the reason for this distance is that, at least in "Impressions of an Indian Childhood," she writes about a developing child whose path of development as a Sioux becomes so pinched off that the older child and adult narrator cannot even repair the discontinuity.

She also writes in English about events that took place when "I knew but one language, and that was my mother's native tongue." The act of rendering her Sioux childhood into English creates its own fiction, for she writes about herself at a time in her life before speaking and writing in English was even imaginable. Like the regionalists, Zitkala Ša depicts a female-centered universe and her own refusal to be silenced, and she triumphs on behalf of the disenfranchised "squaw" when she writes of winning the oratory contest; but unlike the separation of Mrs. Todd from her mother in Jewett's "The Foreigner," a separation that can be eased by telling a comforting story, Zitkala Ša's estrangement from her own mother only deepens as she proceeds with her autobiography. She loses her connection with the world of nature, becoming a "cold bare pole . . . planted in a strange earth."

Henry Adams

Whether or not Adams read Du Bois, for pedagogical purposes we can see the excerpts from *The Education* as thematic variations on the Du Boisean theme of "double consciousness." Like Du Bois, who summarizes nineteenth-century black thinking in 1903, Adams writes as one born in 1838, yet wanting "to play the game of the twentieth" century. *The Education* is another book in the tradition of Franklin's *Autobiography* but interesting because of the new directions Adams takes.

As it happened, he never got to the point of playing the game at all—he lost himself in the study of it, watching the errors of the players—but this is the only interest in the story, which otherwise has no moral and little incident. It is a story of education—seventy years of it—the practical value of which remains to the end in doubt.

The development of self-reliance in the American writer and thinker leads Adams to write that "every one must bear his own universe." Unlike Franklin, Adams does not become a politician but rather finds literary symbols that, as the headnote to Adams in *NAAL* asserts, make *The Education* to many readers "the one indispensable text for students seeking to understand the period between the Civil War and World War I." Students can see this clearly in Chapter I, where Adams writes, anticipating modernism, that the twentieth century is a world without design: "Often in old age he puzzled over the question whether, on the doctrine of chances, he was at liberty to accept himself or his world as an accident. No such accident had ever happened before in human experience. For him, alone, the old universe was thrown into the ash-heap and a new one created." And Adams traces his perception to early events (railroad and telegraph) that presented his six-year-old eyes with a "new world." Even as a boy, he developed "a double nature.

Life was a double thing. . . . From earliest childhood the boy was accustomed to feel that, for him, life was double."

Chapter XXV, "The Dynamo and the Virgin," crystallizes the doubleness he feels, presaging modern life in the symbols that express the split between technology and spirituality. Adams writes clearly; students could easily prepare a summary of the argument of this chapter. In class, you can continue to focus on Adams's early modernist ideas: what happens to human energies—symbolized by the force and power of the Virgin and of ancient fertility goddesses—in an age and in a country that replaces human with technological power and is it possible to state, "with the least possible comment, such facts as seemed sure" and to "fix for a familiar moment a necessary sequence of human movement"?

CHAPTER 10

Teaching Notes for Authors and Works: Volume D, American Literature between the Wars, 1914–1945

In moving forward to the Moderns, you probably face at least three different questions right away:

- How and why did these writers see the world differently from writers in earlier periods and centuries—what we might call a thematic approach to understanding modernism.
- How and why did they choose their images and their narrative and poetic forms?
- How might their gender, ethnicity, or class have influenced their writing—how did pluralism, both within American culture and as it derives from international influence (particularly by Joyce, Woolf, and Yeats), emerge as a determining factor and a consequence of modern literature?

Selections from Native American and African American writers allow students to explore these questions, and you can also perceive continuing colonial attitudes (in both white and minority writers) that manifest themselves in racial segregation and discrimination.

BLACK ELK

In opening discussion on the excerpts from this work, you can begin by asking students questions that will help them explore the interesting narrative form. To

the question "Who is speaking?" they may answer, Black Elk. Fine—but who is
narrating? Black Elk or John Neihardt? Make use of the *NAAL* headnote, especially the fact that Black Elk could neither read nor write and spoke little English
when he told John Neihardt the story of his great vision, and talk about the context within which *Black Elk Speaks* was created: Black Elk telling his story to his
son, Ben Black Elk, who then translated it into English for Black Elk's "adopted"
son, John Neihardt, while Neihardt's daughter, Enid, wrote it all down and other
Sioux elders contributed their memories of events. Then, later, Neihardt worked
from his daughter's transcriptions to produce *Black Elk Speaks*. How do the circumstances of composition affect students' perception of authorship of the work?
Discuss differences between Neihardt's work and the work of early-twentieth-century social scientists who often paid Native American informants to tell their stories. Neihardt was himself a poet; in agreeing to tell his story to Neihardt, holy man
Black Elk was recognizing a kindred spirit.

Even so, there had to be limits to that kinship, and the long account called "The
Great Vision" requires some careful preliminary discussion if we are going to
engage with it effectively in an American literature course. We have to decide, at
least tentatively, what we are reading, or listening to, or overhearing: this is a personal experience (spiritual, religious, psychological, carefully allegorical, or some
combination of them all) related across a considerable cultural and linguistic
divide to a white listener who constructs a written, printed narrative that is subsequently collected into a literary anthology and read by ourselves. A lot of transformations are involved here—so many, in fact, that recovering the original intention
and texture of Black Elk's narrative, and its cultural and historical moment, may
be impossible for nearly everyone except an expert in the Sioux peoples of the last
century. Still, we can value the way in which this narrative extends and enriches
our collective sense both of the nature and possibilities of North American storytelling and of the individual self.

Though your students will have some familiarity with the cultural importance of
the Vision Quest among native peoples of the Western Plains, can they speculate
about how the pronoun *I* is used in Black Elk's account and what that pronoun signifies? When he presents himself as one chosen to receive special wisdom from the
Six Grandfathers (most of us have only four), how are these nameless teachers and
their young pupil presented to us? Why don't all these grandfathers have names?
Is this a "spiritual" education in the European or New England sense of the word?
Are power and wisdom achieved through creating or discovering "identity" as a
thing apart? When Black Elk becomes "the spotted eagle floating" and then moves
to the bay horse and finds himself "painted red all over," are these self-aggrandiz-
ing representations? Why might there be so much emphasis on "the earth," the
ground, in Black Elk's vision?

Black Elk Speaks records only the first twenty-seven years of Black Elk's life,
ending with the battle of Wounded Knee. Neihardt ends *Black Elk Speaks* with an
image of drifted snow in "one long grave" at Wounded Knee. Although Black Elk
himself lived another fifty-nine years, Neihardt closes his text with what some
readers have described as Black Elk's spiritual death and the end of tribal independence; for as Black Elk himself states, after the end of Sioux freedom, he and
his people become simply "prisoners of war while we are waiting here."

Black Elk Speaks, therefore, shapes the form of Black Elk's story as Neihardt works to create the full effect of Sioux tragedy in his white readers, just as Black Elk himself was capable of feeling in himself the pain of the people. The act of the bicultural collaborator creates empathy in the modern reader. Furthermore, the act of teaching *Black Elk Speaks* places the instructor also in the position of bicultural translator, using the classroom and discussion of the text as a way to complete the circle between the American undergraduate student and the text that writes Black Elk's name in our canon of collective attempts to define the American identity.

WILLA CATHER

Cather remains a strongly popular author, a centerpiece on many school reading lists, and a favorite among younger students; many of your students will have encountered *My Ántonia* and various short stories by her and will remember them fondly. The ways in which Cather has been classified by critics and literary historians, however—as a latter-day realist, naïve regionalist or local-colorist, pioneer of an American lesbian sensibility, anti-Freudian sentimentalist, austere modernist of the Great Plains—will strike some of your students as confining or inadequate. You might begin there—with this question of whether there is any real need for maneuvering Cather into some aesthetic position next to Fitzgerald or on some literary family tree, with Twain and Stephen Crane down below and, say, Anne Tyler or Grace Paley or Ann Beattie or others branching out at the top.

If students don't like situating Cather in this way, then the conversation can move to a different kind of likening, especially if the two stories in *NAAL*, "Neighbour Rosicky" and "The Sculptor's Funeral," are read together. In both stories, as in so much of her work, Cather takes on a challenge that was faced by literary realists and naturalists a generation before her: how to write about ordinary people, people without schooling or broad cultural experience, in a manner without condescension, without caricature, without sentimentality? In each case, her success may not be complete—what narrative is completely successful? Therefore, the conversation might be less coercive if you find ways of asking your students what works for them in each story and what does not. You could read backward, starting with the endings: the benedictory paragraph that closes "Neighbour Rosicky," and the lawyer Laird's theatrical indictment of the "sick, side-tracked, burnt-dog, land-poor sharks" of Sand City. Do these endings work? Do they fit with the narratives that lead up to them? Do they successfully avoid predictability or cliché? If there is suspense in "The Sculptor's Funeral" or a rising tension like a pot coming to a boil, what is the plot or suspense of "Neighbour Rosicky"?

A more complex kind of questioning and comparison can be opened by staying with "The Sculptor's Funeral," which meditates on the predicaments of the American artist, predicaments that affect Cather and perhaps all writers. Merrick is from Sand City, and yet in some ways he cannot go home; this is the world that produced him, yet also exiled him and cannot understand him or truly receive him again. Does the artist, the writer, the independent thinker drift into a zone apart, a painful or salutary disconnection with roots? If that is a theme in "The Sculptor's Funeral," then how is Cather attempting to come home in either or both of these stories? In other words, how is she implicitly affirming her connection to the Nebraska she herself grew up in, or affirming a distance, or both?

Students will want to talk about characters here, and with these short stories they may have more trouble than usual in talking about characters as artistic creations rather than as actual people. That is a high tribute to Cather's skill as a novelist and as an observer of human nature but is potentially an awkward situation when you're hoping to talk about this art as art, rather than as personal account or a kind of microhistory. One way through the problem: with all of the overarching formulations about the human condition rife during Cather's career—Marx, Freud, various Darwinisms; aesthetic and political manifestos and totalizing statements about what art and fiction should do and what the human condition inexorably was or should be—is Cather's poise, her commitment to narrative that looks (deceptively) like sheer storytelling, a kind of resistance? A refusal to see and portray the world as less complex and minutely interesting than she understood it to be? If we are to understand the durability of Cather and her heartening intractability as a writer in any ex-post literary school or movement, then discussion of this issue might be a good contribution to that understanding.

GERTRUDE STEIN

The Stein entries are going to be a train wreck for students who approach them with their close-reading methodologies fully engaged and hot from deep-meaning searches that they may have conducted with various realists and modernists that have come before in your course. In reading Stein, they don't get it; and some students can become anxious or angry or (worse) quietly demoralized, like those visitors to the Cabaret Voltaire in Zurich, where Dadaism had its birth in the midst of World War I, who couldn't figure out what was going on because they tried too hard to decode the words and action on the stage. Actually, the problem with Stein in this particular context can be just as bad, or worse—because, enshrined in an anthology, discourse that might otherwise beguile or pleasantly dislocate becomes academic text that must be sounded and understood or else all is lost!

Perhaps a way to grow comfortable with Stein, and to get much further in reading these selections, is to back up a bit and converse about those many sorts of cultural experiences in which things *don't* make sense but in which you can have a good time anyway and not worry about "getting it"—because from somewhere you get the message that getting it isn't the point at all. Your students listen to plenty of music and see plenty of video and film that, in a strict sense, they can't decode or fathom and would feel absurd trying to do so. The pictures don't fit the words; the words are sometimes nonsense. Why is it (you might ask) that they—or rather, we—can accept uncertainty and even complete mystification in some art or entertainment experiences, but not in others? Can we take pleasure in adventures such as this, adventures into prose and poetry that seem to escape the usual chore of making sense and being clear? When your students have gone home after a day of classes, barraged by tomes of deadly earnest, highly rhetorical argumentative prose—showing us this and telling us that and proving to us something else—can a yearning arise for an escape into a freer sort of writing, where meanings (in a Victorian or standard modern sense) are less important than the intellectual and psychological refreshment of getting lost?

An approach like this tends to make Stein seem a contingent writer, responding to and in a sense resisting certain mainstream Western habits of prose and poetry (and the perhaps artificial categorical differences between the two), but understanding first what Stein is *not* doing is an an effective way of opening a discussion of what she accomplishes as new American writing.

AMY LOWELL

Following chronologically from poets Masters and Robinson, Lowell will continue to beguile students into believing that the poetry in the 1914–45 period is accessible. Explore both the accessibility and the inaccessibility of imagism by reading Lowell in conjunction with H. D. and Pound. Examine "Meeting-House Hill," "Summer Night Piece," and "New Heavens for Old" as imagist poems. Lowell's inclusion in *NAAL* does not fully resolve the question about which critics remain divided: Is Lowell's poetry any good? Is it too sentimental to be good poetry? And in using the word *sentimental* against her are we mistakenly accepting devaluation of the very concept of the sentimental and its legitimate role in poetry?

Whatever the verdict among your students, including Lowell's voice in your syllabus will make room for early discussions of female mythological characters that will inform much poetry by women and men in the twentieth century (in "The Captured Goddess" and "Venus Transiens"), and will introduce what Baym calls "appreciations of female beauty" in poems by women. Indeed, a few of the poems included here may be considered love poems to specific women or to women in general: "Venus Transiens" and "Madonna of the Evening Flowers."

ROBERT FROST

Like Cather, Frost retains elements of realism, and like her, he portrays moments in which his speaker's perception changes as central to his poetry. Several class periods can be spent on individual poems and representative poems by other twentieth-century poets through the fulcrum of our analysis of Frost. You can prepare for a discussion of "The Oven Bird" by reading "Nothing Gold Can Stay," with its allusion to Eden and human mortality. "The Oven Bird" deserves an important place in our discussion, because Frost's other poems, his essay "The Figure a Poem Makes," many other works of literature by modern writers, and even the concept of Modernism itself seem contained and articulated in the poem's last two lines: "The question that he asks in all but word / Is what to make of a diminished thing." The bird and the poet ask questions that express the central modernist theme: How do we confront a world in which reality is subject to agreement or lacks referentiality altogether? How do we express the experience of fragmentation in personal and political life? How do we live with the increasing awareness of our own mortality—whether we face the prospect of human death (as the speaker does in "Home Burial," "After Apple-Picking," or " 'Out, Out-' "), the death or absence of God (as Frost considers in "Desert Places" and "Design"), or mere disappointment at our own powerlessness (as in "An Old Man's Winter Night" or "Stopping by Woods on a Snowy Evening")?

In regard to "The Oven Bird," ask students to hear contrasting ways of intoning the last two lines. You might read the lines first with emphasis on the phrase "diminished thing," and the pessimism in Frost and in his conception of modern life receives most of our attention. But read them again, emphasizing the infinitive "to make," and the poem seems to reverse its own despair, to create the possibility that creative activity can ease the face of the lessening, the "diminishing," of modern perception.

Other works offer this positive response to the bird's question. In "The Figure a Poem Makes," Frost defines the act of writing poetry as "not necessarily a great clarification" but at least "a momentary stay against confusion." Students who have studied the Volume A and B material may see Frost's solution to his own metaphysical problem as one more variable in Edward Taylor's attempt to sustain a metaphor through the length of one of his *Preparatory Meditations* to arrive at the language of salvation. Frost emphasizes, though, that he wants to be just as surprised by the poem as is the reader. And his description of the thought process that a poem records applies to our own endeavors in the classroom as well—whenever we try to engage students first and then teach them how to order their engaged perception. When Frost contrasts scholars, who get their knowledge "with conscientious thoroughness along projected lines of logic," with poets, who get theirs "cavalierly and as it happens in and out of books," most students prefer to identify with the poets. And Frost might, indeed, be describing an American epistemology, as it works best with students: "They stick to nothing deliberately, but let what will stick to them like burrs where they walk in the fields."

No study of Frost, at any class level, is complete without close analysis of the great poems "Birches" and "Directive." Students at any level profit from line-by-line discussion of "Directive," particularly in contrast with the earlier poem "After Apple-Picking." In this poem, the speaker's troubled sleep results from his realization of the imperfection of human power to "save" fallen apples (or fallen worlds) or to fully complete any task as someone with godlike power (or any "heroic" human being before the modernist era) might have been able to do. "Directive" transcends those limitations, offers a specific path to take ("if you'll let a guide direct you / Who only has at heart your getting lost"), and arrives at a vision of spiritual regeneration unparalleled in any of Frost's other poems: "Here are your waters and your watering place. / Drink and be whole again beyond confusion."

How does Frost contain *both* American Dream and American nightmare? How does his poetry, as he writes in "Two Tramps in Mud Time," allow him to "unite / My avocation and my vocation / As my two eyes make one in sight"? How do Frost's images suggest that, long after the apparent decline of Transcendentalism, the analogical thinking of Emerson and Thoreau would become a permanent part of the American imagination?

SUSAN GLASPELL

Encountered alone, this dramatized version of Glaspell's famous short story "A Jury of Her Peers" may seem like an ordinary script for a half-hour TV detective drama. And time and subsequent imitation of Glaspell have not been kind to the play's Gothic atmosphere: today's students who come to us loaded with latter-day New England horror stories about brutality, madness, and revenge in old farmhouses far off the main roads will not at first find much of interest here. As social observation, however, the play regains interest if it is situated with other imaginative literature about the crisis facing countless women through much of the nineteenth and twentieth centuries, a crisis of isolation, of thwarted creativity, of marriages founded on a lack of understanding or love. Gilman's "The Yellow Wallpaper," Chopin's *The Awakening*, Frost's "Home Burial," Anderson's *Winesburg, Ohio* stories—if some of these are opened along with *Trifles*, students will be encouraged to see the predicament of these women as a recurring important theme, rather than an excuse for a mild dark drama. Then they can think about modern analogues—novels by Stephen King, films by Hitchcock and his many imitators, rural-nightmare shows on network television. Have changes in literary and dramatic style and tastes enhanced our ability to present such predicaments? Or do those changes somehow impede that attention?

SHERWOOD ANDERSON

If students have been reading chronologically through *NAAL*, they will be ready to see Anderson as writing in the fresh wake of Realism, of Naturalism, and of the regionalist and local-colorist traditions. These are traditions that he both respects and resists in achieving an individual voice. Anderson wants to know where it all begins—to focus on a particular house in a particular street—and to try to figure out, by examining origins, who he is and who we are. Anderson's life before he declared himself a writer illustrates a classic theme in nineteenth-century fiction by white male writers; ask your students to recall Irving's "Rip Van Winkle," or Twain's *Huckleberry Finn*. Like the characters in that earlier fiction, Anderson also seems to have suffered a form of amnesia, sudden disappearance, or inexplicable departure, one day, from his life with his wife and his job at the paint firm. In leaving his life in Ohio so abruptly, Anderson expressed the incompatibility of living conventionally and also writing an American book. How does this define the role of the writer, for Anderson? *Winesburg, Ohio*, though fiction, emerges from an autobiographical impulse; and the reporter in that work, George Willard, experiences the young writer's conflict. Later in life, Anderson would write a memoir titled *A Storyteller's Story*; *Winesburg, Ohio*, which tells the story of Anderson himself still within the eggshell, before his "hatching" as a storyteller.

Several related themes characterize the anthologized stories from *Winesburg*. Anderson portrays conflict between inner emotions and outward behavior; Alice Hindman and Elmer Cowley share this conflict although they express it differently. Sexual repression and displaced aggression enter American fiction in *Winesburg*, and each of the anthologized stories shares this theme. In Elizabeth Willard, sexual repression and repressed identity become interconnected, and in "Adventure," Anderson hints at "the growing modern idea of a woman's owning herself and giving and taking for her own ends in life," although his own fiction explores the stunting of women's lives, not their "modern" alternatives. Writing itself becomes the American passion for George Willard; the "queerness" that interests Anderson in some of his characters (Elmer Cowley and Mook in " 'Queer' ") suggests an American illness caused by inarticulate inner lives that the fiction writer might be able to "cure."

At the end of "Rip Van Winkle," Rip takes his place as the "chronicler" or storyteller of the village and thus moves from margin to center in his position in the town. Anderson's portrait of the American storyteller—in his character George Willard and in the events of his own life—addresses the marginality of the white male writer. Anderson's marginality is central to his vision; despite his portrait of the way American life has twisted and thwarted individual development, he chooses to portray it from without, not envision re-creating it from within. Like Huckleberry Finn, George Willard escapes Winesburg and, in the process, becomes capable of telling a story.

WALLACE STEVENS

Poems such as Frost's "The Oven Bird" and "Desert Places" allow students to experience modernist feeling; Stevens translates the central thematic concern of modern writers into an intellectual framework. We can begin by reading "Of Modern Poetry" line by line and make connections between the idea of "finding what will suffice" and making something "of a diminished thing." This poem links modernist thought to World War I, breaks with the realists' "script," and ends with actions that appear referential ("a man skating, a woman dancing, a woman / Combing") but can be understood only as manifestations of what is spoken "In the delicatest ear of the mind," not as semantic symbols.

Students' greatest difficulties in reading Stevens are to move beyond the apparently referential quality of his language and to learn to read it as dynamic forms of abstract ideas. "Anecdote of the Jar" works well to analyze closely. This poem forces students to push beyond the referential features of the language, for its meaning resides not in the jar but in its placement and in the larger design the poem creates and imposes. But that larger design is an arbitrary creation of the poet, not the manifestation of divine presence in the universe; and we can work through other Stevens poems that illustrate the poet's power to make his world's design. "Thirteen Ways of Looking at a Blackbird" can help students see the problem of perception in a modern world in which there is no shared reality; in "The Idea of Order at Key West," the woman makes order out of the diminished thing by singing, thereby becoming "the self / That was her song, for she was the maker"; and "The Emperor of Ice-Cream" proposes as the modernist's reality a world that lets "the lamp affix its beam" to show, as "The Snow Man" states, "Nothing that is not there and the nothing that is." Ask students how the idea that nothing is there—except what the imagination invents—becomes a manifestation of American self-reliance. For Stevens, all forms of order are created by human perception; nature itself reflects human values only as we project our image onto the natural world.

Stevens responds to the oven bird's question in the first line of "A High-Toned Old Christian Woman": "Poetry is the supreme fiction." Nina Baym directs the reader's attention to two repeated activities in Stevens's poems: (1) looking at things and (2) playing musical instruments or singing. Ask students to identify poems in which these activities appear (for the first, see in particular "The Snow Man," "The Emperor of Ice-Cream," "Thirteen Ways of Looking at a Blackbird," "Study of Two Pears," and "The Plain Sense of Things"; for the second, see in particular "A High-Toned Old Christian Woman," "Peter Quince at the Clavier," "The Idea of Order at Key West," "Of Modern Poetry," and "Asides on the Oboe"), and we identify as parallel concepts making music or singing and writing poetry, and perceiving or observing and giving existence to reality. These parallel activities replace the Christian God, create new gods or mythological forms, and allow us to devise our own supreme fiction. The new mythology or fiction, for whom the poet is both creator and secular priest, explains the presence of so much continually unexpected imagery in Stevens. Furthermore, Stevens's own poetry provides an answer to the woman's musings in "Sunday Morning."

In "Sunday Morning," Stevens creates a dialogue between a woman and a narrator, or a dialogue of one that shows the woman thinking within her own mind, and he alters the meaning of Christianity. The poem transforms the religious connotations of Sunday into those of a human-centered "day of the sun," in which, since we live in an "island solitude, unsponsored, free," we invent as our supreme fiction, our god or our explanation for the way the universe works, the very mortality that is the only "imperishable bliss" we know. Stevens proposes making ritual of the diminished thing, creating fellowship "of men that perish and of summer morn," and seeing "casual flocks of pigeons" not as "homeward bound" but rather as nature's "ambiguous undulations." Nature has no message for us; but in the act of writing (and reading) poetry, we can create our own order, one that becomes more beautiful because it is the projection of "man's rage for order" and, therefore, as fragile as human life. "Death is the mother of beauty" for Stevens because it intensifies the act of "arranging, deepening, enchanting night" (in "The Idea of Order at Key West"), the act of taking momentary "dominion" (in "Anecdote of the Jar"), or the "old chaos of the sun." Poetry serves Stevens (from his book of collected lectures *The Necessary Angel*) as a "means of redemption." What should we make of a world in which there is not external order? Project onto it human mortality and make art out of the moment of sinking "Downward to darkness, on extended wings," create a "jovial hullabaloo among the spheres."

The images of the sun that form the focus for the woman's meditations in "Sunday Morning" also provide Stevens's central image in other poems. Build class discussion around a group of these poems ("Gubbinal," "A Postcard from the Volcano," "The Sense of the Sleight-of-hand Man"), and examine the way Stevens builds his real image of what the supreme fiction might look like on the sun itself. In "Sleight-of-hand Man," he writes, "The fire eye in the clouds survives the gods." The supreme fiction takes the form of human flesh in "Peter Quince at the Clavier." Give students time to work through the experience of Stevens's concept of the supreme fiction. For many, reading Stevens will seem like heresy, a fundamental challenge to their own religious practice. Allow them to compare notes on their various perceptions of Stevens's work. Use class discussion as an exemplum of modernist thought; a class of any size may approach "Thirteen Ways of Looking at Stevens," or "a visibility of thought, / In which hundreds of eyes, in one mind, see at once."

ANZIA YEZIERSKA

Yezierska writes powerfully about the contrast between immigrant expectations and immigrant reality and between the rhetoric of democracy and its broken promise for the immigrant poor. "The Lost 'Beautifulness' " raises these issues painfully and clearly and promotes extensive discussion in the classroom. Ask students to derive two sets of assumptions from the story. The first set includes assumptions about class that Hannah Hayyeh makes, for example: (1) that poverty doesn't mean a person can't also have beauty in life; (2) that even though someone is poor doesn't mean she can't have a rich friend, that friendship can cross class lines; and (3) that "making money ain't everything in life." Explore how Hannah comes to hold these assumptions, what happens to disillusion her with respect to each one and whether students share any of them.

The second set includes assumptions about America and the meaning of democracy, for example: (1) "democracy means that everybody in America is going to be with everybody alike"; (2) it's possible to assimilate into American values—as Hannah tells her husband, "so long my Aby is with America, I want to make myself for an American"; (3) merit is recognized, as in "such a tenant the landlord ought to give out a medal or let down the rent free"; and (4) even a "hungry-eyed ghetto woman" can be an "artist laundress"—the American Dream takes many forms, but even a ghetto laundress can have her dreams. The second set will be harder for students to dislodge, in terms of their own dreams and their assumptions about their own future. However, in the early twenty-first century, even middle-class students are more realistic about the hollow ring of some of these assumptions and will observe the validity of the landlord's corrective truth: "in America everybody looks out for himself."

Compare the ending with the narrator's behavior in Gilman's "The Yellow Wallpaper," and ask students to comment on the effectiveness of the course of action Hannah chooses to follow. Examine the final scene as a moment of imagistic prose, in which the insignia of the Statue of Liberty, the gold service stripes, and the "assurance of the United States Army" that Aby Safransky possesses contrast with the image of broken Hannah in her eviction from her apartment, from her dreams of beauty, and from all things she believed were American.

WILLIAM CARLOS WILLIAMS

How does Williams answer the question, What to make of a diminished thing? We can begin with "A Sort of a Song," which directs its reader to write a poem about the thing. Make nothing of it but the thing itself. Because there may not be meaning, don't insist on it. And we can talk about characteristics of Williams's poems, trying to elicit, in discussion, some of the central features of imagism: exactness, precision, compression, common speech, free verse. "The Red Wheelbarrow," "The Widow's Lament in Springtime," and "Portrait of a Lady" work well for this discussion. We can analyze "Spring and All" closely, suggesting that the process Williams describes becomes, in part, analogous to the creation of a poetic image. Some students have difficulty understanding the concept of the image; and in teaching Williams, you might take time to talk about the eidetic faculty—what happens in the mind when we read a visual description. "Portrait of a Lady," read aloud with appropriate emphasis ("Agh!"), can help them "hear" another kind of image.

You can then talk about some themes in Williams—love and death—and how the poems strip those themes of sentimentality. What happens to Williams's view of human life in poems such as "Death," "The Dead Baby," and "Landscape with the Fall of Icarus"? Compare Williams and Frost; students may suggest that, despite his objectivity, Williams lacks the pessimism of some of Frost's poems. How does Williams's use of poetic technique develop his themes? Critics often compare Williams with Whitman. Ask students to discuss this connection. Several modern poets try to write longer poems, perhaps with the epic form in mind.

EZRA POUND

We read a few Pound poems to see how he uses the image: "In a Station of the Metro" and "The River-Merchant's Wife: A Letter" work well, although students sometimes have difficulty actually seeing Pound's image in the first poem. Does the poem's second line work only if one sees a contrast between the faces and the black bough? Does Pound assume light-skinned faces? "To Whistler, American"; "A Pact"; and "The Rest" are easily accessible to students; but what response do they have to "Hugh Selwyn Mauberley (Life and Contacts)" or *The Cantos*? How do students without a classical education understand Pound's dictum to "make it new"?

H. D.

Several strategies for reading H. D. may enlist student interest. With editor Baym's comments about imagism as a guide, trace H. D.'s formal uses of the image in her poetry, and compare her work with that of A. Lowell, Williams, and Pound. Alternatively, move ahead to other women poets whose work reflects H. D.'s influence. For example, Susan Gubar (in "The Echoing Spell in H. D.'s *Trilogy*," in *Shakespeare's Sisters*, 1979) suggests comparing H. D.'s use of the seashell image to Moore's "To a Snail." (See also Moore's poem "The Paper Nautilus.") The last stanzas of "The Walls Do Not Fall" are clearly echoed later in Rich's poem "Diving into the Wreck." Even further, Gubar suggests that to really understand H. D., we need to move beyond discussions of Imagism and Modernism (and psychoanalysis) to exploring "H. D.'s sense of herself as a woman writing about female confinement, specifically the woman writer's entrapment within male literary conventions, as well as her search for images of female divinity and prophecy." Reading H. D. as a feminist modernist and a poet who is trying to express her discomfort with male-defined representations of women and of history may give students another approach to her poetry.

Because H. D. has been fully appreciated only by recent feminist critics who write about Modernism, you or your students may find useful Susan Stanford Friedman's critical biography *Psyche Reborn: The Emergence of H. D.* (1981), in which she traces H. D.'s development as a feminist modernist and in particular H. D.'s interest in a woman-centered mythmaking. From "Leda" to "Helen" to the goddesses Isis, Aset, and Astarte in "The Walls Do Not Fall," students will at least find the female figures to counterbalance the presence of the all-father and Osiris. H. D.'s closing lines of that long poem ("we are voyagers, discoverers / of the not-known, / the unrecorded") have particular resonance for women in a modernist world.

ROBINSON JEFFERS

Jeffers's poetry contrasts sharply with that of both Frost and Stevens; ask students to discuss his ways of transforming poems about nature into philosophical meditations. Jeffers appears to have disdained Modernism; is his poetry traditional? Compare Jeffers's use of free verse with W. C. Williams's poetic line. How is Jeffers's poetry unique? Discuss his use of the physical landscape of the central California coast. Is Jeffers a regional poet? Identify the source of his cynicism and compare it with Frost's pessimistic poems. Jeffers seems to suggest that "what to make of a diminished thing" is to diminish it still further: "We must unhumanize our views a little." Consider what he means by this.

"Shine, Perishing Republic" can be discussed line by line—or alternatively assigned to students to explicate in an essay. The poem stands out in contrast to many of the modernist works we read, both in what it lacks (any sense that classical mythology holds the key to understanding our present) and for what it offers (as a view of twentieth-century American life and values). This poem and others ("November Surf" and "Carmel Point") seem to some students to comment on our own contemporary life. How does "Shine, Perishing Republic" suggest what it meant to be an American in the twentieth century?

MARIANNE MOORE

In *Naked and Fiery Forms: Modern American Poetry by Women* (1976), Suzanne Juhasz describes Moore as "the leading American woman poet" of her generation but not the "leading American poet" and comments on the contrast between Pound, who "does not have to deny his masculine experience, because it is all of mankind," and Moore, who makes "a neat division between 'woman' and 'poet,' with art and artistry belonging to the domain of the latter." Juhasz's framework is useful for reading modern American women poets; she suggests that the second generation (in which she includes Rukeyser, Bishop, Bogan, and Brooks, all anthologized in *NAAL*) continued to separate "woman" and "poet" but that writers at mid-century (Levertov, Plath, and Sexton) begin to function as both "woman" and "poet."

Teaching Moore following Juhasz's framework will help contextualize both Moore's avoidance of women's experience in her poetry and the increasing attention to women's experience by poets later in the century. Indeed, students will find it difficult if not impossible to locate any gendered experience in Moore. She writes either with a gender-neutral first person (in "Poetry," "In Distrust of Merits," " 'Keeping Their World Large,' " and "O to Be a Dragon") or about generic "man" (as in "A Grave" and "What Are Years?"). Only nature is feminized (as in "Bird-Witted" and "The Paper Nautilus").

Editor Nina Baym comments in her headnote that in Moore "the reader almost never finds the conventional poetic allusions that invoke a great tradition and assert the present poet's place in it." In Juhasz's framework, this is because women of Moore's generation could not find or present themselves as part of a great tradition. What Moore does do, like many of her contemporaries, is to reinvent poetry for herself or to find a new form for what she thought poetry should be. Locate and discuss Moore's statements on the act and art of poetry. Analyze in such a discussion "To a Snail." What happens to poetic language when there is an "absence of feet"? Also analyze closely the frequently anthologized "Poetry." Often students have difficulty understanding why a poet such as Moore would write with such passion about the nature of poetry itself. Build on previous discussions of the image to help them find the contrast, in the poem's middle stanzas, between the discursive statements Moore makes ("we / do not admire what / we cannot understand" and "all these phenomena are important") and her use of images drawn from precise observation of the animal world, such as in the poem "The Paper

Nautilus." What does she mean in trying to create "imaginary gardens with real toads in them"? Analyze "Bird-Witted" and "Nevertheless" to see what Moore does with form in poetry.

Comment on the kind of stanza she creates in "Nevertheless" and ask students to locate rhyme in "Bird-Witted" and "The Mind Is an Enchanting Thing." Most will not have discovered rhyme (as students, in reading Frost, do not immediately perceive rhyme in "After Apple-Picking"). What is the effect of the use of rhyme? Compare "Bird-Witted" with Frost's poem. Is "Bird-Witted" a poem about birds or about poetry? What is Moore's "uneasy new problem"? Does one possibility cancel out the other for her?

Which poems illustrate Moore's response to the modern way of seeing the world? Compare "In Distrust of Merits" with Jeffers's earlier "Shine, Perishing Republic." Which poem seems to be more referential? Discuss Moore's views of war as an "inward" struggle in "In Distrust of Merits." How does her image of the world as an "orphans' home" comment on the modernist themes of her contemporaries? Ask students to extend Moore's discussions—of enslaver and enslaved and our being "not competent to make our vows" about not hating—to our own contemporary social and global conflicts, to the resurgence of nationalism in the world, and to the significance of "I inwardly did nothing" in the context of bias incidents and hate speech on college campuses and in U.S. society as a whole.

Eugene O'Neill

Long Day's Journey into Night demonstrates that one of the strong features of twentieth-century American literature is the continuation of what O'Neill's Edmund calls late in the play "faithful realism." But O'Neill's realism differs from that of the late-nineteenth-century writers, even as it seems to extend some of their concerns. In fact, O'Neill's play sometimes seems a compendium or a spectrum of American ideas that long precede the late nineteenth century, for he presents the Tyrones both as deeply conditioned by their past and as characters who face in their daily life (in this classically unified one-day's play) the fragmentation that is one symptom or consequence of modernist sensibility.

Mary's descent into the madness of morphine addiction becomes the play's emblem; and although O'Neill is writing, in part, about his own mother here, he is also sensitive to Mary's position as woman in the American family and in American history. As the play unfolds the history of Mary's medical treatment and of her husband's attitudes toward her condition, students will make connections between Mary Tyrone and both Edna Pontellier and the narrator of "The Yellow Wallpaper." O'Neill suggests that modern life is more difficult for women than for men: Mary might have played the piano, but married instead, thereby depriving herself of the coherence of vocation; in marriage, and especially in marriage to the peripatetic James Tyrone (rootlessness itself becomes a modern condition), she cuts herself off from having woman friends with whom she might ease her loneliness (O'Neill adds early scandal to the fact of marriage as a way of doubly cutting Mary off from other women); and in choosing to ease her loneliness by following Tyrone on his tours, she is forced to reject even the traditional solace of making a home for her children, so that the series of choices becomes irreversible, and her need for something to ease her emotional pain and to dull her perception of her own meaninglessness increases.

Within the family structure, Mary also suffers the anachronism (in the twentieth century) of not being able to move beyond the scrutiny of external forces that seem to control her. When she tells her husband, "You really must not watch me all the time, James. I mean, it makes me self-conscious," she is experiencing the radical emotion that led the deist Founding Fathers to revolution in the 1770s. But, unlike the deists, who experienced a fundamental shift in worldview when they accepted the idea that God might not be watching them all the time and fought for self-determination from the system of divinely ordained British monarchy, Mary Tyrone is only made "self-conscious" by Tyrone's scrutiny.

She suffers self-consciousness and is not inspired by it. She is not self-conscious in a way that leads other modernists to insight; she is only increasingly made aware of her own worthlessness. O'Neill underscores that worthlessness by presenting the role of wife as one based on constant humiliation and defined by Tyrone's need to feel he has made "good bargains" in life—he makes others pay the price he won't pay.

Throughout the play, O'Neill presents Mary as someone living in a dream (especially as she becomes more and more detached by the effects of taking morphine) that might have made sense for Rip Van Winkle but, protracted into the twentieth century, simply increases her sense of disorientation and alienation. She says at one point, early in the play, "None of us can help the things life has done to us. They're done before you realize it, and once they're done they make you do other things until at last everything comes between you and what you'd like to be, and you've lost your true self forever." For students who have studied Irving, the language Mary uses here will seem reminiscent of Rip's "identity crisis" when he returns to the village after his twenty-year sleep. Later in the play, thinking aloud to the hired woman, Cathleen, Mary ties that disorientation to the death of what students might see as her own American Dream. She says, about the fog, "It hides you from the world and the world from you. You feel that everything has changed, and nothing is what it seemed to be. No one can find or touch you any more." Her language clearly echoes Irving's here, but it also conveys the isolation of American self-reliance carried to its historical extreme and epitomized in the role of twentieth-century American wife and mother—Mary must be self-reliant to survive and must do so in a world devoid of human context other than her own family. She asks the play's central question: "What is it I'm looking for? I know it's something I lost."

Her son Edmund, the autobiographical voice for O'Neill himself, is the only character who understands his mother's drug addiction as the play progresses and who suffers the consequences of trying to articulate the kind of pain she feels. In Edmund's statements, students who have read twentieth-century European literature will hear connections to Camus and Beckett. Edmund also feels the absence of home; and referring to his nebulous, nameless lack of power to control his life, he says, "They never come back! Everything is in the bag! It's all a frame-up! We're all fall guys and suckers and we can't beat the game!" Later he calls himself "a stranger who never lives at home." Like Mary, he would like to "be alone with myself in another world where truth is untrue and life can hide from itself," but he chooses poetry rather than morphine to ease his own pain, and then must confront his own failure as a poet. In a scene with his father, Edmund says, "I just stammered. That's the best I'll ever do. I mean, if I live. Well, it will be faithful realism, at least. Stammering is the native eloquence of us fog people!" In depicting Edmund's "stammering," O'Neill underscores both the need to express modern consciousness and the difficulty of finding the words for it. Other twentieth-century writers will take some comfort in making the attempt; Edmund's "faithful realism" prevents him from idealizing his "stammering." In brother Jamie's cynicism ("The truth is there is no cure") and father James's despair ("A waste!, a drunken hulk, done with and finished!"), O'Neill completes his portrait of the disintegration of the American psyche and American family life and yet presents that portrait within the conventions of literary Realism.

T. S. ELIOT

"The Love Song of J. Alfred Prufrock" works well to read closely with students. Find images in the poem that serve as Eliot's "objective correlative" for Prufrock's particular emotions and for the state of feeling in the modern world (as Eliot saw it). *The Waste Land* raises a problem students have with Modernism generally: that so many twentieth-century poets make extensive use of classical allusions or interweave references to Renaissance painters or quote writers in languages other than English. Berating students for not having a classical education doesn't help them much. Discuss the poem in context with "Tradition and the Individual Talent," in which Eliot defends his own method and describes the good poet as the one who is able to "develop or procure the consciousness of the past."

Although Eliot presents a "waste land" as his variation on the "diminished thing" that symbolizes human personality and culture in the modern world, his answer to the oven bird's question is not to make something (entirely) new or to show Stevens's snow man confronting "the nothing that is not there" and inventing a "supreme fiction," but rather to surrender the individual personality of the poet. The poem becomes a medium that expresses the essential history of the culture. Eliot writes in his essay, "Impressions and experiences which are important for the man may take no place in the poetry, and those which become important in the poetry may play quite a negligible part in the man, the personality." How does Eliot depersonalize the poet in *The Waste Land*? He combines traditions from mythology and legend, anthropology (with references to vegetation myths and fertility rites), classical literature and culture (including Shakespeare and Wagner), the Tarot, and comparative religious cultures; and he juxtaposes these traditions with images of isolation, fragmentation, uncertainty, and waste, hoping to use "these fragments" to "shore against" the ruins that are Eliot's variation on Frost's "diminished thing."

CLAUDE MCKAY

McKay is a strong inclusion in any survey of modern American literature, especially if the course is intended to look into complex relationships between form and content in verse. McKay's form choices may come as a surprise, for the notion still seems to run deep (not only among students but also among critics and teachers) that "free verse" or at least unrhymed, loosely metered verse signifies honesty, spontaneity, and emotional intensity; whereas sonnets, rhymed couplets, and other traditional patterns all suggest accommodation to social practices, conventional beliefs, and ordinary values. McKay is a passionate writer and a political radical, and he writes sonnets, uses rhyme royal, and frequently employs forms reminiscent of Pope, Wheatley, and Longfellow. What's going on here? Does compression and control in such forms diminish the strength of their intention? Or does confinement, in some way, seem to increase their heat? Is there an element of defiant performance here, reminiscent of Equiano perhaps, or of Ellison? In other words, does McKay's demonstration of such expertise, in what has been predominantly a white European literary practice, parallel or support some purpose that can be found in the content of these verses?

KATHERINE ANNE PORTER

Porter's fiction shows a vast range of subject, and the selections in the anthology seem so different as to defy comparison. *Pale Horse, Pale Rider* is set in a newsroom of a small American city, where the great drama of World War I is observed, at least at first, from afar. "Flowering Judas" is about life on the edge, dangerous complicity with an apparently doomed revolutionary movement in Mexico. But look at the predicament of the woman at the center of each story and a deep harmony will emerge. The Porter world, whatever the specific scene, is often a world of dislocation, of the self in the predicament of being, or feeling itself to be, a nearly helpless witness to one's own life; the barriers to action or to direct engagement or even to any vital feelings other than profound loneliness can seem too great to cross.

Porter's story of the last months of World War I has maintained its intensity for more than seven decades, and students will probably be drawn into it strongly, once they apprehend the times and circumstances in which the narrative is set. This is a story of war, love, and epidemic, of massive losses not only on battlefields of France and Belgium but also at home. Before getting too far into *Pale Horse, Pale Rider*, you might want to spend some time ensuring that students understand the size of the American Expeditionary Force that broke the long stalemate of the war, the millions of lives wasted since 1914 in trenches along the Meuse and the Somme, and the devastation that a virulent form of influenza brought to field hospitals, rear echelon encampments, and finally to British, French, German, and American cities and towns, in a time when antibiotics and other effective medications were still only a dream. In 1918–19, hundreds of thousands of people died of the disease, and Miranda's grimly described hospitalization really is a trip into the Valley of Death.

But how does such a story avoid the pitfalls of melodrama? Students have been through many overwrought versions of the essential tale before this: the (outwardly) hard-boiled independent woman, lonely at heart; the young hero and the budding romance, cut short by world-scale crisis or catastrophe. To look for answers, you might begin with one of the long, risky paragraphs late in the narrative, describing Miranda's hallucinations under the grip of fever and weakness. In these paragraphs, Porter looks into the inventories of the imagination, the words and images that Miranda's life in journalism, her visits of mercy to hospital wards, and her ordinary citizenship in a wartime America have loaded into her unconscious.

You could begin, for example, with the paragraph beginning with the portentous sentence "The road to death is a long march beset with all evils, and the heart fails little by little at each new terror, the mind lets up its own bitter resistance and to what end?" You might point out that Miranda's dream of Dr. Hildesheim borrows images from a famous anti-German propaganda poster of those years and from accounts often repeated in the popular press of German atrocities in their attack through Flanders and northern France. This is the visual and verbal rhetoric that an ostensibly hardened Miranda has resisted at the opening of the story, as a cynic in a newsroom populated by would-be H. L. Menckens, self-styled tough guys resisting the programmatic emotionalism in the streets. If their bravado has proved fallacious and derivative and thin, what about her own? Structurally, there is a reversal here of an early scene in which Miranda has gone to visit wounded soldiers in a ward and has felt rejected and hypocritical, pretending to an empathy that she did not feel. How does that early scene resonate here? If there is an irony to this arrangement, does it strike you as mechanical, contrived, or richer than that?

Miranda is a new sort of woman on the American scene, an independent professional, working with "the boys" in a profession that until recently had been almost entirely male. She works with language, writing "Ye Towne Gossyp," evidently a chatty column of local scandals, advice, and miscellaneous encouragement—in other words, she writes to amuse, distract, nurture popular beliefs; and she has grown tired of her own voice and the avalanche of telling and exhorting that the war effort has brought on. Where is Miranda psychologically at the end of this story? At some point, you might want to compare the final pages of *Pale Horse, Pale Rider* to the closing of Larsen's *Quicksand*, and consider how surprising or appropriate these endings are to their respective narratives. Or like Marlow in Conrad's *Heart of Darkness*, Miranda nearly dies, but recovers, and goes on into the future neither broken nor consoled, but apparently in some other condition of mourning. Adam is dead, and at the close of the story Miranda is responding to a "dazed silence," a silence that seems to be as much within herself as without. How does this ending compare, say, with the final paragraphs of *The Great Gatsby*? Is Porter contributing to a new and fittingly Modernist way of concluding a narrative about crisis, loss, and survival? In what way might her psychological condition suggest a broader or national response to the end of a terrible war?

ZORA NEALE HURSTON

Hurston worked as an anthropologist as well as a writer and wrote "The Eatonville Anthology" after graduating from Barnard College and returning to her birthplace in Eatonville, Florida, to transcribe the folktales and folkways she remembered from childhood. Like her later *Mules and Men* (1935), both the "Anthology" and the essay "How It Feels to Be Colored Me" explore origins of consciousness—both collective and individual—that Hurston transforms into mythology, her attempt to explain the creation of the universe, to understand why the world is the way it is. Mythology does not overpower Hurston's fiction; rather, it empowers her use of folk history. Ask students to locate suggestions of mythology in "The Eatonville Anthology"; see, in particular, the opening of Section XIV: "Once 'way back yonder before the stars fell all the animals used to talk just like people." Are there important differences between Hurston's handling of talking-animal folktales and the way Harris told them in the previous century?

The Gilded Six-Bits

Like most of the African American women writers represented in NAAL, Hurston was a risk taker—so much so that her reputation has gone through some dramatic swings in the past forty years. In this story she steers very close, perhaps dangerously so, to certain stereotypes that have been widely exploited over the years. Students who have followed recent controversies about BET and the Def Jam comedy forms will already be aware of the complexities of telling this kind of tale: how it is interpreted can depend very much on who is reading it, and in what context. Where are the stereotypes in "The Gilded Six-Bits"? Is Hurston playing along with them? Subverting them? Correcting them? What kind of audience is this story implicitly intended for and in what kind of political and moral context? Does the story take unexpected turns—not in plotting but in tone? In what ways does Hurston distinguish her own voice, her own perspective, from that of Missy May and Joe Banks?

NELLA LARSEN

Like Larsen's protagonist Helga Crane, Quicksand itself is fast-moving and rest-less, and your students may have responses at the ready in regard to its pace and its surprising leaps among settings and social classes. Larsen plunges her heroine into many different arenas where African American identity is being prescribed, reinvented, and liberated or neglected to find its own way: a repressive school in the South, the Black Belt in Chicago where Richard Wright situated Native Son, upscale communities within the vibrant culture of Harlem in the twenties; then Copenhagen and a personal experience a bit like Josephine Baker's in Paris; then Harlem again and finally a marriage and an exile into the rural South, where the novel reaches its eerie end.

Students may find this journey dizzying, headlong, and be inclined to explain it away as reflective of Larsen's own life. To suggest that there is control here, and direction, and a stylistic roving here to parallel the leaps around the map, you might ask them what novels or stories Quicksand reminds them of—as a narrative of growing up, a story of a young independent woman trying to find her way, a story of being a stranger in every community you encounter, of being driven by a name-less yearning. The answers may lead back into NAAL if you're reading Quicksand as part of a sequence in the anthology: students may recall Edna's predicament in The Awakening, moments in Yezierskas's "The Lost 'Beautifulness,' " Chesnutt's "The Wife of His Youth," and episodes and narrative strategies in Hart Crane, Garland, Cather, and other American naturalistic authors. Larsen's is a literate book, in uneasy conversation with an American literary tradition, predominantly white, with which, like Helga Crane, Larsen has to achieve some mix of accommodation and individuality. In a sense, the conflict here—a stylistic and thematic conflict—may prove more interesting than the plot and the major character herself. Is Larsen's portrait of Helga reminiscent of Edna Pontillier? You might note how often Helga feels faint or physically ill at moments of crisis relating to herself, her hopes, her feeling of entrapment, and compare those moments to ones in which Edna is overcome by fever or heat or fatigue just when she seems to be on the cusp of an important recognition. The conversation may range outward from the reading list in the course, and encompass other novels and stories that students often have in common. What about other literary characters of the twenties? Fitzgerald's Nick Carraway in *The Great Gatsby*; or the people in "Winter Dreams"; or Carrie Meeber in Dreiser's *Sister Carrie*, who also drifts into Chicago and is swept away by happenstance and luck; or Isabel Archer in "The Portrait of a Lady"? It's likely that your students will have encountered many stories about young people driven by a deep dissatisfaction with their own circumstances and by yearnings that are a mix of the superficial and the spiritual, the material and the profound. *Quicksand* is a story in dialogue with those other stories, affirming that the African American experience both is, and is *not*, a story that modern readers will find familiar and classifiable as a tale of the American Dream—of making it and of being accepted, of coming home.

Once the kinship of *Quicksand* has been glimpsed, you and your students may want to engage tough questions regarding Helga's appeal as a protagonist. Is she likeable? How much empathy are we supposed to feel with her? Some of your students may find her too headstrong, too fast and passionate and abrupt and self-centered in her choices, perhaps an African American forebear of the Scarlet O'Hara that Margaret Mitchell would create about ten years later. Difficult, hard-to—love heroines take hold in American letters around the end of the nineteenth century: Dreiser's Carrie, Wharton's Lily Bart and Fleda Vetch, Frederic's Celia Madden, Norris's Trina Seipp, and closer to Larsen's time, Fitzgerald's Daisy Buchanan and Nicole Diver. So unpleasant leading women are familiar in American letters—but what are the risks of assigning these difficult qualities to a mulatto protagonist?

If students feel empathy with Helga—and it's likely that they will—then some attention can be paid to her story as potentially tragic—what missed opportunities and strategic or moral mistakes lead her into her final disaster. Are her crucial decisions foolish ones—quitting the school in Naxos, turning down the marriage proposal of Axel Olson, losing or turning away from other bright and well-heeled suitors back in America? When Olson paints her portrait, and Helga sees there "some disgusting sensual creature with her features," has Olson revealed a kind of truth that Helga does not want to face? Or has Helga encountered and been repelled by a deep-lying European assumption about the "real" nature of African American women?

When in a kind of spell Helga marries the Reverend Pleasant Brown and passes away from us in a long giddy sleep of empty rural life and endless child-bearing, is Larsen dealing out retribution like the ending of a Greek tragedy? Is this the ending you were expecting? What are the implications and dangers of portraying a "down home" resolution as a kind of disaster, perhaps a fate worse than death for such a heroine? You may find that in the closing pages, many of your students were poised for Helga's death, a suicide like Edna's or a succumbing to disease, to provide a tidy close to this wandering tale. They may be irked by what they encounter instead. Why *doesn't* Larsen end the story with Helga's death? What unfinished struggles are suggested by the ending we do get, with Helga returning to a species of physical if not psychological health as Mrs. Brown and bearing her fifth child?

DOROTHY PARKER

Parker has been experiencing renewed attention in recent years, but more as a victim of an odd literary context and period than as a writer whose talent came to full flower. If students show interest in the Algonquin Round Table and the *New Yorker* group of the twenties and thirties, you might recommend that they look at the film *Mrs. Parker and the Vicious Circle* (1995) or consult James R. Gaines's *Wit's End: Days and Nights of the Algonquin Round Table* (1977), a highly readable short book that describes Parker's world as one in which talent was suborned into superficial display. Students may want to talk about wit and irony (by Parker or other modern practitioners) and whether these strategies take a reader, or a writer, anywhere worth going. Does Parker's humor have connections to the general tradition of American humorist writing? Can students talk about the ways in which Parker achieves her linguistic effects, both in her short poems and in "The Waltz"? What kind of audience seems implicit here? Can they comment on the suggestion that in Parker's poems, "wit and elegance costume moods of emptiness and despair"? What happens if we compare Parker's "The Waltz" with Gilman's "The Yellow Wall-paper"? Where does the Parker legacy show up, in contemporary American humor and satire?

E. E. CUMMINGS

Consider what it would mean to ask whether Cummings is a "serious" poet. Describe the ways in which he experiments with language in poems such as "anyone lived in a pretty how town" or "my father moved through dooms of love," and consider their effects. Ask students to read "Buffalo Bill's" or " 'next to of course god america i" out loud and discuss what happens to poetry that is meant to be read, not spoken. Locate modern themes in Cummings; place him in context with Frost (compare "pity this busy monster,manunkind" with Frost's "Departmental"), Jeffers ("i sing of Olaf glad and big" with "Shine, Perishing Republic"), or Moore ("Poem,or Beauty Hurts Mr. Vinal" with "Poetry").

JEAN TOOMER

Discuss "Georgia Dusk" as a variation on Emerson's call for an American poet a century earlier. What, for Toomer, will be the characteristics of that "genius of the South"? And what will be the literary tradition for that "singer"? Locate Toomer in the context of other black writers or writers about black experience in *NAAL*, for example, Harris and Chesnutt. What does it mean, in Toomer, to make "folk-songs from soul sounds"?

Analyze "Fern," first from the narrator's point of view and then focusing on Fern herself. What is happening within the speaker as he imaginatively recreates Fern? What is the literary analogue in Toomer for Du Bois's "double consciousness"? How does Toomer evoke "the souls of black folk" in this excerpt from *Cane*? Place Fern herself in the context of other works by American male writers, such as Poe's "Ligeia" or Anderson's "Mother." Toomer gives Fern a moment of speech when she asks, "Doesn't it make you mad?" and then his narrator interprets what she means. Does he give her voice? Consider the last sentence in "Fern": "Her name, against the chance that you might happen down that way, is Fernie May Rosen." What, in this sentence, gives the reader more clues to Fern's identity than Toomer's earlier idealization of her? Is there any "real" Fern beneath Toomer's portrait of her as his narrator's muse? Note Toomer's reference to the black woman who "once saw the mother of Christ and drew her in charcoal on the courthouse wall." The allusion is one piece of evidence to suggest that black women, as well as men, have tried to record their visions; they have been artists as well as inspirations for art.

GENEVIEVE TAGGARD

If you have brought Juhasz's framework into your presentation of women poets (see discussion of Moore), Taggard's poetry will seem quite in advance of her generation, because much of her poetry derives from women's experiences (as in "With Child" and "Mill Town"), and particularly women from poor and working-class origins. Indeed, Taggard's poetry poses a challenge in defining aesthetic Modernism. In response to Frost's famous question in "The Oven Bird," "What to make of a diminished thing?" Taggard would seem to answer: sing! strike! move! In Taggard, poetry and politics become intertwined and women participate in both (as in "At Last the Women Are Moving" and "Mill Town"). Even more startling in Taggard is the presence of class politics. More than any other poet in the 1914–45 period (with the exception of black poets S. Brown and Hughes), Taggard's poetry addresses class issues; indeed, her poetry gives voice to working-class women and men, and like Brown and Hughes, she privileges "everyday" experience (as in "Everyday Alchemy").

To demonstrate the contrast between a white male poet's apolitical approach and Taggard's interweaving of one woman's experience with the experience of class and with politics, read "A Middle-aged, Middle-class Woman at Midnight" against Frost's "An Old Man's Winter Night." In Taggard's poem, age, cold, and anxiety about the state of the world allow her "middle-class woman" speaker to cross class boundaries and align her own struggle to sleep ("A woman took veronal in vain") with the "stink of poverty": "I hope the people win."

As part of your discussion of Taggard, ask students to think about the relationship between poetry and politics. In Latin America, poetry has long served political ends and has a vital life among people outside the college classroom. In the United States, many people believe that poetry (and all art) should have nothing to do with politics. Taggard is herself aware of her departure from convention in this regard. For Taggard, poetry must move people, and must move them collectively.

F. SCOTT FITZGERALD

Students who have read *The Great Gatsby* will sense that in some ways "Winter Dreams" is a compact version of Fitzgerald's most famous novel and that obsessions and mixed emotions that characterize Nick Carraway are also present here, in Dexter Green and the nameless narrator, who often sounds like Nick in his uncanny mix of adulation and contempt for what he sees in the world of the rich and the glamorous. To start the conversation a bit enigmatically and get the students from fresh perspectives, you could put two famous epigrams on the board. One from Nietzsche:

In the end one loves one's desire, not the thing desired.

and one from Oscar Wilde:

There are only two tragedies in life: one is not getting what one wants, and the other is getting it.

After the class probes the truth of these epigrams, you might test them on values of Dexter and the narrator of "Winter Dreams." Does Dexter love Judy Jones? Is the fascination with her or with a life and a social class that she represents? If she had not been out of reach or mercurial in Dexter's adolescence and young manhood, would he have pursued her as hotly? In his emotional turmoil at the end of the story, what is going on? Is Dexter's regret for lost time and lost opportunity, for a life with Judy that he never had, entirely an experience of pain? Or do you sense a pleasure lurking somewhere in his nostalgia, a final superiority—of himself over Judy or of men over "women" as the upper classes in the early twentieth century had constructed women—as lovely and ephemeral acquisitions? Some students will recall moments in *The Great Gatsby* that resonate strongly with "Winter Dreams"—the moments where Nick imagines Gatsby acquiring Daisy after so much longing . . . and feeling regret and a measure of disappointment that the quest is now over. Nick himself, as the narrator of Gatsby, has similar moments with Jordan Baker: his desire for her rises when she moves out of his reach.

All of which can lead up to a more complex conversation, about the narrator of "Winter Dreams" and his unsteady empathy with Dexter Green. There are moments when this narrator seems superior to and dismissive of this Black Bear Lake world of golf and fashion and money and a bit contemptuous of young Dexter for falling for it. At other times, however, the narration seems as breathlessly credulous as Dexter does—or a strange commingling of the two sentiments, the wonder and the contempt. Ask a student to read aloud the paragraph that begins section II of "Winter Dreams," searching for the tone of it. What do your students hear in these lines? Something like the uneasy voice of Nick at the opening or closing of *The Great Gatsby*? Why does Fitzgerald favor this predicament, the hero on the edge of the glamorous life, looking at it with these conflicting emotions, suffering from and in an odd way delighting in his exile? When Dexter says, at the very end, "That thing will come back no more," does he believe that wholeheartedly? Has he stopped looking for the glamorous and impossible dream? Will he ever be capable of loving a woman for what she is, not what she represents as a status symbol? Are Fitzgerald's narratives unique because they tell stories of growing up? Or is it that the major characters in them never quite grow up as much as they tell themselves they have?

"Babylon Revisited" comes from an array of stories about men and women who have made it, people who have lived beyond the year or two of glory that Gatsby achieved before he died, perhaps mercifully, in his own West Egg swimming pool. These are stories of people who move unhappily through glorious locales: the Riviera and Paris, the comfortable private places in midtown Manhattan, the exclusive resorts of Switzerland. An opening question for your class: what differentiates this kind of story from the modern trash novel, the kind sold in drugstores or

beach-supply shops, about the woes of being a supermodel, a Hollywood sex symbol, a magnate in fashion or the perfume trade? If students grope for an answer,
you might grab a paragraph or two and suggest the difference: no matter how dis-
sipated or dislikeable the Fitzgerald protagonist or how unsympathetic—or
voyeuristic—we might feel toward the general situation that the story offers us,
there are gorgeously phrased moments of insight about human nature, the mingled
emotions of going back and coming home, the internal conflicts of wanting and *not*
wanting in the same instant. As flush times and bad times come and go, Fitzgerald's reputation will have to rely on his prose to carry him through, and with the
sound and pace and agility of his prose your discussion can begin and end.

LOUISE BOGAN

Bogan is hard to categorize, which may be an inconvenience for critics but is
possibly a testament to her versatility, her range of voices and tastes, and her quest
to express the many dimensions of modern experience by using a variety of vocabularies and forms. By this point in the course, students will have a number of
strong American poets in mind already; and if their experience does not include
much Auden or Yeats (writers whom Bogan admired), they may have fresh recol-
lections of Dickinson and Whitman—who are often played off as opposites in later
nineteenth-century American verse. When does Bogan sound like Dickinson?
When like Whitman? When the voice is reminiscent of Dickinson, are the themes
similar as well? When she works in the long, free-verse lines of Whitman, is she
playing ventriloquist or is she adapting Whitman's free, buoyant voice to a different purpose? In sum, does Bogan seem like an imitator of yesterday's poetry? Or
does she transform these established voices into something unique and new?

WILLIAM FAULKNER

As students begin to read *As I Lay Dying* they experience fragmentation and dislocation. After assigning only the first five or ten monologues, you could spend
much of the first class period allowing them to discuss the expectations they bring
to a novel as readers and how *As I Lay Dying* disrupts those expectations. The initial confusion they feel as a result of Faulkner's disparate narrative sections and
points of view can help them understand Modernism as a challenge to their ways
of seeing the world. If allowed to express their own disorientation, they begin to
use Faulkner's novel as an exploration of ways of knowing (epistemology) as well
as of ways of being (ontology) in a disordered universe.

We begin with a preliminary discussion of the book's title in light of earlier thematic discussions of Modernism. What does the reader expect, given this title? And
how does the novel, from its opening sections, thwart those expectations? Who *is*
the "I" of the title? Just Addie Bundren? What or who else does that first-person
point of view include? And how does the past tense of the title create a preliminary
absurdity before the reader begins the novel? In eliciting students' initial confusion
about opening sections, try to give them the experience of posing Faulkner's own
questions as he lets his characters speak. What do they know as they read, and how
do they know it? You might closely read Darl's opening section. Where does
Faulkner "locate" the reader? Part of what "lies dying" for readers new to Faulkner

is any reliance on the author as someone who will facilitate knowing. Faulkner shows readers only what his characters know, not what readers may feel the need to know.

As students proceed through the novel (over the span of an additional two or three class periods), you can spend class time describing what Faulkner is doing. A class might want to consider novelistic conventions—character development, plot, use of a narrator, chronology, narrative form—and assess the extent to which Faulkner adheres to or deviates from traditional elements of the novel. In the collective act of description, students make numerous statements about *As I Lay Dying*: they note the number of narrators (fifteen by the novel's end) and sections (fifty-nine separate monologues); they distinguish among the narrative voices by making descriptive observations: Darl has, by far, the most sections; some central characters—Jewel and Addie—have only one monologue; monologues by Darl, Jewel, Dewey Dell, Anse, Vardaman, Cash, and Addie create a nexus of family dynamics; other characters—Cora, Tull, Peabody, Samson, Whitfield, Armstid, MacGowan, Moseley—express a wide range of possible social responses to the Bundrens. These descriptive statements may make some students feel that they have "figured out" the novel; and you may observe that their attempts to "solve" the novel may be premature and may actually be covering over their uneasiness as readers, lest they become lost in a work without omniscient authority.

They also establish collective understandings about the characters in the novel that become shared facts and that serve as a prelude to interpretation. The attempt to bury Addie becomes the family members' ostensible reason for the journey to Jefferson, which provides Faulkner with his novel's narrative structure; but most of the Bundrens also have other reasons for the trip. Cash wants the free ride back to Tull's, where he is supposed to work on his barn, and he dreams of a "talking machine." Vardaman remembers something in a store window (the toy train) that Santa wouldn't have sold to town boys. Anse wants to get some new teeth. Dewey Dell hopes to buy a drug-induced abortion. Darl twice narrates events at which he could not have been present and in other sections appears to "know" things that others have not told him (he knows Dewey Dell is pregnant and that Anse is not Jewel's father). Among all of Addie's survivors, Jewel seems best able to feel the depths of his connection to his mother, to mourn her death, and to achieve emotional resolution. (At the end of Cora's section just preceding Addie's monologue, Addie tells Cora that Jewel "is my cross and he will be my salvation. He will save me from the water and from the fire," and indeed, Jewel first saves Addie's coffin in the ford, and later from the fire Darl has set to Gillespie's barn.)

The group effort to figure out what can be known in reading the novel becomes a pedagogical analogue to the Bundrens' own journey. The parallel tensions of burying Addie (for the Bundrens) and figuring out what is happening in the novel (for the members of the class) comment on the act of modernist reading: without the storyteller/guide of traditional narrative, the task of arriving at an understanding of Faulkner's text (analogous to bringing the coffin to Jefferson) places much of the burden of creation on the act of reading itself.

As a result of description, students move toward interpretation. The elements of form they observe lead to their perceptions of character. For example, they note the repetition in the form of the images Jewel and Vardaman create as a way of grieving for Addie: "Jewel's mother is a horse" and "My mother is a fish." Then they can ask, which image works best to help the character resolve grief? In responding to the question, they explore the relationship between image and feeling, between word and meaning, between the novel as a form and the attempt to order the fragments of human consciousness.

Central to exploring Faulkner's search for theme, meaning, and order is Addie's single monologue, placed off-center in the novel in the second half, long after Addie has died and the Bundrens have begun their journey to Jefferson. To what extent does Addie exist in the novel? Although she gives the other characters their ostensible reason for action, she herself does not act. Neither does she speak, except to acknowledge Cash as he builds her coffin. Her monologue in the novel may appear to give her a voice, but her death has already silenced her and prevents her from making her genuine presence known. She exists for others as their own projected need. Interestingly, what occupies her thinking in her monologue is the uselessness of words. Discuss Addie's various statements about words: "words dont ever fit even what they are trying to say at"; a word is "just a shape to fill a lack"; a name is a "word as a shape, a vessel . . . a significant shape profoundly without life like an empty door frame"; words are "just sounds" that people have "for what they never had and cannot have until they forget the words." In the narrative structure of Faulkner's novel, Addie is herself "just a shape to fill a lack."

The visual image of the coffin that appears in Tull's third monologue typographically disrupts, once again, the reader's expectations; for although Faulkner has violated readers' expectations of linearity and wholeness in narrating As I Lay Dying, he at least uses words. With the visual image of the coffin, followed later by Addie's description of words, Faulkner creates a series of concentric visual images or shapes that serve both to contain his novel's meaning and to express the limits of narrative form. In Faulkner's thinking, each of the following is associatively synonymous: the visual figure of the coffin, the name Addie, the narrative form he has chosen for the book (it is spatial, a world laid out by compass and rule), and the book itself. As I Lay Dying effectively becomes Addie's coffin, a fiction in which she is silenced by the title; and like her family in Jefferson cemetery, she might be listening to the other fifty-eight monologues, but she'll "be hard to talk to."

As I Lay Dying can have a profound effect on students who are themselves struggling to emerge from silence and to explore the world's order and form, to discover whether it has any or whether they must join the human collective task of making form and meaning. Students may empathize with Addie's silence and may find it reflected in Vardaman's obsession with his mother as a fish or in Cash's inability to speak except to focus on the coffin's construction or need for balance. As I Lay Dying demonstrates the novelist's own struggle to emerge from silence, and students may believe that it is only partly successful or that Faulkner is saying that it is possible to achieve only partial success.

In evaluating the relationship between the construction of form—as a coffin or a novel—and of meaning, ask students to think about Darl. Is he crazy? If so, what makes him crazy? Interestingly, Darl has by far the least difficulty with silence; he can speak for others as well as for himself. Is he a mere scapegoat at the novel's end? Do the other members of his family believe he "knows too much"? Or has he

failed in some basic way to create a form for what he knows? Darl is the only character who cannot make a connection between himself and some concrete object.
He has no coffin, horse, fish, abortion, or reason to go to town. Students may find
it difficult to believe that Darl "goes crazy" at the end of the novel, in part because,
in many of his monologues, he closely resembles a traditional omniscient narrator,
one whose own identity does not intrude. Who then is Darl? If he cannot express
his connection in terms of an image, a form—coffin or novel—his knowledge and
creativity become destructive. Darl simply cannot "be contained" in a form; therefore, as Cash realizes at novel's end, "this world is not his world; this life his life."
In Darl's failure to achieve a form for human consciousness, Faulkner implies his
own struggle for meaning. What to make of a diminished thing?—make something
of it, find a word to fill the lack, write a novel that will reconcile human need for
form with the formlessness of human consciousness. Cash's briefest monologue
locates *As I Lay Dying* in the progression of Faulkner's career as a novelist: "It was-
n't on a balance. I told them that if they wanted it to tote and ride on a balance,
they would have to." *As I Lay Dying* rides precariously, a book about silent knowing necessarily told in words. Expecting to be told, students emerge from *As I Lay
Dying* with the uneasy knowledge that words no longer—for the Modernist—carry
ultimate authority. As Addie expresses it, "the high dead words in time seemed to
lose even the significance of their dead sound." Perhaps literary authority itself is
at least a part of what "lies dying" in Faulkner's modern fictional universe.

HART CRANE

Crane can be hard to engage with in a quick-moving survey course. His prosody
varies; as a visionary poet and a twentieth-century bard, he takes on immense subjects; his verse presents a first-time reader with a bewildering range of moods and
temperaments; and the story of his short, turmoiled life can shadow the poetry so
much that the verse can become subordinate to the biography, mere exhibits in an
investigation of the man. If you want students to appreciate, on the fly, Crane's
ambitions as a poet and the variety of voices that he mastered, the best beginning
might be to take two extended stanzas from two different parts of *The Bridge* and
examine them closely and comparatively. For instance, you might have students
read carefully, perhaps aloud in class, the first stanzas of "Powhatan's Daughter"
and "Cutty Sark"—rhymed, formal, grand-style verse, and Cummings-like, unpredictable, wide-open lines. Why the difference? Do other voices resonate in these
different stanzas? In other words, are these different voices in some ways a kind of
incantation, calling up not just different historical moments, but different eras in
the history of the American imagination? Can a poet or a poem encompass such
diversity? Whitman tried to embrace all of American experience, but his prosody
did not show this kind of variety. What do students think of Crane's experiment,
not just in seeing but in creating one long poem in such a variety of styles?

ERNEST HEMINGWAY AND THOMAS WOLFE

Hemingway and Wolfe are near neighbors in *NAAL*, and there is much to be
gained in looking at them together if one of your objectives is to help students
increase their awareness of the variety of literary styles that were applied to mod-

ern experience. Students can see here a spectacular contrast, opposite ways of refreshing American narrative catching the feel of contemporary life: Hemingway the minimalist, the stoic, the great doubter of emotional and intellectual display, and Wolfe, the ecstatic describer, the lover of adjectives and unending periodic sentences, the believer in saying. Judging by the post-1945 prose fiction that is included in *NAAL* and other canon-making anthologies, Hemingway seems to have won the face-off: Vonnegut, Carver, Beattie, Silko, and many other contemporary writers show his influence. Why did the Hemingway style prevail? What was it about modern experience that made minimalism appropriate or more so than Wolfe's ebullience? If students need some coaxing to engage in these speculative questions, you might ask them to compare the closing paragraphs of "The Lost Boy" and "The Snows of Kilimanjaro." They are both elegiac in a sense, both about loss, death, and the problem of understanding the meaning of one human life. But the tonal and thematic differences will be strongly apparent, and contrasting the passages can open up a broad discussion about saying, and *not* saying, as literary and artistic values.

STERLING A. BROWN

Brown chooses the principle of contrast between white man and black man as his subject in "Mister Samuel and Sam" and "Master and Man." In these poems, the differences between white and black are settled by the common denominators of death and harvest time; and yet as the poems appear to resolve differences, they also end by highlighting the inequalities within those common denominators (both Samuel and Sam may die, but the harvest is more bounteous for the Master than for the Man). Other poems (such as "He Was a Man") also derive their form from the principle of contrast; but the holding back of detail in early stanzas typical of a ballad about the life of a man yields to more detail, and the ballad's "story" turns out to be the progress by which this "man" is reduced to not a man in the eyes of white people. The promise of unfolding in the ballad form is negated (and demonstrated by the poem's consistent use of negatives—"It wasn't about," "Didn't catch him," "It didn't come off")—by the poem's ultimate irony, that it's impossible to write a story of a man's life when he isn't viewed as a man. Thus the title's assertion ("He Was a Man") becomes the poem's primary message. "Break of Day" continues the ballad/blues form and a variation on the same theme: "Man in full" becomes "Long past due" by the poem's end.

LANGSTON HUGHES

Before the Harlem Renaissance writers of the 1920s (Hurston, Toomer, S. Brown, Hughes, and Cullen are all associated with this period), most black writing took the form either of the slave narrative of the middle nineteenth century or of "racial uplift" literature or polemical writing characteristic of the turn of the twentieth century (and represented in *NAAL* by Washington and Du Bois). While most African American writers wrote for white audiences, Hughes may be the first African American writer to view his white reader's interest, and his role as speaking voice, as a form of encounter not unlike those early encounters between Europeans and native peoples during the period of exploration and colonization. You can begin teaching Hughes with "Visitors to the Black Belt" and discussing the two-sided perspective this poem gives about Harlem. More than an exercise in language ("Across the tracks" versus "here on this side of the tracks"), the poem ends with a simple question and answer that resonates with the problem of postcolonialism. "Who're you, outsider? / Ask me who am I." In these lines, the poet teaches the reader, by means of the expected question, how to ask the speaker who he or she is rather than to assume he or she already knows. If the outsider learns to know his or her place as outside, then the person on the inside ("To me it's *here* / In Harlem") has room to define himself. So Hughes is pleading with his white audience not to draw conclusions about black life without asking him, without allowing him, to define its reality and meaning and—in other poems (such as "I, Too"; "Refugee in America"; "Madam's Calling Cards"; and "Democracy")—what it means to be an American.

The other side of the experience of encounter involves the responsibility it places on the poet. Echoing Whitman in "I, Too" and self-conscious about both calling for a black American poet and responding to that quasi-Emersonian call in "Note on Commercial Theatre," Hughes responds very simply: "I reckon it'll be / Me myself! / Yes, it'll be me." From the perspective of literature of encounter, if Hughes can imagine a white readership "encountering" black experience and black art with genuine interest (perhaps for the first time on a large scale during the Harlem Renaissance), then he has the responsibility to make certain that experience and that art don't become "colonized," commercialized ("You've taken my blues and gone—"). The person who recognizes that colonization is taking place must struggle against it, especially by resisting being appropriated in a white someone else's image. Thus Hughes moves beyond S. Brown, whose poetry stresses contrast and counterpoint, to include contradiction and the two-way experience of encounter.

Students will also find in Hughes's work an appreciation for black women's struggles and an attempt to represent women's experiences. In one of his greatest poems, "Mother to Son," he also connects his own answer for the modernist question to a woman's voice and a woman's experience. If you read this poem closely with students, you might focus on the contrast between the mother's description of the stairway itself and the image she arrives at ("Life for me ain't been no crystal stair") as a controlling metaphor for her vision. The poem shows the mother arriving at modernist order in the chaos of "sometimes goin' in the dark" by making this particular image. Ask students to consider the numerous connotations of the image of the "crystal stair" as well as the way Hughes is experimenting with levels of diction, in effect raising the level of diction in this phrase. Raising the level of diction and "racial uplift" become ground notes in his work; see, for example, "Genius Child," in which Hughes moves beyond protest to a transcendent belief in the "genius" of black life ("*Kill him*—and let his soul run wild!").

And in the Alberta K. Johnson poems (here represented by "Madam and Her Madam" and "Madam's Calling Cards"), Hughes demonstrates the complexity of the relationship between black woman and white woman. When Alberta responds to her Madam's profession of love by saying "I'll be dogged / If I love you," Hughes is making a simple statement of fact: if relationship with the Madam means that Alberta Johnson has to work even harder, she will indeed be "dogged," for it will kill her; and indeed, Alberta must stop short of "loving" the woman she works for if she is to love herself at all. And that she does love herself is clear in "Madam's Calling Cards": "I hankered to see / My name in print." Both like and unlike Yezierska's characters, Alberta Johnson wants to be an American but doesn't consider herself an immigrant: "There's nothing foreign / To my pedigree."

JOHN STEINBECK

This is a selection from an enormous novel, a favorite on high school English and social studies reading lists—so there's a good chance that several students in a sizable class will know *The Grapes of Wrath* and show enthusiasm for revisiting it. The chapters in *NAAL* are a core sample of an epic story, and attention to Steinbeck's expository style—its poise, its linguistic simplicity, its lack of ostentation in imagery—could open up into a speculative discussion about what kinds of narration are appropriate to this or that moment in modern cultural history. Compare the opening of Chapter 12 to the opening of Fitzgerald's "Winter Dreams" or Porter's *Pale Horse, Pale Rider*. Students can make headway in this comparison by focusing first on verb choices. If these other beginnings, elegant yet uneasy, suggest a psychological unsettledness in passing from youth into age, safety into war and then into prosperous peace, why might Steinbeck tell this tale of economic disaster and mass deracination with such understatement, letting accumulations of details, rather than heated metaphor, do the telling? When Steinbeck intrudes into the tale to comment or moralize, what language and sentence structures does he favor, and why?

COUNTEE CULLEN

He rhymes, he scans, he sounds Shakespearean here, like Keats or Tennyson or Dickinson there—it's not surprising that Cullen's achievement, in his brief life, should have gone through a phase of dismissal after his death. When critics call, as they periodically do, for rough and flamboyant authenticity, such "Phi Beta Kappa verse" can look contrived, a performance to please a wrong audience. To read Cullen that way is to miss the intensity of his struggle within and against a tradition, to master it, join it, and resist it all at the same time. If that description suggests an irrational or paradoxical drive, then it is also human and rich—and because of those conflicts you might consider reading Cullen in light of other conflicted American masters, like Bradstreet and Dickinson, both of whom seem to resound in the *NAAL* selections. You could start with the last two quatrains of "Uncle Jim," quatrains that your students might guess were straight out of Dickinson if they came upon them in another context. Where are the similarities closest? What about the final lines, which veer away from Dickinson's world and look to a different tradition, an African American and family source of wisdom? You could move from here to the ending of "Incident," and again ask how the poem is and is *not* a contemplation in the Dickinson manner. If students sense that Cullen is in a "lover's quarrel" with a literary tradition that both schools him and excludes him, and if they have some experience with canonical British writers, you might try "Yet Do I Marvel" as a poem that pushes back, as it were, against the sonnet tradition of Shakespeare and Milton. Look at the grammar and syntax here: they seem defiantly unmodern at times and far from an African American vernacular. And all this about Tantalus and Sisyphus—is this the kind of allusion that overshadowed English verse more than three hundred years ago? What is Cullen doing? What opposite or conflicted motives might cause him to speak from the heart in such a voice?

D'ARCY MCNICKLE

McNickle's short stories are an early, tentative effort to bring Native American experience into reconciliation with the forms of the modern short story and the tastes of a wide audience. "Hard Riding" is a bit like folktales in the European and Native American tradition, tales in which a know-it-all intruder finally recognizes that people he takes for rustics are cleverer than he is or in which characters who pride themselves on rationality are tripped up by people or animals who are not "reasonable," yet wise. What other stories in the American literary tradition follow this pattern? Are there moments, for example, in Irving and Twain that echo here, as well as moments in the Native American trickster tales? We can focus on point of view and the possible reasons why a Native American writer would tell "Hard Riding" from the point of view of a white official from the Indian Service. Brinder Mather has been on the reservations for five years. When we look at the "crazy Mountain Indians" through his eyes, what do we see? Do these people turn out to be crazy and fulfill his expectations? Later, when he finds himself puzzled or outfoxed by the elders of this people, how does he react? When he says to them, "Boys, you should of elected me judge of your kangaroo court. I would have made a crackerjack," what does he intend? A backhanded compliment? About the last line of the story: what point of view is implied there? Why, suddenly, do we shift to the Indian perspective—and what might be suggested about how people from different cultures can know each other?

RICHARD WRIGHT

Since "The Man Who Was Almost a Man" was published within a year of his great novel *Native Son*, we can look for similarities in theme and in the motivation of characters. This is a story of a crisis brought on by desperation and sudden bizarre circumstance, a crisis that could change or ruin a young man's life forever. In some ways the story reads like a prologue to *Native Son*: set in the Deep South, the tale ends with a potentially dangerous protagonist, in isolation, heading off into the darkness of his fate—perhaps to a place like Chicago. Discuss what "being a man" means to Dave Saunders. Why does the gun represent manhood to him? Does a black boy in the 1930s South automatically get "to be a man like anybody else" or does he have to make that happen? Why does he want the power to "kill anybody, black or white"? How does Dave Saunders move beyond Washington's views of black identity in *Up from Slavery*? Is Dave another heroic fugitive, like Douglass? Does he have a destination at the end of the story?

CARLOS BULOSAN

Bulosan writes about cultural and psychological predicaments and in a sense, from a literary predicament as well. In telling of ordinary people from traditional cultures adjusting to life in America and being changed so much by that experience as to be unable to go home again imaginatively or psychologically, he offers a prose style strongly reminiscent of Hemingway, especially when Hemingway is writing about country people, Italian soldiers, untutored Spanish peasants, Native Americans, or others from beyond his own upbringing and social class. Hemingway's simple prose emphasizes a distance between the teller and the people told about. Does Bulosan's similar style enhance a sense of empathy and understanding with his characters? Establish authorial distance *from* those characters? Oscillate between those two conditions? Does the style, in other words, get us close to Bulosan's relationship to his own heritage, or heritages—Filipino and American? What about Bulosan's use of lines that can read like clichés? "He was like a man who had emerged from light into day, and found the light as blinding as the darkness." "The entire district was quiet as a tomb." "He stood between them, trembling with indecision." How appropriate are such sentences in their respective contexts? What do they suggest about the characters who experience these enormous disruptions in personal identity, or who bear witness to those changes?

MURIEL RUKEYSER

As the headnote points out, Rukeyser saw no conflict between polished, sophisticated verse and art that is politically engaged. Ask students to compare their evaluation of Rukeyser's poems to the way they responded to Taggard or Hughes. Does Rukeyser succeed, in their view, in writing political poetry in a high style? Can Rukeyser reach audiences she might want to reach—and can we tell who those audiences might be?

Poems, for Rukeyser, seem to be one way of making sense of the wars she has lived through. And notice, with students, the range of Rukeyser's historical and political themes. Questions that may draw the most interest, however, involve her development as a stylist, as a creator of poems, over such a long career. It's a sad fact that for convenience critics often classify a poet on the basis of what he or she publishes in the first collections and alter that classification only grudgingly, as an artist matures and takes on new voices and experiments. Ask students to compare the poems in *NAAL*—not in regard to theme or embedded politics but as assemblages of words and sound. What changes in Rukeyser's voice? What dialogue does she engage in, with major voices in the American poetic tradition?

CHAPTER 11

Teaching Notes for Authors and Works: Volume E, American Literature since 1945

Prose since 1945

EUDORA WELTY

"Petrified Man," like many of Welty's great stories about small town Southern life, is a comic marvel but a challenging narrative. As students become happily lost in the blather of the beauty shop, they may miss the fact that there is a plot here, and a meditation on the entanglements of truth, human nature, and the arts of telling. The story is almost entirely dialogue, and Welty gives us very few cues as to where we are or what to think of these people, other than the cues they give about themselves. Discuss the relationship that emerges for us between Leota and Mrs. Fletcher. Does Mrs. Pike exist? At what point do our suspicions begin to rise? Also, you might want to discuss at some point the undercurrent of violence in "Petrified Man." How does Leota's story show her attempt to gain control over her own life? Is she successful? Who is Billy Boy? Why is Leota she taking care of him? And why does Welty give him the last word, the cliché comeback, "If you're so smart, why ain't you rich?"

INTRODUCING STUDENTS TO CONTEMPORARY AMERICAN DRAMA

An introductory course in American literature, especially in twentieth-century or contemporary literature, offers students a unique opening into the experience and meaning of drama as an American literary form. American writers have certainly produced great plays before the contemporary period; and drama served a vital function for Americans as early as Tyler's *The Contrast,* when delighted audiences flocked to view Jonathan's comic rendition of what an "American" in 1787 might look like. Few of your students, however, will have thought much about the uses of drama in their own lives.

One way of beginning is simply to ask students to talk about drama in general. What do they associate with drama? Almost all of them will have read Shakespeare in high school; they may have learned, as a result, that drama belongs to an elitist category of literary forms. Are any students willing to challenge that impression? Others may recall acting in less serious high school plays: comedies, musicals, or plays written especially for high school acting. A few may have written and/or acted in original plays as children or may have parents who participated in community theater groups. Others may associate a family trip to New York City to view a Broadway play as some initiation rite into adult life and culture. Some may associate drama with television situation comedies. Even with this limited range of responses to the experience of drama in their lives, you can begin to explore the variety of functions drama serves. What are some of the differences between literature that one reads, often alone in a room, and a play that may be "taking place" before the viewer's eyes, as that viewer sits in a group with others? Is a play "shown" or "told" when the performers stage it? What kinds of effects does the stage play make possible? And what does it mean to dramatize?

Contemporary drama may elicit students' ability to engage in the reading process more readily than contemporary American poetry, which often seems deliberately to distance the reader with its private meanings, idiosyncratic uses of language and imagery, and sense of barriers between speaking voice and reader of the text. Drama, however, seems to require a viewer; a play creates audience in the process of making character, situation, scene, and dramatic effect; the student, in the act of reading, becomes a collaborator in creating a visual image of the scene.

The plays included in Volumes D and E of *NAAL,* by their very choice of subject matter and realistic treatment, may particularly elicit the student's capacity to become engaged, to become created or re-created as audience. When O'Neill explored American family life in *Long Day's Journey into Night,* he did not exhaust our increasing fascination for the function and fate of the American family. Perhaps the crisis in family life for late-twentieth-century Americans brought on the crisis of consciousness that earlier in the century we associate with World War I and the question of the death or absence of God or design in the modern world. Family life provides a central focus in the work of Williams and Miller. If the American family is dead or absent, who or what "mirrors" an American identity that continues to evolve?

Tennessee Williams

The loss of "Belle Reve" seems to establish the tarnished American Dream as one of Williams's central themes in *A Streetcar Named Desire.* Some students may see Blanche DuBois as a conventional symbol for the loss of that dream: as an unmarried, aging belle, she worries about her clothes, her appearance, and her ability to attract men and uses alcohol to ease her loneliness. But is the loss of desirability, or desire itself, the play's subject? Does Blanche want to find an object for her desire, or to be a desired object?

Williams might have made desire itself a symbol; instead, throughout the play, he focuses on explicit sexuality. What particular scenes define desire as sexual in the play? Ask students to discuss in particular the relationship between Stanley and Stella. Their attraction for each other is sexual, and most students will equate sexuality with heterosexuality and, as it is presented in this play, with a hierarchy of physical dominance (the men in the play, especially Stanley, use physical abuse as part of sexual power; see Stanley's comment to Blanche, " 'Oh! So you want some roughhouse!' ").

But this play revolves around that moment in Blanche's past when she married a "young boy" who tried to find "help" in Blanche for his homosexuality. When she discovers him with "an older man who had been his friend for years" and that day tells him how much he disgusts her, he blows his head off. For most students, presuming that heterosexuality is "normal" and homosexuality "deviant," this moment will establish Blanche's tragedy as a conventional one—she has loved young and lost—and the moment in which homosexuality enters the play will quickly recede. Raise the possibility that from this moment on, Blanche's sexual identity becomes ambiguous, despite the fact that Williams has made her a woman in the play, and suggest also that although Stanley and Stella both seem secure in their gender identities, their very insistence on continuing to reaffirm their sexual relationship by means of violence—thereby asserting Stanley's "manhood" and Stella's "womanliness"—begins to raise the question of the origins of gender determination as well.

What would it mean to say that Blanche's sexual identity becomes ambiguous in the play? Near the end she tells Mitch, "I don't want realism, I want magic! . . . I don't tell truth, I tell what *ought* to be truth." What are Blanche's props for her "magic"? Ask someone to study her array of furs, costumes, jewelry, and perfume in the play; she wears all of the trappings of gendered femininity, like the legendary Mae West (the statuette Mitch wins for Blanche at the amusement park). But her success in establishing her appearance depends on her avoiding the sun and even electric light. Without the costumes, who would Blanche be? What would it mean to call her a "woman"? And who are her consistent objects of desire? Williams is exploring the way female identity is made, not born.

Ask students to think about Stanley's response to Blanche. What motivates Stanley to rape her? What does she represent that makes him want to humiliate her? Blanche sees Stanley—with his phallic "genius"—as subhuman; Stanley sees Blanche as undermining his control over Stella ("You remember the way that it was? Them nights we had together? God, honey, it's gonna be sweet when we can make noise in the night the way that we used to and get the colored lights going with nobody's sister behind the curtains to hear us!"). But Stanley is also acting out of a variation on homophobia—or is homophobia a variation on misogyny? Stanley hates Blanche because she insists on wearing women's costumes and yet refuses to define herself as degenerate or to excuse her sister for her submission to Stanley. In raping Blanche, he is raping the wearing of women's costumes, the flaunting of sexuality by women (or by men who refuse to be "phallic"). No wonder that Stella tells Eunice, "I couldn't believe her story and go on living with Stanley." The sexual "stories" Blanche and Stanley tell totally contradict each other. Blanche exhibits desire without violence; Stanley achieves his through violence and humiliation.

Ask students to talk about Stella's grief at the end of the play: "What have I done to my sister?" How has she betrayed Blanche? Has she also betrayed herself? In what version of sexual desire does the "truth" lie? The play ends with Stanley and Stella, having eliminated Blanche from their world, returning to their hierarchical heterosexual roles: Stella weeps in luxurious abandon, Stanley unbuttons her blouse. Is this desire? or a more destructive lie than Blanche's "magic"?

JOHN CHEEVER

Cheever makes an excellent foil for Williams, and he offers a demonstration of how postwar American literature has brought us a proliferation not only of regional works but of different possibilities regarding the presentation of temperament. Rightly or otherwise, Williams has become associated with hot climates, hot passions, overt sexuality, and spectacular (if not always eloquent) breakdown scenes in which primordial desire and deep pain are exhibited and confessed. Cheever's associations are in some ways the opposite: his landscape, physically and psychologically, is often the suburban landscape of southern Connecticut and Westchester County, New York—upscale neighborhoods two hours or less by train or car from New York City, landscapes in which urban comforts blend (sometimes attractively, sometimes grotesquely) with a real or contrived pastoral setting, and in which people may try to balance and sustain their inner lives in part by keeping their lawns, houses, and outward personalities well tended.

The classic Cheever breakdown, so strongly contrasted with Williams's, is of a sort he associated with prep-schooled, Ivy League–trained professional men and their façade-conserving wives: a sudden wave of anomie, of deracination, an unexplained compulsion to take on or persist in some bizarre or self-destructive activity, or to quietly tear the fabric of the artificial life that surrounds them and their families. Students can work back and forth between Cheever and Williams, strengthening their own powers to compare and discuss works in light of one another and musing on how deep the class differences and region differences still run in contemporary America. Does even madness have its local rules, its cultural shape, its regional identity?

BERNARD MALAMUD

"The Magic Barrel" also works well with *A Streetcar Named Desire*, because there are similarities between the works that help students formulate their questions. Salzman's idea of Paradise is to find a good woman for Leo, the rabbinical student, and to keep Leo away from his own daughter, Stella, a "fallen woman." (Is Williams's Stella also "fallen"?) When Leo falls in love with Stella's picture and arranges to meet her at the end of the story, Malamud depicts their meeting in "fallen" terms: Stella is dressed like a streetwalker, Leo runs forward "with flowers outthrust" (or as if he and Salzman had exchanged places, and Leo is now a cupid or the FTD florist's winged messenger bearing flowers), and Salzman, convinced that there is no good man, chants prayers for the dead. But Leo pictures in Stella "his own redemption"; and Malamud suggests that although Leo becomes less than a rabbi by the end of the story, he becomes consequently more of a man, more of a human being. Simply loving, in this story, does re-create Paradise because it makes it possible, once again, for Leo to love God—and even to create God in a human image. In Malamud's terms, Leo's love for the fallen Stella makes him a good man; and although Salzman mourns, the story has a happy ending. Less is more for Leo. As he becomes the "diminished thing" in Salzman's eyes, he is more capable of human love. In short, this is a parable, and students will enjoy speculating on Malamud's connections to some of the oldest kinds of storytelling in the Western tradition.

RALPH ELLISON

Students by this point in your course will have much to say about the use and abuse of symbolism; and to draw them into the power of *Invisible Man* and to encourage them to read the entire novel, it's worth pausing to see how Chapter I works both as an allegory and as a splendid piece of realistic narrative. Compare Ellison's protagonist with Dave Saunders in Wright's "The Man Who Was Almost a Man." The two might seem incomparable in educational background and social possibilities; yet, how are they up against similar barriers? In the Prologue to *Invisible Man* the older protagonist writes, in retrospect, "responsibility rests upon recognition, and recognition is a form of agreement." How is this observation relevant to his experiences as a young man in Chapter I? How does the boy's attempt to deliver the speech he himself has written comment on the literary tradition of American black writers? What are the symbolic and real obstacles he must overcome in trying to find his voice and to express his point of view? What might it take for the white men at the smoker to "recognize" and "accept" the invisible man? Is the white woman in a better position than the black boy? Does either have power in the world of the back room?

With Ellison's "Cadillac Flambé," we have another story suggesting a parable, a chapter of a novel that was evidently never completed, a story again saturated with symbolism. Students who have had an experience with *Invisible Man* will find themselves on familiar ground here, and may want to talk about similarities between moments in that book and the pace and structure of "Cadillac Flambé." There is an eerie mix of the believable and implausible here: the basic story, an enraged and (possibly) insane African American burning his car on the lawn of a complacent white senator, sounds like something pulled from the headlines—but the long orotund speeches and the tableau-like scenes give the narrative an aura of the surreal. Students may want to speculate on why once again (as in *Invisible Man*) Ellison chooses a narrator who witnesses and does not act, who tells vividly but seems to withhold judgment or repress anger.

Are we on familiar ground here in other ways: a narrator on the edge of the experience witnessing drastic action by others who, in a sense, act and are sacrificed for him? Is there anything of Nick Carraway in Ellison's teller? What about the speech? If it is not plausible that an incensed man could be so eloquent for so long (with the firetrucks and the police on the way), why does Ellison seem to suspend time and disturbances so that Minifees can get it all said? If there is an allegory lurking here, you can test for it by speculating on the names in the story—Sunraider, Minifees, Fleetwood—and the metaphors and similes favored by the narrator.

SAUL BELLOW

One of a handful of American Nobel Prize–winners, Bellow has a reputation for being dauntingly intellectual: in a Bellow story, one ordinary-looking man, not especially successful or even known, walking down one New York street on one ordinary day will open up as a cosmos, an inner world where Conrad, Marx, Hegel, Henry James, Condorcet, and a mob of other thinkers and public and private personalities will riot and conjoin in amazing thought patterns. The worst and saddest mistake to make in reading Bellow, or in presenting him to a college class, is to take cadenzas of this kind as some sort of showing off, for usually the opposite is true: throughout his career, Bellow has been writing good-natured, human satires about the seductions of the intellect, how we hunger to know so much, and how little good it does in handling the streets of modern America or the big questions about the human condition. At the end of his most celebrated novel, *Herzog,* a compulsive professorial letter writer, arguer, and last-word seeker decides to just shut up and not even tell his cleaning lady what to do; other Bellow heroes resort ultimately to one sort of silence or another, yet rarely is it a silence of defeat or of contempt for other human beings. James's old adage, that literature is a celebration of life, is strong throughout the Bellow canon; and "Looking for Mr. Green" has cosmic dimensions that need to be brought out along with a celebration of ordinary experience: that even in the most absurd human jobs and errands and activities, wonderful things can take place.

Arthur Miller

Death of a Salesman gives American family life itself the power to create character—almost as if the play were about the inability of any playwright to invent roles he or she has not already played or watched in the tragedy of family life. The family is both the play and the playwright. And in this play, the family prescribes certain roles for each of the four main characters that they continue to reenact in the process of discovering what they are. Students, following Linda's cue, will focus on Willy Loman himself: "Attention must be finally paid to such a person." Why doesn't Loman accomplish anything? Why does he have such trouble really talking to his sons? Neither of his sons is able to catch on. How do they all get derailed? Unlike Mary Tyrone or Blanche DuBois, Linda Loman has no identity of her own. Is *Death of a Salesman* realistic in its portrait of Linda? What was her role in Loman's decline? Miller implies that Linda has kept her husband from going to Alaska and "conquering the world"; is she to blame or has she seen inadequacies in her husband that he was unable to recognize in himself? Does she never criticize Loman or want to defend Biff against his father? Who raised these children, anyway? Is the role of American father as provider a myth without basis in fact? Who *does* "provide" in this play? And what is Miller indicting? Capitalism? Family life in general? American fatherhood?

Grace Paley

A conversation about Paley can range far: into modern writers and American politics, the status of women in urban cultural and professional contexts, the transformations and development of realist motives as they interconnect in various ways with ideas associated with Modernism and Postmodernism. If you are uneasy about classifying Paley in one clutch or another of contemporary writers (and she resists classification), you might enter this tale as a story about storytelling—not a self-indulgent or self-promoting exercise about individual genius or the supposed magic of fiction but about writers and intended audiences; about whether any mode of narration can achieve simple and profound truth; and about whether all this making of fiction really serves any purpose in a world grown so complex, changeful, and forgetful of the struggles and the rich inner life of the private self. Some of your students have probably been wondering about such issues all term, and Paley can bring those concerns eloquently into the open.

It's a disarming tale that students will probably like very much, as it respects and celebrates creative intentions that in other circumstances are scorned or condescended to: pleasing people whom you love, sharing the heartfelt perception with a father or mother, respecting the life and thoughts of fairly ordinary human beings—people who may not belong in art films but who nonetheless are capable of powerful insight. There is a kinship evident here not only between Paley, Malamud, and Bellow, but also between Paley and American writers at least as far back as Rebecca Harding Davis, and students will help you speculate on those relationships.

KURT VONNEGUT

Vonnegut's vogue may be somewhat diminished; he was *de rigeur* reading among college students in the 1960s, when his simple prose style and his bizarre plots and puppetlike characterizations were seen as refusals of a clumsily elaborate tradition in American fiction, a fiction as hard to penetrate and as irrelevant as most other social and artistic traditions were seen to be in those times.

This speech by Vonnegut is an effective introduction to the Vonnegut style, and specifically to his attempts to adapt an American humor tradition, exemplified most handsomely in the speeches and sketches of Twain, to outrageous realities in the modern condition. You might open by making note of the impossibility and absurdity of the actual situation of the speech: a talk about the evils of nuclear weapons, delivered to a liberal New York audience, is actually preaching to the choir. These people have heard it all before, been scared, or numbed, by the accounts of the devastation and long-range consequences of atomic warfare. How is anyone to reach them and how is anyone to say anything about this subject that would not be a waste of time? Vonnegut veers outward from the immediate subject, however, to muse about many other human brutalities, old and new. What ultimately proves to be the intention and subject of his talk? What familiar strategies from the American humor and satire traditions does he make use of in this presentation?

JAMES BALDWIN

"Going to Meet the Man" is an imaginative leap as well as a political risk: an African American writer exploring, from the inside, the mind of a Southern white racist. Furthermore, brutal as he is, Jesse is not portrayed without a measure of sympathy: Baldwin presents him as the victim of an upbringing in a deep, inescapable culture of race hatred, culminating in a lynching that, for all the talk around him and *from* him about the nonhumanity of black people, terrifies him and awakens in him a human empathy that he seems to be spending the rest of his life trying to suppress. The small-town world that Baldwin creates is rich and intense; and sexuality, racist dogmas, direct firsthand experience, and deep, almost wordless anxiety and guilt seem to contend in the consciousness of this protagonist. Nonetheless, we now read in an era when writers and directors are regularly chided for straying too far from home territory and for presuming to imagine the psychological life of someone from the other gender or from a different race or culture. Does Baldwin succeed at this difficult and dangerous artistic feat? Is a bold act of understanding like this, published in the very midst of the civil rights struggle of the 1960s, an important political or moral act or a gesture that resonates beyond the usual reach of imaginative fiction?

Flannery O'Connor

In "Good Country People," Mrs. Hopewell says, " 'Everybody is different. . . . It takes all kinds to make the world,' " but she doesn't really mean it. She would prefer that all the world, and especially her daughter, be "good country people" like herself. What would it mean for Hulga to take her mother as her model? Contrast the two sets of mothers and daughters depicted in the story. What are Hulga's "crimes"? What makes her unforgivably "different" to her mother? What is Hulga looking for in Manley Pointer? What does she find? Look at the mother-child imagery of Pointer's "seduction." What do Manley and Mrs. Hopewell have in common? As unlikely as it might have seemed, Hulga has chosen as a love object a person who both infantilizes her and tries to idealize her—someone whose psychological connection with her resembles her mother's own. And what is the story's final betrayal? Is it possible for Hula to escape being her mother's daughter?

Ursula K. Le Guin

Students who have been moving through the fiction chronologically, worrying over the symbolic dimensions or pretensions of various writers before this point, may panic when they get to this story; so it's a very good idea to try to relax them and suggest that "Schrödinger's Cat" may be a tale about *not* knowing rather than a story with all sorts of concealed profundities. Le Guin is writing about a paradox that shadows the life not only of the writer interested in science, science fiction, and fantasy but of any sentient person who tries to understand worldly experience: that there are powerful and seductive theories out there that are imaginatively almost ungraspable or that threaten to overthrow or render absurd any attempt to make sense of our own situation. The story is in some ways about quantum physics, a body of thought that most of us outside that discipline do not understand at any level beyond the superficial. The story is about that puzzlement, about what can happen to our imaginative life when we try to grasp the principles of uncertainty, of the inherent instability or contingency of what (for several centuries) we had taken (again, perhaps without much real understanding) as the fixed laws by which the universe operates.

Nonetheless, this story (as well as the other Le Guin selection, "She Unnames Them") seems lighthearted, playful: this is not a portentous allegory, but something like a giddy hallucination or reverie of a sort that an informed modern consciousness might undergo in a hypnagogic state or a daydream. You might ask students to toy with the first long paragraph—what's going on there? What is the tone? What kinds of expectations are set up in this moment? What kinds of expectations and readerly habits do we need to drop to move on into the story? If students seem tense, draw them into a recognition that they deal with surrealism, crazy visual situations, and narrative discontinuities all the time: in rock videos and in big-budget films that they queue up to see on summer weekends. If they can surrender their interpretive anxieties in those situations, then why not here? The answer, of course, is that when a narrative moves into a classroom or an anthology, it becomes a "text," and what would beguile and amuse before becomes threatening now. That's an idea very much worth developing, in regard to Le Guin and many other texts that you have been encountering this semester.

PAULE MARSHALL

Marshall's "Reena" is about several different kinds of isolating conditions: being a single professional woman in America, being black, having Caribbean roots, and living in a borough of New York. The narrative has a remarkable arrangement, with the narrator maintaining a Cather-like reserve, withholding judgment and generalization, and the main character talking at length and eloquently about herself and life as she has seen it. Part of the connection between them, the teller and the hearer, has to do with a shared loneliness, a failure to find lasting love. This is a powerful theme in works by Morrison and Walker as well: so powerful that controversies have broken out from time to time about whether America's prominent black women writers are somehow unjust in portraying men in their culture or revealing problems and discords that should not be made public in this way, in imaginative fiction that can be read widely, and perhaps predominantly, outside that culture.

What are the major themes of the story? Is Reena heroic in some way, a casualty of the American urban black experience, or a victim of some kind of modern dislocation that is presented here as transcending culture and race? Does the story seem an act of sharing, celebrating the commonality we may have in feeling lost and having to create value as we move along through life? Or does the story emphasize the essential privacy and specialness of the experience of being black and a woman in the modern United States?

DONALD BARTHELME

Before you launch into Barthelme, it might be a good idea to encourage students *not* to feel frustrated if they don't get it, don't see some special significance in "The Balloon" or sense that the narrator has a palpable emotional stake in the telling of the story. The voice here is classic Barthelme, and times change.

Barthleme's heyday was during the period of happenings, put-ons, and general resistance against notions that logic, literary and artistic conventions, official analyses and histories, and other attempts to guide cultural conduct or individual thought were really worth anyone's time. In the history of the modern short story, overtly engaged tellers are a strong tradition, running back to Wharton. In the narratives of Fitzgerald, Ellison, Malamud, Bellow, Baldwin, Paley, and others, we can imagine the narrator as passionately engaged in an act of remembrance, a variant of Coleridge's Ancient Mariner, telling the tale because he or she is compelled to do so. Against this tradition of passionate engagement, Vonnegut and Barthelme offer resistance, and in that sometimes overheated context, the drably objective voice of "The Balloon" could seem radical or refreshing. There is a tradition behind that too: some of your students may recall Mersault in Camus's *The Stranger* or the voice in Samuel Beckett's *Malloy* or some of the postwar essays and plays of Jean-Paul Sartre. As in those earlier texts, the mood of Barthelme's tale is unsettling not because of what happens (which is not much) but the matter-of-fact way in which those events are received and remembered.

Your students may want to know right away what you think the balloon signifies, or argue the matter among themselves—but it might be well to duck that question for a while and attend first to the style of this narrative. If you have been suggesting that hearing a work, apprehending a tone, is very important to opening its meaning, this is a good place to try out that principle. Ask a student to read a bit of "The Balloon" aloud, giving it the tone that he or she thinks is appropriate. Ask other students if they agree with the reading, and to try their hand at a sentence or two. If you hear lassitude or melancholy evolving in that succession of readings, ask where it's coming from, where in the words on the page. Focus on the verbs in one of those longer paragraphs. What kinds of verb choices does Barthelme favor? Compare the paragraph you chose to a passage of similar length from Bellow, Baldwin, Le Guin, Fitzgerald, or some other author whose verbs can dance and buzz on the page. One of the oldest rules in creative writing workshops is to try for interesting verb choices—yet Barthelme favors variants of *is* and *was*, passive expressions, verbs with little or no vividness or action. Why does he do so? Is this story about a balloon at all? Or about habits of response, the way that overworked or overwhelmed people respond ritualistically to anything new?

You can spread out from here into speculations about this story as a commentary on contemporary everyday urban life and the possibility that cities and city habits can condition us to take everything as only a minor variant on the routine. Oh. Look. A giant balloon. Uh huh. What else is new? A massive, mysterious thing appears over midtown, and the reportage from this narrator is even duller than a weekend local newscast or a talk show on a Sunday afternoon. Predictable interpretive arguments break out and fill hours and pages, and to no avail. How do they parody the arguments that jam our printed pages and daily lives—arguments even perhaps about the meaning of short stories like this? The last words of "The Balloon" are "awaiting some other time of unhappiness, some time, perhaps, when we are angry with one another." Does this narrator sound as if he would be capable of any emotion as strong as anger? What, if anything, might it take, to bring his energy levels up, cause him to speak and act as if he cared about what he was seeing and doing?

TONI MORRISON

You may find that your students have previous experience with Morrison, because *Sula* and *Song of Solomon* have become regulars in advanced high school courses and freshman English sections. It is likely, however, that they haven't previously read a work as concise as this by Morrison. Since at least the 1980s, her work has defied easy categorization; so rather than begin with possible connections between this story and American Realism and Naturalism, you might ask what other narratives *Recitatif* reminds them of—other works by Morrison or works by other fiction writers, dramatists, or screenwriters. The tale has many kin in contemporary American literature: after all, it is a story of two women, formerly childhood friends, who meet by chance and struggle to rediscover some key memories, evade some other ones, and find grounds for intimacy and empathy despite the effects of time and personal experience. There are stories and films in profusion that cover such ground, but rarely in this way and with the themes that Morrison emphasizes here.

Twyla and Roberta don't struggle to impose meaning on life, but rather to find meaning within their personal experience, to accept and engage with the realities that have overwhelmed them since childhood and to discover, as Twyla puts it, "How to believe what had to be believed." Circumstances change and they change again: the late sixties culture gives way to the materialism of the seventies and eighties, and each of these people is carried along and to some extent transformed.

Can students see any connection between that general theme and Twyla's emphasis on food and her interest in matching up "the right people with the right food"? Why does she stay at the demonstration, carrying her sign, even when the disorder of the group has made her own placard meaningless? Words seem to fail her, and cultural correlatives (like Jimi Hendrix) keep changing, and people not only shift social classes but shift values and attitudes along with those classes. But is this a pessimistic story? Or do identity and friendship show themselves as transcendent somehow, undamaged in their essence by change? And why is the story called *Recitatif*, which, as the headnote observes, is a narrative that is sung in a free-form way? Is there a suggestion, implicit in this title, that the music of experience is more important than wordy, prosy explications?

JOHN UPDIKE

Updike will be well known to you not only for his best-selling novels and respected short stories but also for his enormous literacy and accomplishments as a critic of art, film, poetry, fiction, and American culture. The challenge in teaching one short work by him lies in conveying the range of cultural experience that can make itself felt within a fairly conventional-looking tale of middle-class trouble. To show how this story might stand apart from a legion of tales about "middleness," separations, divorce, and the failure of love, why not start from the beginning and end and work toward the middle? Turn to the last paragraphs and talk a little about the risks inherent in closing a story with a question like *"Why?"*

Can a story about a middle-class family bear the weight of a question like that? What does the young boy mean by that question, and what does his father hear in it? This is a breakthrough moment, but a breakthrough from what kind of confinements? Turn to the opening pages, then, and look at two passages: one of descriptive narrative and one of human speech. What kinds of details does Updike pack into his opening paragraph, and *why?* What kinds of language—what vocabularies—are Joan and Richard using when they speak to each other? What are the effects of those word choices? If this is a couple encumbered, and perhaps undone, by the bric-a-brac of ordinary routine, acquisitions, and professional aspirations, are they encumbered also by a baggage of English words? If your students have read Wharton's "Souls Belated," ask them to review that story with an ear for the

words that are used there in tense, important conversations—and then to speculate on ways in which American realists, bygone and contemporary, understand
language as central to the fabric of reality.

PHILIP ROTH

As is true in many of his novels and stories, Roth mixes broad comedy with a
serious moral and identity crisis in "Defender of the Faith." The historical context
is crucial to understanding what is at stake here, and you might want to spend
some time describing the odd season between VE Day (the surrender of Nazi Ger-
many) and VJ Day (the surrender of Japan). Millions of American troops, in
Europe, in the Pacific, and at home, were expecting an all-out assault on the
Japanese mainland, and redeployments and high anxiety were everywhere. There
was also significant tension between combat veterans and new recruits—the men
who had seen battle, and those who had passed through four years of war in relative safety. Within such a context, how is the story like a situation comedy? What
are the somber issues that lurk within it? Why name the protagonist Marx? In the
middle of the twentieth century, what "Marxes" did the American public know, and
love, and fear? What do these mixed associations suggest about the sergeant's
evolving impression of his own identity, as an American, a soldier, and a Jew?

What are the risks of portraying Grossbart as an operator and a cheat? What ethnic stereotypes does Roth use here, perhaps dangerously? What are possible reactions from within Roth's own ethnic group, and from non-Jewish American readers? What similarities do you see between his predicament and that of Captain
Vere in Herman Melville's *Billy Budd*?

How is this story interesting as a crisis in the formation of an American Jewish
identity, an identity complicated by Nazism, the Holocaust, and the experience of
service in the U.S. Army overseas and coming home again? As members of other
American minority groups enter military service and experience combat, are similar stories possible now, about the unfinished process of becoming American?

AMIRI BARAKA (LEROI JONES)

In the fifties and sixties, Baraka's relationship with experimental writers and was
complex, and *Dutchman* might be read as a commentary on that unpredictable mix
of intimacy, exploitation, and hostility that, as a black artist among white artists
and literary camp followers, he experienced firsthand. However, some of the continuing power of the play is that it looks at more dimensions of urban and interra-
cial experience than just the literary. Quick, false pretenses of mutual understanding, racial stereotyping, hostility lurking just below the relative quiet and
businesslike onrush of New York life—they are all here, and they suggest strong
connections to the tradition of literary naturalism. To engage with this play, students might want to start with its cadenza passage, the long burst of eloquence
from Clay just before Lula stabs him and the others in the subway car throw his
body off the train. Is this mere street-talk brutality or does the language and
cadence of Clay's rage have its literary kin and comparisons? Baraka is a poet as
well as a dramatist, and his personal artistic rebellion is an informed and thought-

ful one. Have students read a few selections of Ginsberg's *Howl*, or other high-intensity poetry from the Beats, and see if there isn't a resemblance there—a resemblance that can help locate *Dutchman* in a particular period of American letters and set it apart from the work of Baraka's contemporaries.

N. Scott Momaday

In the selections from *The Way to Rainy Mountain*, Momaday interweaves a Kiowa past to which he is connected by his bicultural memory, family, and tradition and a Native American literary future (or "renaissance," in the terms of critics) that re-creates in words a culture that exists only "tenuously," in memory. It proves to be Stanford-educated Momaday's thorough acculturation in what his nineteenth-century predecessors would have called "white" or "government" education as well as his command of the English language that makes both possible at once: the preservation of the past and a vision of a future for Native Americans. Unlike most of the Native American texts included in *NAAL*, Momaday's is not transcribed from a non-English language or from an oral performance—although he collects Kiowa tales and myths, with his father as translator—and he is writing simultaneously to native peoples and Euro-Americans. He is also writing for himself, and for others like himself who want to hold on to a Native American heritage. This can include students, even white students, in the American literature classroom.

In some ways, *The Way to Rainy Mountain* becomes a "final exam" of the new Native American materials in *NAAL*, a way of testing students' knowledge and integration of their earlier readings. For understanding the form of the poem requires at least some acquaintance with American Indian myths and history. The poem begins with Momaday's contemporary rendition of the Kiowa myth of creation—an emergence myth, like that of the Pima "Story of the Creation" included in Volume A. He traces the migration of the Kiowas and the legends they make, such as the legend of Tai-me, and their relation to other gods in the sky; he gives his grandmother, Aho, a position of reverence and a godlike voice from Kiowa history; he relates the development and loss of the Sun Dance ritual, what his grandmother remembers as "deicide"; he works through (with his father's help in translation) a series of Kiowa myths, counterpointed (or as if in encounter with) other voices—a voice of family and cultural history, and a third personal voice of reflections on his place in the schemes of history and myth; and he ends with a poem, "Rainy Mountain Cemetery," which conveys his own vision.

The Native American poet in the late 1960s has been to the mountain, an Indian Moses, and has brought back his vision of "the early sun," on the mountain that "burns and shines," in an image of a new dawn approaching "upon the shadow that your name defines"—an unmarked dark stone that must serve as the marker for the beautiful woman buried in an unmarked grave near his grandmother's house, for all of the unmarked dead Kiowas, for the end of Kiowa culture itself. It is as if, for Momaday, the end of the Sun Dance ritual—like the end of the Ghost Dance religion (both of which occurred in 1890)—required a new vision a century later, and the Native American poet writes a version of the Messiah Letter, one that combines myth, song, and rituals of ceremonial prayer.

GERALD VIZENOR

Written with humor and reserve, Vizenor's story is in some ways about words and about living in two different cultures, in which the relationship between language and identity is entirely different. Vizenor portrays reservation life as a world of near silence, where words are spoken rather than written or read, and where utterance has great importance and sometimes mystical power. To go into the outside world, however, is to enter a gale of talk and print, where people "talk and talk" like the blond anthropology student, and where everything is analyzed verbally. Even the "sovereign tribal blank books" sold by mail order from an abandoned car transmogrify once they enter the white world: schooled in Samuel Beckett and the supposed eloquence of empty pages, professors do critiques of the books and teach them in California classrooms.

The comedy here is broad, but it may touch on an abiding predicament of being a Native American *and* a writer, a member of a group that understands the power of silences and not saying, and the practitioner of an art that believes in saying endlessly. The paradox is real: language itself, any language, can get in the way of true expression and the culturally based inner life. Students will know the stereotype of the silent Indian all too well; he appears in forms ranging from Tonto through Kesey's Chief Bromden. This story can open some new perspectives, not only on cultures that favor reticence and silence but on the transcultural problems inherent in seeking always to penetrate the unsayable with torrents of words.

STEPHEN DIXON

The headnote to Dixon draws attention to the cultural moment in which he situates himself as a writer: a resemblance between his work and Beckett's, and Dixon's association with both phenomenology and the so-called literature of exhaustion. However, some of your students may want to affirm (as they may have affirmed in other highly theorized literary periods) that a work of imaginative literature has to do more than demonstrate an esoteric and possibly transient literary or philosophical doctrine. To look for the life and originality in Dixon, you might consider pushing beyond the proffered guidance to consider how he compares to other writers who have put such heavy emphasis on dialogue and so little stress on interior monologue or careful, overt analysis of family relationships and other ordinary human situations. Dixon's analogues in American literature run back at least as far as Norris and Stephen Crane and the other naturalists and come forward through Hemingway, Vonnegut, and Mamet. In such company, how does Dixon establish an individual voice and perspective?

RUDOLFO A. ANAYA

If they have read Cahan, Yezierska, Bulosan, or other authors of the immigrant experience before coming to Anaya, students may be eager to contrast this good-humored tale of school chaos to tales that come earlier in *NAAL*. Once again we have a story about mutual misunderstandings—but here they unfold without lasting trauma. "The Christmas Play" reads like an affectionate reminiscence: the children swear in Spanish, and their "Anglo" teacher is oblivious; Miss Violet herds and strong-arms the class into cooperation, yet no harm is done, and an atmosphere of mutual respect and even affection seems to pervade the narrative. How is this accomplished? If students have trouble talking about that, you might begin by comparing the first paragraph of the story to the last, to see how the motif of the school as "tomb" has evolved in the intervening pages. Bulosan uses the tomb comparison as well in "Homecoming," and you can compare the ways in which the old simile is used and developed by each author. How does Anaya help us differentiate these children in a quick and busy story? In what spirit are these children attending school, and in what spirit are they being taught? What are the cues that promote those impressions?

THOMAS PYNCHON

The short story "Entropy" includes some classic Pynchon themes and strategies: the high-intensity anxiety about nearly everything in human experience, from worldly human foibles to frightening laws of physics and uncrackable conundrums in epistemology. We also have the fast-moving, sometimes eloquent, but essentially flat characters orating and tearing about in the foreground: if asked for analogues, and encouraged to be freewheeling, some of your students will suggest similarities with the Simpsons, other dark-toned comics by Matt Groening and Berke Breathed, and some of the more bizarre Hollywood dystopic comedies. Pynchon has been around long enough and has been popular enough to have had his admirers and imitators in television and film.

After students recognize that Pynchon operates on certain wavelengths familiar to them from popular culture, you might ask what he adapts from conventions of narrative and what he resists. For instance, it's a commonplace assumption that good stories run on characterization; that personages presented to us should be compelling somehow, or complex; and that what they do and how they fare should matter to the reader. Is that true for this Pynchon story? If it doesn't play by the conventional rules, then what does it do instead to hold the reader's attention? To approach the question from a different side: it's often (and rather gloomily) observed that Henry Adams's law of acceleration has proved true for human culture, that sheer speed and change have caused us to blur distinctions that used to be respected, and that motion and metamorphosis have taken the place of substance in art, in letters, in the self. Is that a Pynchon theme? In other words, does this tale seem to be a symptom of such a problem, a commentary on that problem, or somehow both?

RAYMOND CARVER

The headnote points out that when Carver died in 1988, his work was widely admired and imitated in academic circles; but since critical attention has focused on Carver as a refuser of many narrative conventions and a practitioner of a "stripped down" minimalist sort of realism, students may wonder what is going on here beyond a gesture of resistance against other kinds of fiction that were in favor in the seventies when Carver began to publish his collections. Your class is not likely to be interested in a transient and parochial dispute, and the challenge may be to open up "Cathedral" as a story that does take chances and that affirms the validity of engaging with the world imaginatively.

Since Carver is usually classified as a latter-day realist, students may be reluctant to see any symbolic dimensions to the key action in the story: the rediscovery of the majesty of a cathedral, not by seeing but by moving the hands and feeling. A little nudging of the story to bring out those dimensions will open up the possibility that even a work as austere as this can resonate in this way and can be about the recovery of the capacity for wonder, even in times of disbelief. The magic, if we can call it that, may lie in how we perceive and how we refresh our own ways of examining the world.

TONI CADE BAMBARA

You can expect that your students will come to Bambara with other African American writers and stories in mind: there's a good chance that some of them will have read James Baldwin's "Sonny's Blues," Toni Morrison's *Sula*, Zora Neale Hurston's *Their Eyes Were Watching God*, or other works favored in high school classes and entry-level college courses as glimpses into modern African American experience and experimental literary forms. An opening question, therefore, about the form of "Medley" could bring out generalizations (half remembered from some other context) about resemblances between this tale and the forms and improvisations of modern jazz. An observation like that can be helpful, but it can also beg some important questions having to do with the realist tradition and certain basic expectations and practices in storytelling. To be absolutely true to life as we know it, true to the meanderings, cadences, and interludes of ordinary experience can be to tell no "story" at all. Analogues from the world of music may not answer the question: does "Medley" go anywhere or say anything?

If students find that problem interesting, then a good way to proceed might be to start with a specific, limited passage and work outward. "Medley" is in some ways a story about telling stories, and there are several moments when Sweet Pea, our narrator, muses on the talents of other people as tellers of tales, and of the worth of any story, told badly or well. The paragraphs about Hector as a "bad story-teller," omitting and blurring the details of his reminiscences from the funeral business, offer much to talk about, especially if some attention is paid to Hector as "an absolute artist on windows," clearing the dirt away so that something, however mundane, can be seen clearly, as if for the first time. To what extent is that the experience of reading "Medley"? If some readers find the pace and direction of the story puzzling or exasperating, are they missing what the story is really about—-the commingling of a lot of different experiences (emotional, aesthetic, mundane) in one consciousness and the way that these apparently miscellaneous experiences create one identity and voice?

MAXINE HONG KINGSTON

Kingston's "[Trippers and Askers]" can work exceptionally well in your class, if you are opening questions about how to create a distinct voice and a coherent identity out of the vast array of experiences in modern American culture. Kingston's thinking about this problem is anything but reductive: she recognizes that the contemporary artist, whatever his or her ethnicity and cultural preferences, constantly engages with high art and pop, the classic and the transient, the subtle and the banal. Wittman may be a Chinese American, but he lives in a vibrant city; and its changefulness, color, and life appeal to him deeply. His problem—funny and perhaps tragic in the same moment—is finding a way to speak, to love, and to be within a culture that both inundates him and marginalizes him. One good place to start might be with the title of the chapter—a phrase from Whitman's "Song of Myself"—and with the resonant pun in Wittman's name: is he a latter-day Walt Whitman also seeking to weave a song of himself out of everything he has seen and experienced as an American? What are the risks to this would-be bard? Part of the suspense in this story lies here, in the risk that Wittman faces of becoming nothing as a result of his trying to say and encompass everything. Is this a noble artistic quest? A mad one? An act of artistic courage? Of cowardice?

The headnote points out a Joycean quality in the narration, reflecting the melange of vocabularies and experiences with which Wittman tries to speak to himself and to create himself as an artist and as a lover: you might ask your students whether this wide-ranging, all-mixing vernacular suggests personal chaos, or the possibility of some kind of resolution, a composite and resilient identity well suited to life and writing in a composite and quick-changing American landscape.

DIANE GLANCY

It is possible that because of previous experience with contemporary writers who address a Native American ethnicity students may be puzzled by Glancy's work, which may seem to violate borders among literary modes and between private experience and publishable art. The most important border crossing—or violation, as some of your students might see it—may involve the moral and political predicament of a Native American writer and the kind of license usually accorded to poets of white ancestry and middle- or upper-class schooling. Glancy doesn't avoid or soft-peddle the paradoxes and problems within contemporary Cherokee and Native American culture; she talks about alcohol abuse and sexism within those communities and mordantly about the pretentiousness she sees among other Native American writers, who "play Indian" (in Scott Momaday's phrase) to awe and profit from a largely white American literary culture. She is particularly tough on "Indian intellectuals" and their "surreal coyote tales" in "Jack Wilson"; and students may want to talk about their own predicament as readers, as they eavesdrop on this open-ended and important quarrel among Native American writers. Who is Glancy implicitly writing to and for? Do we hear her? Or do we *over*hear her? Do your students think that the time is right for such internal conflicts to be explored in the open, i.e., in the bookshops, colleges, and literary journals of mainstream America?

GLORIA ANZALDÚA

NAAL offers Anzaldúa in several roles—as polemical poet; writer of personal reminiscence; editorialist on the problems of literary, linguistic, racial, and sexual identity. In *"La conciencia de la mestiza"* the personal alienation moves through layer after layer of complexity: the essay offers little hope that anyone in her predicament can shake off these constraining special traits and dive happily into some available group identity. Students may be puzzled by these sustained refusals and want to debate the importance of any single characteristic as a source of specialness or exile. The essay moves back and forth between English and varieties of New World Spanish: what is suggested psychologically by these different voices in what purports to be nonfiction prose, a perspective from one writer? The end of the essay may draw attention as yet another invocation of nature and the earth as a source of redemption, consolation, welcome. Where have we seen this before? How does Anzaldúa arrive here, compared to Thoreau's arrival in the final pages of *Walden*? The close of Whitman's "Out of the Cradle"? Nick Carraway's wish for oneness with something primordial and natural at the end of *The Great Gatsby*? "How to Tame a Wild Tongue" offers sharp observations about the freedom and cross-pollination of Spanish in North America. How does that modern history compare to the history of American English, as celebrated by Whitman and Twain?

Barry Hannah

Any college undergraduate or advanced high school student will have plenty of experience with narratives of Vietnam, to the extent that these students may want to speculate on the legitimacy, ethics, and authenticity of some of these works. If you are ranging through some of these Volume D or E entries more or less chronologically, you may have already opened questions about relationships between war and imaginative literature: when does high-spirited narration become exploitation? When does empathy become voyeurism? Some students may land hard on the fact revealed in the headnote that Hannah did not serve in Vietnam and that like many other contemporary writers he makes his professional home in a college academic department. The problem is not a trivial one: what credentials do we require, or should we require, of fiction writers, screenwriters, dramatists, and directors who try to engage with a large-scale historical crisis? In regard to Vietnam, one motif that has become standard is a contrast of the knowable "home" world with the surreal or nightmarish world of combat on the other side of the planet. To what extent does Hannah escape that convention or work within it?

Alice Walker

Walker's depiction of her mother-daughter bond differs considerably from O'Connor's. While Mrs. Hopewell defines herself and her daughter by listening to the voices of conventional "good country people," the mother who narrates "Everyday Use" listens to her own inner voice and creates her own values. How are Dee and Maggie different? What explains Dee's decision to rename herself Wangero? How do the quilt's values change for her and what do they mean to Maggie and the narrator? What does Walker mean by valuing "everyday use," even though the quilts may be, as Dee claims, priceless?

Ann Beattie

Beattie's "Weekend" alludes to the film of the same name by Jean-Luc Godard, and what violence takes place in this *New Yorker* story takes place only in the language and as disjunction. Houseplants play a significant role in this story (the contemporary writer's concession to the loss of the external green world?), and Lenore projects and simultaneously contains her own violent fantasies when Beattie writes about her that she "will not offer to hack shoots off her plant for these girls." Otherwise, nothing happens in this story; Lenore, the "simple" character, asks Beat-tie's quintessential contemporary question, "Why do I let *what* go on?" Ask students how they interpret Lenore's statement that she is "simple." What does it mean to be simple in contemporary life? "It is true; she likes simple things." Yet Lenore's life and Beattie's "Weekend" are more complex than that; does the word *simple* for Lenore allow her to defend against noticing the full extent of the lack of communication between her and George? "Weekend" presents a simple world of women, in which women are out of place; all of George's guests are "girls," and living with George without being married offers Lenore only the illusion of choice.

George joins a large list of contemporary characters who drink their way through their fictions; and as George drinks, Beattie shifts to passive voice: "another bottle has been opened." The point of the sentence seems to be that no one knows who has opened the bottle; agency unknown reflects the postmodern dysfunction.

How do students respond to Lenore's last action in the story, as she moves next to George on the couch? Beattie writes that Lenore leans her head on George's shoulder "as if he could protect her from the awful things he has wished into being." Lenore ends by giving George credit for wishing the existence of "awful things" in the world. Is this what Beattie means by simple? Does Lenore stay with George because she can attribute to him the agony of not being in touch? Because she can listen to him teach that "there can be too much communication between people" and, therefore, not have to look too closely at herself? Does *simple* mean attributing the state of the contemporary world to some other, human, agency, rather than focusing more clearly on the unknown agency of passive voice?

DAVID MAMET

Students will find Mamet familiar territory for several reasons. Several of his plays and screenplays have been made into successful films, which have been in the video stores for years. *House of Games, Glengarry Glen Ross, The Verdict,* and a number of others were box-office successes—to the extent that the Mamet style of hard-boiled language, laconic conversation, and unprincipled, ruthless action have been widely imitated in Hollywood films and television dramas. The proliferation of Mamet imitations, in fact, may cause students to wonder what is special about Mamet.

If you have been doing a chronological survey of the nineteenth century, then your students will recall the heyday of literary Naturalism, and they will have no trouble seeing a relationship between Mamet's work and selections from Dreiser and Stephen Crane. You may want to have a freewheeling conversation about whether the usual dates assigned to Naturalism (c. 1890–c. 1920) make sense at all, if Naturalism went to the movies and entered pop literature and culture rather than gave way to other literary movements. You can also return to the dilemma raised by Norris: that a naturalistic narrative or drama isn't a breakthrough from art into truth but a mode that is stylized in a variety of different ways.

Have two students read, with some conviction, a page or two of dialogue from this play, and see if they hear the odd cadences of a classic Mamet exchange—the repetitions, the little rituals that sometimes make his supposedly realistic characters seem to speak like creatures from some other planet. This will lead into broader speculations about whether the literary arts can ever, in any mode, represent things as they really are and human behavior as we really know it.

You can open some long-lasting perceptions if you come at this Mamet play comparatively—as a colder, more cynical reprise of Miller's *Death of a Salesman* or as a modernization of the themes in *Babbitt* or even *The Great Gatsby*. If you are feeling daring at this point in the course, you might ask about recent films that students have seen, films that seem somehow to borrow Mamet-type characters, speech patterns, and situations. You may hear about a number of films that you haven't seen, haven't heard of, or simply don't want to see: *Clerks, Chasing Amy, Pulp Fiction, Blue Velvet, The Comfort of Strangers,* and others that, as the students describe them, might astound you. But the conversation will be worthwhile if students become more aware of modern cross-pollination between the supposedly separate worlds of art and popular culture.

LESLIE MARMON SILKO

At that point early in "Lullaby" at which Ayah does not want to think about her dead son, she thinks instead "about the weaving and the way her mother had done it." Craft defends against sorrow, for Ayah, and for Silko, who weaves the loss of Pueblo culture into Ayah's lullaby at the end of the story. Yet the promise passed down from generation to generation of Pueblo children from their mothers has been broken: "We are together always / There never was a time / when this was not so." Ask students to explore thematic similarities between Silko's story and others in Volume E of *NAAL*. Like Walker and Beattie, Silko also portrays the family in dissolution; however, Ayah has lost her children to the Bureau of Indian Affairs and to cultural assimilation with white people. It is not possible for her to reclaim them or to restore her sense of family. The loss of the possibility of family affects the relationship between Ayah and Chato; and Chato and many other native American men in "Lullaby" turn to alcohol to numb their despair. Ayah does not drink; her experience makes the men afraid of her and to look at her "like she was a spider crawling slowly across the room."

Ask students to compare Ayah with the mother in Zitkala Ša's "Impressions of an Indian Childhood" and to compare Zitkala Ša's portrait of the removal of Sioux children from their reservations with Silko's almost a hundred years later. Ask students to examine the problems in the mother-daughter relationship that Walker portrays in "Everyday Use" when Dee also "emigrates" to another culture.

JUDITH ORTIZ COFER

As a new writer in *NAAL*, and inevitably as a representative of contemporary American narrative fiction practiced by Latina writers, Cofer presents a story that students may find to have an unsettling blend of warmth and loneliness, a mixed atmosphere which they may want to explore. Several themes here can allow for connections between "The Witch's Husband" and other postwar narratives: relationships between the old and the young; between women and men; between female protagonists and a cultural heritage that defines, empowers, and at the same time impedes or restricts. We have a woman at the center of the tale, but not a woman operating on her own, in isolation from family love and support. Compare the situation of the protagonist in "Witch's Husband" to the predicament in Kingston's "[Trippers and Askers]," Glancy's stories of contemporary Native American life, or even Porter's *Pale Horse, Pale Rider*. The "I" of Cofer's story is very much part of a "we," and the story is in great part about coming to terms with the joys and woes of that belonging. Compared to classic and modern American narratives about women within and resisting domestic and family situations (*The Awakening,* "A Conversation with My Father," "The Lost 'Beautifulness,'" "A New England Nun"), how is a resolution achieved in "Witch's Husband"? Is the supernatural element, as a story within the story, an evasion of the major dilemma facing the protagonist, or a way of addressing it?

SANDRA CISNEROS

A bit like Chavez, Cisneros is crossing borders as a writer: writing in English for an English-speaking audience and writing about a world that is in some ways between worlds, the experience of growing up Hispanic in various places in the United States. She takes risks in other ways, writing from *within* that world and entirely within the consciousness of her protagonist, whose sensory experiences and clipped phrases and clauses can convey (at the outset) a sense that she does not really understand her own cultural situation. How is the growth and change conveyed? What stays constant, conveying some continuity of self? Are these stories nostalgic in some way for the experience of girlhood? As Cisneros presents it, what are the costs and the gains of growing up and coming to terms with your own ethnicity in a world that both is and is not your own?

LOUISE ERDRICH

Erdrich is one of the most widely respected contemporary Native American writers; and this story is packed with incident: violence, natural catastrophe; tense confrontations; and at the center, a woman of mystery. So much is going on here that a reader can go with the flow and drift into an assumption that "Fleur" is an unspooling of personal experience, raw narration, whose only source—for event, character, and form—is Chippewa life in northern Minnesota. Part of the challenge of teaching Erdrich, therefore, is to encourage perceptions that this is a highly literate writer, "literate" not just in Native American lore, history, and contemporary experience but in techniques of modern American fiction, the predominantly white traditions of telling. Cather is here, and Faulkner, and O'Connor, and Hemingway, and many others as well—but to discuss Erdrich's implicit conversation with such other writers is not to present her work as ancillary to this tradition.

In looking into Erdrich's originality and understanding how her voice, by building on other voices, becomes strongly her own, you might look at the long card game in the middle of the story, which can seem an extended calm. What is it doing there? What suspense does it create? What mysteries does it raise? What does it suggest about life in this place and the consolations and frustrations of living this way as woman or man? What about the final section of the story, the last paragraph block, which, like some closings in Conrad, seems to suggest that truth disappears under a cloud and that no amount of imagining or telling can ever recover it? If that's so, then what is a story like this for in the modern Native American tradition and in Erdrich's dialogue with her predominantly white audience?

RICHARD POWERS

Galatea 2.2 can work very well indeed as a late stop in a survey tour through American literature. This is a "novel of ideas," but unlike so many of that sort, it offers plausible and compelling characters and real emotional impact. Thoughtful and intensely literate (more about that intensity below), it takes us into dilemmas that haunt the enterprise of the course you are teaching, and the complex underlying hope that the arts, imaginative experience, a reading of the "greats" in *NAAL* or out beyond it provides any kind of genuine wisdom, or even viable delusions to help us move through the turmoil and knowledge storms of contemporary life.

But *Galatea* 2.2 is not an exercise in postmodern cynicism. In fact, it questions the glibness and superficial nihilism of people who have had too much "theory" and too little of anything else, including life. The novel instead takes us compassionately into a pathless wood. It tells of an innocent mind (in this case, a neural network created in an artificial-intelligence center) undone by the shock of the real, a final, massive dose of the daily chaos and mayhem to which most of us have become inured and which is customary in the halls and classrooms of the "literary" in only measured and mollified ways. One troubling question that looms at the end of the novel, therefore, is whether a life in the arts—the life that the narrator has constructed for Helen and for himself—is worth anything at all.

Even so, the selection can have lasting positive effect, if one of your objectives has been to help students read courageously and on their own, venture into new art where much remains mysterious, where there are no headnotes or published commentaries to tell us what it means. There are no thorough studies in print yet about *Galatea* 2.2; and if the book's reputation grows, years will nonetheless go by before professors have combed through it. We have to improvise, like the narrator himself, and know that *not* knowing is a condition we may never escape.

The voice of this narrator is saturated with literary echoes because, like Helen, he has been "programmed" that way, intoxicated from an early age with the idea that canonical literature expresses what Richard Wilbur called "the humane unity of a people" and the idea that remembering is a way of connecting, to the texts themselves and to others who have known them and have thought about them. That faith is called into question in the final pages of this novel—and if your students are worried about *not* understanding this or that literary or scholastic reference, then it's important to face questions that the novel engages with deeply: what are we doing when we read imaginative literature? What does it teach us? Is the practice antiquated, elitist, wrong somehow in the contemporary world? What does it mean to know things that come from novels and books and plays?

First, it might be a good idea to survey and acknowledge the cluttered landscape of the selection, which is representative of the novel's fullness. Much of the action is set at a big American university, where people hustle around and conversations are rushed and projects spring up in close proximity, where old friends share the same hallways as strangers, where thousands of students flood into life every autumn. Your students know this world firsthand, and they may appreciate the authenticity of the atmosphere that the narrative evokes. The selection offers a sizable batch of characters glimpsed and recollected: Lentz the cognitive neuroscientist and project leader, whose wife, Audrey, with advanced Alzheimer's disease, lives in an institutiton; Diana Hartrick and her two sons, the precocious William and his brother Petey, who has Down's syndrome; the Taylors, an English professor and his wife who have both died before the action begins; and others known to us only by initials, chief among whom are "C," the former lover whom the narrator has treated too much like Helen, nurturing and teaching too avidly; and "A," the brilliant, theory-loving graduate student with whom the narrator subsequently falls in love. The episodes in the novel are short, and the action moves abruptly from context to context.

If all that is confusing, does it also suggest the countless studies and contemplations and private lives that unfold in a single setting? Does it suggest too our intellectual life, a movement through a funhouse of possibilities where we choose, perhaps arbitrarily, what to take in and what to pass by? In other words, is the experience of getting lost in this text parallel to the narrator's own dilemma, and Lentz's, and Helen's? Can anything be said about the pattern of these characters—brilliant people who are closely connected to people who have in a sense lost their minds or had their mental circuitry impaired by disease or bad genetic luck? People who want to think programmatically like machines and machines who with their naïve curiosity seem at times more human than the humans around them? "A" has reduced all of literary study to algorithmic process, and this reduction is getting her ahead, professionally. Helen however finds that kind of interpretive process reductive and appalling; and after offering a brief, meaning-packed answer on the final test, she shuts herself down. Because there are ironies and paradoxes everywhere in *Galatea 2.2*, it's important that students be encouraged to see those dilemmas as open-ended and connected to contemporary experience, if they are going to move from here into literary and cultural adventures by themselves.

One way of opening up the selection might be to pick a short passage that seems configured to puzzle anyone who reads it and to consider not the answers but rather the pleasures and pains of that puzzlement. You might start with the paragraph that begins:

> She wanted to know whether a person could die by spontaneous combustion. The odds against a letter slipped under the door slipping under the carpet as well. Ishmael's real name. Who this "Reader" was, and why he rated knowing who married whom. Whether single men with fortunes really needed wives.

If it's late in the term and your students trust you, you might ask how many of these allusions ring a bell. Depending on how advanced they are in their reading of Anglo-American literature, some members of your class may see Dickens here, or *Jane Eyre* and *Pride and Prejudice* and *Wuthering Heights* and *As I Lay Dying* and *Gulliver's Travels*, all of which are still standard fare in undergraduate novel courses. But because not many of them are likely to hear the echoes from *The Ambassadors* and *Middlemarch* and *Ulysses*, you might have some fun thinking together about how "major" fiction gets sorted out into age groups and academic levels—Dickens for high school, Austen for sophomores, Joyce for seniors and graduate students, and so on.

This conversation could gain momentum if you highlight questions that pervade or underlie this playful, meditative paragraph: *why* are such things remembered? Why are they taught? What do we gain by knowing such things? What pleasure, embarrassment, or combination of emotions do we experience when we recognize that such things are in the mind? If students draw a blank in regard to these references, ask them to write a similar paragraph of their own, with sentences that suggest cultural references that they think everyone in their own peer group knows—details and important lines from films, music, television, pop culture of any variety. Then pose variants of the questions above: why do they know such things? What do we signify to each other when we reveal that we know them? What are the private pleasures and advantages of having such things in mind? A conversation like this can approach core questions in *Galatea 2.2*. What body of reference or experience do we have in common now, and is it sufficient? What does culture mean, and what worth does it hold in a rapidly expanding and ramifying world? If as the narrator observes, the annual book production worldwide is approaching one million titles per year, how can anyone, or any university or group of editors, propose the Great Stuff, or contrive a literary and cultural history that makes any sense at all?

At the end of the novel, the scientist Lentz gets the good lines and the last words. "Why do we do anything? Because we're lonely," he says; and the very last line of the book: "Marcel, don't stay away too long." Marcel is Lentz's nickname for the narrator, another literary allusion: Marcel Proust, the French autobiographical novelist, gave his life to remembering his personal past and questioning the worth of remembering. What meaning is packed into that last line? Friendship, love, mutual understanding—are these values that the narrator has given up on, now that Helen is gone? Or does this final line keep a door open, affirm that possibilities remain unexplored, that disbelief is not a point of arrival? We end this formidable novel of ideas with a simple oblique expression of friendship. What do your students think of that, as a valid ending to a novel about reading and the motions of the mind?

SUZAN-LORI PARKS

Parks's play is a meditation on cultural history and the effect that canonical personages and events have on the individual imagination. *The America Play* is a drama for Americans, for people raised in a deep familiarity with Lincoln, the cavalcade of presidents, the drama of the Civil War, and the legacy of Lincoln as a *literary* subject. The play suggests ways in which we as an audience are shaped and shadowed by that collective experience and the way the experience transfigures as specific groups of "ordinary people" within the culture, especially African Americans, live with and negotiate this legacy.

If this is a play to be performed, what kind of setting would be most suitable for it? A big Broadway stage? A warehouse space with a few seats? What impression do you get about the intended audience and cultural location? Does it seem like a play for everyone? If not, whom does it seem to be for?

To sense how *The America Play* dialogues with canonical works about Lincoln, you might ask students to read aloud the first long passage in Act 1 and compare it, for sound, to passages in Whitman's "When Lilacs Last in the Dooryard Bloom'd." Are the Foundling Father's words a parody of Whitman? A kind of homage? Some combination of parody and homage? You can widen the discussion by asking for impressions on how the longer speeches in *The America Play* are intended to be listened to. If Whitman often repeats himself, lulls or beguiles a reader into a different kind of reading or hearing than might be true with other poets, like Dickinson, what about the way that the Foundling Father's or Brazil's words seem to roll through the mind?

Are the acts of the play thematically connected? Why does the vignette of the Foundling Father, the ordinary man who impersonates the Great Man, give way to the dialect interactions of Lucy and Brazil? Why is the catastrophe of Lincoln's assassination reiterated throughout the play? Why do we replay cataclysmic events over and over, and what happens to our response as we watch and reenact? How is this a play about change—the evolution of American legends, the transformation of those legends, depending on who is telling, and who is listening?

Poetry since 1945

As the period introduction observes, many of these writers learned their craft while majoring in English or studying with professors of English in colleges and universities. Contemporary poets have created their own industry and their own markets for their products by giving readings, teaching in writers workshops, staffing creative writing programs, and writing book reviews and media commentary to promote the readership for their work. Both as students and as consumers, then, we are all likely to encounter living poets; indeed, we may argue that our poets are made and not born, and that for reasons we may not yet understand our poets serve a socially and culturally useful function. Ask students to consider whether as consumers and present or future taxpayers (who fund some of the grants that keep poets alive), they are getting anything that is useful to them. What are, or ought to be, the "uses" of poetry in contemporary American life? If you read "Rip Van Winkle" with students a semester ago, ask them to consider whether the role of the American writer has changed since Irving's time (see the discussion of "Rip Van Winkle" in this guide). Do we still need poet-chroniclers to tell us where we have been, where we are going? Do we trust them? What might we plausibly want our poets to do for us, that they seem not to be doing at present?

You might begin by asking students to survey the table of contents for the "Poetry since 1945" section and to identify poets and poems they recognize. Those works can become useful starting points for the rest of us, and you can then ask students to identify the areas of contact they may have with the large body of texts included here. You can then work from their responses to the question concerning the uses of poetry to help match them up with unfamiliar poets or poems. If someone believes, for example, that poetry should make us aware of the fragility of our environment, you might encourage them to try Snyder or Kinnell. If students want to hear a strong woman's voice, Rich or Lorde can be presented. Much as contemporary poets from all ethnic and regional backgrounds may be said to write for all of us, it can seem helpful to students interested in finding common ground to know what regions or ethnic groups individual poets represent.

Or they may identify with biographical details. Does it matter that Duncan never met his mother because she died at his birth, or that Bishop lost both parents by the time she was five and was raised by relatives? That Berryman, Plath, and Sexton committed suicide? That Lowell and Roethke suffered nervous breakdowns? That Niedecker wrote "on the margins" of literary culture? That Hayden was raised by foster parents? That Rich, Lorde, Duncan, Ginsberg, and Merrill made lesbian and gay choices in their personal lives? That in the midst of the civil rights movement, Baraka changed his name from LeRoi Jones? Assign students the task of reading one new poet carefully based on biographical information; then ask them to write briefly, perhaps in class, about their reading experience. To what extent does familiarity or strangeness motivate or influence their choice?

Consider also your own training and tastes in the very diverse world of contemporary American verse. What works for you? Having been taught to close-read individual poems, be sure to pass that skill on—and the all-important balance of confidence and uncertainty that ought to go along with it. What kind of training did you have and what would you like your students to have if they are to continue to be vigilant, sensitive, open-minded readers? Do you want them to be able to move beyond close reading to see larger intersections between poems and poets, between poetry and prose, between poetry and contemporary culture, between poetry and politics? Are any students willing to challenge your own approach with their own? Do any wish to read their own poems to the class?

STANLEY KUNITZ

Kunitz is a good place to begin when surveying poetry since 1945, as he brings many classic American voices forward, blended and transformed, as he builds a body of verse with amazing range of subject and sound. If students hear Whitman in the cadences and language of "Father and Son" and "The Wellfleet Whale," where do these and other poems turn in new directions or break away from that Whitman voice? If "After the Last Dynasty," in its austerity and echoes of a classical Chinese and haiku tradition, ends with a paradox and a question, what is the sequence of perceptions that arrive there? Are incongruous literary artifacts in evidence here—Stevens perhaps, or W. Williams? When Kunitz ventures imaginatively and physically into the heart of New England—to fish, to walk the beach, commune with a dying whale—what does he take with him that is old and new, familiar and out of place? Where does "The Wellfleet Whale" echo Whitman's "Out of the Cradle Endlessly Rocking," and where and how does Kunitz's poem break away?

MARY OLIVER

Because Oliver is very much a New England pastoral poet, it makes sense to encourage students to read her with other such poets in mind. The long, rich tradition of Anglo-American pastoral poetry can actually be a burden for the individual modern artist, if the quest is to achieve an original voice among so many other writers, living and dead, working in similar modes. Students who are comfortable with the overt control and polish of Frost, Wilbur, and Bishop may be disconcerted by the apparent freedom and spontaneity of Oliver's lines. If the objective is to distinguish Oliver's voice, you might begin with "The Black Snake" as a rewrite of or response to William Stafford's famous short elegy "Traveling through the Dark," which takes similar risks with a similar situation: an animal found dead along a highway, a poet trying to bear witness without descending into bathos or forced consolations. In some ways, Oliver goes further with her contemplation than Stafford does, saying things that he left unsaid. Does that pattern, of venturing into the unsayable, continue in Oliver's other poems? In "In Blackwater Woods" she opens a pastoral poem with prosody adapted from William Carlos Williams— not a poet known for conspicuous spirituality or for general truths garnered or glimpsed from observations of nature. How does Oliver transform the Williams voice for her own purposes? If we set Oliver's "Landscape" alongside Wilbur's "The Beautiful Changes," what differences emerge having to do with the way nature is imagined and poems are made?

CHARLES WRIGHT

As a poet, Wright loves to mix it up, blending in one poem a wide range of experiences, memories, and knowledge. Students may enjoy talking about the apparent miscellany of subjects and allusions in "Poem Half in the Manner of Li Ho" and "North American Bear" and consider whether they have encountered any other poets who bring such incongruities together: a Tennessee boyhood, ancient Egyptian and Chinese literature, modern history, Greek mythology. Does this work? What does it suggest about a modern consciousness, a modern education? Does Wright seem pretentious? Do his poems welcome the reader to make such leaps, and prepare the way? In the lines of the poems, how does that happen? What does Wright like to do at the very ends of stanzas? You might look at the closing verses of each stanza in "North American Bear," and compare these to closing lines in poems by Stevens and Lowell. Some of these lines are apparently unfathomable, disappearances into a mist. What do such closings suggest about Wright's temperament, recurring themes, and idea of a poem?

CHARLES SIMIC

If Simic's verse is characterized by short, flat, declarative sentences, and by opening stanzas that seem dead set against overtly poetic effects, then students may want to look for and discuss moments where these poems seem to shift suddenly in pace, language, and theme. Where does Simic suddenly introduce a haunting memory or frightening personal experience, and to what effect? When he moves to a moment that seems Gothic, lurid, or surreal, how has the poem earned our willingness to go there with him, to sense or accept a connection between the ordinary, the diurnal, and the concealed? Simic is an intensely well-read poet; and like many postwar writers, his verse rings with the sounds and experiments of others. Where might you hear touches of Lowell here, or Bishop, or Plath, or Ginsberg, or other poets associated with the Confessionals, the Beats, and other schools of verse from the last fifty years of the twentieth century?

ROBERT PINSKY

The headnote for Pinsky suggests relationships between his work and poetry of Bishop and Williams; but what students may find most striking—and initially daunting—about Pinsky's work is his vast range of associations and allusions, his apparent faith (a bit like Bellow's) that everything is connected somehow to everything else and that finding and relishing those connections is a source of consolation and hope. A contemplation of an ordinary imported shirt will take you, imaginatively, to the other side of the world, to moments in American history, to other American and British poets—and from George Herbert to "a Black / Lady in South Carolina." Students can enjoy a ride with Pinsky if they first can see that his leaps and allusions are *not* pretentious, not proffered to make students feel ignorant and small and to give professors something to footnote. These poems celebrate the act of thinking and the motions of the informed, experienced mind. A good way to proceed, therefore, might be to ask students to read passages from the long poem "At Pleasure Bay" aloud and with a bit of feeling, *not* stopping to worry about "Ibo dryads" or "the Soviet northernmost settlements" but thinking instead about a poetry that tries to cross boundaries of culture, time, and private experience. A poem like this finds its subject and its metaphors everywhere, as if the speaker were a bard for the whole human race. Does the poem succeed? Does Pinsky take us places, imaginatively and intellectually, where other contemporary poets fear to go?

BILLY COLLINS

Because Collins began a term as poet laureate of the United States in 2001, students may want to know what the fuss is about—in other words, what distinguishes his work, and why he would be chosen from thousands of living American poets. Since newspaper reviews of Collins often use the word *accessible* to describe his verse, you could have a freewheeling discussion about "accessibility" as a virtue or a weakness in contemporary art, and why it is that some critics use the term as a pejorative. When you encounter poems like these in a tour through contemporary verse, a tour that involves many forays into the opaque, are you suspicious or disappointed when you read verse that you *can* understand, more or less, on the first or second reading? Collins favors familiar words and opening situations, and his poems often begin with lines that suggest oral discourse rather than laboriously crafted verse. But where and how do the poems change and complicate? Students could do some core sampling here, reading the first stanza and a stanza that comes much later in one of the longer poems ("Tuesday, June 4, 1991" and "Osso Buco" would work well for this) and speculate on the process by which the poem gets from here to there. Logic? Free association? Some complex intuitive process? Compared to Rich or Graham or other contemporary poets, how does Collins dramatize the motions of the mind? If the language is not complex, and if the metaphors are easy to crack, is there a psychological complexity here that is worth our attention? How might we describe that?

LOUISE GLÜCK

If Glück is read in a clear context, as a poet establishing one voice self-consciously amid a chorus of postmodern American verse and within a well-established and academically sanctioned poetry tradition, your students will probably have much better luck with her work than if she is read alone or in a scattering of American poets from the late nineteenth century into the late twentieth. Glück writes very much in the wake of other writers—Dickinson, Williams, Plath, and Lowell—and her strategy of *not* saying, of closing a poem with a mysterious and personal image or an emotion only partially expressed, achieves importance as a kind of resistance, as a rejoinder to the Lowell-Plath way of closing poems with a kind of crushing finality. To be mystical, Glück leaves things open-ended: hers is a kind of agnostic mysticism. Students may want to talk not only about the contextual specialness of her vision to compare it to contemporaries (Wilbur, Dickey, and Rich would work well for contrasts) but also about whether they find this kind of indeterminate spirituality convincing and sufficient as poetic discourse. In other words, Glück can be a very good mirror to the reading self, as it considers what it requires from contemporary poetry.

JORIE GRAHAM

Graham's long poem *The Dream of the Unified Field* offers an intense tour through Graham's major themes and her strategies as a poet. But because Graham's longer poems are adventures in intuitive connection, moving among personal experiences, cultural history, and many geographic locations, care should be taken when transforming her work into a classroom text. *The Dream of the Unified Field* is a labyrinth, an adventure in the labyrinth of the mind—and we need to assure students that getting lost is part of the experience of reading it. Students might feel a bit easier about making this journey if they have recently discussed some other long poems in *NAAL*, several of which echo here: Eliot's *Waste Land*, Lowell's "The Quaker Graveyard," Levertov's "September 1961," Wilbur's "The Mind-Reader," and Rich's "Snapshots of a Daughter-in-Law." Compared to one or more of these, how does Graham's poem move from one thought or memory to the next? The poem is in seven sections: what can we say about the breaks? Are the sections thematically or stylistically distinct? An intensely personal poem at many points, *Unified Field* ends with a long quotation—with additions and imaginative leaps—from the diary of Columbus, a document of encounter and conquest like those in the opening sections of *NAAL*. What is this doing here? Has this entire poem been about discovery, about wonder and concealed riches? Can we describe the relationship of this ending to the main body of the poem? We have "snow . . . coming down harder" in the opening lines, "downdrafts of snow" in the middle of part 2, a "midwinter afternoon" in part 5, and "blinding snow" at the very end. Should we consider the poem as woven together visually, like a vast painting? Are there other motifs and connections that draw it together? What kind of dominion does Graham achieve, here and in the other representative poems, over her wide range of personal experience and literary and cultural education?

JOY HARJO

The first inclination of the class may be to talk about Harjo's prosody as a continuation or modernization of Native American songs and chants of the sort represented in Volumes A and B. This is a starting point; but you may want to help students see that there is a broad and paradoxical literacy behind and within Harjo's poems and that these poems, though private in their demeanor, speak to a varied audience. She is writing contemporary poetry in English; and like Kingston,

Glancy, Bambara, and others, she seeks to achieve a voice reflecting the totality of her experience as an American of mixed racial and cultural heritage.

Some questions to get the conversation moving can center on the variety in Harjo's prosody: do these variations reflect shifts in mood, subject, and voice? There is considerable emphasis on sound—as an effect but also as a subject. Talk, radio noise, church voices, sudden silences—all are accorded special eloquence and spirituality. Does a pattern of hopes and beliefs emerge among these poems? Or do they read as a preamble to a spiritual breakthrough, rather than as a breakthrough in themselves?

Rita Dove

The headnote for Dove suggests connections to the early work of Bishop, a poet known for meticulousness, craft, and an unsettling mix of detachment and passionate engagement in regard to her subjects. How would your students describe Dove's emotional presence in her own poems, especially in the endings of those poems? Why does she break the "Adolescence" reminiscence into several parts, rather than embrace the whole experience in one wide, passionate poem as Whitman or Ginsberg might? When she writes about Benjamin Banneker, what is her stake in that act of imagination? Why does she emphasize the mundane in Banneker's life, rather than the Banneker one might find in the college history books? Students might want to compare this poem to others in which a poet imagines a figure from history—for instance, Kinnell on St. Francis, Sexton on Plath, Lowell on Jonathan Edwards, or Harper on Charlie Parker.

Alberto Ríos and Lorna Dee Cervantes

As Hispanic American writers, Ríos and Cervantes draw attention to the specialness of their cultural heritage—and one challenge in reading them, especially at the end of an academic term, is to recognize the importance of that heritage but also to see their work as interesting in ways that extend in several directions. If you decide to read them together, you may need to make clear that the intention is not to ghettoize, but to compare experiments in form: Ríos is represented here by long poems that favor four-stress and five-stress lines; Cervantes's poems seem quicker in their sound and movement from one perception to the next. But Cervantes's "Visions of Mexico While at a Writing Symposium in Port Townsend, Washington" expands in ways that recall Whitman. Ask students to describe the overall difference in the voice of these two poets—and to talk about moments when each poet seems to rebel against his or her own patterns.

Another rich subject for speculative conversation: the details from ordinary life that these poets focus on. Ask students to compile a quick list of mundane objects and experiences that turn up in the work of these poets, and then to discuss what might be intended by these observations. An affirmation of a kind of citizenship, or commonality with others within or beyond a minority community? A commentary on the preoccupations of everyday life? A suggestion that something special lurks just beneath the surface of the ordinary? Once you have gathered a set of such speculations from your students, you might look for reverberations of other American poetic voices in the works of Ríos and Cervantes. Whom do they seem to have read and valued, and whom do they reflect and quarrel with in their own verse?

CATHY SONG AND LI-YOUNG LEE

Once again, the value of thinking of these two Asian American poets together is to highlight their commonalities, their differences, and their complex and varied use of several traditions. Thanks to the popularity of haiku as a poetic form (and writer workshop exercise) through much of the past century, and of Japanese and Chinese prints as both art and decor in American galleries and hallways, Asian American poets may be linked, fairly or otherwise, to a tradition that is both a treasure and a burden. That tradition is rich and subtle—but what are the dangers of echoing it or borrowing from it? If the canonical American tradition seems dramatically different from the Chinese or Japanese tradition in verse, what reconciliation or combinations are possible, without being typecast by a diverse contemporary audience? Ask students to compare two poems about solitude—Song's "The White Porch" and Lee's "Eating Alone." In each poem, what does each speaker describe herself or himself as being momentarily separated from? Family? Outsiders? The encumbrance of culture? What combination of separateness and connection are they yearning for in each poem?

CHAPTER 12

Examination Questions
and Essay Topics

In previous chapters, the teaching notes offer many questions that can be adapted as writing topics. Similarly, exam questions and essay topics offered in this chapter can also work well as subjects for class discussion. Our intention here, however, is to suggest questions that encourage students to venture out beyond the normal range of classroom presentations and conversations and to try their hand as individual readers and thinkers.

Within each historical period, the exam and essay questions are organized into two groups. "General Questions" addresses literary, historical, and genre connections among texts and authors. "Questions about Individual Authors and Works" focuses on the interpretation of specific texts and includes problems and topics that either situate these texts within their own literary traditions or promote comparisons across traditions.

Volume A: Literature to 1700

General Questions

1. The earliest literary works we have from this period, the Native American creation stories and trickster tales, come down to us in translation, and from cultures and times that can seem remote. Are there advantages to reading the creation stories as *one* narrative? What about the trickster tales? Write an essay about the

value and drawbacks of combining the stories as we think about them and of seeing them as separate and distinct from one another.

2. Write an essay contrasting the Pima Stories of the Beginning of the World with creation stories from Egyptian, Greek, Chinese, or Norse mythology. Compare the mysteries that are explored by these stories and the emphasis they place on the importance of human beings in the larger scheme.

3. Most of these Native American narratives are received as anonymous works—attributed to a people rather than to a single author and historical moment. Most of the accounts by European voyagers and colonizers, however, have names and dates attached and often center on the adventures and thoughts of one author. Write an essay about these differences—the ownership of narrative, the concern with time—and how they might connect to different ways of perceiving the American landscape.

4. Wayne Franklin calls the period of European discovery and encounter a "many-sided process of influence and exchange." He also writes that "much of what was new . . . came about through struggle rather than cooperation." Choose either statement and write a short essay in which you comment on its accuracy by citing references to specific writers and narratives included in the period.

5. The period introduction identifies three purposes of European colonization. Referring to at least two of these purposes, describe how they are reflected and varied in individual texts from the time.

6. Much of the literature of encounter and discovery includes inventories of one kind or another. Choose inventories from three of the writers we have read and describe what these inventories imply about the author's values and his conception of the New World and its inhabitants.

7. Choose several significant moments of encounter from different narratives included in this section and describe the different perspectives from which Europeans and native peoples view each moment.

8. Research the myths of Doña Marina and Pocahontas and report on their cultural survival in Mexico and North America.

9. Viewing the encounters as moments of communication, interpret how each side views the other and what messages they convey in their own behavior. Ground at least part of your reconstruction in a reading of the Stories of the Beginning of the World.

10. Describe some of the central principles of Puritan ideology and illustrate their significance in specific literary works. Choose from among the following: (1) New World consciousness, (2) covenant theology, (3) typology, (4) innate depravity, and (5) irresistible grace. A few of the writers who address each of these con-

cepts, and whom you will need to discuss, include (1) Bradford and Bradstreet; (2) Bradford and Wigglesworth; (3) Bradstreet (in "Here Follows Some Verses upon the Burning of Our House"), Edward Taylor, Winthrop, and Wigglesworth; and (4) Edward Taylor and Wigglesworth.

11. Trace the connection between the Puritan reliance on written covenant, as in "[The Mayflower Compact]," and their uneasiness in their literature regarding personal vision.

12. Compare Bradford's metaphors to Morton's. Why does Morton resort to a different trove of analogies than Bradford does? What do these choices say about their temperaments and belief systems?

13. Identify and discuss literary texts that reveal stresses on Puritanism or that illustrate schisms within Puritan and colonial consciousness.

14. Describe the contrast between the personal and the didactic voice in Puritan and early colonial literature.

15. Trace the power of the written convenant in colonial and early American literature, beginning with "[The Mayflower Compact]."

Questions about Individual Authors and Works

NATIVE AMERICAN STORIES OF THE BEGINNING OF THE WORLD

1. Locate and read other Native American creation stories and discuss them in light of the Iroquois and Pima stories included in *NAAL*.

2. The Judeo-Christian accounts of the beginning of the world place emphasis on a grand design and purpose and on an essential order in the natural world. Do these Native American creation stories put similar importance on the centrality of humankind and on an overall plan? Where do you see similarities and differences in regard to this theme?

NATIVE AMERICAN TRICKSTER TALES

1. Write about the concept of the trickster as a way of explaining or imagining the natural world. Is the trickster malevolent, an embodiment of evil? How is the landscape around the storyteller and listener transformed or energized by imagining the trickster as an abiding presence?

2. Write an essay in which you imagine the intended audience of these tales, and compare their culture-based expectations to those of a specific storyteller from the European tradition: Bradford, Mather, or some other white writer who narrates with a specific purpose and to a particular culture.

3. There are comic moments in these tales; but comedy and fear are often closely connected—sometimes we laugh at things that in some dimension frighten us. What might be frightening about these tales? What in the cosmology of the Native American teller and listener might be threatening about the trickster and the trouble he causes?

4. Write an essay about the mingling of total irreverence and the sacred in two of these narratives. What does the bawdiness accomplish? Is it comic relief as in a Shakespeare drama or other European-style narrative? Or does the mingling of the irreverent, the scatological, and the sacred work in a different way?

Christopher Columbus

1. Discuss how Columbus's expectations, "thinking that I should not fail to find great cities and towns," reflect the contrast between European ideas of greatness and a more indigenous perspective on "great" civilizations in the New World.

2. Despite the fact that this material is translated and that five hundred years have passed since Columbus's voyages, can you discern a voice here or an imaginable personality? What moments in his letters give you those clues?

Bartolomé de las Casas

1. Write an essay about the moral outrage which Casas shows in his *Very Brief Relation*. Where is it grounded? Is it based in a traditional faith? In a kind of secular or nonsectarian humanism? Look at the details that he offers and the adjectives he uses, and try to describe his moral position.

Bernal Díaz del Castillo

1. Write an essay about irony in *The True History of the Conquest of New Spain*. Where do you see it? Does it seem intentional or inherent in the enormous events that the *True History* relates?

2. More than other narratives of encounter, Díaz del Castillo's becomes a narrative of witness. Locate and discuss several moments in the narrative where he demonstrates his self-consciousness and responsibility about his role as witness.

Álvar Núñez Cabeza de Vaca

1. Focusing on the texts of Cabeza de Vaca and Díaz del Castillo, write an essay that brings into focus the lives of native women in North America.

Garcilaso de la Vega

1. Remembering that this was an age of warfare and religious persecution throughout western Europe, what might Vega's intentions be in offering an account of suffering and near-martyrdom in a far-off place? How does this account contribute to the literary record of first encounters in the Caribbean?

THOMAS HARRIOT

1. Locate moments in Harriot in which his intentions seem to be in conflict as he reports of the encounter between the English and Native Americans.

SAMUEL DE CHAMPLAIN

1. Read Champlain's descriptions of American Indian agricultural life. Summarize the portrait of native life (food, customs, housing, activities, manners, relationships between men and women, domestic arrangements) that Champlain offers. What are the indications that Champlain is looking at this culture objectively or empathetically?

2. Evaluate the narrative voice in which Champlain describes the Native Americans he encounters. Can we trust his account? What evidence might you offer to support your position?

JOHN SMITH

1. The settlement of the Middle Atlantic lands is often contrasted with the settlement of Massachusetts Bay: the Virginia colonies are described as secular and materialistic in their purposes, rather than religious and spiritual. Where are the indications of Smith's motives and aspirations as he describes the Jamestown area to an English audience? What specifically excites him about the prospect of colonies in this region?

2. Near the beginning of the excerpt from the Third Book, Smith writes: "Such actions have ever since the world's beginning been subject to such accidents, and everything of worth is found full of difficulties, but nothing [is] so difficult as to establish a commonwealth so far remote from men and means and where men's minds are so untoward as neither do well themselves nor suffer others." What is he talking about? What assumptions is an observation like that based on? Can you think of modern intercultural misunderstandings that parallel the problem that Smith believes he is facing here?

3. At the end of the excerpt from the Third Book, Smith writes, "Thus you may see what difficulties still crossed any good endeavor; and the good success of the business being thus oft brought to the very period of destruction." Locate other passages in which Smith expresses his concern for the reputation of the business endeavor in which he is engaged or in which he uses metaphors from the world of work or business to describe his activities.

WILLIAM BRADFORD, THOMAS MORTON, AND JOHN WINTHROP

1. Write an essay comparing these three writers as literary stylists. What are the stylistic qualities that make Morton the odd man out in this group? How can we differentiate Bradford and Winthrop from each other as Puritan writers?

2. Write an essay describing the Winthrop legacy in American public discourse, especially the president's Inaugural Addresses, State of the Union Addresses, and other speeches to the American nation. Find three recent addresses and compare their style and content to Winthrop's "A Model of Christian Charity."

ANNE BRADSTREET

1. Write a close reading of a single lyric poem. Depending on how much analysis you have already done in class, choose from among the following: "The Prologue," "The Flesh and the Spirit," "The Author to Her Book," "Here Follows Some Verses upon the Burning of Our House," and "As Weary Pilgrim."

2. Describe a sequence of stanzas from "Contemplations" and discuss the thematic and stylistic relationship between these stanzas and the entire poem.

3. Compare the imagery of "To My Dear and Loving Husband" with Taylor's "Huswifery." How does the imagery characterize each poet's work?

4. Discuss the extent to which Bradstreet's poetry reflects Puritan thinking. Analyze in particular the way Bradstreet reflects her own spiritual and metaphysical fears in the process of describing an actual event in "Here Follows Some Verses upon the Burning of Our House."

5. Describe the tonal and rhetorical differences among Bradstreet's three elegies for her grandchildren, and suggest reasons for these differences.

JACOB STEENDAM AND ADRIAEN VAN DER DONCK

1. Consider the last twenty lines of Steendam's "The Praise of New Netherland" and the closing paragraph of Van Der Donck's "Of the Wood, the Natural Productions, and Fruits of the Land." As texts written for an audience in the Netherlands, how do they conclude and what concerns and interests do they appeal to?

2. Compare Van Der Donck and Smith as promoters of settlement and colonization.

MICHAEL WIGGLESWORTH AND EDWARD TAYLOR

1. Adapted from John Stuart Mill, a familiar assumption about poetry holds that "Rhetoric is heard; poetry is overheard." Compare the voices of Wigglesworth and Taylor. Does the distinction apply to either or both of these poets? Write an essay comparing the publicness and privateness of Wigglesworth and Taylor, and describe how their different intentions are reflected in their verse forms, imagery, and rhetorical style.

2. The first generations of New England Puritans are often remembered as people who favored plain speech and simple design. Write an essay about *The Day of Doom* as a Puritan poem—in its subject and also in its voice.

3.Write a close reading of any of the poems from *Preparatory Meditations*. Identify the central metaphor or series of related metaphors and describe the process by which Taylor develops each metaphor into an address to his own salvation.

4. If you have studied English Metaphysical poets (especially Donne, Jonson, Herrick, or Herbert), choose an interesting poem by one such poet and compare its theme and structure to a similar poem of Taylor's.

5. Discuss Taylor's use of objects from the natural world or of secular experience in "Upon Wedlock, and Death of Children"; "Upon a Wasp Chilled with Cold"; or "A Fig for Thee, Oh! Death" and examine the relationship in the poem between earthly life and spiritual salvation.

6. Discuss the extent to which Taylor's poetry reflects specific concepts of Puritan theology.

MARY ROWLANDSON AND COTTON MATHER

1. In Rowlandson's *Narrative,* locate three passages that seem to vary or conflict in portraying her view of her captors. Write an essay discussing and accounting for these differences.

2. Rowlandson and Mather, following a Puritan pattern of thought, attribute certain worldly events to Divine Will or supernatural causes. Compare passages in which such attributions are made, and make distinctions about their thinking and their rhetorical style.

Volume A: American Literature 1700–1820

General Questions

1. Identify the literary forms available to eighteenth-century American writers. What limited their choice? How did they invent within these forms?

2. Describe some important differences between Puritan thinking and eighteenth-century deist thinking, and discuss literary works that illustrate these differences.

3. Describe the way the concepts of the self and of self-reliance develop and find expression in American literature of the eighteenth century and the Revolutionary period. Identify those specific figures or works that you see as significant and explain their contributions.

Questions about Individual Authors and Works

SARAH KEMBLE KNIGHT AND WILLIAM BYRD

1. By modern standards, or even those of the nineteenth century, these travel writers do not travel far. Compare ways in which Knight and Byrd emphasize the

oddness or otherness of the places they visit and how each traveler affirms the values and practices of home.

2. Write an essay in which you compare Byrd's *The Secret Diary* with a work by any of his New England contemporaries. What relationship does Byrd assume between the private and the public self? Between the worldly and the religious self? How do those relationships contrast with ones you see in major Puritan writers?

JONATHAN EDWARDS

1. People often see "A Divine and Supernatural Light" as coming from a completely different sensibility than does "Sinners in the Hands of an Angry God." Do you agree? Do these works resonate with one another in any important way? Do they give indications of coming from the same theology and individual mind?

2. Discuss Edwards's manipulation of biblical language in "Sinners in the Hands of an Angry God." What specific transformations does he perform? And how does his use of language in the "Application" section of the sermon differ from and comment on the earlier doctrinal section?

3. Edwards and Franklin were contemporaries. Explain, with specific references to their works and more general comments on their ideas, why this fact might seem startling.

4. Write a brief comparative analysis of form and function in Taylor's poems and Edwards's sermons. (Students need to see the way each of these Puritans tried to demonstrate or even "prove," in Edwards's case, spiritual salvation and the way each associates being saved with the authority of being able to find the right language.)

BENJAMIN FRANKLIN

1. Explain why the eighteenth century was called the Age of Experiment and consider the relevance of this term as a description of Franklin's writing.

2. Evaluate metaphors that Franklin uses in Poor Richard's maxims in "The Way to Wealth." Count and categorize the metaphors; summarize your findings. What are their origins and how does he use them?

3. What is the "religion" Franklin "preaches" to his readers in Father Abraham's speech? How do you explain Franklin's use of religious metaphors in his writing?

4. Discuss several permanent contributions Franklin made to American life, ranging from the practical to the ideological.

5. Choose any single section or aspect of *The Autobiography* as the basis for analysis. Or contrast Franklin's choice of focus in its four parts; consider the significance of his choice to address the book to his son; read closely the letters that begin "Part Two" and comment on their significance to *The Autobiography* as a whole; discuss Franklin's various practical attempts to alter his moral character.

6. Following notes from class discussion, explain the various ways in which Franklin's *Autobiography* may be seen as "self-invention."

JOHN WOOLMAN

1. Compared to Edwards's *Personal Narrative,* Woolman's *Journal* pays more attention to ordinary experience: family, town life, the details of growing up. How does Woolman give importance to these details? Why would they matter to him but not to Edwards? Choose two paragraphs from Woolman and two from Edwards, and compare them for language use and rhetorical style. Like the Puritans, the Society of Friends emphasized simplicity in ordinary life and personal deportment. Why then the differences in vocabularies and sentence structure?

JAMES GRAINGER

1. Write an essay on the relationship between style and subject in *The Sugar Cane.* When does the style seem appropriate to the subject? When do conflicts arise?

2. In a history of Anglo-American literary discourse about race, how would you locate *The Sugar Cane*? What do you think it represents in a larger narrative of Africans and Europeans interacting in this hemisphere?

SAMSON OCCOM

1. In his account of his life, Occom writes from two perspectives: as a minister and as a member of a minority group in the larger culture. Do these perspectives come into conflict in his narrative? Where and how?

2. Occom's narrative has come back into print only recently. In your opinion, what is the best way to read it: as a stand-alone work or as a work that converses with or responds to other autobiographies and personal narratives of the eighteenth century? If you feel that the work stands alone, then offer a close reading to support your position. If you see it as part of a conversation, then choose another autobiographical account and show how that dialogue enriches the reading of both authors.

J. HECTOR ST. JOHN DE CRÈVECOEUR

1. Witnessing slavery firsthand leads Crèvecoeur to lament the "strange order of things" in Letter IX from *Letters from an American Farmer.* How does he reconcile his view of slavery, and of the great contrast between lives of plantation owners and slaves in Charles-Town, with his portrait of America as a place where humankind can be renewed?

2. Crèvecoeur was one of the first writers to see America as a place where dogmatic disputes and sectarian violence could be permanently overcome—not by other idea systems but by the landscape and life within it. Describe his argument, the evidence he offers, and the European historical experience that he turns to for contrast.

3. Compare Woolman's and Crèvecoeur's understanding of "strangers" and their place in "American" society.

JOHN ADAMS AND ABIGAIL ADAMS

1. Compare one of Abigail's letters to John with one of Bradstreet's poems to her husband, "absent upon public employment." How are sentiments expressed and constrained in both of these texts?

2. The letters that pass between John and Abigail offer us a private view of the writing and signing of The Declaration of Independence. Examine the hopes these writers have for independence and describe those that are not explicit within the document itself.

3. How do the Adams letters reflect values in transition—changes that would reverberate in nineteenth-century American public and cultural life?

ANNIS BOUDINOT STOCKTON

1. Write an essay comparing Stockton and Bradstreet as love poets, and suggesting how cultural circumstances are reflected in their respective styles.

2. Write an essay about Stockton's imagery. Compare similes and metaphors in the ode to Washington with those in the ode to sensibility, and account for the variations you observe.

THOMAS JEFFERSON

1. Write an essay about similarities you see between the rhetorical strategy of The Declaration of Independence and sermons, speeches, and public discourse from the American Colonial period.

2. Based on class discussion, recapitulate the ways The Declaration of Independence uses rhetorical style to achieve its power.

3. Describe the evidence of Franklin's interests in "self-invention" in *The Autobiography* and suggest ways in which Jefferson, with the assistance of Franklin, carries these interests into the political sphere of The Declaration of Independence.

4. Write about the rhetorical strategies used in the antislavery grievance from The Declaration of Independence, a section that the Continental Congress eliminated from its final version.

5. Describe the ways in which Franklin and Jefferson reflect the legacy of Puritan thinking.

OLAUDAH EQUIANO

1. Equiano's prose style is powerful. Choose one or two paragraphs and write an essay about the ways in which he structures his sentences, chooses analogies, and selects vocabulary. At times his prose is highly formal, even ornate. Why? How might his style reflect his situation, or predicament, as a writer?

2. For many years, Equiano lived in a paradoxical condition: as a slave in North America and virtually as a free man on his voyages and sojourns abroad. Do you see this strangeness reflected in the personality that he constructs in his *Narrative* and in the language and style with which he writes it?

3. Reread in the early chapters of Bradford's *Of Plymouth Plantation* the portrait of life aboard the *Mayflower* with Equiano's account of life aboard the slave ship. Consider the various meanings different colonial authors attribute to the word *removal*.

PHILIP FRENEAU

1. Although Freneau's "To Sir Toby" is ostensibly about a sugar planter on the island of Jamaica, examine the poem for evidence that Freneau is also writing about southern slavery. Locate references to slavery in his other anthologized poems and summarize the way slavery, for Freneau, contradicts eighteenth-century principles of reason and human rights.

2. Evaluate the language of Freneau's historical poems in comparison to specific passages in Paine or Jefferson, and speculate on the relative effectiveness of political and poetic voices within the context of American revolution.

PHILLIS WHEATLEY

1. Locate and discuss imagery in Wheatley's poems that directly or indirectly comments on her experience as a freed slave.

2. In the Wheatley poems that address others—students, General Washington, a painter, the earl of Dartmouth—how does Wheatley present herself? How does she create or suggest a personality within the formal context of these poems?

3. Should Wheatley's poetry be considered an important point of origin for African American verse? Why or why not? Can you talk about specific qualities or moments in Wheatley's poems to support your position?

ROYALL TYLER

1. How seriously should we take *The Contrast* as a social commentary? Write an essay about ways in which the play asserts itself as imbued with serious themes—and ways in which it undercuts or limits those implications.

2. Where does the legacy of *The Contrast* turn up in contemporary comedies, on either the stage or the screen? Select two of these recent plays or films and compare specific characters or plot situations to similar elements of Tyler's play.

SARAH WENTWORTH MORTON

1. Does Morton succeed in resisting or individualizing the highly formal style that she has inherited from the eighteenth-century English poets and within which she works? Is she able to express her gender or her American identity in her verse? Discuss specific poems and passages in answering this question.

2. Read carefully Morton's poem "The African Chief." Does the poem achieve or convey empathy for its subject? Or is it what Randall Jarrell called (in another context) "just an excuse for some poetry"? Talk about specific moments in the poem in answering this question.

SUSANNA ROWSON AND CHARLES BROCKDEN BROWN

1. How would you account for the enormous popularity of *Charlotte,* which went through two hundred different editions before 1900? Does it successfully merge the sensational with the didactic? Where, for you, are the novel's best moments? Where are its worst ones? Discuss one scene in detail and comment on its dramatic power and its rhetorical strategies.

2. Is *Charlotte* a feminist document? Why or why not? Discuss specific chapters that influence your thinking about this question.

3. The excerpts from Brown's *Wieland* also show signs of didactic intentions. Compare those moments to similar ones in *Charlotte.* Which do you find more convincing as instruction about human nature, and why?

Volume B: American Literature 1820–1865

General Questions

1. Why were the American landscape and political experiment especially suited to a flowering and transformation of European-style Romanticism? What problems did artists and writers face in adapting English romantic themes and tropes to the American scene?

2. Discuss the following statement with reference and relevance to specific literary works: The Puritans were typological, the eighteenth-century writers were logical, but the early-nineteenth-century writers were analogical in their way of knowing and expressing what it means to be an American.

3. Discuss changes in the concept of the American self in the early nineteenth century. Locate your discussion within specific works by Sedgwick, Bryant, Emerson, Thoreau, Hawthorne, and Melville.

4. Cite some key differences between early-nineteenth-century writers and their eighteenth-century predecessors. Focus on the concept of self-invention and, in specific literary works, discuss the early-nineteenth-century evolution of this concept.

5. Examine the work of one or more American Romantic and nineteenth-century painters (Thomas Cole, Albert Bierstadt, George Caleb Bingham, George Inness, Frederic Church), and discuss stylistic and thematic similarities that you see between the work of these painters and literary works of the period.

6. Consider literary portraits of women engaged in heroic struggle or of escaping slaves portrayed as heroic fugitives. Compare portraits by Stowe, Fuller, Jacobs, and Douglass with Hester Prynne in *The Scarlet Letter* or Thoreau's autobiographical narrator in *Walden*.

7. It may be possible to sort major writers of this period into two groups: those who advance particular doctrines and systems of thought, and those who question or critique those doctrines or who suspect any systematic or totalizing view of the world. Which of these writers seem to you most interested in arriving at some coherent view of experience? Which are temperamentally more interested in questioning such coherent views—and the possibility of seeing the world through what Fitzgerald would later call "a single window"?

8. American realists made different choices of language and genre than did their contemporaries and immediate predecessors. Write about a text by any of the following authors and explore elements of realism in their work: Stowe, Thorpe, and Davis.

Questions about Individual Authors and Works

WASHINGTON IRVING

1. What kind of relationship does Irving suggest between himself and the stories that he tells? Compare the end of "The Legend of Sleepy Hollow" to the end of Rowson's *Charlotte* and write an essay about the different ways in which these stories are offered to the American public. Why do you think Irving takes the stance that he does?

2. Compare Freneau's and Irving's uses of the historical situation as the subject of imaginative literature.

3. Discuss several different ways in which "Rip Van Winkle" addresses versions of the American Dream.

4. Compare Rip Van Winkle with Franklin's Father Abraham in "The Way to Wealth." What do the two have in common?

5. "Rip Van Winkle" is an early work that casts the American woman as the cultural villain. Analyze the character of Dame Van Winkle in the story and discuss the significance Irving attributes to her death.

6. What happens if we try reading "The Legend of Sleepy Hollow" as an allegory—about city ways and country ways, about common sense and "education"? Is that pushing the story too far for the sake of literary analysis? If the story does work as an allegory, in what spirit is it offered?

James Fenimore Cooper

1. In the Leatherstocking Tales (of which *The Pioneers* is one novel) Cooper is often said to be doing the traditional cultural work of an epic writer: helping a new culture to lay claim to an ancient or dying tradition. Where do you see this under way in these excerpts?

2. Write an essay about Chapter III (the pigeon massacre) as a critique of Old World and Native American ways of living in a natural context.

The Cherokee Memorials

1. Based primarily on direct references or inferences you can draw from the Cherokee Memorials, write an essay in which you describe the Cherokees' particular economic, cultural, and political situation in Georgia at the time of the writing of these Memorials. If you consult any historical source(s) to verify your inferences, provide appropriate citations.

2. Summarize the argument or arguments that the Memorials urge on members of the Senate and House.

3. What are the rhetorical strategies of the Memorials? Why might those strategies be especially effective in speaking to a white audience in Washington, D.C.?

Catherine Maria Sedgwick

1. Compare Sedgwick's prose style to Cooper's. In the evolution of a vernacular suited to portraying ordinary American life, what are the advantages of Sedgwick's strategy? If you compare her portraits of domestic life to Rowson's, what differences become clear?

2. In Sedgwick's work, do we see indications of the inadequacy of literary eras and "ages" (like the Age of Romanticism and the Age of Realism) for classifying and describing individual talents? In what ways might Sedgwick be ahead of her time? In what ways does she seem very much a writer of the early nineteenth century?

William Cullen Bryant

1. In his essays, Emerson calls for the emergence of an American poetics. Focusing on Bryant's *The Prairies,* describe ways in which Bryant might meet Emerson's demand. In what ways does Bryant move away from imitating British poetry and address American themes? In what ways does he play by the familiar rules of the epic tradition?

2. Bryant is writing about a wilder and less imaginatively tractable landscape than Wordsworth and Coleridge wrote about in the early years of English Romanticism: the woods and prairies were not domesticated and were not haunted by "ghosts" of a kindred race and culture. Describe ways in which this situation proves advantageous to Bryant and difficult for him to work with.

WILLIAM APESS

1. Write an essay in which you explore "An Indian's Looking-Glass for the White Man" as an American work. To what extent does it address familiar American themes? To what extent does the emergence of a Native American literature in the English language coincide with and contribute to the emergence of an indigenous (as distinguished from imitative) American tradition?

2. Compare Apess's "Indian's Looking-Glass" with Douglass's "Meaning of July Fourth for the Negro."

3. Bryant wrote his poem "The Prairies" within a year of Apess's "Indian's Looking-Glass." Read "The Prairies" with Apess's perspective and comment on Bryant's portrait of "the red man" in light of Apess's text.

CAROLINE STANSBURY KIRKLAND

1. Write an essay comparing Kirkland's prose style and treatment of subject matter to Sedgwick's. In what ways do these two writers resist modes of description and narration that you see in Irving and Cooper?

RALPH WALDO EMERSON

1. Discuss what Emerson means in one of the following statements from *Nature:* (1) "The use of natural history is to give us aid in supernatural history. The use of the outer creation, to give us language for the beings and changes of the inward creation" or (2) "A man is a god in ruins. When men are innocent, life shall be longer, and shall pass into the immortal as gently as we awake from dreams."

2. Trace Emerson's thinking, image patterns, and particular forms of expression in one of the poems.

3. Compare an Emerson paragraph with an Edwards paragraph. What are the differences in structure? In argumentation? Does Emerson play by the rules that you were taught in composition classes? If not, then how does Emerson make his own strategy work?

4. Explain why the poet is so important for Emerson, summarizing his argument in "The Poet." Does his idea of a poet have a certain gender? Where do you see indications that it does or does not?

5. Discuss the way Emerson uses analogies. Choose several analogies he creates in *Nature* and explain their significance.

6. Explore any one of the following central concepts in Emerson's work in the context of your reading: the spiritual vision of unity with nature, the significance of language in achieving spiritual vision, basic differences between thinking and writing by means of analogy and by means of discursive logic, the theme of self-reliance, and the significance of self-expression.

7. Explain how Emerson's philosophy, as he expresses it in *Nature*, represents a culmination of what it means to be an American in his time and place.

Nathaniel Hawthorne

1. Explicate character, theme, language patterns, style, use of point of view, setting, or design in any particular short story or in *The Scarlet Letter*. (The problem with assigning one of these topics, of course, is that you then have to deal with the standard interpretations students are likely to find if they go straight to the library. If you use a version of this question, you might use it in in-class writing where the only book available is *NAAL*.)

2. What are the problems with assigning any of the following classifications to Hawthorne's work: Puritan, anti-Puritan, transcendentalist, antitranscendentalist, romantic, realist? Cite specific works, characters, and passages to frame your answer.

3. Are some Hawthorne stories more fablelike than others? Choose two stories that illustrate your response to this question and write about them.

4. Explain what Melville means by Hawthorne's "blackness" in his essay "Hawthorne and His Mosses" and discuss it with specific reference to any two of the stories in the text (or any three with reference to specific characters in *The Scarlet Letter*).

5. Explore the moral ambiguity in any given Hawthorne character or work. What does reading "Rappaccini's Daughter" (or "The Minister's Black Veil" or "Young Goodman Brown") do to the reader's ability to discern "good" and "evil" characters?

6. Consider Hawthorne's presentation of women in his fiction. What attitudes inform his portraits of Beatrice Rappaccini or of Hester Prynne?

7. Consider the relationship between "The Custom-House" and *The Scarlet Letter*. Where does the narrator stand in each work? In what ways might we consider "The Custom-House" an integral part of the longer fiction? Consider the particular use of "The Custom-House" as a way of "explaining" or delaying the fiction: might "The Custom-House" serve as Hawthorne's "black veil" in facing his readers?

8. Given the autobiographical references in "The Custom-House," consider the possibility that each of the major characters in *The Scarlet Letter* might also be aspects of the narrator's own persona. Discuss ways in which Hester Prynne, Arthur Dimmesdale, Roger Chillingworth, and Pearl complement each other thematically.

9. Given your earlier study of Puritan literature, trace elements of Puritanism in Hawthorne's stories or *The Scarlet Letter* and discuss the extent to which Hawthorne himself embraces or critiques Puritan ideology. (Compare actual Puritans you have studied with Hawthorne's fictional characters: Anne Bradstreet with Hester Prynne; Edward Taylor with Arthur Dimmesdale; Jonathan Edwards with various ministers in Hawthorne, or with the narrator himself.)

10. Locate references to childhood in *The Scarlet Letter* and, focusing on Pearl, discuss Hawthorne's portrait of what it might have been like to be a Puritan child.

11. To lighten up the class a bit, screen a few scenes from the recent Hollywood film *The Scarlet Letter*. Ask students to comment on whether certain big (and unintentionally hilarious!) scenes catch the spirit of Hawthorne's novel. *Viewers' note*: the novel that you know doesn't start until about an hour into the film. The final ten minutes—featuring a big Indian fight, a bit of New Age catharsis by Dimmesdale, and an ending that you won't believe—can be a good place to start a lively conversation and inspire some comparative essays about characterization and major themes.

HENRY WADSWORTH LONGFELLOW

1. Longfellow sought to be a poet for the American people: to inspire his nation, unite it, and help it imagine itself as a coherent culture with a historical legacy. Write about two of his poems in detail and talk about ways in which they make his poetic mission clear.

2. Write an essay comparing "The Slave's Dream" to S. Morton's "The African Chief."

EDGAR ALLAN POE

1. Summarize Poe's theory of aesthetics as he expresses it in "The Philosophy of Composition" and discuss his application of that philosophy in "The Raven." Given Poe's delight in wit and practical jokes, do you think that he means everything that he says in "The Philosophy of Composition"? Are there elements of self-parody in "The Raven"?

2. Explicate a short lyric ("To Helen") and discuss Poe's creation of a persona.

3. Discuss "The Sleeper," "The Raven," "Annabel Lee," and "Ligeia" in light of Poe's statement in "The Philosophy of Composition" that "the death, then, of a beautiful woman is, unquestionably, the most poetical topic in the world—and equally is it beyond doubt that the lips best suited for such topic are those of a bereaved lover."

4. Explain what Poe means by his attempt to achieve "unity of effect," and trace the particular ways he manages this in "Fall of the House of Usher," "The Man of the Crowd," or "The Masque of the Red Death."

5. Poe almost never writes about American settings or cultural contexts. Why not? Write an essay distinguishing his kind of Romanticism from that of Bryant, Whittier, or Longfellow.

Abraham Lincoln

1. Lincoln's prose style changed permanently the nature of American public speech. In the American literary tradition, what roots does he draw on and what traditions does he break from? Find passages from earlier public or political prose (Winthrop, Paine, Jefferson, Edwards) to make the comparison clear.

2. Comparing the 1858 "House Divided" speech to the Second Inaugural Address, do you see any differences in strategy, style, temperament? If so, describe those differences and speculate on causes and motivations.

Margaret Fuller

1. Read Margaret Fuller's "The Great Lawsuit," published the year before Emerson published "The Poet." Focusing on comparison with Emerson, discuss Fuller's critique of the masculine assumptions of her generation of intellectuals.

2. At one point in "The Great Lawsuit," Fuller writes prophetically: "And will not she soon appear? The woman who shall vindicate their birthright for all women; who shall teach them what to claim, and how to use what they obtain?" Why was the time right for Fuller to expect an appearance "soon" of this new empowered woman? Had literary culture in some ways prepared the way? Had it created obstacles that Fuller's new woman would have to overcome?

3. Write an essay comparing Fuller's expository style to Emerson's or Thoreau's. Where does she draw on Transcendental modes of discourse? Where does she break radically from those modes, and why?

Harriet Beecher Stowe

1. Write an essay about Tom, whose fame underwent dramatic changes from the middle of the nineteenth century to the middle of this one. Why might Tom have been an appropriate "hero" for the historical moment in which Stowe created him? Are the other African American characters in *Uncle Tom's Cabin* constructed in similar ways, for similar purposes? How do you account for variations?

2. Write an essay about the white characters in *Uncle Tom's Cabin*. Why would this particular array of characters serve Stowe's purposes?

Fanny Fern

Compare Fern's rhetorical strategies to those of Fuller, or compare both of them to Emerson. Is Fern implicitly criticizing a style of argument, as well as the subjugation of women? Cite and discuss specific passages in Fern's essays to support your answer.

HARRIET JACOBS

1. Compare Linda Brent with Hester Prynne in *The Scarlet Letter.* See especially the following quotation from *Incidents,* which equates unwed motherhood with stigma: "My unconscious babe was the ever-present witness of my shame."

2. Write a paper comparing Jacobs and Douglass and based on the following central quotations from each narrative: "Slavery is terrible for men; but it is far more terrible for women" (Jacobs) and "You have seen how a man was made a slave; you shall see how a slave was made a man" (Douglass).

3. Explore the particular obstacles Linda Brent faces and their significance for women at the end of the twentieth century: sexual harassment, poor mothers' legal rights, and difficulties for advancement when faced with responsibilities and care for children.

4. Jacobs ends her narrative "with freedom, not in the usual way, with marriage." Comment on the implication here that freedom matters more to Linda Brent than marriage. To what extent does *Incidents* suggest that the "life story" is different for enslaved women than for free (white) women?

5. Identify the contradictions implied in Dr. Flint's promise to Linda that if she moves into the house he has built for her, he will "make her a lady."

T. B. THORPE

1. Without explaining the humor of "The Big Bear of Arkansas," can you describe it as a literary experience? Does it seem to be written from within the culture it talks about, or from the loftier view of an outsider? How well does this narrative stance work? Write an essay offering speculative connections between this early work of Southwestern humor and comic styles in modern America.

HENRY DAVID THOREAU

1. Discuss one of the following statements from *Walden:* (1) "Every morning . . . I got up early and bathed in the pond; that was a religious exercise, and one of the best things which I did" or (2) "I fear chiefly lest my expression may not be *extravagant* enough, may not wander far enough beyond the narrow limits of my daily experience, so as to be adequate to the truth of which I have been convinced."

2. Cite several points of philosophical and stylistic connection and divergence between Emerson's *Nature* and Thoreau's *Walden.*

3. Discuss in detail one point of significant resemblance between Franklin's *Autobiography* and Thoreau's *Walden* and one point of contrast.

4. Explain specific ways in which Thoreau's *Walden* may be considered a "practice" of Emerson's theory. Emerson, whose philosophy influenced Thoreau, wrote that "words are also actions, and actions are a kind of words." Write an essay on

Walden in which you demonstrate Thoreau's insistence on the truth of this statement or apply the same quotation from Emerson to "Resistance to Civil Government," paying particular attention to the relationship between self-expression and personal conscience.

5. Explore any of the following central concepts in Thoreau: the spiritual vision of unity with nature, the significance of language in achieving such a vision, the theme of self-reliance, the use of analogy as meditation (perhaps contrasting Thoreau with Edward Taylor), and the significance of self-expression.

FREDERICK DOUGLASS

1. Discuss the extent to which Douglass may be considered a Transcendentalist in his view of human nature and the future of the United States.

2. Compare Douglass's *Narrative* with Franklin's *Autobiography,* narratives about self-creation and about the possibilities open to the individual man or woman.

3. Douglass writes parts of his slave narrative as a series of incidents or adventures. Discuss ways in which those various incidents and adventures are made to cohere.

4. Compare Harriet Jacobs's *Incidents in the Life of a Slave Girl* with Douglass's *Narrative.* Was the model of "heroic fugitive" possible for female slaves? Jacob's *Incidents* depicts the network of relationships within the slave community and between black and white communities. Look for evidence of such a network in Douglass's *Narrative.* What explains Douglass's lack of attention to emotional connections?

5. In his prefatory letter to the *Narrative,* Boston abolitionist Wendell Phillips compares Douglass with the signers of The Declaration of Independence: "You, too, publish your declaration of freedom with danger compassing you around." Does the *Narrative* share formal similarities with The Declaration of Independence as well as rhetorical ones? Compare Jefferson's characterization of the British king and his itemizing of grievances with the design and structure of Douglass's *Narrative.*

6. Compare *A Narrative of the Captivity and Restoration of Mrs. Mary Rowlandson* with *Narrative of the Life of Frederick Douglass, an American Slave.* What formal, thematic, and historical continuities exist between these indigenous genres?

7. In "The Meaning of July Fourth for the Negro," Douglass writes that the reformer's heart "may well beat lighter at the thought that America is young" and that "were the nation older," its "great streams" may dry up, leaving "the sad tale of departed glory." Explain why Douglass takes hope from America's youth, and contrast this expression with the twentieth-century poet Robinson Jeffers's sentiments in "Shine, Perishing Republic."

8. Trace Douglass's views concerning the role of reform and dissent in the American republic in "The Meaning of July Fourth for the Negro."

Walt Whitman

1. Write an essay in which you describe the place and effect of "Facing West from California's Shores" within the context of *Leaves of Grass* ["Song of Myself"].

2. Focusing on the following two quotations, discuss thematic, philosophical, and technical connections between Emerson and Whitman: from *Nature:* "I become a transparent eyeball. I am nothing. I see all"; and from "Preface to *Leaves of Grass*": "[the greatest poet] is a seer . . . is individual . . . he is complete in himself. . . . What the eyesight does to the rest he does to the rest." Where does Whitman break with Emerson's practice, if not from Emerson's ideals and theorizing?

3. Compare Emerson's "The Poet" with "Preface to *Leaves of Grass*." In what ways does Whitman claim to embody Emerson's idea of the American poet?

4. Choose one of the following quotations from *Leaves of Grass* ["Song of Myself"] and discuss it by suggesting several ways in which it describes what Whitman is attempting in the poem: (1) "I know I am solid and sound, / To me the converging objects of the universe perpetually flow, / All are written to me, and I must get what the writing means"; (2) "I am an acme of things accomplish'd, and I am an encloser of things to be"; (3) "I know I have the best of time and space, and was never measured and never will be measured."

5. Discuss Whitman's poetry as a culmination in the development of American identity. How does Whitman contribute to the ongoing evolution of self-reliance? Of human freedom? Of concepts of democracy?

6. Write an essay about "Out of the Cradle Endlessly Rocking" and the traditions of the Anglo-American elegy. What rules and expectations does Whitman follow here? Which rules does he break, and how and why?

7. Trace Whitman's various responses to the Civil War throughout the poems anthologized from *Drum-Taps*. Compare and contrast Whitman's war poems with the anthologized lyrics from Melville's *Battle-Pieces*.

8. Do a study of Whitman's use of the catalog as a poetic device. Then illustrate, by means of close analysis, the effects Whitman achieves in a particular catalog from *Leaves of Grass*.

9. Alternatively, study and illustrate Whitman's use of parallel construction as a poetic device, and comment on its various effects.

Louisa Amelia Smith Clappe and Bayard Taylor

1. Write an essay about the kind of imaginative excitement that each of these travel writers finds in the American West.

2. What kind of audience is implied by each of these texts? What are the differences?

HERMAN MELVILLE

1. Write an essay about "Benito Cereno" as expressing that "power of blackness" that Melville ascribes to Hawthorne's work. In pursuing that "blackness," what happens to the treatment of black slaves as characters in fiction?

2. Writing about "Benito Cereno," Newton Arvin noted that "the story is an artistic miscarriage, with moments of undeniable power." Evaluate the fairness of this statement given your own reading of the story.

3. How well is "Bartleby, the Scrivener" grounded in the actualities of modern-style work? Is the narrator himself a victim of the same misery that may have undone Bartleby? Write an essay about this story not as about "ah, humanity!" but as about the frustrations and balked emotions of the modern urban workplace.

4. Part of what fascinates the reader (and possibly Melville himself) about Bartleby is his inscrutability—and possible banality. Describe various "walls" that Bartleby may be trapped behind and explore ways in which the story's structure or design reinforces the reader's inability to penetrate those walls.

5. Choose any one of the following moments of dialogue in Melville and use it as a prism through which to "read" the work in which it appears: (1) "Ah, Bartleby! Ah, humanity!"; (2) " 'Follow your leader' "; (3) "God bless Captain Vere!"

6. If in some ways Billy is Adam or Jesus Christ and Claggart is Satan or the serpent, then is Vere to be understood as Pontius Pilate? What are the limits and complications of reading him that way?

7. Explore the two kinds of justice Melville sets in opposition in *Billy Budd, Sailor,* and discuss the moral, political, and thematic implications of Billy's execution.

EMILY DICKINSON

1. Read carefully a group of Dickinson poems with related themes—the natural world, death, traveling, private experience, art and its value—then write an interpretation of one of the poems that includes your expanded understanding of the way Dickinson uses the theme in other poems in the group. Some specific groupings: (1) poems of loss and defeat: 49, 67, 305; (2) poems about ecstasy or vision: 185, 214, 249, 465, 501, 528, 632; (3) poems about solitude: 280, 303, 441, 664, 754, 1099; (4) poems about death: 49, 67, 241, 258, 280, 341, 449, 510, 712, 1078, 1732; (5) poems about madness and suffering: 315, 348, 435, 536; (6) poems about entrapment: 528, 754, 1099; and (7) poems about craft: 441, 448, 505, 1129.

2. Dickinson's poems 130, 328, 348, and 824 all contain references to birds. Discuss how they are observed in each poem; or study one of the following groups of poems and trace the recurring image pattern: (1) a bee or bees in 130, 214, 216, 348; (2) a fly or flies in 465; (3) butterflies in 214, 341, 1099; and (4) church imagery or biblical references in 130, 216, 258, 1545.

3. Locate images of size, particularly of smallness, in Dickinson's poetry. Working out from 185, trace evidence that Dickinson perceived a relationship between "size" and literary authority. Alternatively, locate images of authority in the world (king, emperor, gentlemen) and contrast these with images Dickinson uses to create her own persona as poet.

4. Many Dickinson poems illustrate change in the consciousness of the poet or speaker. Choose a poem in which this happens and trace the process by which the poem reflects and creates the change.

REBECCA HARDING DAVIS

1. Compare the relationships between Hester and Dimmesdale in *The Scarlet Letter* and between Hugh Wolfe and Deborah in *Life in the Iron-Mills*.

2. Recall what Thoreau has to say in *Walden* about the "lives of quiet desperation" most men lead. Might Hugh Wolfe, like Thoreau, have chosen to simplify his life and retreat to a pond outside of town? Compare the conditions under which Wolfe makes his art with those Thoreau describes.

3. Study Davis's references to Deborah, who is generally depicted as being a "thwarted woman" who leads a "colorless life." Contrast her with the korl woman. Discuss the distance Davis creates between the real and the ideal woman in Wolfe's life.

HARRIET PRESCOTT SPOFFORD

Write an essay comparing Spofford's "Circumstance" to other works in the American gothic tradition; consider works by Poe and Hawthorne especially. Does Spofford take chances that these earlier writers did not?

Volume C: American Literature 1865–1914

General Questions

1. Compare the humor in Twain's "The Notorious Jumping Frog of Calaveras County," Harte's "The Outcasts of Poker Flat," and Freeman's "The Revolt of 'Mother.'"

2. Writers following the Civil War put irony to new thematic uses. Compare the way in which irony is used in Bierce's "Occurrence at Owl Creek Bridge," James's "The Jolly Corner," and Crane's "The Open Boat."

3. Write an essay on point of view in regionalist and local-color fiction from this period. In which texts does the narrator look *at* the major characters from an omniscient perspective? In which texts does the narration unfold through the eyes of a character? What characters are excluded from sharing the point of view, and why? What effects do these varying strategies have on the fiction and its major themes?

4. Write an essay discussing differences in the portrayal of women characters and women's experience in the local-color writers Harte and Garland, regionalist writers Freeman, Jewett, and Chopin, the Asian American author Sui Sin Far, and the New York ethnic writer Cahan. Looking at these portrayals as a group, what generalizations occur to you about the status of women in various communities in late-nineteenth-century America?

5. Although this period was the heyday of Realism and Naturalism, many writers continued to use dreams and fantasy as important elements in their work. Discuss Bierce's "Occurrence at Owl Creek Bridge," Jewett's "A White Heron," Gilman's "The Yellow Wall-paper," James's "The Jolly Corner," and Wovoka's vision of the Messiah, focusing on how the use of dream, vision, or altered perception affects the realism of the fiction.

6. Many late-nineteenth-century writers wrote in response to contemporary social conditions. Present a composite picture of their concerns by discussing the following group of texts: Charlot's "[He has filled graves with our bones]," and Garland's "Under the Lion's Paw."

7. Examine political discourse of Cochise, Charlot, Washington, and Du Bois in the context of political discourse in earlier periods of American literature. What similarities and variations do you see? How do Washington and Du Bois respond, implicitly and otherwise, to new and prevailing literary styles of the late nineteenth or early twentieth centuries?

8. In your library, consult a standard literary history for its general discussion of local-color and regional writing at the end of the nineteenth century. These summaries are rarely more than a few pages long. Then analyze any story in *NAAL* by Jewett, Chopin, Freeman, Chesnutt, Harte, Garland, or Oskison in light of the historical commentary, and discuss differences you see between the story and the general descriptions.

9. Research a regional writer from this period (1870–1914) from your home state or region. Write an essay analyzing one of the sketches or stories by this writer.

10. Referring to Twain's "Fenimore Cooper's Literary Offenses," and James's "The Art of Fiction," construct a theory of Realism that accommodates premises in several of these texts. Then choose one story by each writer, and see how thoroughly each plays by these rules.

11. Turn-of-the-century critics used the phrase *new realists* to describe the work of naturalists S. Crane, Dreiser, and London. Choose a work of fiction by any of these writers and consider the accuracy of the phrase. Based on your analysis, would you identify Naturalism as a new genre or a derivative one (a "new" Realism)?

12. Whether in anticipation of or in the general climate of Freud's *The Interpretation of Dreams* (1900), sexuality concerns several writers of the 1865–1914

period. Analyze sexual imagery or attitudes toward sexuality in several of the following works: James's "The Jolly Corner"; Jewett's "A White Heron"; Chopin's *The Awakening,* "At the 'Cadian Ball," or "The Storm"; Freeman's "A New England Nun"; and Wharton's "Souls Belated."

Questions about Individual Authors and Works

MARK TWAIN

1. Many readers of *Adventures of Huckleberry Finn* consider the ending flawed— Hemingway, for example, said that Twain "cheated"—while others have praised it. Write an essay about the appropriateness of the novel's ending, focusing on Huck's treatment of Jim and on Huck's moral complicity with Tom.

2. The theme of pretending is one that unifies *Adventures of Huckleberry Finn,* although the word *pretending* takes on several meanings and levels of significance as the novel unfolds. Describe three of these, and illustrate each by analyzing a specific character, scene, or incident from the novel.

3. If one were constructing a list of "classic" American books, *Adventures of Huckleberry Finn* would probably appear on it. Write an essay about ways in which Twain explores American experience in new ways.

4. Explore the relationship between the possible symbolic importance of the river and the design and structure of the novel.

5. Analyze Twain's portrait of Jim in light of your reading of Douglass. Is *Adventures of Huckleberry Finn* in some ways a slave narrative? Does Twain use the discussion of slavery as a pretext to write about other issues?

6. Explore the novel as a presentation of mid-nineteenth-century attitudes toward children and child rearing.

7. Write an essay about Twain's humor, focusing on "The Notorious Jumping Frog of Calaveras County" or "Fenimore Cooper's Literary Offenses" and one or two incidents from *Adventures of Huckleberry Finn.*

8. Discuss Huck Finn's language in the opening passages of *Adventures of Huckleberry Finn.* Discuss how Twain uses Huck's style as a way to construct his character.

9. Compare Huck Finn's speech with dialects spoken by other characters in the novel. Compare Twain's depiction of dialect in general with that of Harte, Harris, or Jewett.

10. How does Twain portray Tom Sawyer? Is he model, rival, alter ego, or mirror for Huck? Does he develop in the novel?

11. Write an essay about the development of Jim as a character. Does he change over the course of the novel? Compare his portrait with portraits of black characters in the Harris tales or in Chesnutt's "The Goophered Grapevine."

12. Write an essay about the plot of *Huckleberry Finn*. If the novel were more tightly plotted, would it be better? In what ways is a loose structure advantageous?

13. For generations, *Huckleberry Finn* has been read as a moral breakthrough in American letters. Lately, that kind of reading has become more controversial. What are your own perceptions on this question, and where are they grounded in the novel?

NATIVE AMERICAN ORATORY

1. Compare the rhetorical strategy of Charlot to that of William Apess in "An Indian's Looking-Glass for the White Man."

2. Compare Charlot's rhetorical construction of "the white man" with rhetorical constructions of "King George" in The Declaration of Independence.

3. Write an essay about the role that Native American oratory can or should play in a history of modern American literature. What can be learned from these transcribed speeches? What stylistic and moral attention needs to be paid to them, and why?

SARAH MORGAN BRYAN PIATT

1. Compare Piatt's way of facing the challenge of the graveyard elegy to that of Emma Lazarus. How does each poet attempt to make this old subject fresh? How do these poems respond to mainstream and male-dominated American poetic practice, as exemplified by Longfellow and promulgated by Emerson?

CONSTANCE FENIMORE WOOLSON, CHARLOTTE PERKINS GILMAN, AND HENRY JAMES

1. Write an essay comparing "Miss Grief" to "The Real Thing," as meditations on the artifice of realism. Which do you find more thoughtful about this paradox, and why?

2. Both of these stories are first person narratives; the artist speaks of a personal experience pertaining to professional practice. Compare the prose with which these stories open and close. What does that prose suggest about the voice and personality of the speaker?

3. Examine Gilman's "Why I Wrote *The Yellow Wall-paper?*" and James's "The Art of Fiction" and discuss points of convergence and divergence, as explanations of fiction's urgency and role.

4. How does Gilman's Realism differ from that of James? Does the narrator of "The Yellow Wall-paper" recognize any correspondence between her own perception and external reality?

5. Consider "The Yellow Wall-paper" as Gilman's portrait of the American woman as writer. What does the story suggest about the literary authority of the woman writer? What obstacles stand in the way of her creation? What is her ultimate work of art?

6. Compare Gilman's narrator and Chopin's Edna as potential artists. What kinds of perceptions empower them? What stands in their way?

7. In "The Art of Fiction," James writes, "A novel is in its broadest definition a personal, a direct impression of life." With this quotation as your point of reference, analyze the particular "impression" James is trying to create in *Daisy Miller*, "The Real Thing," or "The Beast in the Jungle."

8. James has often been called a psychological realist who was more interested in the development of consciousness than in portraying character types and social reality. Discuss the extent to which this observation holds true in *Daisy Miller* or "The Beast in the Jungle."

9. Although *Daisy Miller* appears to focus on the portrait of Daisy herself, a reader might argue that James's real interest is in Winterbourne. Rethink the events of the story as Daisy herself might have viewed them, and suggest ways in which the author of "A White Heron" or of "A New England Nun" might have differently handled both the story and the portrait of Daisy.

10 . Reviewing the James stories for his interest in convention and social forms, write an essay on one or two scenes that exemplify James as a careful observer of social practices.

11. James is often credited with perfecting the use of point of view as a narrative device. Choose one incident from "The Beast in the Jungle" and analyze his use of point of view in that story. What does it reveal? What does it conceal? How does it achieve its effectiveness? What is its significance in terms of the story's themes?

12. Write an essay about James as a writer of horror stories. As a realist, what Gothic or horror traditions does he draw on? How does he transform and modernize the idea of evil?

SARAH ORNE JEWETT

1. Compare Jewett's Sylvy in "A White Heron" with May Bartram of James's "The Beast in the Jungle."

2. The tree, the hunter, the cow, and the heron all seem to possess mythical significance in "A White Heron." Choose one to discuss in relationship to Sylvy and explore the way Jewett combines elements of folk or fairy tale and literary realism.

3. Read Thorpe's "The Big Bear of Arkansas." Viewing the Southwest humorists as precursors of the late-nineteenth-century local-color writers, contrast Thorpe's attitude toward the bear hunt with Jewett's attitude toward Sylvy's search for the bird in "A White Heron." Or imagine "A White Heron" told from the point of view of the young ornithologist and explain why this other story might have been accepted for publication in the sporting magazine of the Southwest humorists, *The Spirit of the Times*.

4. Unlike Twain, Gilman, and James, Jewett did not write essays about writing or reading. Fill in the gap in literary history, using the two anthologized stories as a foundation, and write the essay that wasn't: "How to Tell a Story," by Sarah Orne Jewett. You may also choose to title the essay "Fiction-Writing and Fiction-Reading" or "The Art of Fiction." Compare the relationship between Edna Pontellier and Mlle. Reisz in *The Awakening* with the relationship between the narrator and Mrs. Todd in Jewett's "The Foreigner."

KATE CHOPIN AND MARY E. WILKINS FREEMAN

1. These two authors are often classified as local colorists or regionalist writers. What do you see as the implicit emotional relationship between each of these authors and the place they write about? Are their ambitions the same? Do you find *local colorist* a descriptive term, or a limiting one, for describing these texts and authors?

2. *The Awakening*, "A New England Nun," and "The Revolt of 'Mother' " regularly appear as important moments in the history of American feminist literature. Compare the ways that each work investigates the predicament of a woman in a domestic setting.

3. Both "The Revolt of 'Mother' " and "A New England Nun" portray women who triumph over the material conditions of their existence. Describe the nature of that triumph and the process by which they achieve it.

4. Examine the use of the window and the barn doors as framing devices in the two anthologized stories. Compare form in Freeman's fiction with form in Gilman, James, or Jewett.

5. Compare Oakhurst in Harte's "The Outcasts of Poker Flat" and Freeman's Adoniram Penn. Do they triumph or are they defeated men?

6. Describe the character of Mlle. Reisz in *The Awakening* and compare her with Louisa Ellis in Freeman's "A New England Nun." How does Chopin limit Mlle. Reisz's possibilities and influence on Edna in her novel?

7. Edna Pontellier is caught in the contradictions between the way others see her and the way she sees herself. Identify several moments in which this becomes apparent and show Edna's growing awareness of the contradiction.

8. Discuss the women of color in *The Awakening*. What does their presence and their treatment in the novel suggest about Edna's (and Chopin's) attitudes toward human development for nonwhite and poor women?

9. Some readers have described Edna's death in *The Awakening* as suicide; others view it as her attempt at self-realization. Argue the relative truth of both interpretations.

10. *The Awakening* contains elements of Regionalism, Realism, and Naturalism. Identify these by choosing exemplary characters or scenes from the novel and by basing your distinctions on close analysis.

11. In "At the 'Cadian Ball," Chopin explores the dimensions of sexual power and desire conferred by racial and class status and marked by dialect. Identify the numerous among the characters that can be understood in terms of power dynamics and explicate those dynamics.

CHARLES CHESNUTT AND HAMLIN GARLAND

1. Consider the ending of "Under the Lion's Paw" and the ending of "The Wife of His Youth." Garland ties up the loose ends; Chesnutt leaves huge questions unanswered. Why do these stories conclude so differently? What does each ending suggest about the kind of "realism" espoused by each author?

2. After generations of dialect humor in American newspapers and magazines, what are the risks of Chesnutt's narration of "The Goophered Grapevine"? How successful is the story in overcoming those risks?

3. Explore the way in which Chesnutt manipulates point of view in "The Goophered Grapevine" and the effect this has on the story's ending.

4. Read the Uncle Remus stories by Joel Chandler Harris, and compare Chesnutt's use of the folk tale and the folk narrator with that of Harris.

5. Compare Irving's use of folk materials early in the nineteenth century with Chesnutt's use of folk materials in "The Goophered Grapevine."

6. Write an essay about "The Wife of His Youth" as a possible act of resistance by Chesnutt against the relative innocuousness of the local-color tradition in which he usually worked and with which he was commonly associated. In what ways is this story a critique or confirmation of the idea that place determines identity? What difficult problems does it raise regarding the migration of African Americans to other regions and the establishment of new identities and social orders?

7. Compare Garland's portrait of the women in "Under the Lion's Paw" with Freeman's in "The Revolt of 'Mother.'" How does each author present women's ability to confront poverty?

8. Garland's narrator views his characters from the outside. Review specific scenes in the story to show how this outsider's view predetermines the reader's understanding of the characters' actions.

9. Are the characters in "Under the Lion's Paw" individuals or types? What would be the advantages or disadvantages of stereotyping in a story with these intentions?

EDITH WHARTON AND SUI SIN FAR

1. Write an essay comparing Wharton and Sui Sin Far as authors of realist fiction, with special interest in the predicament of women. Compare the challenges and complications of the setting that each author observes, and the challenge of making these narratives important to a broad audience.

2. Some of the wit and poignancy of "Mrs. Spring Fragrance" stems from Far's portrayal of Chinese-American society as a hybrid, a mix of traditions and social practices. Write an essay about how the narrator situates herself with regard to the story, and compare that point of view to the perspective favored in "Souls Belated."

3. For much of the twentieth century, critics regarded Wharton's short stories as exercises in the mode of Henry James. What are the significant differences between "Souls Belated" and James's "The Jolly Corner" or "The Beast in the Jungle"? Write an essay comparing Wharton and James as prose stylists, and as presenters of interactions between men and women.

BOOKER T. WASHINGTON AND W. E. B. DU BOIS

1. Write an essay about the convention of regarding these writers as political opposites. How appropriate do you think that assumption is, and why? What aspects of these texts are you thinking about as you form your opinion?

2. The structure and rhetorical strategies of *The Souls of Black Folk* are markedly different from those favored by Washington in *Up from Slavery*. Write an essay describing some of these differences, and consider the relationship of these strategies to the intentions of each author.

CHARLES ALEXANDER EASTMAN

1. Research Elaine Goodale (perhaps by reading *Sister to the Sioux: The Memoirs of Elaine Goodale Eastman,* 1978, edited by Kay Graber), and construct a portrait of the young white women who became missionaries to the American Indians in the West.

2. Calling the adherents of the Ghost Dance religion "prophets of the 'Red Christ,'" Eastman writes about what he calls this religious "craze": "It meant that the last hope of race entity had departed, and my people were groping blindly after spiritual relief in their bewilderment and misery." Set this comment against

Captain Sword's account of the Ghost Dance religion and evaluate it in terms of the confusion that becomes evident among "hostiles" and "friendlies" during the Ghost Dance War.

STEPHEN CRANE

1. Compare "The Open Boat" to "The Blue Hotel" as fables about the human condition. Which one seems to you more like a fable or a lesson? What differences do you see in the way in which irony is presented and handled in each narrative?

2. Despite the apparent irrationality of its characters, "The Blue Hotel" moves logically and inexorably toward its conclusion. Study the evidence of irrationality in the story's portraits of human behavior; then describe the linear progression by which the Swede's initial comment—" 'I suppose there have been a good many men killed in this room' "—comes to control events.

3. In "The Bride Comes to Yellow Sky," Jack Potter's marriage appears to alter forever Scratchy Wilson's perception of reality. Argue that for Crane marriage itself becomes an external force. Does the story's humor mitigate the oppressiveness of this force?

4. Explore relationships between Crane's poems and his fiction. Does Crane's choice of the lyric poem allow him to develop aspects of his major themes that his fiction does not fully explore? How do his choices in language and form reflect his temperament and prevailing themes?

THEODORE DREISER

Describe the portrait of family life that Dreiser presents in "Old Rogaum and His Theresa." Would it be legitimate to categorize this story as a work in the naturalistic tradition? What are the problems or limitations in doing so?

JOHN M. OSKISON

1. Write a research paper in which you locate "The Problem of Old Harjo" in the history of intervention in the lives of Native Americans in the nineteenth century. Cite evidence from other anthologized texts, including Apess's "An Indian's Looking-Glass," Eastman's *From the Deep Woods to Civilization,* Wovoka's vision, and Zitkala Ša's "Impressions of an Indian Childhood."

2. Explore Apess's figure of speech, the "Indian's looking-glass," as it applies to "The Problem of Old Harjo." To what extent does Harjo possess the cunning of the powerless? To what extent is Harjo the powerless character in the story?

NATIVE AMERICAN CHANTS AND SONGS

For most students writing about these transcribed oral works, the best strategy might be to read them in a broad context, rather than isolate them from each other or as a group away from the other materials in *NAAL.* In many cultures, chants and songs have done similar important kinds of cultural work: they can encourage resolve, peace of mind, a sense of group identity, connection with the past and with the divine. They also can provide solace or other sorts of escape from the verbal and psychological turmoil of ordinary life and the moment of order and a consolation that can come from saying and hearing the same things again and again. What, then, are the resemblances between some of these chants and nineteenth-century poetry by white Americans? Are some New England poets seeking these same values? When Du Bois turns to the "chants and songs" of African Americans as a focus for his meditations on being black in a predominantly white America, does he search for qualities similar to ones in these Native American texts?

Henry Adams

1. Henry Adams writes in his *Education* that "From earliest childhood the boy was accustomed to feel that, for him, life was double." Explain the significance of Adams's particular kind of "double vision." Compare it with the internal contradiction Edna Pontellier feels in *The Awakening* and the "double consciousness" of Du Boisean black identity.

2. What happens to Adams's perception of design and order in the universe over the course of his *Education*? How does it happen that "he found himself lying in the Gallery of Machines at the Great Exposition of 1900, his historical neck broken by the sudden irruption of forces totally new"?

3. Explain and comment on the following statement from *The Education*: "Adams began to ponder, asking himself whether he knew of any American artist who had ever insisted on the power of sex, as every classic had always done; but he could think only of Walt Whitman; Bret Harte, as far as the magazines would let him venture; and one or two painters, for the flesh-tones. . . . American art, like the American language and American education, was as far as possible sexless."

4. The anthologized chapters from *The Education* contain much evidence that Adams viewed himself as a transitional figure. Identify several points at which he "broke his life in halves again," and trace his progress from his early sense that the eighteenth century was his companion to his entrance into the twentieth century at the close of Chapter XXV.

5. What, finally, does Adams mean by an "education"? Is he seeking the same kind of experience and wisdom that Emerson or Thoreau sought? Do his expectations determine his self-described "failure"?

6. In American literary culture, trace the sources of Adams's habit of organizing experience into dualities and oppositions. Adams thinks in dialectics. Who else in the American traditions thinks that way? How might this habit of mind predetermine what he sees when he looks at modern technological power?

Volume D: American Literature between
the Wars, 1914–1945

General Questions

1. At the end of Frost's poem "The Oven Bird," we find the following lines: "The question that he frames in all but words / Is what to make of a diminished thing." With reference to works by other poets and prose writers, explain how this statement expresses a common theme in twentieth-century American writing.

2. Compare an early-nineteenth-century poem (such as Bryant's "Thanatopsis") with an early-twentieth-century poem (Frost's "Directive" or Robinson's "Luke Havergal"). Discuss how these poems reflect shifts in perspective, and in ideas about what constitutes poetry.

3. Choose three twentieth-century works and show how they implicitly respond to the following quotation from Stevens's "Of Modern Poetry": "The poem of the mind in the act of finding / What will suffice. It has not always had / To find: the scene was set; it repeated what / Was in the script."

4. Explain the parallel concerns in the following statements: (1) "The poem is a momentary stay against confusion" (Frost, "The Figure a Poem Makes"), (2) "These fragments I have shored against my ruins" (Eliot, *The Waste Land*), and (3) "Poetry is the supreme fiction, madame" (Stevens, "A High-Toned Old Christian Woman").

5. Examine twentieth-century modernist lyric poems in traditional forms by Robinson, Frost, Millay, Bogan, Parker, McKay, and Moore. How do these poets reconcile traditional forms with twentieth-century themes?

6. Many modernist lyric poems are themselves about poetic form and intention. Compare some of these poems by Frost, Stevens, Williams, Bishop, Wilbur, and Dove.

7. Examine the modern use of traditional metric forms. Analyze what Frost does to and with iambic pentameter in "Desert Places" or how Stevens uses it in "The Idea of Order at Key West."

8. In the headnote to Marianne Moore in *NAAL*, Nina Baym writes, "Pound worked with the clause, Williams with the line, H. D. with the image, and Stevens and Stein with the word; Moore, unlike these modernist contemporaries, used the entire stanza as the unit of her poetry." In an out-of-class essay, choose poems by each of these writers that will allow you to further explain the distinctions Baym creates in this statement. In British poetry, Robert Browning was a master of the dramatic monologue—a poem in which a speaker, different from the poet, reveals much about his or her own character in a speech to somebody else. Find and discuss dramatic monologues by three twentieth-century American poets. You might look at Stevens, Pound, Eliot, McKay, Hughes, and Wilbur for starters. Write an essay about how they adapt and develop the dramatic monologue as a form.

9. Several twentieth-century American poets have attempted to write epics. Research features of epic poetry, and write an essay about epic characteristics in Pound's *The Cantos*, H. D.'s *The Walls Do Not Fall*, Eliot's *Four Quartets*, and Hart Crane's *The Bridge*.

10. Compare the realism of a twentieth-century story with the Realism of Twain, Jewett, James, or Wharton. Analyze Faulkner's "Barn Burning" or Ernest Hemingway's "The Snows of Kilimanjaro," paying particular attention to the twentieth-century writer's innovations in point of view or use of symbolism.

11. In Suzanne Juhasz's framework for twentieth-century women poets (see the discussion of Marianne Moore in Chapter 7 of this guide), she suggests a progression from Moore to Rukeyser to Plath and Sexton to Rich in terms of the particular writer's willingness to write about women's experience in poetry. Choosing specific poems for your focus, trace this progression and comment on its effectiveness.

12. Many writers between 1914 and 1945 wrote poetry that may have been influenced by the values of Modernism, but which reflects other artistic traditions and intentions. Write an essay about poems by Taggard, Rukeyser, S. Brown, and Hughes that show a complex relationship to literary Modernism.

13. While writers like Pound and Eliot were concerned with tracing the origins of modernist consciousness in classical mythology, other writers were more interested in becoming assimilated into American society. Identify and discuss issues of importance to writers, fictional characters, or lyric voices who concern themselves with issues of immigration and assimilation.

Questions about Individual Authors and Works

BLACK ELK

1. Arnold Krupat (in "The Indian Autobiography: Origins, Type, and Function," *American Literature*, 1981) has written that "to see the Indian autobiography as a ground on which two cultures meet is to see it as the textual equivalent of the 'frontier.'" Write an essay in which you comment on this statement and its significance for understanding *Black Elk Speaks*. In writing your essay, pay particular attention to the way this text challenges the expectations of a white listener or reader.

2. In the second edition of *Black Elk Speaks* (1961), John Neihardt changed the title page of the text from "as told to John Neihardt" to "as told through John Neihardt." Explain the significance of this change and the relationship it suggests between Neihardt and Black Elk, and between Neihardt and *Black Elk Speaks*.

3. Compare this excerpt from *Black Elk Speaks* with two other American texts: Franklin's *The Autobiography* and the *Narrative of the Life of Frederick Douglass, an American Slave*. Focus on what constitutes a life-transforming moment for Franklin, for Douglass, and for Black Elk.

4. Compare Zitkala Ša's autobiographical writing and narrative voice with that of Black Elk. Both writers were Sioux; evaluate their respective roles as "holy man" and "teacher," comment on their different experiences with biculturalism, and compare the points at which they break off their autobiographical accounts.

EDGAR LEE MASTERS

1. Where does Masters seem to position himself in regard to the various voices in *Spoon River Anthology*? Does he seem to be among them? Above them? What are the problems that arise when an artist seeks to speak as or for the common man or woman and how does Masters overcome those problems?

2. Write about irony in *Spoon River Anthology*. Does it have the same effects as irony in the works of S. Crane? In Robinson? Do the implications of the dramatic irony change from one poem to the next or over the course of several of these poems?

WILLA CATHER

1. "The Sculptor's Funeral" and "Neighbour Rosicky" tell of individuals in small communities, people who live out their lives without being understood, sometimes without companionship or love. Compare Cather's stories to other works which visit this predicament—poems of Robinson and Frost, stories by Freeman, Gilman, Chopin—and describe what is special or unique about Cather's experiments in this territory.

2. To what extent are these stories reflexive—in other words, stories about the predicament of the artist? Write an essay making a case for that kind of reading, and indicating the limits or qualifications that you think such a reading should have.

AMY LOWELL AND CARL SANDBURG

1. Pound referred to Lowell's poetry as "Amygism," perhaps as a way of belittling its value, perhaps to distinguish it from "Imagism," a larger movement which Lowell helped to champion. Locate essays on Imagism in the influential magazine *Poetry* (for example, F. S. Flint, "Imagism," and Ezra Pound, "A Few Don'ts by an Imagist," both in the March 1913 issue), Lowell's own anthologies (see the *NAAL* headnote for Lowell), or other references that clarify the terms *Imagism* and *Amygism*. Compare Lowell's images with those of Pound and W. Williams. What qualities or tastes distinguish Lowell's verse from these others?

2. As American Modernist poets, should Lowell and Sandburg be seen as opposites? Are there moments where Sandburg's verse shows the influence of Imagism, moments where Lowell, like Sandburg, responds to the legacy of Whitman? Write an essay comparing the styles of Lowell and Sandburg, and speculating on causes for these differences and similarities.

3. Sandburg may continue a poetic tradition that begins with Whitman, but does he also draw on experimentation by other American poets? Locate moments in the

Sandburg poems where you see influences from other American poets and talk about how Sandburg blends them.

Gertrude Stein

1. In characterizing her "description of the loving of repetition" in *The Making of Americans,* Stein writes,

> Then there will be realised the complete history of every one, the fundamental character of every one, the bottom nature in them, the mixtures in them, the strength and weakness of everything they have inside them, the flavor of them, the meaning in them, the being in them, and then you have a whole history then of each one. Everything then they do in living is clear to the completed understanding, their living, loving, eating, pleasing, smoking, thinking, scolding, drinking, working, dancing, walking, talking, laughing, sleeping, everything in them.

How does this statement of purpose compare to Whitman's in the opening stanzas of "Song of Myself"? Is Stein's intention of a "complete history" the same as Whitman's? Write an essay describing the implicit relationship of each poet to ordinary American experience.

2. Discuss Stein's sentence structures in the excerpts from *The Making of Americans* and *Tender Buttons.* Locate similar sentences, identify points of transition in the prose, note the appearance of new and startling words, and comment on this prose as an aesthetic experiment or an act of persuasion.

3. Jewett, like Stein, lived for many years with a woman (Annie Adams Fields, the widow of Hawthorne's publisher James T. Fields) and wrote much about relationships between women in her fiction. Reread Jewett's "The Foreigner" and compare Jewett and Stein as writers about relationships between women.

Robert Frost

1. Write about the narrator's perceptions about death in "After Apple-Picking"; "Stopping By Woods on a Snowy Evening"; "Home Burial"; " 'Out, Out-' "; and "An Old Man's Winter Night." How does each poem serve as a buffer against mortality and meaninglessness?

2. Write about two of the following poems to show how Frost's poetic techniques serve as his own "momentary stay against confusion": "Once by the Pacific," "Desert Places," "Mending Wall," "The Wood-Pile," or "Design."

3. Illustrate how Frost's statement in "The Figure a Poem Makes" applies to "Home Burial": "The possibilities for tune from the dramatic tones of meaning struck across the rigidity of a limited meter are endless."

4. Discuss Frost's use of the sonnet form in the following poems: "Mowing," "The Oven Bird," "Once by the Pacific," and "Design."

5. One of the most striking characteristics of Frost's poetry is his creation of a speaking voice. Examine the following poems and describe the relationship between speaker and hearer: "The Pasture" and "The Tuft of Flowers."

6. Examine the image of loss of Paradise, or the Fall, in "Fire and Ice," "The Oven Bird," and "After Apple-Picking."

7. Choose one of the following poems not anthologized in *NAAL* for further close analysis: "A Minor Bird," "The Investment," "The Hill Wife," or "The Cow in Apple-Time."

8. In "The Gift Outright," Frost has written a small history of American literature. In the poem, he personifies the American land as female. Trace the imagery of sexual conquest in the poem, and explore what it reveals about Frost's conception of the American poet.

9. "Directive" advises its readers to get lost to find themselves. How does this poem reflect Frost's twentieth-century worldview? What are the relative values of disorientation and reorientation? How does "Directive" offer a modern version of the American dream?

SHERWOOD ANDERSON AND ANZIA YEZIERSKA

1. Do you see modernist concerns in *Winesburg, Ohio* and "The Lost 'Beautifulness' "? Or would it make more sense to think of Anderson and Yezierska as a latter-day local-colorists or realists? In answering this question, make specific reference to the selections in *NAAL*.

2. To what extent are Anderson and Yezierska writing as outsiders, introducing their readers to communities and ways of life unknown to many of them? What strategies do these writers employ to engage this larger, uninitiated American audience?

3. Read another story from Yezierska's collection *Hungry Hearts* and explore her themes of class difference and disillusionment with American promise (as she expresses them in "The Lost 'Beautifulness' ").

WALLACE STEVENS

1. One of the most famous lines from Stevens, and one of the most enigmatic, appears in "Sunday Morning": "Death is the mother of beauty." Summarize the thinking process by which the speaker in this poem transforms Sunday morning from a day of Christian religious observance for the dead into a very different kind of celebration.

2. Discuss carefully the sun imagery in stanza VII of "Sunday Morning." Then write an interpretation of "Gubbinal" that builds on what you have observed.

3. Both "Anecdote of the Jar" and "Study of Two Pears" center on an inanimate object. Discuss the meaning these two poems share, and the syntactic and semantic techniques Stevens uses to create that meaning and make pears and a jar interesting as subjects for poetry.

4. Discuss the technical experiment in Stevens's "Thirteen Ways of Looking at a Blackbird." How do other Stevens poems help us understand what this poem is about?

5. "The Idea of Order at Key West" contains two poems or singers: the woman who sings, and the poem's speaker. Describe the relationship between them, and comment on Stevens's use of these two voices—one of which is heard, the other only described.

6. Compare poems of Frost and Stevens, focusing on one of the following pairs: Frost's "Desert Places" and Stevens's "The Snow Man" or Frost's "Directive" and Stevens's "A Postcard from the Volcano." In what ways do Frost and Stevens contribute to modernist ways of knowing the world?

7. Examine poems in which you see activities of (1) looking at things or (2) playing musical instruments or singing, and explore the significance of the activity in Stevens's poems.

Susan Glaspell

1. Write about ways in which *Trifles* extends, alters, or refreshes themes in Chopin's *The Awakening*, Gilman's "The Yellow Wall-paper," or Yezierska's "The Lost 'Beautifulness.' "

2. Write about *Trifles* as a commentary on isolation in the rural New England landscape. Compare Glaspell's exploration of this subject with similar moments in Robinson and Frost. How far back does this theme go, in the literature of New England, and where do we see it continuing in contemporary popular literature?

William Carlos Williams

1. At the end of "To Elsie" Williams writes, "No one to witness and adjust, no one to drive the car." Describe how he arrives at this image; then comment on how this image addresses Frost's concerns in "The Oven Bird" or "Desert Places" and Stevens's in "A High-Toned Old Christian Woman" or "Of Modern Poetry."

2. In "A Sort of a Song," Williams writes, "No ideas but in things." Write an essay about the anthologized poems that appear to be about things rather than ideas: "The Red Wheelbarrow," "Death," and "Burning the Christmas Greens." What do these poems achieve?

3. Some of Williams's poems directly or indirectly address the writing of poetry. Discuss what the following poems tell us about his poetic theory: "Portrait of a Lady," "Spring and All," and "The Wind Increases."

4. Discuss Williams's word choices in "To Elsie."

5. Describe the form Williams invents in "The Ivy Crown." Discuss the effects this form has on the reader. How does the form contribute to a reader's understanding of the poem?

6. Compare the two Williams poems that derive from paintings by Brueghel: "The Dance" and "Landscape with the Fall of Icarus." Locate copies of these paintings in your library or on the Web, and look at them carefully. Why might these works interest a contemporary American poet? What relationship does Williams achieve between the visual and the verbal experience? Is it necessary to know these paintings to understand and appreciate the poems?

ROBINSON JEFFERS

1. Compare Jeffers's use of nature in his poems with Frost's. Choose one of the following pairs: "Once by the Pacific" and "Shine, Perishing Republic" or "Birches" and "Hurt Hawks."

2. In several poems Jeffers takes birds as his central symbol. Write a close reading of "Vulture" in the context of his other bird poems, "Hurt Hawks" and "Birds and Fishes."

3. Unlike most of his contemporaries, Jeffers locates many of his poems in an actual place: the central California coastline. Study his references to Point Lobos, Carmel, and Monterey. Then discuss "Carmel Point," paying particular attention to the significance of a particular place to his mood and imagination.

MARIANNE MOORE

1. Moore's work resembles that of Stevens in its interest in ideas. Choose one of the following pairs of poems, focusing on your analysis of Moore, and discuss the resemblance: "The Idea of Order at Key West" and "A Grave" or "Of Modern Poetry" and "Poetry."

2. Moore experiments with form and line lengths in "The Mind Is an Enchanting Thing." Write about this poem, paying close attention to the relationship between form and meaning. How does "O to Be a Dragon" serve as a postscript to such a discussion?

3. Like Jeffers, Moore also writes poems about birds. Compare "Bird-Witted" with "Hurt Hawks."

4. Study Moore's work for explicit statements about what poetry is and does. Evaluate these statements in light of class discussion and construct a prose version of her poetic theory.

5. Discuss one of the following poems by Moore with the aim of describing the poem's form and demonstrating the relationship between form and meaning in the poem: "To a Snail," "Poetry," "The Paper Nautilus," and "Nevertheless."

EUGENE O'NEILL

1. Discuss what O'Neill's character Edmund calls "faithful realism" in *Long Day's Journey into Night.* Is this play a work of realism? In what way does it extend or transform the concerns of the earlier realists to include twentieth-century concerns?

2. O'Neill suggests that modern life is more difficult for women than for men. Discuss continuities between the predicament of Edna Pontellier in Chopin's *The Awakening* and Mary Tyrone in *Long Day's Journey into Night.*

3. If you have studied early-nineteenth-century American literature, try reading *Long Day's Journey into Night* as the culmination of themes and concerns that have set a direction in American fiction from "Rip Van Winkle" on. What does the play have to say about versions of the American Dream, about individual identity, about self-reliance, about social exclusion, and about the development of consciousness?

T. S. ELIOT

1. Eliot writes, in "Tradition and the Individual Talent," that the individual personality and emotions of the poet recede in importance and his meaning emerges from his place in cultural tradition. He writes that "no poet . . . has his complete meaning alone." Examine his use of classical allusions in "Sweeney among the Nightingales." What does a modern reader need to know to understand the allusions and how does that understanding enhance our meaning of the poem?

2. Describe the progression and interconnection of images and themes in *The Waste Land,* locating the central image in each of the five sections of the poem.

3. Eliot himself considered *The Waste Land* to be "a poem in fragments." Explain why this is an appropriate description of the poem, how it addresses Eliot's twentieth-century worldview, and how he attempts to resolve the fragmentation at the end of the poem.

4. Describe carefully the persona of the speaker in "The Love Song of J. Alfred Prufrock" by examining the way he sees the world.

5. Like Williams, Eliot tried to achieve exactness and compression in creating his visual image. Find "Preludes" in the library and analyze Eliot's use of the image in that poem.

6. Eliot dedicates *The Waste Land* to Ezra Pound, who offered suggestions for revision. Read Pound's "Hugh Selwyn Mauberley," published just before *The Waste Land,* and locate similarities between the two poems.

Claude McKay

1. Write an essay in which you discuss ways in which McKay refreshes and personalizes traditional poetic forms. Is it legitimate to call McKay a modernist poet? Why do you think so? Make reference to specific poems in preparing your answer.

Katherine Anne Porter

1. One of Porter's recurring themes is the alienation or disconnection of the self—particularly of intelligent and independent women—from the rest of the world and a lack of genuine understanding or companionship or trust. Compare the predicament of one of Porter's heroines to that of some other isolated or misunderstood women we have looked at recently: Daisy Miller, May Bartram, Edna Pontellier, Mary Tyrone. Are there differences? Are men or is a male-dominated world the fundamental cause of the disconnection of Porter's women?

2. Write an essay comparing Porter's prose style and rhetorical strategies to those of Chopin, another Southern writer who wrote of women in grim predicaments. What differences to you see in the ways they handle expository prose and begin, pace, and end a narrative?

Nella Larsen

1. Write an essay about Helga as an American protagonist. What do you see as her literary ancestry? In what ways is she an unprecedented or daring creation?

2. Write an essay about this question: Does Larsen achieve sufficient artistic distance between herself and her own heroine? Choose, analyze and evaluate specific moments which support or complicate your answer.

3. Write an essay about the way that *Quicksand* concludes. Compare its ending to the final scenes of *The Awakening*.

Zora Neale Hurston

1. Write an essay about the ways in which Hurston makes use of myths and archetypes. What emotional or psychological impact does mythology bring to "The Eatonville Anthology" and "How It Feels to Be Colored Me"?

2. Compare "The Gilded Six Bits" to Mark Twain's "Notorious Jumping Frog of Calaveras County" or a "Mr. Rabbit" story by Joel Chandler Harris. At what points in "The Gilded Six Bits" does Hurston emulate or pay homage to these older tales? At what points does she seem to resist or transform a literary folktale tradition dominated, up to that time, by white men?

3. During her lifetime, Hurston enjoyed a measure of fame, followd by a long eclipse. She died in poverty and obscurity. How do you account or this rise, fall, and posthumous rise in her reputation? How does her literary work reflect or conflict

with the narrative or the American civil rights struggle or with the establishment of an African Amreican voice in our literary history?

Edna St. Vincent Millay and Dorothy Parker

1. Write an essay about wit and irony as important dimensions of Parker's verse, and as a presence in poems of Millay. Compare the effects and the inferences, and speculate on the advantages, and risks, of wit as a rhetorical strategy in poems by modern American women.

2. When Millay and Parker write about "The Sex Situation" or "Almighty Sex," are they referring to the same array of problems and challenges? Are they endemic or culture based? What differences do you observe in their perspectives and how are they reflected in the style and language of their verse?

E. E. Cummings and John Dos Passos

1. Write an essay comparing Cummings to Sandburg and Whitman as observers of ordinary American life. Pay special attention to the implicit attitude conveyed with regard to middle-class or working-class people as subjects in the verse.

2. Throughout his career, Cummings attempted to distinguish his verse by ignoring or defying conventions in punctuation and capitalization. Write an essay that looks carefully at passages where you see this strategy at work, and comment on the effects—in regard to the specific lines you choose, and overall as a hallmark of Cummings's poetry.

3. Do you see similarities between Dos Passos's stylistic experiments in "The Big Money" and the voices achieved by Cummings and Sandburg? Write about the similarities and differences, and speculate on the large—scale cultural forces to which these authors might be responding together.

Jean Toomer

1. What is the literary analogue in Toomer's *Cane* for Du Bois's "double consciousness"? How does Toomer evoke "the souls of black folk" in this excerpt from *Cane*?

2. Place Fern herself in the context of other works by American male writers, such as Poe's "Ligeia" or Anderson's "Mother." How does this tale continue or transform a conversation between American writers and the larger culture, about the valuation of women?

F. Scott Fitzgerald

1. Write an essay about Fitzgerald as a nostalgic author. With what mix of emotions does he describe a personal and collective past? What moments in personal experience does he find most evocative? How does he make this nostalgia inter-

esting or important to readers in different historical periods, with different backgrounds?

2. Fitzgerald is famous as a prose stylist whose sentences can convey conflicting perspectives, tension between romantic and cynical inclinations. Write an essay about the opening paragraphs of "Winter Dreams" and "Babylon Revisited." Analyze the prose and describe the complexity of the voices that you find there.

3. In Hemingway's "The Snows of Kilimanjaro," the narrator/protagonist recalls his friend Julian, a pseudonym for Fitzgerald, and his friend's fascination with the rich. Hemingway writes, "He thought they were a special glamorous race and when he found they weren't it wrecked him just as much as any other thing that wrecked him." Consider Hemingway's description of Fitzgerald as an interpretation of what happens in "Babylon Revisited." Fitzgerald made an often-quoted remark that "There are no second acts in American lives." Is this a theme in "Babylon Revisited"? If so, how is it developed and made interesting?

4. Compare the opening page of "Winter Dreams" to the opening page of a Porter story or Hemingway's "The Snows of Kilimanjaro." Describe the differences and suggest what they imply about the different ways in which these writers worked as modern artists.

GENEVIEVE TAGGARD

1. Locate other poems from the 1930s in the anthology, read Taggard's poems from the 1930s, and explore to what extent this period of national economic depression provided a context for the themes and forms of its poetry.

2. Taggard, unlike Moore and Rukeyser, seems to have no difficulty writing about women's experience. Write an essay about her representations of women's experience.

3. Compare Taggard's poem "A Middle-aged, Middle-class Woman at Midnight" with Frost's "An Old Man's Winter Night."

LOUISE BOGAN AND STERLING BROWN

1. In the midst of an era of free verse, Bogan and Brown both chose to write in rhyme and favored tight stanzaic forms. Write an essay comparing Bogan and Brown as contrarians: speculate on why each of them resisted the trend away from traditional form. How does their prosody reflect their key interests and values, and their respective conceptions of what modern poems are and should accomplish?

2. In "Cassandra" Bogan speaks through the persona of a seer from Greek mythology; in "Mister Samuel and Sam" and "He Was a Man," Brown uses personae of a different sort. Write about ventriloquism in these three works, and the stylistic and thematic advantages of assuming these voices.

WILLIAM FAULKNER

1. Keep a journal of your thoughts, frustrations, and insights as you read *As I Lay Dying*. In particular, note your use of visual reading skills. Does the novel allow you to develop visualization as a reading technique, and if so, how? Pay close attention to Faulkner's effects on your actual reading process.

2. Often the use of the journey as a plot device in a novel implies character development. Which character(s) develop in *As I Lay Dying*? Consider carefully the evidence of character development, or lack of it, and discuss how Faulkner's use of character affects interpretation in his novel.

3. Faulkner said that he wrote *As I Lay Dying* from start to finish in six weeks, and that he didn't change a word. While Faulkner was known to exaggerate, he conveys an essential fact about this novel: that he wrote it easily, quickly, and as if it were the product of a single action. Explore the ironies inherent in such a description of the novel's creation. Compare Faulkner's description of how he wrote *As I Lay Dying* with Addie's statement "I would think how words go straight up in a thin line, quick and harmless, and how terribly doing goes along the earth, clinging to it, so that after a while the two lines are too far apart for the same person to straddle from one to the other."

4. Throughout *As I Lay Dying*, Faulkner's characters use measurement and geometry as a way to depict the world, and Faulkner himself created a map of Jefferson County that "located" the Bundrens' journey within the larger world of his fiction. Find the map on the flyleaf of an edition of *Absalom, Absalom!* Consider Faulkner's use of spatial form and spatial relations as a unifying element in *As I Lay Dying*.

5. In class we have discussed *As I Lay Dying* as an epistemology, a set of ways of knowing the world. Explore the idea of the novelist as a carpenter and *As I Lay Dying* as one of the tools—rather than one of the products—of Faulkner's trade.

6. Critics have often commented on Faulkner's use of comedy in *As I Lay Dying*. Think about the various meanings of comedy and evaluate the extent to which *As I Lay Dying* may be considered a comic novel.

7. Examine *As I Lay Dying* from the point of view of family dynamics or social process. Is "Bundren" an identity these family members all share? What is the ontology, the way of being a Bundren? To what extent is Faulkner commenting on the American, especially the southern, family? Evaluate the perspectives with which the outsiders in the novel view the Bundrens. Which is reality? How does Faulkner demonstrate his characters constructing it?

8. Critics often associate Faulkner's portrait of the Snopeses with his perception that the "New South" following Reconstruction had lost its values. Consider this proposition with regard to "Barn Burning."

HART CRANE

1. Write an essay about Crane's use of the sacred. Compare this usage to the role of the sacred in poems of Eliot or Stevens.

2. Crane's verse forms are enormously varied. From two poems, choose stanzas that seem antithetical in their formality, and write about them, describing the advantages and difficulties of each strategy, and possible relationships between form, tone, and theme.

ERNEST HEMINGWAY AND THOMAS WOLFE

1. Write an essay comparing the prose style of Wolfe to that of Hemingway. What are the crucial differences? Could the story of "The Lost Boy" be told in a Hemingway style? What would be the effects? What about the possibility of "The Snows of Kilimanjaro" retold in the style of Wolfe? What conclusions do you draw about the suitability of each style to each narrative?

2. In writing workshops and literary magazines after World War II, the Hemingway legacy was much more palpable than Wolfe's. Write an essay suggesting reasons why Hemingway became the more influential stylist.

LANGSTON HUGHES

1. Discuss what Hughes's poetry tells a reader about his theory of poetry.

2. Place Hughes's work in the context of black musical forms invented in Harlem in the early twentieth century. Is black poetry the way Hughes writes it, like jazz, a new genre? What are its characteristics? If "black poetry" is a genre, does Countee Cullen write in it?

3. Hughes's poetry is open to the experiences of women. Analyze "Mother to Son," "Madam and Her Madam," and "Madam's Calling Cards" and explore the ways he transforms women's experiences into emblems of African American experience.

4. Would you describe Hughes's poetry as modernist in its themes, use of images, and style? Locate specific points at which you can see Hughes's modernism, and demonstrate it in an essay.

RICHARD WRIGHT AND JOHN STEINBECK

1. Although Wright's work appeared later than that of the poets of the Harlem Renaissance, he reflects some of their concerns. Trace the theme of manhood in poems by Sterling Brown and in Wright's "The Man Who Was Almost a Man." What do these texts suggest about manhood as an American experience?

2. Wright's story makes significant use of dialect; even the title, in its original form, was in dialect. What are the challenges of writing in this voice, and how does the legacy of American fiction support or complicate that strategy?

3. Like Wright, Steinbeck is often regarded as a modern practitioner of literary naturalism. Write an essay comparing the narration of *The Grapes of Wrath* to the narration of "The Man Who Was Almost a Man." What differences do you see in the way these narratives are told? What indications do you see of the author or narrator's relationship to the major characters?

4. Wright and Steinbeck were both writing in an age of film, and both of these authors had firsthand experiences with studios and movie-making. Write an essay about "camera work" in these two narratives: panoramic shots, close-ups, sudden changes of angle and perspective. How would you compare the cinematic style of these two writers?

CARLOS BULOSAN

1. Write an essay which reads Bulosan as continuing a legacy extending back to Yezierska, Cahan, and Chesnutt. What are his contributions to a tradition of narratives about American minority experience?

2. Write about the challenge of point of view in Bulosan's stories—the balance of distance and empathy that he tries to achieve in relation to his own protagonists. Compare this strategy to that of two of the following authors: Woolson, Dreiser, Cather, Fitzgerald.

Volume E: Prose since 1945

Although the teaching notes for this period include questions that can work either as discussion openers or as essay topics, ambitious papers about postwar and contemporary literature may gravitate toward several important and open-ended questions:

- The continuing relevance of genres, modes, and literary traditions: where do we see their continuation and development? Where do we see indications that this legacy is being rejected or radically reconstructed?
- The coexistence of the printed word with other media. It is no secret that since the 1960s, many electronic-based arts and entertainments have entered the competition for our time and attention. How has written literature adapted? How has it implicitly or explicitly recognized this revolution—as competition, complication, or enhancement?
- Canons, continuity, and diversity. The recognized diversity of American culture creates enormous richness and vitality in our literary life—but it obviously poses challenges for the construction of conventional literary history. What efforts do writers make to cross boundaries and reach different communities of readers? How is American literary culture avoiding fragmentation?

General Questions

1. Explore the variety of themes and techniques by which late-twentieth-century writers of fiction depict their own life stories in imaginative literature. You might include the following authors in your discussion: Ralph Ellison, Saul Bellow, Toni Morrison, Rudolfo Anaya, N. Scott Momaday, Sandra Cisneros, and Richard Powers.

2. Is heroism possible in contemporary society, as it is portrayed by our fiction writers? Discuss the possibilities for heroism in the following heroes or antiheroes: Miller's Willy Loman, Roth's Sargeant Marx, Baldwin's Jesse, Erdrich's Fleur, Kingston's Wittman Ah Sing.

3. In their efforts to record and understand the mysteries of life, many contemporary writers show special interest in the grotesque, the inexplicable, or the fantastic. Discuss this dimension of the following works: Welty's "Petrified Man," Malamud's "The Magic Barrel," O'Connor's "The Life You Save May Be Your Own" or "Good Country People," Pynchon's "Entropy," and Le Guin's "Schrödinger's Cat."

4. White middle-class suburban life and marriage become a central subject for several contemporary writers. Discuss the different treatment of this subject in the following works: Cheever's "The Swimmer," Updike's "Separating," and Beattie's "Weekend."

5. While contemporary writers no longer take upon themselves the responsibility for "defining" what it means to be an American, many continue to reflect on what Norman Mailer once described as "the forces now mounting in America" and "the intensely peculiar American aspect" of contemporary life. Discuss commentaries on recent or current American life in the following works: Ellison's *Invisible Man*, Miller's *Death of a Salesman*, Baldwin's "Going to Meet the Man," Reed's "The Last Days of Louisiana Red," Erdrich's "Fleur," and Mamet's "Glengarry Glen Ross."

6. Betrayal by mothers—or by sisters—is one variation of the exploration of the influence of family on contemporary life. Stella, at the end of *A Streetcar Named Desire*, cries, " 'Oh God, what have I done to my sister?' " Explore relationships between women in (for example) Welty's "Petrified Man," T. Williams's *Streetcar*, O'Connor's "The Life You Save May Be Your Own" and "Good Country People," Morrison's "Recitatif," Walker's "Everyday Use," and Cisneros's "My Lucy Friend Who Smells Like Corn."

7. Examine as a group the anthologized stories by these twentieth-century southern writers: Porter, Wolfe, Welty, and O'Connor. Do these writers alter the nineteenth-century concept of regionalism, and if so, how? If not, how do they extend the genre? How are twentieth-century regional writers also modernist writers?

8. Among contemporary writers, perhaps dramatists perceive most clearly the possibility for tragedy in American character and American life. The heroes and antiheroes of fiction seem to disappear, or take on tragic dimensions, in the work of Williams, Miller, Baraka, Mamet, and Parks. Describe carefully one of the char-

acters from their plays as a tragic hero, paying particular attention to the way the dramatic form enhances or frustrates such a reading.

9. Is it possible, and useful, to talk about a Native American voice in contemporary poetry and fiction? What would you say are thematic and stylistic characteristics of that voice? If you write about contemporary poets, consider especially Glancy, Harjo, and Ortiz. If you write about prose, consider Silko, Vizenor, and Erdrich.

10. Compare the way Williams constructs Blanche DuBois's southern speech with the way Faulkner, Welty, or O'Connor do for their southern characters in the anthologized stories.

11. A number of contemporary prose writers write about the challenge of writing, of being an artist within their own group or in and for the larger culture. What do these writers have to say about that challenge? What similarities in theme do you see among them? Consider Kingston, Bambara, Carver, and Reed.

12. Read a play by Lillian Hellman (*The Little Foxes, The Children's Hour*), Lorraine Hansberry (*A Raisin in the Sun*), Ntozake Shange (*For Colored Girls Who Have Considered Suicide*), Marsha Norman (*'Night, Mother*), or Wendy Wasserstein (*The Heidi Chronicles*) and compare it with one of the plays in *NAAL*.

13. Locate and read one of O'Neill's earlier "expressionistic" plays written during the 1920s and compare it with *Long Day's Journey into Night*.

14. Read the anthologized selections by Cheever, Updike, Carver, Barthelme, and Beattie. Based on these stories, identify formal and thematic features of these stories by writers who have appeared often in *The New Yorker*. Then read a short story published in *The New Yorker* during the past year and evaluate its similarities to these works.

15. One of the central questions for readers of *Black Elk Speaks* involves understanding the meaning of biculturalism. Explore the concept of biculturalism for contemporary Native American writers: Momaday, Silko, Vizenor, and Erdrich. Alternatively, consider the meaning of cultural assimilation for members of minority groups in America and examine the following works and their treatment of assimilation: Ellison's *Invisible Man*, Walker's "Everyday Use," Silko's "Lullaby," and Anaya's "The Christmas Play."

16. Write an essay comparing Cofer's "The Witch's Husband" with Paley's "A Conversation with My Father." Focus on what the younger narrators seem to learn from their interactions with older people. What remains mysterious in each of these narratives?

17. Write about ways in which Powers's *Galatea 2.2* comments on the experience of reading literature in college, and compare his perceptions with your own.

18. Write an essay about the implicit audience for Anaya's "The Christmas Play" and Anzaldúa's "How to Tame a Wild Tongue." Whom do you assume these works were written for? What kinds of accommodation, or resistance of accommodation, do you see in each of these texts?

19. What are the pros and cons of grouping writers like Anzaldúa, Cisneros, Cofer, and Anaya as "Latino writers," or Song and Lee as "Asian American writers"? Write an essay about this strategy, explaining and defending your views with reference to writers from early periods in American literature.

20. Readers have sometimes complained that the plays of Mamet, the narratives of Carver, and other contemporary works are too much like everyday life and language, or ordinary reportage, to qualify as "literary." Choose two contemporary texts from *NAAL* and comment on the mingling or the tension you see there in regard to artifice and truth.

21. American playwrights have often used siblings within a family to stand for divisions within the self or for two opposing forces. Consider the relationships between James Jr. and Edmund in *Long Day's Journey into Night,* Blanche and Stella in *A Streetcar Named Desire,* and Biff and Happy in *Death of a Salesman.*

Volume E: Poetry since 1945

General Questions

1. Test the accuracy of the following statements by and about poets based on your own careful reading of the selections in *NAAL.*

- *Niedecker:* "Like other experimental American poets, she uses the space of the page to suggest the movement of the eye and mind across a field of experience."
- *Penn Warren:* "What poetry most significantly celebrates is the capacity of man to face the deep, dark inwardness of his nature and fate."
- *Oppen:* "Oppen's distinctive measure, with its hesitancies and silences, becomes itself a measure of language's capacity to say with clarity what is real."
- *Jarrell:* "He is master of the heartbreak of everyday and identifies with ordinary forms of loneliness."
- *Wilbur:* "The most adequate and convincing poetry is that which accommodates mixed feelings, clashing ideas, and incongruous images."
- *Ammons:* "Ammons has often conducted experiments with poetic forms in his effort to make his verse responsive to the engaging but evasive particularity of natural process. This formal inventiveness is part of the appeal of his work."
- *Levertov:* "Her overtly political poems are not often among her best, however; their very explicitness restricts her distinctive strengths as a poet, which include a feeling for the inexplicable, a language lyrical enough to express wish and desire, and a capacity for playfulness."

- *Rich:* "Our culture, she believes, is 'split at the root'. . . ; art is separated from politics and the poet's identity as a woman is separated from her art. Rich's work seeks a language that will expose and integrate these divisions in the self and in the world."
- *Snyder:* " 'I try to hold both history and wildness in my mind, that my poems may approach the true measure of things and stand against the unbalance and ignorance of our time.' Throughout his life Snyder has sought alternatives to this imbalance."
- *Plath:* "Seizing a mythic power, the Plath of the poems transmutes the domestic and the ordinary into the hallucinatory, the utterly strange."
- *Harper:* "Harper writes poems to remember and to witness, but at times the urgency of the content overpowers his form and his language cannot sustain the urgency the poem asserts."
- *Ortiz:* "His sense of contemporary life, especially its absurdities, is acute. But the America he travels conceals within it an older landscape, one animated by spirit."
- *Dove:* "The experience of displacement, of what she has called living in 'two different worlds, seeing things with double vision,' consistently compels this poet's imagination."

2. Niedecker and Oliver both present poetry about significant landscapes, poetry that might be called pastoral. Compare the technical or formal features of their attempts to create a spirit of place in their work.

3. Many of Bishop's poems concern themselves with loss and exile, yet the tone of her poems is often one of reserve, of detached observation. Is such a tone appropriate to Bishop's themes? Where do you see tone and theme combining (or contrasting) most effectively in these poems?

4. Brooks and Dove wrote sequences of poems based on life in African American communities. Compare Brooks's anthologized poems from *A Street in Bronzeville* and Dove's poems from *Thomas and Beulah.* How do these poets make use of the technique of collage? What are their technical and thematic differences?

5. Write an essay about four contemporary American poets, responding to Randall Jarrell's observation "the gods who had taken away the poet's audience had given him students."

6. What are the oppositions and tensions that energize and shape Lowell's poetry? Do you see resemblances between his worldview and that of Henry Adams or other New England writers? Talk about specific poems that show these structures and conflicts.

7. Almost as if they were poetic "siblings," Levertov, Duncan, and Creeley trace their formative influences to William Carlos Williams and H. D. Choosing representative poems by each of these three, related by their choice of literary models, explore "family" influence. You may choose to trace the influence of Williams or

H. D., or you may focus instead on the "sibling" qualities of Levertov, Duncan, and Creeley.

8. A number of American poets seem to favor austerity—short lines, sparse use of metaphor, a stance of cool detachment. Others have favored long lines, lavish use of images and allusions, and overt emotional intensity. Creeley, Jarrell, Simic, and Cervantes may seem to belong to the former group, Ginsberg, Lowell, Roethke, Graham, and Ortiz to the other. Write an essay about two contemporary poets who strike you as having markedly different, or even opposite, literary voices. Describe differences, making specific reference to poems by each writer, and then speculate on possible similarities.

9. Ginsberg's use of long lines was a deliberate experiment for him, the "long clanky statement" that permits "not the way you would *say* it, a thought, but the way you would think it—i.e., we think rapidly in visual images as well as words, and if each successive thought were transcribed in its confusion . . . you get a slightly different prosody than if you were talking slowly." Read *Howl* and other anthologized poems, paying particular attention to Ginsberg's use of the long line.

10. O'Hara wrote about his work, "The poem is at last between two persons instead of two pages." Explore your own sense of audience and connection with O'Hara's poems, then consider whether his statement also applies to other contemporary American poets.

11. Kinnell and Levine have written of Whitman's influence on their work and their influence on each other. Choosing specific poems as the basis for your commentary, examine thematic and formal connections between Kinnell, Levine, and Whitman.

12. Ashbery is often spoken of as associated with the "language" poets, including Charles Bernstein, Lyn Hejinian, and Michael Palmer. Locate the work of one of these poets and read representative poems in light of Ashbery's work.

13. Many of Charles Wright's poems depict in detail an actual American landscape. Close read one of Wright's poems and examine the relationship between internal and external "landscape" in his work. Would you call Wright a pastoral poet? Where are his roots and forebears in the American literary tradition?

14. When Collins was appointed as a poet laureate, there were comments about how "accessible" his poetry is—and sometimes the description was not intended as a compliment. Write about Collins as an accessible poet: what strengths do you discover in his clarity? When you read him in the context of other contemporary poets, does his work seem sufficiently rich and multidimensional? In framing your answer, develop readings of at least two of Collins's poems.

15. Write an essay comparing Simic's "The White Room" with Robert Frost's "Directive" and Lowell's "Skunk Hour." Think about these poems as soliloquies or

elegies, and comment on how Simic's tone and implications vary from those of Frost and Lowell.

16. Write an essay about the way the supernatural is invoked in Kunitz's "Quinnapoxet," Graham's "The Dream of the Unified Field," and Wright's "The Appalachian Book of the Dead VI." Describe the mixture of belief and disbelief that you find in the work of each of these poets.

17. In one of the poetry seminars that Lowell taught at Boston University, both Plath and Sexton were students. All three of them knew Wilbur, who also frequented the Boston area in the fifties and sixties. Imagine that some or all of these people have gone out for coffee one night after class and write a conversation they might have had. What might they have had to say to each other about their work?

18. More than any other contemporary American poet, Rich has located and explicated women's lives and their relationships to each other, to their communities, to history. Her poems also reflect her "understanding of change as the expression of will and desire." Write an essay in which you trace the continuum of women's relationships to each other that appear in Rich's poetry and in which you also locate the poems along the timeline of composition dates that Rich provides, examining evidence of what she has termed, in an essay by the same title, "When We Dead Awaken: Writing as Re-Vision."

19. Consider the appropriateness of Lorde's own phrase to describe her poetry: "a war against the tyrannies of silence."

20. Locate Ortiz within the Native American tradition of literature as represented in *NAAL*. What themes, forms, and images link his work with earlier Native American writers or with contemporaries Silko or Erdrich?

21. Explore the themes of Ortiz's poetry: traveling, the power of storytelling, dislocations of American Indian identity, exploitation of the American land.

22. Explore the connections Dove draws between individual moments of her personal history and larger historical forces. Compare her use of black history with that of other anthologized black women poets: Brooks and Lorde.

23. The Latino writers included in *NAAL* intermix Spanish phrases and lines in their work. Choose one or more of these writers (Ríos, Cervantes), and discuss the effects and effectiveness of the inclusion of Spanish in the work.

24. Like other contemporary American women poets (for example, Rich and Dove), Song writes about family ties and ancestors. Explore the power of family in Song's work.

25. Find examples of the use of traditional poetic or metric forms by post-1945 poets and describe the relationship between form and meaning. Choose, for exam-

ple, the following sonnets or near sonnets: Jarrell's "Well Water" or Brooks's "kitch-enette building."

26. The following poems all reflect the autobiography of the poet: Bishop's "In the Waiting Room," Lowell's "My Last Afternoon with Uncle Devereux Winslow," Ginsberg's "To Aunt Rose," Merrill's "The Broken Home," O'Hara's "In Memory of My Feelings," and Plath's "Lady Lazarus." Choose one of these poems for close analysis, locating it in the context of autobiographical poems by other writers.

27. Poems that are addressed to or are about family members tell us a great deal about differences between contemporary poets as well as family relationships in the twentieth century. Explore one of the following groups of poems: (1) mothers: Brooks's "the mother" and Rich's "Snapshots of a Daughter-in-Law"; (2) fathers: Roethke's "My Papa's Waltz," Berryman's *Dream Song* 384, Merrill's "The Broken Home," Wright's "Autumn Begins in Martins Ferry, Ohio," Plath's "Daddy," and Lee's "The Gift" and "Persimmons"; and (3) sisters: Song's "Lost Sister."

28. Poems addressed to other contemporary poets, living or dead, can tell us about the poet writing the poem and the poet honored by the dedication. Choose any of the following poems for close analysis, working within the context of the anthologized work by the poet to whom the poem is dedicated or addressed: (1) Bishop's "The Armadillo," for Lowell; (2) Lowell's "Skunk Hour," for Bishop; and (3) Sexton's *Sylvia's Death,* for Plath.

29. Contemporary poets have written about nature in many different ways. Explore some of the variations: does nature become the object of perception and the reason for precision in language? does it serve as the symbolic projection of human emotions and fears? does it provide an alternative world within which the poet can locate a coherent vision? Choose several poems from the following list: Bishop's "The Moose," Dickey's "The Heaven of Animals," Ammons's "Corsons Inlet," Wright's "A Blessing," and Plath's "Blackberrying."

30. Locate and read statements on poetry by post-1945 poets; then review particular poems in light of the poets' statements. Choose, for example, Levertov, "Some Notes on Organic Form," from *Poet in the World*; Snyder, "Poetry and the Primitive," from *Earth House Hold*; Rich, "When We Dead Awaken," from *On Lies, Secrets, and Silence.*

31. Poets often first publish their poems in small books or collections. Find and read one of the following titles, study the order of poems in the collection, and then analyze the poem included in *NAAL* within the context of the other poems with which it was originally published. The titles of the anthologized poems appear in parentheses.

- Bishop, *Geography III* ("In the Waiting Room," "The Moose," or "One Art")
- Lowell, *Life Studies* ("Memories of West Street and Lepke")

- Brooks, *A Street in Bronzeville* ("kitchenette building" or "a song in the front yard")
- Wright, *The Branch Will Not Break* ("A Blessing")

32. Read the anthologized poems from one of the following connected poem sequences and describe intertextual connections within these sequences: Brooks, *A Street in Bronzeville*; Berryman, *Dream Songs*; Rich, *Twenty-One Love Poems*; or Dove, *Thomas and Beulah*. Or extend your reading to include all of the poems in the Brooks, Rich, or Dove sequences and consider them as a single connected work.

33. What do contemporary poets have to say about some of the traditional themes of poetry: love, death, loss, or the passing of time? Choose and discuss two or three poems from one of the following groups:
- Love: Niedecker, "[Well, spring overflows the land]"; Lowell, "Skunk Hour"; Creeley, "For Love"; Rich, "A Valediction Forbidding Mourning"; Snyder, "Beneath My Hand and Eye the Distant Hills. Your Body."
- Death: Jarrell, "The Death of the Ball Turret Gunner"; Berryman, No. 384; O'Hara, "The Day Lady Died"; Merwin, "For the Anniversary of My Death"; Sexton, "The Truth the Dead Know" or "Sylvia's Death"; Harper, "Deathwatch"; Wright, "The Appalachian Book of the Dead VI."
- Loss: Roethke, "The Lost Son"; Bishop, "One Art"; Jarrell, "Thinking of the Lost World"; Merrill, "Lost in Translation"; Merwin, "Losing a Language"; Levine, "Animals Are Passing from Our Lives"; and Song, "Lost Sister."
- The passing of time: Bishop, "In the Waiting Room"; Hayden, "Middle Passage"; Lowell, "Memories of West Street and Lepke"; Pinsky, "A Woman"; Graham, "The Dream of the Unified Field"; Collins, "Forgetfulness."

Questions and Topics Related to American Literary Traditions

1. In *Of Plymouth Plantation*, Bradford writes, "But here I cannot but stay and make a pause, and stand half amazed at this poor people's present condition; and so I think will the reader, too, when he well considers the same." With this quotation in mind, examine *Narrative of the Life of Frederick Douglass*. Look for patterns in the two prose texts: How does each construct an audience? On what terms does each writer convey a sense of beginning, of "new world," both in historical and in literary terms? What specific material and ideological circumstances oppress the writers of these texts? In what way does each text establish questions that later writers will address? How do the texts differently deal with the problem of literary authority? What are the didactic purposes of the narratives?

2. Bradstreet and Wheatley were the first white and black American women to publish poetry. Examine Wheatley's poems in light of Bradstreet's "The Prologue." Can you find any evidence of conscious encoding in Wheatley's poems? Is she aware, as Bradstreet was, that as a woman or an African American her poems might be "obnoxious" to "each carping tongue"? Compare in particular the formal elements of Wheatley's poems with some of Bradstreet's, especially stanzas from "Contemplations," "The Flesh and the Spirit," and "As Weary Pilgrim."

3. Consider the extent of Bradstreet's and Wheatley's acceptance of received theology by examining one of the following pairs of poems: "Contemplations" and "Thoughts on the Works of Providence"; "The Flesh and the Spirit" and "To the University of Cambridge, in New England"; and "As Weary Pilgrim" and "On the Death of the Rev. Mr. George Whitefield, 1770."

4. Polemical writers in each literary tradition use rhetorical language to move their audiences. Choose works from the following writers as the basis for cross-traditional analysis: Edwards, Occom, Jefferson, Apess, Fuller, Charlot, Washington, and Du Bois. Consider ideological similarities between Edwards's "great revival" thinking in "Sinners in the Hands of an Angry God" and Apess's looking-glass in "An Indian's Looking-Glass for the White Man," or discuss the radicalism (for their contemporaries) of Jefferson, Fuller, or Du Bois.

5. Show how the lyric poem develops across historical periods in the works of each of the following groups of writers: Bradstreet and Taylor; Emerson and Whitman; Wheatley, Brooks, and Lorde.

6. Demonstrate how concepts of black identity determine prose forms in works by the following writers: Douglass, Jacobs, Chesnutt, Hurston, Toomer, Ellison, and Walker.

7. The genre of autobiography reveals many differences between writers from separate literary traditions. Examine segments of some of the following autobiographical narratives, choosing figures from each tradition, and outline contrasts in social position and economic class, educational background, audience, or didactic purpose: Edwards's *Personal Narrative,* Franklin's *The Autobiography,* or Hawthorne's "The Custom-House"; Jacobs's *Incidents in the Life of a Slave Girl* or Hurston's "How It Feels to Be Colored Me"; Equiano's *The Interesting Narrative,* Douglass's *Narrative,* Eastman's *From the Deep Woods to Civilization,* or Momaday's *The Way to Rainy Mountain.*

8. Some writers, while not choosing the genre of autobiography, still include enough autobiographical allusions in their poetry or fiction to tantalize the reader or critic. Consider the use of autobiographical material in literature outside the genre of autobiography from several traditions, perhaps choosing from among the following lists: Taylor, Thoreau, Whitman, Melville, or Robert Lowell; Bradstreet, Dickinson, Gilman, Porter, Levertov, or Rich; Wheatley or Brooks; Sterling Brown, Hughes, Ellison, or Harper.

9. In an out-of-class essay, consider points of connection, useful contrasts, or central themes in each of several works that may be considered focal points for their respective literary traditions: Douglass's *Narrative,* Twain's *Adventures of Huckleberry Finn,* Chopin's *The Awakening,* and Momaday's *The Way to Rainy Mountain.*

10. Examine a play by Glaspell (such as *Trifles*) or Hansberry (such as *A Raisin in the Sun*) in the context of class discussion of O'Neill's *Long Day's Journey into Night* or Baraka's *Dutchman*.

11. Choose an important writer in an American minority tradition, or in the tradition of American women authors. Write an essay in which you compare the perspective a reader achieves in examining a particular text within the context of the writer's literary tradition with the perspective he or she might have in placing the text within the context of the writer's white male contemporaries. Useful writers for this assignment include Jewett, Cather, or Welty; Hurston, Brooks, or Walker; Chesnutt, Brown, Hughes, or Richard Wright; or Eastman, Zitkala Ša, Momaday, or Erdrich.

12. Write an essay about the following lyric poems from different literary traditions: Frost's "The Gift Outright," Brooks's "kitchenette building," Rich's "Diving into the Wreck," Ortiz's "Poems from the Veterans Hospital," Ríos's "Madre Sofía," Cervantes's "Visions of Mexico," Song's "Chinatown," and Lee's "Persimmons." Focus on the disparate voices and perspectives the poems reveal.

13. Examine characters who have been created by writers of the opposite gender. Compare a male protagonist created by a woman writer, such as Mr. Shiftlet in O'Connor's "The Life You Save May Be Your Own," with a female protagonist in a male writer's fiction, such as Hawthorne's Beatrice Rappaccini, James's Daisy Miller, or O'Neill's Mary Tyrone.

14. Compare black characters created by white writers with black characters created by black writers, in pairings such as Melville's Babo and the autobiographical persona in Douglass's *Narrative*; Stowe's Eliza and Linda Brent in Jacob's *Incidents in the Life of a Slave Girl*; Twain's Jim and Chesnutt's Uncle Julius.

15. Compare women characters created by male writers, such as Irving's Dame Van Winkle, Hawthorne's Hester Prynne, James's Daisy Miller or May Bartram, O'Neill's Mary Tyrone, Toomer's Fern, Faulkner's Addie Bundren or Dewey Dell, or T. Williams's Blanche DuBois, with women characters created by female writers, such as Stowe's Eliza, Jewett's Sylvy, the narrator of Gilman's "The Yellow Wallpaper," Chopin's Edna Pontellier, Porter's Miranda, or Walker's Mama.

16. Read works by writers outside the list of major authors in the literary traditions approach that illuminate questions of cross-gender or cross-racial interest or that increase our understanding of the development of literary traditions and explain how and why they are significant. Choose from the following list: Rowlandson's *A Narrative of the Captivity and Restoration* (to examine a Euro-American woman's view of Native American men), Poe's poems and stories about women, Davis's *Life in the Iron-Mills* (to raise issues of class and working conditions in pre-Civil War industrialism), Harris (for a white man's transcription of black folk life), H. Adams's "The Dynamo and the Virgin" from *The Education* (for

a white male writer's sense of woman as a source of symbolism), Anderson's "Mother" from *Winesburg, Ohio* (to compare a woman character by a writer who deeply influenced Faulkner with one of Faulkner's own female characters), Williams's "Portrait of a Lady" (a poem that raises questions of literary convention), H. D.'s "Leda" or "Helen" (a woman poet's sense of woman as a source of mythology), Parker's sketches (for an example of humor in the white women's tradition), Wolfe's "The Lost Boy" (another example of a writer using autobiographical material in a genre other than autobiography), Crane's "At Melville's Tomb," Berryman's "Homage to Mistress Bradstreet," Ginsberg's "On Burroughs' Work," and Sexton's "Sylvia's Death" (for questions of literary influence).

17. Write an essay about the southern tradition as represented in *NAAL*. Focus in particular on those writers who do not figure as major authors in any literary tradition, such as Smith, Byrd, Thorpe, Wolfe, Penn Warren, or Dickey. What generic or thematic concerns link some of these writers? Can you describe the development of southern literature in a chronological reading of the representative figures in *NAAL*? In examining writers from the literary traditions, to what extent are their works informed by southern history or identity? Consider minority writers in the context of their chronological contemporaries. Are Douglass, Hurston, or Richard Wright anomalous in their respective literary periods when we consider them as southern, rather than as black or women writers? Consider writers in different genres, such as Byrd and Jefferson, Poe and Douglass, Faulkner and Wolfe, Dickey and Warren, and Welty and Walker. Are these writers so diverse in form and theme that their southern ties become negligible, or does that southern heritage link them significantly despite their differences?

18. Define a literary tradition on your own according to genre or theme. Defend your list of writers and works, and choose for class analysis a particular work that both represents your larger list and illustrates its central concerns.

19. Study the Jewish writers represented in *NAAL*: Lazarus, Yezierska, Rukeyser, Malamud, Miller, Bellow, Roth, and Ginsberg. Choose a representative text for close analysis and view it either within the context of other works in the tradition, with works by the writer's contemporaries from a variety of traditions, or paired with a significant work from another tradition.

20. Study the relationship between marginality and vision or social stigma and literary authority in works by white male writers: (1) The colonial period appears to be unique in American literature in that it did not produce white male writers who considered themselves marginal (with the exception of Williams and Woolman, who were not part of the Puritan community). Speculate on some of the reasons why this is the case. Might the absence of men who wrote against the established ideology have somehow made it easier for Bradstreet to write at all? (None of her contemporaries chose to establish himself or herself as marginal, perhaps leaving the possibility open to a woman; and in Puritan culture, where marginality might lead a man to predict his own damnation, a woman—a flawed version of

an already flawed creation—might have less to lose by embracing marginality.) (2) Many white male writers in the early nineteenth century wrote as if they were marginal. Choose representative texts (by Irving, Hawthorne, Thoreau, Whitman, or Melville) and consider what the marginal characters in these fictions have to say about the relationship between white male authors and marginality. (3) Examine Twain's Huck Finn or James's John Marcher as representative of lonely, isolated, and marginalized characters. (4) Twentieth-century white male authors frequently explore the theme of social difference. Some created their most powerful fictions based on this theme. Examine the theme in Anderson, Jeffers, O'Neill, Faulkner, Bellow, or Tennessee Williams and speculate on the white male writer's fascination with marginality.

Index

Page numbers in boldface indicate main discussions of works and authors.